Due to urbanization and gentrification, the lines between the urban and suburban realities continue to blur. As a result, churches must rethink their missional strategies and retool for greater relevance in their communities. *A Heart for the Community* will inspire you with new models and expose you to current best practices for reshaping your church's response for building relational bridges of hope with those yet to be reached in your community and beyond.

Dr. Larry Acosta, *President, Urban Youth Workers Institute*

The single word change in the titles *A Heart for the City* in 1999 to *A Heart for the Community* in 2009 speaks volumes about the gospel taking root and flourishing in Chicago, the consummate "city of neighborhoods." John Fuder and Noel Castellanos have both broadened their lens and opened our eyes. Suburbs are included now because they are no longer the escape from cities, but the extension of them. Chicago has gone from being the city with the second largest Polish population in the world, more than 800,000 when I began ministry there more than forty years ago, to an equal number of Spanish speakers today. Nations are still coming to neighborhoods in Chicago, but also to the suburbs and collar counties as in every American city. But the range of ministry models introduced in this book also proves my thesis that city ministries in America have become the R & D unit for the growing urban mission task on all six continents. Urban ministry has become the front line of world mission today. In this book we witness an ecclesial flower garden of the Holy Spirit's gifts, called and active in practical ways we could only dream about a few years ago. I'll look forward to carrying this book all over the world to encourage but also to expose urban ministers and missionaries to the practical tools for credible, faithful, and sustainable witness to our Lord Jesus Christ. Thank you John, Noel, and Moody Publishers. That this should appear on the 50th anniversary of my own graduation from MBI only increases my appreciation.

Ray Bakke, *Chancellor, Bakke Graduate University, Seattle, Washington*

A Heart for the Community will challenge any serious Christians to take seriously Jesus' call to unity so that the full effect of the gospel's power can be visibly seen in a world that desperately needs a message of hope, healing, and spiritual transformation.

Dr. Tony Evans, *Pastor, Author, Speaker*

What a valuable, hope-giving resource! The contributors to *A Heart for the Community* are no arm-chair theorists, but practitioners who have responded to the call to build bridges of love and reconciliation . . . And they provide us with the inspiration and models to do the same.

Dr. Crawford W. Loritts, Jr., *Author, Speaker, Senior Pastor of Fellowship Bible Church, Roswell, Georgia*

How thankful I am that these writers have demonstrated by personal experience that the gospel works—whether in the suburbs or the inner city. To our shame, we have often run from the challenges of the inner city instead of embracing these opportunities to prove the integrity of the gospel message. This book not only teaches us how ministry can be done in unlikely places, but why our efforts are both rewarding and fruitful if we follow the model of Jesus who lived and died among those who needed Him the most.

Dr. Erwin Lutzer, *Senior Pastor, Moody Church, Chicago*

A Heart for the Community covers a broad range of critical contemporary issues in a highly accessible fashion. The authors are rich in frontline experience and thoughtful in their theological reflections. This book will be a great asset to anyone seeking to join God in His mission of community transformation.

Dr. Amy L. Sherman, *Author and Director, Sagamore Institute Center on Faith in Communities*

The challenge of urban ministry in the 21st century differs vastly from urban ministry of the previous century. Our urban centers continue to change and develop while maintaining their strong influence upon American society. Drawn from a wide range of practitioners, *A Heart for the Community* may prove to be the manual and text for the 21st century urban minister. This book is a worthy testament to the exciting work of the Christian Community Development Association and a needed encouragement for those on the front lines of ministry.

Soong-Chan Rah, *Milton B. Engebretson Assistant Professor of Church Growth and Evangelism, North Park Theological Seminary, Author of* The Next Evangelicalism

Timely, targeted, thorough, touching, transforming.

Tom Steffen, *School of Intercultural Studies, Biola University*

A Heart for the Community is just that — a book that draws our hearts into the communities, urban and suburban, that God loves. This collection of essays takes a new look at critical issues in the city, taking seriously the current major demographic shift as more people move into the cities while poverty moves to the suburbs. The approach is to see this shift not as an obstacle but rather as an opportunity for reconciliation. The various authors offer their unique perspectives on the changing city. *A Heart for the Community* will be an excellent resource both for students and for practitioners seeking to make a difference for God's kingdom.

Jude Tiersma Watson, PhD, *InnerChange/CRM, Associate Professor of Urban Mission School of Intercultural Studies, Fuller Theological Seminary, Pasadena, California*

A HEART FOR THE COMMUNITY

New Models for Urban and Suburban Ministry

A HEART FOR THE COMMUNITY

General Editors
JOHN **FUDER** & NOEL **CASTELLANOS**
Foreword by
JOHN **PERKINS**

MOODY PUBLISHERS
Chicago

Library of Congress Cataloging-in-Publication Data

A heart for the community : new models for urban and suburban ministry /
John Fuder and Noel Castellanos, general editors.
    p. cm.
  Includes bibliographical references.
  ISBN 978-0-8024-9131-2
  1. City churches. 2. Suburban churches. 3. Church work. I. Fuder,
John. II. Castellanos, Noel.
  BV637.H43 2009
  253--dc22
                    2008054598

Editor: Cheryl Dunlop
Interior Design: Smartt Guys design
Cover Design: Paetzold Associates
Cover Image:: iStockPhoto

This book is printed on acid free recycled paper containing 30% PCW
(Post Consumer Waste) and manufactured in the United States of
America by Thomson-Shore.

We hope you enjoy this book from Moody Publishers. Our goal is to provide high-quality, thought-provoking books and products that connect truth to your real needs and challenges. For more information on other books and products written and produced from a biblical perspective, go to www.moodypublishers.com or write to:

Moody Publishers
820 N. LaSalle Boulevard
Chicago, IL 60610

1 3 5 7 9 10 8 6 4 2

Printed in the United States of America

To my wife of thirty years, who sacrificed countless hours of our time together so I could work on this book. I love you, Nel. You are still and always will be the best "gift" God has ever given to me (Phil. 2:2).

And to the "urbies" of MGS, both past and present, whose tribe is steadily increasing. You have encouraged and blessed me more than you will ever know. May you take your places and thrive in ministries like these in cities all over the world (Jer. 29:7).

JOHN

To my wife, Marianne, who has been my partner in ministry and parenting for the past twenty-five years in the barrios of East San Jose, California, and La Villita in Chicago—it has been a real ride! Your love for Christ and gift of harmony are an inspiration to me.

To my children, Noel Luis, Stefan, and Anna, I love you more than you'll ever know, and I am so proud of how you are growing up to be young men and women of character who are working to own your faith. You inspire me to stay young and always strive to use all of my God-given potential for His glory.

Finally, to all of my extended family, thank you for your love and support. When you have a Mexican-American and Italian-American extended family, there are many people to thank! Mom and Dad, I am especially proud of your example as followers of Christ.

NOEL

CHICAGO CITY MINISTRIES

1 Rogers Park: Youth With A Mission
2 West Ridge: South Asian Friendship Center
3 Uptown: Emmaus Ministries
4 Albany Park: Bridge City Church
5 North Center: Young Life
6 Lakeview: Chicagoland Community Church
7 Logan Square: River City Community Church
8 Austin: Circle Urban Ministries
9 Garfield Park: Bethel New Life
10 Bridgeport: New Life Community Church
11 West Pullman & Roseland: Salvation Army
12 South Loop: South Loop Community Church

IRVING PARK
13 Chicago Tabernacle
14 Lydia Home

NEAR NORTH SIDE
15 Moody Bible Institute
16 By The Hand Club For Kids
17 Park Community Church

HUMBOLDT PARK
18 La Casa Del Carpintero
19 New Life Covenant

LAWNDALE
20 Lawndale Community Church
21 The House
22 Christian Community Development Association

SUBURBAN MINISTRIES

23 South Barrington: Willow Creek Community Church
24 Elgin/Aurora/Carpentersville/Montgomery: Riverwoods Christian Center
25 Bolingbrook: New Song Church
26 Dolton: Lorimer Baptist Church
27 South Holland: Living Hope Community Church

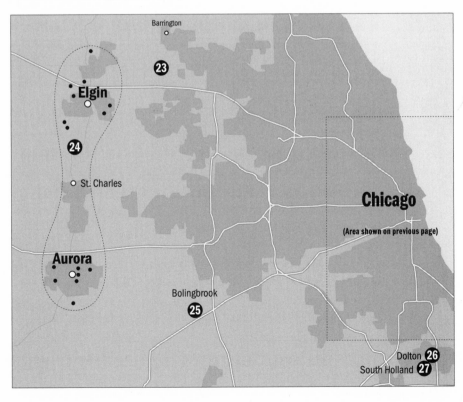

CONTENTS

PART 1: CRITICAL ISSUES

PART 2: CHURCH-PLANTING MODELS

PART 3: MINISTERING TO SUBURBAN NEEDS

PART 4: PARACHURCH MINISTRIES

About the Contributors

DAVID ANDERSON is a psychologist and Executive Director of Lydia Home Association. He received his B.A. in community health at Northern Illinois University and his Psy.D. from the Chicago School of Professional Psychology. He has been married for twenty-five years to Karen and has two birth children (Nathan and Audrey), one adoptive child (Connor), and one foster son (Nick) who has two children of his own.

DAVE AND ANGIE ARNOLD live in Albany Park, a neighborhood in Chicago's Northwest Side, which is the nation's third most ethnically diverse zip code and port of entry to immigrants and refugees. They were married in March 2000. Dave received his Bachelor of Science degree in pastoral ministry from Taylor University in 1998, and his Master of Theological Studies degree from Michigan Theological Seminary in 2005. Angie received her Bachelor of Urban Ministry degree from Moody Bible Institute in 2009. Together, in 2005, they founded Bridge City Ministries, a vibrant, grass-roots ministry that focuses on planting ethnic house churches and organic churches in Albany Park, throughout Chicago, and to the ends of the earth.

ALVIN BIBBS has a Master of Arts degree in Christian leadership development from Fuller Theological Seminary. He is the Executive Director of Multi-Cultural Church Relations for the Willow Creek Association in South Barrington, Illinois. He is assisting the WCA in developing a more ethnically diverse movement in order to serve prevailing churches around the country. His role has special emphases geared toward the values of radical compassion, racial reconciliation, social justice, and leadership development for the sake of the Church.

NOEL CASTELLANOS has worked in full-time ministry in urban communities since 1982. He has served in youth ministry, church planting, and community development in San Francisco, San Jose, and Chicago. Noel is a highly sought after speaker, motivator, and mentor to young leaders throughout the USA, and has a deep passion to serve and invest in the lives of emerging leaders. After serving on the Board of the Christian Community Development Association for many years, he has established the new CCDA Institute, which is working to equip emerging church leaders in the philosophy of Christian Community Development, and currently serves as the Chief Executive Officer of CCDA. He and his wife, Marianne, have three children, Noel Luis, Stefan, and Anna, and make their home in the barrio of La Villita in Chicago.

SCOTT CLIFTON was born and raised on the East Coast. He has been married to Linda for seventeen years and together they have three adventurous boys, Ben, Danny, and Jonathan. He and his family lived in west London for about four years prior to coming to the Windy City. They are proud owners of a registered bungalow in the Mayfair neighborhood in north Chicago. He received his undergraduate degree at the University of Delaware and his master's degree at Westminster Theological Seminary.

CLIVE CRAIGEN has spent nearly twenty years of his life in urban ministry, both working with youth and in church planting. He received his B.A. from Grace College and his M.A. in inner city studies education from Northeastern Illinois University. He is also a graduate of the DeVos Urban Leadership Initiative (Chicago 2000). He currently serves as Assistant Professor of Urban Ministry at Moody Bible Institute, co-shepherds a house church in Chicago, and works as a student mobilizer for Go2 Church Planting Ministries.

JACKSON CRUM is the lead pastor of Park Community Church. Park is located in the city of Chicago with one of their campuses in a changing area that was previously part of Cabrini-Green. Jackson is married to Donna and they have two sons.

TONY DANHELKA is an ordained minister and a co-founder of Riverwoods Christian Center in St. Charles, Illinois. He and his wife, Donna, moved to the Fox River Valley in 1976 to begin and develop the mission of Riverwoods. They have one son, Anthony David, known to many as TJ. Tony's heart is to partner with local Fox River Valley Churches to come together across cultural and denominational lines in unity to better address efforts of strategic prayer, caring through community development, and sharing the Good News of Jesus Christ.

WILFREDO DE JESUS is Senior Pastor of New Life Covenant Ministries, one of the fastest growing churches in Chicago. New Life is a vibrant and caring church that is reaching out to the community. Wilfredo De Jesus received a Bachelor's degree in Communications from Trinity University and a Master's degree in Christian Ministries from North Park Theological Seminary. Wilfredo resides in Chicago with his wife Elizabeth and their three children, Alexandria, Yesenia, and Wilfredo, Jr.

LUKE DUDENHOFER is pastor at the Bridgeport location of New Life Community Church, a multi-site church in Chicagoland. Serving in this role since 2002, Luke desires to be used of God to lead a reconciling church, where spiritually lost people are united to God through faith in Jesus and culturally diverse people are united to one another as a community in mission for Jesus. Luke is a graduate of Moody Graduate School. He and his wife, Melissa, have three adopted children and live in the Bridgeport neighborhood.

JOHN FUDER received his Ph.D. from Biola University and has been a professor since 1994 at Moody Bible Institute's Graduate School in the heart of Chicago. He spent twelve years with CityTeam Ministries in San Jose, California, and two years with Impact Ministries in Chicago. For his doctoral research he worked with people on skid row in Los Angeles. Doc Fuder lives in Chicago's Edgewater community, is married to Nel, and has three children and one grandchild. He is the author of *Training Students for Urban Ministry* and the general editor of *A Heart for the City*.

"Coach" **WAYNE GORDON** is founding pastor of Lawndale Community Church and chairman/president of the Christian Community Development Association (CCDA). He is a graduate of Wheaton College and Northern Baptist Theological Seminary. He received his Doctor of Ministry degree from Eastern Baptist Theological Seminary. Wayne and his wife, Anne, have raised their three children in the Lawndale community. He is also the author of the inspiring book *Real Hope in Chicago*.

JOHN GREEN is the Founder and Executive Director of Emmaus Ministries, an evangelical ministry of Roman Catholic and Protestant Christians reaching out to men involved in prostitution. He has an M.A. in educational ministries from Wheaton College and was ordained to the permanent diaconate in the Catholic Church in May of 2002. John is a frequent speaker on issues relating to male prostitution and urban ministry. He and his wife, Carolyn, and their four children, Jonathan, Daniel, Peter, and Claire, attend Our Lady of Lourdes Catholic Church.

DANIEL GUTE grew up in Guatemala, Central America, the son of missionaries. He is a graduate of the Moody Bible Institute, Wheaton College, and Trinity Evangelical Divinity School. He has served on the pastoral staff of Lorimer Baptist Church in Dolton, Illinois, since 1983. He and his wife, Diann, have three children, Sarah, Derek, and Melinda.

As a Salvation Army officer, **MAJOR DARLENE HARVEY** has served as a pastor in Oak Creek and Green Bay, Wisconsin; Divisional Youth Leader in Indianapolis, Indiana; in community development and projects in South America; as Family Care Director at The Salvation Army College for Officer Training; and presently is working on the Kroc Center project. She holds a B.S. in sociology and a Master's in Church Management from Olivet Nazarene University. She and her husband have two sons.

MAJOR DAVID HARVEY has always been passionate about program and community development. Before becoming a Salvation Army officer, he was a Community Center Director and Youth Director in Dearborn, Michigan. As a Salvation Army officer, he has served as a pastor in Oak Creek and Green Bay, Wisconsin; Divisional Youth Leader in Indianapolis, Indiana; Territorial Youth Secretary in South America; Curriculum Director at The Salvation Army College for Officer Training; and presently is the administrator for the Chicago Kroc Center. He earned a B.A. in business from Asbury College and a Master's in Church Management from Olivet Nazarene University. He and his wife have two sons.

DANIEL HILL is the Founding and Senior Pastor of River City Community Church, located in the Humboldt Park neighborhood of Chicago. Prior to starting River City, Daniel launched a dot-com in the nineties before serving five years on the staff of Willow Creek Community Church in the suburbs of Chicago. Daniel has his B.S. in business from Purdue University, his M.A. in Biblical Studies from Moody Graduate School, and his certificate in church-based community and economic development from Harvard Divinity School. Daniel is married to Elizabeth, who is a Professor of Psychology at Chicago State University.

JUANITA IRIZARRY currently serves the Christian Community Development Association (CCDA) as its Institute Director, coordinating trainings across the country to educate CCDA members in the key principles of Christian Community Development. She also teaches nonprofit management at DePaul University and urban studies at Eastern University and does nonprofit strategic planning consulting through Najera Consulting Group. She has a Master of Public Administration from Harvard University, has a Bachelor's degree in history/political science and Spanish from Greenville College, and has completed sixty hours of graduate study in urban planning and policy with concentrations in housing and community development at the University of Illinois at Chicago.

PHIL JACKSON has more than twenty years of experience working with youth and young adults. He currently serves as pastor for The House Covenant Church, Chicago's first all teen and young adult hip hop church, and is an associate pastor for Lawndale Community Church. He is an author of *The Hip Hop Church* and is also a contributing author of chapters for various other books, as well as an editor for Crossway Publishing's *Urban Devotional Bible*. Phil and his wife, Kim, have been married since 1985 and have three children.

SARAH JAMES received her B.A. at the University of Indianapolis in Elementary Education. Sarah came to Chicago to get her Master's degree in urban ministry at the Moody Graduate School. She is the Director of By the Hand Club for Kids, an after-school program in Chicago that serves over 600 children in under-resourced neighborhoods. Sarah has recently been given guardianship of two brothers from Cabrini-Green, Keewaun (fourteen) and Trayvon (ten).

DAVID AND BETH KANELOS have served as Young Life Area Directors since 1985, reaching out to a multi-culturally diverse population of urban teenagers on Chicago's North Side. In 2004, they received the Young Life "Senior Staff Award of Excellence" in honor of their years of commitment to one community. David received his B.A. from Western Michigan University, and did graduate work in counseling at DePaul University and in theology at Fuller Seminary. Beth has a B.F.A. from the University of Illinois. David and Beth raised their son and daughter in Chicago.

GLEN KEHREIN, along with his wife, Lonni, and family, have lived on Chicago's West Side since the early 1970s when they founded Circle Urban Ministries (www.circleurban.org). Glen and Lonni's journey has taught them principles of racial reconciliation, urban ministry, and redemption. Other writings of Glen's can be found in *Restoring Communities at Risk*, *Heart for the City*, and *Breaking Down Walls*.

MARY KIM is a graduate of Moody Graduate School with a Master of Arts in Biblical Studies. She was born in Seoul, Korea, but moved to Los Angeles in 1980 with her Salvation Army parents and two brothers to open the Korean ministry of the Salvation Army in the United States. Mary has served on two summer mission teams to the Republic of Georgia. She is currently a student at The Salvation Army College for Officer Training in Chicago's Lakeview neighborhood.

Native to Chicago's Far South Side, **TOM KUBIAK** has a burden to see Christ's true Church engaged in the ministry of reconciliation throughout the city—vertically and horizontally. He rejoices in God for his lovely wife, Joanna, and their children, David, Leah, and Sarah. They relocated to the city-center South Loop in 1999. Tom is the founding pastor and preaching elder of this integrated, nondenominational, neighborhood ministry.

ISAÍAS MERCADO is a graduate from McCormick Seminary in Chicago with a Master of Divinity and a Doctorate of Ministry degree with an urban ministry concentration. He is the Founding and Senior Pastor of The Carpenter's House, a thriving bilingual church in the Near Northwest Side of Chicago. Rev. Mercado also serves as the Vice President of the Latino Leadership Foundation, a nonprofit ministry that supports Latino Christian leaders in their efforts to impact the barrios of our nation with the gospel. He has been married to Lucrecia for twenty years and has three children, Alexis, Isaías, and Emmanuel.

SAM NAAMAN and a group of missionaries started the South Asian Friendship Center in the heart of the Indian Marketplace in Chicago. His wife, a doctor, also serves at the center. This is the first center of its kind to reach Muslims and Hindus in North America. He teaches at the Moody Bible Institute in the department of World Missions. Sam and his wife, Debbie, have two sons, Blaise and David.

WINFRED NEELY is Professor of Pastoral Studies at the Moody Bible Institute, and Church Planting Pastor of Living Hope Community Church in South Holland, Illinois. He holds the Doctor of Ministry degree from Trinity Evangelical Divinity School, Deerfield, Illinois, and degrees from Wheaton College Graduate School and Trinity International University.

MARY NELSON is President Emeritus of Bethel New Life, where she served for twenty-six years. Bethel pioneered in faith-based creative community-based efforts to build healthier, sustainable, and equitable communities on Chicago's West Side. She serves on the Boards of Sojourners and Christian Community Development Association. Mary has her Ph.D. from Union Graduate School and six honorary Ph.D.s, and is now doing consulting, writing, and teaching in faith-based community development. Mary lives, works, and worships on the West Side of Chicago. She is on the faculty of ABCD Institute (Northwestern University), CCDA Institute, and SCUPE.

JON PENNINGTON is Coordinating Pastor of Chicagoland Community Church in the center-city Chicago neighborhood of Lakeview. He is a graduate with a Master of Divinity from Southwestern Baptist Theological Seminary in Ft. Worth, Texas, and has a B.A. in history from Morningside College in Sioux City, Iowa.

Jon also serves as the next generation facilitator for the new work team of the Chicago Metropolitan Baptist Association. Jon is married to Alana, and is father of three children.

MARTY SCHOENLEBER was the founding pastor of New Song Evangelical Free Church in Bolingbrook, Illinois. He received his B.A. in ancient history from the University of Maryland and the M.Div. from the International School of Theology in San Bernardino, California. Currently he serves as the Church Planting Missionary Consultant for the Great Lakes District of the Evangelical Free Church.

BRAD STANLEY is the founder of Youth With A Mission Chicago and has been its Director for the last seventeen years. Based in the Rogers Park neighborhood, Brad has helped to develop and facilitate evangelism, discipleship, and practical helps ministry among the city's diverse ethnic and subculture communities. Brad and his family have worked with Youth With A Mission for the past twenty-two years and have served in more than twenty nations.

In 2001, **AL TOLEDO** sensed the Lord leading him and his family to leave New York, where he was an Associate Pastor at the Brooklyn Tabernacle, and begin a work in the city of Chicago. In January 2002, the Chicago Tabernacle, a multiracial church of about four hundred, was birthed.

PAMELA TOUSSAINT is a graduate of Fordham University with a BA in communications/journalism. She has written extensively for numerous periodicals such as *Decision, Discipleship Journal, Spirit-Led Woman,* and *Black Enterprise.* Pamela has authored and coauthored many books to literary acclaim, including *Signs of Hope in the City, Boys into Men,* and *Great Books for African-American Children.* She has been featured in *Charisma* magazine, on *Joni, Paula White Today,* and *Focus on the Family Weekend.*

DONNITA TRAVIS is Executive Director and Founder of By the Hand Club. After serving as a volunteer with children in Cabrini-Green for five years, Donnita stepped down as president of an advertising agency in 2001 to establish By the Hand. Located in the Cabrini-Green, Altgeld-Murray, Austin, and Englewood neighborhoods, By the Hand is dedicated to helping more than six hundred children have new and abundant life. Donnita was in advertising for eighteen years, received her M.B.A. from Northwestern Kellogg School of Management in 1995, and was named to Today's Chicago Woman "100 Women Making a Difference" in 1998.

Foreword

would like to congratulate John and Noel on both the vision and the will to pull together a book like this. At this point in the history of the church, it is desperately needed. At a time when the church and the general population are moving back to the city, a book that reaches across racial, cultural, and economic barriers like this is of critical importance. I pray that this book will reach a diverse audience and people all across America will be exposed to and adopt its message. All the writers have a clarity and vision that make this a practical community development textbook. By looking at the history of these people and their ministries we can learn about the problems of our cities and the strategies of attacking those problems.

This book is absolutely timely. I know the people who have made contributions personally and they all either currently are or have been committed to the area in which they have written about. I just know it's going to be an asset to the individuals and organizations that make up the Christian Community Development Association because they are all true Christian community developers. Of course my great desire is that the church would reflect true "holistic" Christian community development, evangelism, social responsibility, and justice. Most of all we need to break through our racial and cultural barriers that inhibit us from carrying out Christ's Great Commission to bring the gospel to Jerusalem, Judea, Samaria, and to every ethnic group on earth.

Today, we face some of the most severe economic challenges in our nation's history, with millions of Americans facing poverty and brokenness like never before—in the city and in the suburbs. In the midst of this crisis, the church must be a bearer of good news that offers hope and that addresses the real needs of the people we serve. We must also seize the opportunity to make racial bigotry and hatred a thing of the past. And, with our nation's first African-American president, Barack Obama (also from Chicago), in office, we have an opportunity to confront racial prejudice and injustice in new ways. I believe *A Heart for the Community* provides us with examples of these new approaches that will be essential for the entire church to embrace and understand.

There is a new awakening in the Christian community, and this book represents the voices of that awakening. It seems right that like the first volume, *A Heart for the City*, written over ten years ago and launched at our annual CCDA conference held at Moody Bible Institute and Moody Church, this new edition focuses on examples of whole-gospel to whole-person ministry. This book represents a Kingdom partnership between Moody Publishers, Moody Bible Institute, and the Christian Community Development Association, all located in one of the world's more diverse cities, Chicago.

Finally, I would like to congratulate John and Noel for taking on this project and challenge. Both of these men are my friends, and both are providing essential leadership to prepare Christians to minister effectively in communities across our nation: John, as a professor in Moody's graduate school, and Noel, as the CEO of CCDA, which is inspiring and training Christians to give their lives to ministering in under-resourced communities throughout our country.

Dr. John M. Perkins, President
John M. Perkins Foundation for Reconciliation & Development, Inc.
1831 Robinson Street, Jackson, MS 39209
info@jmpf.org

Preface

The brisk Saturday morning betrayed our senses. A group of about twenty unsuspecting passengers boarded a bus for a leisurely Saturday tour of Chicago's so-called inner-city ministries. Our host, Dr. John Fuder—looking more like a professional backpacker and mountain climber than a professor—greeted us with furtive smile and restrained energy.

Once on the bus, John solemnly and passionately prayed for our time. He set a tone that was to be a defining moment for most on that tour.

John paints a picture of the city with his hands. He gestures widely with enthusiasm about the great legacy of Dwight L. Moody and his longing for those who live in the brownstones, under the el, in cardboard boxes, in hovels and holes. It doesn't take long before you see that D. L. Moody infected John. Or at least they caught the same bug.

John is known for his passion. It can be downright annoying at times. It's annoying because he's as real as the people he's trying to help.

First stop, not far from the Moody Bible Institute: Cabrini-Green. While gentrification takes place before our eyes, what was at one time a massive housing project is smaller now, but still home to thousands of children. As John explains the plight of single-parent kids, drugs, prostitution, violence, and unemployment that characterizes so many who live here, a young woman appears out of nowhere. She is standing on the corner. The bus door opens and John invites her on the bus. Sarah, a misplaced Midwesterner, introduces herself and her life. She came to Moody as a student and volunteered at "Kids' Club" (now By the Hand Club), an area ministry that tries to help Cabrini kids. After completing her master's degree, she caught the bug too. She's been serving with By the Hand Club for more than seven years and is now on staff. She talks about "her boys," both in middle school. She's taking one of them to get tennis shoes today because he got all C's on his report card. She's afraid for them. Just letting them go home through the halls of those projects would make a strong man quake.

We stop at places like this all day long. International pockets of populations, areas known for drugs and violence, gang neighborhoods, ethnic sections that are frozen in time, political neighborhoods like Louis Farrakhan's Nation of Islam,

Jesse Jackson's Operation PUSH, Chinatown, and on and on we go.

Quietly, subversively, we're getting infected.

It is a fact that most of humanity lives in large cities. Long before we were worried about sprawl, millions of people were cloistering in cities. With the crush of humanity, the crushing effects of sin and sadness press in too. And each one of these precious people is made in the image of God.

Something about the American spirit is forever reinventing things. We can't settle down. We've got to be creating something new. But let's not pass over those who have gone before us doing incredible work. The bus stops in this book will take you to places not on the architectural tour. It's not as glamorous as a boat tour at night. But it's right here, under our nose. It's right outside your door. And it's in a downtown near you.

By the way, all of us on that tour were spent when the day was done. When you see the needs of the community right in front of you, only a stone wouldn't cry. Thanks, John.

Take a tour. Step on and off the bus. Move in and around to see these people's lives. Ask God to shake you up and toss you out—out into a reality where most of humanity lives. Our city—Chicago—desperately needs Christ. Yours does too. How about getting on the bus?

"And He was saying to them, 'The harvest is plentiful, but the laborers are few; therefore beseech the Lord of the harvest to send out laborers into His harvest'" (Luke 10:2 NASB).

Dr. Michael Easley
President Emeritus
Moody Bible Institute
November 2008

Acknowledgments

The privilege has been mine, a second time, to serve as the general editor of a book with Moody Publishers. I am very grateful to Greg Thornton, Vice President of Publications, and his entire team for helping to make this project a reality. Coupled with your professionalism, you all exemplify humble servant hearts, and are a pleasure to work with.

This volume, *A Heart for the Community,* is a companion to the first edition, *A Heart for the City* (1999). A decade later, its scope is intentionally wider, so as to include a number of church-based models that are dealing with "urban" issues in suburban settings. Together, these books total fifty-eight chapters, using Chicagoland as a laboratory to display relevant ministry themes and transferable principles.

A Heart for the Community, though, by design, reflects a strategic partnership between Moody and the Christian Community Development Association (CCDA). It has been an honor to co-edit this book with Noel Castellanos, CCDA's Chief Executive Officer. Nel and I have known him and Marianne since our City Team days together in the mid-1980s in San Jose, California. Our lives are richer because of John (who wrote the Foreword) and Vera Mae Perkins, Coach and Annie Gordon, Glen and Lonni Kehrein, et al. Thank you all for your faithfulness to Christ and the community over the long haul. Your example is worth emulating.

I would be remiss in not giving some love to my loyal faculty assistants who have labored tirelessly on this project behind the scenes for almost two years. Sarah Milano, Susannah Martinsen, Daniel Snoek—you guys are the best! I could not have done it without your help. Also, to my dean(s) and colleagues at the MGS, and your spouses, comrades in the calling of training ministry practitioners. Bless you for putting up with my passionate, seemingly one-track focus on the city, racial justice, and the poor for so many years! You also are gifts to Nel and me, and we need and love you all.

And to those contributors to this edition, who, like the first volume, work in many of Chicagoland's finest ministries and are the very heartbeat of this text, thank you for putting up with my incessant phone calls and e-mails to try to keep us on deadline! I deeply respect your lives and ministries and sincerely pray that God will use and bless this second work as He did the first.

Finally, to Ray Bakke (who wrote the Foreword for the first edition), long-time Chicago and Moody alum, friend and advisory board member of CCDA: It began with you, brother, more than ten years ago, on a place mat (which I still have) at Ann Sathers' on the North Side. Even the Heart for the City bus tour, which so deeply impacted Michael Easley and became the Preface to this book, has its roots in your car, with Joe (who did the Preface in the first volume) and Martie Stowell and me. An undeserving mantle passed, of a great love for and knowledge of our city. You infected me, and now your legacy lives on in countless others. We are all so very grateful.

JOHN FUDER

fter writing one chapter in A *Heart for the City* more than a decade ago, I am thrilled to be working this time around as co-editor with Dr. John Fuder on a follow-up effort, *A Heart for the Community.* Along with being excited to be working on this project with my good friend of more than twenty years, I am also convinced that the partnership between Moody Bible Institute, Moody Publishers, and the Christian Community Development Association (CCDA) is an important and timely one. In the city of Chicago, no other Christian educational institution is situated physically like Moody Bible Institute, in the center of the city. The opportunity that provides for training and developing students is unprecedented—and, in Chicago, CCDA's partner ministries often provide the frontline church and parachurch organizations where these students can learn and serve.

In my role as CEO of CCDA, I have the privilege of seeing some of the most effective and inspiring ministries around the country working with the poor; not just to provide relief or bandage solutions, but to bring about transformational change in people's lives and in restoring communities. Right here in Chicago, we are blessed to have some of the leading examples of churches and ministries that are addressing and confronting the new realities of the poor in our nation—both in the heart of the city and in the surrounding suburbs, which represents a tremendous change in the demographics of poverty, not only in Chicago but across our country.

To help us understand these changes and the new approaches that are making a difference for the Kingdom, we have a great team of contributors that have much to teach us. I am grateful to each one of them for making this volume a strong resource for anyone with a heart to minister among the poor.

I must also acknowledge the leadership of CCDA, our Chairman Emeritus, Dr. John Perkins; our President, Dr. Wayne "Coach" Gordon; our Board Chairperson, Dr. Barbara Williams-Skinner; and our Vice-Chairman, Dr. Luis Carlo. They, along with our entire board, have given me the time and the freedom to work on making this project a reality. And I thank each one of my staff at CCDA, who work tirelessly to serve me and all of our members.

Finally, I want to thank my wife, Marianne, and my children, Noel Luis, Stefan, and Anna, for their love and support, which has made it possible for me to pursue my passion of living and ministering in the barrio for so many years.

My prayer is that *A Heart for the Community* will inspire and equip Christians everywhere to get fully engaged in the ministry of restoring under-resourced communities for the glory of God.

NOEL CASTELLANOS

Part One

CRITICAL
ISSUES

JOHN FUDER received his Ph.D. from Biola University and has been a professor since 1994 at Moody Bible Institute's Graduate School in the heart of Chicago. He spent twelve years with CityTeam Ministries in San Jose, California, and two years with Impact Ministries in Chicago. For his doctoral research he worked with people on skid row in Los Angeles. Doc Fuder lives in Chicago's Edgewater community, is married to Nel, and has three children and one grandchild. He is the author of *Training Students for Urban Ministry* and the general editor of *A Heart for the City*.

Introduction to Critical Issues

John Fuder

A BOOK IS BORN

I t all started more than two years ago in the Commons of the Moody Bible Institute. First, a passing conversation with Greg Thornton, Vice President of Publications for Moody Publishers, about another edition of *A Heart for the City*, in partnership with Christian Community Development Association (CCDA).

Shortly thereafter was a brainstorming session with Noel Castellanos and Glen Kehrein. What would make this edition distinct from the first? What new paradigms should be addressed? What significant issues sit on the horizon for urban ministry practitioners in this generation?

Though far from exhaustive, this Critical Issues part of the book captures most of those new topics. Other subjects that follow, in succeeding sections, include church planting and the suburbanization of poverty.

A PASSION IGNITED

When my family moved to Chicago in 1993, and I began teaching at Moody the following year, one of my first responsibilities was to develop the field education (internships) program for the Graduate School.

I began by meeting with a former staff member of the undergraduate Practical Christian Ministries (PCM) department who knew Chicago well. I asked her if she could identify the top one hundred church and parachurch ministries in the city that had been impacting and mentoring Moody students in recent years.

During the summers of 1994 and 1995, I visited all one hundred of them, fifty per summer, several a day. In the process, I fell in love with Chicago, cultivating a deep heart for this city. Amazingly, I do not recall any of those being new church plants. Now, fifteen years later, some of the most vibrant models of ministry in Chicagoland, and across urban America, are church planting models. I say "Chicagoland" to include the suburbs, because the suburbanization of poverty is here to stay.

Numerous times a year I have the privilege of leading three- to five-hour "Heart for the City" tours with Moody students, staff, donors, local businessmen, pastors, and ministry leaders. We start the tour by looping around what is left of the Cabrini-Green low-income housing projects, nearly across the street from MBI's campus. By "what is left" I mean that most of the high rises have been torn down in the past five years and have been replaced by multi-site townhomes and condominiums, with price tags approaching one million dollars.

The inevitable question posed on nearly every recent tour is, "Where are all the poor people going?" Some choose to resettle in other Chicago Housing Authority (CHA) buildings, scattered throughout the city. But the deeper, more challenging response to that question is simply, "Coming soon to a suburb near you."

CULTURAL EMPHASIS

Coming to teach in the Moody Graduate School, I inherited a course called Research Methods. Like many graduate level or seminary classes it was heavy on quantitative methodology.[1] Over the years, the course morphed into Research Project Seminar, in a more focused attempt to equip students to write their theses.

But still there remained the persistent plea, "Hey Doc, why can't we take another Bible class instead?" Undaunted by such a no-confidence vote, I sought to introduce more qualitative methodology,[2] and the course was reborn as Community Analysis. In its essence, it is now a class in cultural exegesis. You can read more about the adventures of Moody students diagnosing the needs of diverse people and places throughout the city in chapter 3.

A primary reason for this course adjustment was a point made by Dr. Leith Anderson, noting that "pastors are trained in exegesis but rarely in ethnology" (the study of ethnic groups and cultures).[3] But the concurrent, equally opportune moment is the relentless progression of the United States as a laboratory of the nations.

In an article, "Why Is America a Mission Field?" a good friend and former colleague at Moody, Dr. Marvin Newell, writes:

In John 10:16, Jesus says, "I have other sheep, which are not of this fold . . ." (NASB). Those "others" are no longer geographically distant, but simply culturally distant. This is the crucial point that all North Americans need to understand. People of other ethnicities are no longer separated from us by an ocean. They are right here among us, just down the street.[4]

TODAY'S URBAN ISSUES

Gentrification

Dr. Bob Lupton, a much-respected CCDA board member and urban ministry practitioner in Atlanta for more than thirty years, has been a voice as strong as any other in the past decade to highlight the strategic phenomena of gentrification in urban America. Quite honestly, most of us urban practitioners did not even initially understand the meaning or significance of the word!

In his recent excellent book *Compassion, Justice and the Christian Life*, Bob has a chapter entitled, "Toward a Theology of Gentrification." The term *gentrification*, he informs us, "comes from the old English word 'gentry,' the land-rich ruling class of the sixteenth century who controlled the economy by virtue of their land holdings."[5]

"Gentrification," he continues, "by contemporary definition, is the restoration and upgrading of deteriorated urban property by the middle classes, often resulting in displacement of lower-income people."[6] This pattern is not unique to Chicago. It is playing out in cities across America.

These economic factors seem to be changing the landscape of our urban communities overnight, yet this "displacement of lower-income people" has within it a Kingdom purpose for our generation.

Many of the ministry models highlighted in the following pages are included because they are seizing this missional opportunity. The city and suburbs alike are a shifting mix of classes, cultures, and ethnic groups.

The Latino Explosion

The African-American community was significantly highlighted in our first book, *A Heart for the City*.[7] More than one-third of the chapters were authored by African-Americans and/or focused on black communities or populations.

Now, ten years later, this book, *A Heart for the Community*, more fully acknowledges the burgeoning Hispanic demographic. Newly released figures from the U.S. Census Bureau reflect that the Hispanic community exceeds 15 percent of the total U.S. population, surpassing the African-American numbers, which stand at a little over 12 percent.[8] Of particular interest is the strategic and volatile issue of immigration.

A recent Pew Research Center report speculates that by 2050 nearly one in five U.S. residents will be an immigrant, and that the Hispanic numbers will double, to reach nearly 30 percent of the population.[9]

Coming to Chicago from Los Angeles and learning a new city, I have sought to heed the sound advice of many to keep "a Bible in one hand, and a newspaper in the other."[10] That, however, has translated into bulging file folders full of newsprint!

Included in that collection is a University of Notre Dame study projecting Chicago's rapidly growing Latino community at over three-quarters of a million, plus numbers exceeding eight hundred thousand in the suburbs.[11] More specifically, a report by the Chicago Council on Global Affairs states that one in six area residents are of Mexican descent, with those numbers expected to double by 2030.[12]

Scripture is replete with God's heart for "the stranger," the foreigner, the immigrant.[13] Every child of God on this earth is a "resident alien,"[14] and we are exhorted to "administer true justice" for the vulnerable.[15] We may never run out of places to apply that mandate in this generation.

Muslims Among Us

A projected 285,000 Muslims live in Chicago.[16] Some believe the number is even higher. Estimates vary widely of the numbers of adherents to Islam across the country, but the most commonly accepted figure is around six million.[17] Although these numbers are mere percentage points of the total population, their rapid growth and perceived militancy is a concern for many.

Larry Poston and Carl Ellis, in *The Changing Face of Islam in America,* point out that "Islam is now coming into its stride, and Christians are beginning to watch with anxiety as Muslims close the gap."[18] But rather than live in fear, and treat Muslims among us as "Christianity's most dangerous enemy,"[19] we should see that we have gained, on our watch, a mission field in our own backyard.

This is far more than just one of many "Critical Issues" in our book. It is rather an entrustment to God's people, in our age, "for such a time as this" (Esther 4:14). Poston and Ellis aptly write,

> *Let us resolve to do good to the Muslims we meet, helping them to adapt and adjust to American culture, aiding them in learning our worldview, customs and language. In the process of teaching and serving them, we can do what will ultimately prove to be the greatest good we can possibly perform for them: sharing the good news of salvation.*[20]

"Coach" **WAYNE GORDON** is founding pastor of Lawndale Community Church and chairman/president of the Christian Community Development Association (CCDA). He is a graduate of Wheaton College and Northern Baptist Theological Seminary. He received his Doctor of Ministry degree from Eastern Baptist Theological Seminary. Wayne and his wife, Anne, have raised their three children in the Lawndale community. He is also the author of the inspiring book *Real Hope in Chicago*.

CHAPTER 1

GENTRIFICATION:

The Good News and the Bad News

Wayne L. Gordon

Introduction: The Enemy Among Us?

Gentrification. A dreaded word to many of us in urban ministry and a major issue. But why? Is gentrification really so bad?

I am writing this chapter from the perspective of a Christian community developer and a pastor. Christian community development is a philosophy of ministry among the poor that works to help people lift themselves out of poverty. The roots of Christian community development stem from John Perkins and his three R's, which are relocation (living in the community of need), reconciliation, and redistribution. Christian community development has evolved into eight principles, the three R's plus five others: being church based, empowerment, holistic approach, leadership development, and listening to the community.[1]

GENTRIFICATION: A WORKING DEFINITION

Gentrification is practically understood as the process by which middle-income professionals buy and restore homes in depressed communities. It's the return of the gentry, the landowners, to a community. In Chicago we have often watched gentrification with pain and disillusionment. We have watched buildings being purchased by people we never expected to be interested in Lawndale, a largely African-American community on the West Side of Chicago, including new business owners, outside developers, and speculators. These speculators seem to be coming into poor neighborhoods for the sole purpose of making money.

Gentrification is driven by the market forces in real estate development. Real estate developers have great vision when they see vacant lots and abandoned buildings in the same communities often targeted by those of us doing Christian community development in urban ministry. It is in these underserved and under-resourced neighborhoods that new opportunities arise for developers to come and grow. It appears that only the real estate developers have the understanding and knowledge to redevelop and to rebuild many of the poor communities.

It is surprising that many of us doing Christian community development actually use some of the same jargon as outside developers. Our scriptural text comes from Isaiah 58:12, the theme verse for the Christian Community Development Association (CCDA): "Your people will rebuild the ancient ruins and will raise up the age-old foundations; you will be called Repairer of Broken Walls, Restorer of Streets with Dwellings." Rebuild, raise up, repair, restore: these are the buzz words most of us use in our ministry in under-resourced communities. As we live and work in poor neighborhoods, it has always been our goal to rebuild our communities and to restore the streets where people live, walk, and play.

In many ways gentrification is the secular response to dilapidated neighborhoods. Yet when we as urban workers see outsiders coming in and making profits at the expense of our community and neighbors, we often become outraged. It is through these eyes that I would like to discuss gentrification in this chapter. Let those of us doing urban ministry rework our understanding of gentrification using the philosophy of Christian community development. Let us rethink gentrification together and look at how we can use this powerful force within the context of our philosophy of ministry.

SIGNS OF GENTRIFICATION

We know that gentrification is coming to our neighborhood when we see billboards that say, "We buy ugly houses," when there is new interest in vacant land and abandoned buildings, when a new business such as a Starbucks starts up, and grocery stores move in and begin to operate. When after years of neglect there seems to be new attention given to our community by local government officials and the business community. New fire stations, police stations, public transportation improvements—these all are signs that something is about to happen. The market forces of real estate developers have now seen our neighborhoods as viable workplaces where money can be made.

It may very well be that public policy of rebuilding neglected communities makes good sense for increasing the tax base and for reducing crime, gang activity, decaying buildings, and more. Not only is this a sign of gentrification but it actually serves as a catalyst for gentrification. The reality is that the community changes but the people in the neighborhood don't; they are simply displaced and the problems just move to another community. Gentrification is very different in different cities and communities; I will be speaking from the perspective of my experience in Lawndale on Chicago's West Side.

THE LAWNDALE STORY

When Lawndale Community Church began in 1978, we had almost no services within our community. We could not even buy a pair of shoes in North Lawndale; there were no McDonald's restaurants in our community, no chain grocery stores, no restaurants in which to sit down and eat with our families. It was a barren place lacking many of the services that a healthy community has.

Part of the mission of Lawndale Community Church has been to redeem the Lawndale Community; we have sought to bring Christian holistic revitalization to the lives and environment of our residents through economic empowerment, housing improvement, educational enrichment, quality affordable health care, and Christian discipleship.[2] These are at the very heart and soul of Lawndale Community Church's mission. We started Lawndale Christian Health Center to serve the health care needs of the people of our neighborhood. We also established Lawndale Christian Development Corporation to provide housing and encourage economic development and to help restore our community to a healthy, stable, and sustainable neighborhood. We have worked hard not to do this in isolation but always within the context of our community. One of the key components of Christian community development is listening to the community. It was the residents who dreamed most of the ideas and the desires for our neighborhood.

We have envisioned a future where Christian values undergird the attitudes and actions of our community residents. We see the future when existing residents are empowered to live in harmony and security; when vacant lots and abandoned buildings are converted into new and affordable homes and rehabbed apartments; when the majority of homes are owner occupied; when high school and even college graduations are expectations; when job skills and employment opportunities abound; when all people have quality, affordable health care; and when Jesus Christ is seen as Lord. This is the vision of what we would like to see happen in our inner-city communities.

The problem seems to be as we start seeing this vision begin to happen, others also see this and jump in with a different purpose and with seemingly unlimited resources. Then panic begins to come over us as we watch outsiders buying and selling property and new housing being developed by outsiders with no community connection. We name the force of gentrification as a negative option for us, instead of embracing it as a means to help us. We cannot do all the development in a large community like Lawndale. With fifty thousand residents, a small church is clearly unable to bring about the kinds of systemic change that is needed for our neighborhoods to be sustainable and see the quality of life improved.

Many inner-city neighborhoods have become poor by such things as white flight, years of neglect, deteriorating rental properties, abandoned buildings, and vacant lots. People like Glen and Lonni Kehrein, Thomas and Tracy Worthy, Richard and Stephanie Townsell, Ted and Shelly Travis, Jim and KJ Swearingen, Noel and Marianne Castellanos, Anne and me, and many others have moved into these under-resourced communities and made huge impacts. It is through Christian community development and relocated urban ministers that many of these positive changes have begun.

HARNESSING GENTRIFICATION

Bob Lupton from Atlanta has encouraged us in CCDA to harness the forces of gentrification for justice and for the good of our community.[3] Bob has helped us to rethink gentrification and how we might come alongside some of the secular market forces that are working to change our communities. One of the distinctives of Christian community development is our philosophy of living in the community in which we serve. In the truest sense of the word this is gentrification. We, from the outside, have been relocating and moving into poor communities all across the urban landscape for more than thirty years. We normally see this as good, with many inner-city neighborhoods benefiting around the country from like-minded urban ministry people who have moved into the communities and raised their families.

In Lawndale for the first twenty years of our church presence, no one was developing any housing except Lawndale Community Church, mostly through Lawndale Christian Development Corporation and one other nonprofit housing group. It was after our gaining momentum and beginning to focus on housing with scale that others took notice. Actually we became a victim of our own success. As we were successful in building new houses, the market forces noticed us and began to work in our neighborhood. Simultaneously came rebuilding of the old Sears & Roebuck headquarters in the northern part of Lawndale.

More than twenty years after Sears closed its headquarters in Lawndale, it contracted the Shaw Company to come in and tear down the existing buildings and build new housing. Nearly four hundred units of rental and owner-occupied housing was built. This brought national and local attention to our community. Lawndale Community Church was providing housing on the southern edges of Lawndale and the Shaw Company was developing housing on the northern edge of Lawndale.

Others began to see the opportunity and potential for development. Lawndale has a large number of vacant lots, including more than one thousand owned by the city, and dozens of abandoned buildings ready to be developed. A ministry such as ours cannot buy all the property. One hundred million dollars would not be enough for us to prevent gentrification ourselves. Therefore the key question becomes, How do we use the gentrification process for our mission and the good of our community? Let us first look at gentrification in general.

What to Do

So how can we embrace the forces of gentrification when they come into our community? First of all, in the Church it is very important for us to remember the very essence of who we are as the body of Christ. We need to ask ourselves, Why did we come to our communities in the first place? Proverbs 31:8–9 says, "Speak up for those who cannot speak for themselves, for the rights of all who are destitute. Speak up and judge fairly; defend the rights of the poor and the needy." It is our mission to speak up for the poor and the hurting people of our communities. The Great Commandment is to love God with all of our heart, soul, and mind and to love our neighbors as we love ourselves (Matt. 22:34–37). One of the negative outcomes of gentrification often is that the poor are displaced. This has created a new phenomenon in our landscape of poverty by moving it to the outer parts of our cities. The suburbanization of poverty is taking place all over America. We are called to speak up for the rights of the poor and build a strategy that might help the disenfranchised people of our communities and not allow them to just be the pawns of gentrification. This is where our heart, mission, and actions come together as Christian community developers.

As the Church it is important for us to do what we should do best: pray, fast, and seek God as Nehemiah did when he heard of the walls of Jerusalem lying in ruins (Neh. 1:4–11). It is imperative for us to get involved in the community, to investigate what is happening. For those of us living in inner-city neighborhoods, it is essential that we stay put and encourage those in our church and ministries to stay in the community if possible. This is not the time to sell our houses and move to the suburbs, but to stay as the local stakeholders, possibly even using this opportunity to start a local business. When we in Lawndale saw these forces coming we took six weeks to pray, fast, and talk on a weekly basis in the evenings through what was happening in our neighborhood. We invited Bob Lupton to come and talk about gentrification and how we might work alongside this new economic force for the betterment of our community. Clearly the most important thing for us is not to panic but to trust God and continue doing Christian community development.

Gentrification often brings a vicious cycle to the poor. With the inflated property values of more desirable property, higher taxes often push working-class people out of ownership. Speculators buy and flip properties with absolutely no regard for the community; their only goal is to make a quick dollar. Instead of being alarmed we must creatively embrace these market forces and begin to find new partnerships and new ways to do ministry.

Our Key Initiatives

After several months of study and discussion concerning gentrification the people of Lawndale Community Church decided to focus on several key initiatives to work creatively with the forces of gentrification. First, we would encourage home ownership by church members and other community residents. We would increase our production of affordable housing and rehab more abandoned buildings. We did this through the Canaan homes program at Lawndale Christian Development Corporation, helping working-class people own their own homes.

Second, we partnered with a local group, United Power for Action and Justice (the local Industrial Areas Foundation) in Chicago, to build new homes in our community. This was called the Ezra homes program and we built more than one hundred new affordable homes for existing residents of our community.

Third, Lawndale Community Church, in an effort to help our members own a home, began a down-payment assistance program. Anyone who was active in Lawndale Community Church would have their down payment matched dollar for dollar up to three thousand dollars. My wife Anne's uncle had passed away and left our church some money. We creatively put twenty-five thousand of that into a down-payment assistance fund. Oh how shortsighted we were—twenty-five thousand was not nearly enough. More than thirty-five people from our church took part in this program. We spent more than one hundred thousand dollars matching money so first-time home buyers in our church could buy a home.

It was exciting as others were gentrifying our neighborhood to see local people take control of their own destiny and buy their own homes. Everyone was required to take home ownership classes, which helped people to understand what it means to own a home and to gain important skills of ownership. These classes helped people understand taxes, down payments, closing costs, and other vital information of owning a home. We are pleased that of the more than 150 new homes in our community affiliated with our ministry, there have only been six foreclosures.

A fourth strategy that proved to be very significant was to increase affordable rental housing in our neighborhood. Lawndale Christian Development Corporation has developed more than three hundred units of rental housing and has its own property management company to manage these. We are now developing more than one hundred units of affordable rental housing that will be completed within the next two years.

Fifth, we began to improve the area by helping and supporting community-owned businesses. This became a major goal of Lawndale Community Church, and we have been making it a priority. We opened Lou Malnati's Pizzeria in 1995 and it continues to be a beacon of light in our community. Since that time we have established and helped several local businesses that are striving to compete in the marketplace: a barbecue restaurant, a fence business, a landscaping business, several contracting businesses, an interior decorator, and an event planner. These are all new businesses that have been established by people in our local church. As a church we have helped all of them in different ways, from buying buildings for them to operate from to giving small grants that help people start their business.

Sixth, we have kept a close watch on all of the real estate movement in the community. By signing up with a local Realtor, I receive a listing daily of all the new housing and land that comes up for sale. This includes a description of the property, the address, and the asking price.

Partnership

A central aspect in making a difference when neighborhoods are being gentrified is to partner with other groups. Lawndale Community Church partnered with United Power for Action and Justice with the goal of building more than three hundred homes in North Lawndale. Earlier we partnered with twenty-five other churches in the Westside Isaiah plan to build more than two hundred affordable houses for ownership. We have recently gathered ten churches to partner with us to build forty units of affordable rental housing on the land where Dr. Martin Luther King and his family lived here in Lawndale. We also partnered with Chicago Housing Authority (CHA) in a recent development called Fountain View where thirteen of the fifty units were sold to CHA. Former CHA residents have moved into our community and now live alongside more stable families.

Real estate developers can be good partners. A real estate developer at one of our partner churches came and walked the neighborhood with us, helping us immensely. He saw many things that as urban ministers we were unaware of, and his expertise helped us make more informed decisions. We cannot live and work in isolation; we do not have the ability or the skills to do development on a large scale. Partnering helps us to be more effective.

As the faith community, get involved in the neighborhood, and as often as possible join block clubs and attend community meetings. Encourage your church members to participate when the city hosts hearings regarding new opportunities for development. As a ministry be a part of the neighborhood and participate with the people as new initiatives come to the area. It is important to be considered a friend and partner in the community. To be a good neighbor.

Lawndale Christian Development Corporation has partnered with the Local Initiatives Support Corporation (LISC) and the McArthur foundation for a program called New Communities. We are the lead agency and with our neighbors are looking at our community and striving to plan for the future. More than three hundred community residents in the last five years have participated in dreaming and planning for the future of our neighborhood. We put together a plan of what we hope to see Lawndale look like in ten years. This has been done by community residents, not outsiders. We named this plan "Faith Rewarded." Instead of lamenting about how others are developing our community, we took the bull by the horns and made our own plan, realizing that we could build upon the assets of the people and our community that were already present.

Difficulties and Struggles

This has not been an easy process for us here in Lawndale. We have met many obstacles along the way, some of which have been very discouraging to us. Community residents have protested with signs and called us names, using racial slurs because of what we have done. We have been accused of selling out to developers when we have partnered with them. We use the community workforce as much as possible and also keep the neighborhood people well informed about developments, but our motives are sometimes questioned. The emotional pain of this is difficult to express.

There is just not enough money to do all the developments that our community has been dreaming. It is easy to get discouraged when we see outside developers come into our community with apparently unending resources and money oozing out of their pocketbooks.

The recent housing crisis has also affected all of us. Lawndale Christian Development Corporation has fifty lots that we hope to build on, but it is becoming harder for us to maintain the lots and to pay the taxes just to keep them. Gangs and violence have increased in the last five years. We have a long way to go until our neighborhood is what we dream of. Christian community development is not an easy task, but it is one that we feel called to complete.

Now the Good News

It is imperative for us not to see gentrification as the enemy but to embrace it. A new study that has just come out by the University of Pittsburgh, the University of Colorado at Boulder, and Duke University examined more than 1,500 neighborhoods across the United States. They used the census data from 1990 and 2000 and found some amazing things. One thing that's clear is that African-American high school graduates were less likely to move out of a gentrifying neighborhood than they were to move out of a similar neighborhood that did not gentrify.

As urban ministers we have been working hard to improve the quality and value of education. If we are going to redevelop our communities for the very people we have been serving, then gentrification helps us to keep them from leaving to a greater extent than an ungentrified neighborhood. Other signs show how gentrification is helping and not hurting. Our neighborhood in the height of its population in 1960 had more than 120,000 people. The 2000 census showed we were under 50,000 people. This means that we have the capacity to bring in 50,000 new neighbors. These new neighbors can be from various races and ethnic backgrounds. They can come alongside our existing community residents without displacing the residents. Our goal is and always has been community development and housing improvement without displacement. We continue to work hard at that goal.

At Lawndale Community Church we have helped more than 150 young people go away to college and graduate with the exciting aspect of seventy-five of them moving back into our community here on the West Side. These are the future leaders, coming back to their community, and they want it to be a place where they can raise their families. Studies have also shown that many neighborhoods are being gentrified by middle-class African-Americans and middle-class Hispanics moving into neighborhoods within cities. This is a very positive thing as they come alongside many of the people left behind in our neighborhoods.

Lawndale has proved to be a stubborn and reluctant partner with the forces of gentrification and developers coming. When we have developed new houses we have sought to build them in a way that gentrifiers would not be attracted to them. The new Ezra homes are very affordable with no basements, smaller square footage, less brick, and fewer amenities to keep prices low. We have fought hard against those gentrifying forces that displace people. We have come alongside people at risk of eviction, striving to help them to be able to stay and to continue to own their homes. On the other hand, sometimes we have seen a family that has owned its own home in our community and paid off the mortgage choose to sell it for several times the initial investment, reaping the benefit of a new market demand. This gives residents flexibility to pick a new community or invest again in their own neighborhood. Our vision has been for stable, sustainable communities. When we see these improvements come, we embrace the development.

With the recent housing crisis, gentrification in Lawndale has come to an abrupt halt. Now we see not a continued string of openings but a cycle of closings. Starbucks, the ten-screen movie theater, two chain grocery stores, video stores, and banks have closed their doors and left our community again. For many this has brought disillusionment and a new loss of hope. Concurrently the Chicago Housing Authority has been tearing down high-rise public housing buildings and displacing the poor. This brings new people with federal Section 8 vouchers, which provide people with affordable rents through subsidies based on income, flowing to our community. More poor people have been moving into Lawndale.

The Zechariah 8 community is still the dream of Christian community development, where old men walk with canes and young children play in the city street; and where God dwells and is honored in the city. We continue to work, long, and pray for this in our communities.

CONCLUSION: CONTINUING TO LOVE

As CCDA'ers and urban workers we do not think of ourselves as gentrifiers, but when you boil it down, that is what we have been doing for a decade. We have principles that hopefully have helped us to treat the poor with dignity and help them to dream their own future and destiny. It is our prayer and hope that our representation of dealing with gentrification will encourage you. Dream and think creatively as gentrification comes to your community. We at Lawndale Community Church are committed to our neighborhood and to the people of our community. We are ready and willing to embrace our new neighbors, to love them into the Kingdom and help them find a personal relationship with Jesus Christ. We are called to love all of our neighbors, no matter what their race, ethnic background, or religious affiliation might be. We have a new window of opportunity to buy more property, to establish new businesses, to build more affordable houses, and to help more people buy their own home. These people become the stakeholders of our neighborhood.

We here at Lawndale Community Church will continue to love God and continue to love our neighbors here in our neighborhood. We will walk beside all people in our community, and as Tom Skinner has taught us, we will "continue to continue" loving God and loving our neighbor.

REFLECTION QUESTIONS

1. Has gentrification come to the neighborhood of your ministry or church? How has it hurt the community, and how has it helped?

2. How can you protect the poor of your community from displacement?

3. How can you help community residents purchase homes in your community?

NOEL CASTELLANOS has worked in full-time ministry in urban communities since 1982. He has served in youth ministry, church planting, and community development in San Francisco, San Jose, and Chicago. Noel is a highly sought after speaker, motivator, and mentor to young leaders throughout the USA, and has a deep passion to serve and invest in the lives of emerging leaders. After serving on the Board of the Christian Community Development Association for many years, he has established the new CCDA Institute, which is working to equip emerging church leaders in the philosophy of Christian Community Development, and currently serves as the Chief Executive Officer of CCDA. He and his wife, Marianne, have three children, Noel Luis, Stefan, and Anna, and make their home in the barrio of La Villita in Chicago.

CHAPTER 2

WORKING TOGETHER TO RESTORE OUR COMMUNITIES:

Networking and Collaboration

Noel Castellanos

INTRODUCTION: DREAMING BIG DREAMS

Driving on Upper Wacker Drive these days it is impossible to miss the construction of the new Trump Tower skyscraper right on the Chicago River. It continues to rise into the sky at an impressive pace. I am awed when I think about the complexity of building something this huge: all of the people and details that must be coordinated, all of the egos that must be stroked, and all of the issues that must be dealt with in order to make a project like this work. The number of architects, politicians, bankers and financiers, building inspectors, lawyers, city workers, developers, contractors, and the hundreds of subcontractors that it takes to get a building like this constructed is mind-boggling!

With a project of this immensity, collaboration and partnership are essential. Not even a rich, powerful, egotistical, visionary real estate mogul like Donald Trump could realize his dream of seeing another world-class skyscraper fill the Chicago skyline without an array of partners with diverse resources, abilities, connections, and experiences.

In the same way, the task of seeing the Kingdom of God reign in our city can never be accomplished by any one great church or by any one visionary pastor. It will take the entire body of Christ working together to see the gospel truly impact our city. It will also take great humility to admit our need for one another. Deep wisdom is needed to figure out how to work side by side with others of different beliefs and perspectives for the sake of the Kingdom—but it can be done in the power of God's Spirit, and for His glory.

Not long ago, an unusual group of leaders was called to meet together at Moody Bible Institute (MBI) to talk about safety and violence issues in our public schools. The mayor's office contacted MBI to ask for help in bringing together key youth pastors and nonprofit leaders working with school-aged kids. They knew the value of seeing churches engaged in the process of addressing the increase of violence in our schools, in collaboration with the police and with local schools. The twenty-five or so leaders in attendance all voiced their willingness to work with the city and the school board, and to work with one another to seek the peace of our city. Since arriving in Chicago eighteen years ago, I have attended countless meetings of this sort, all aimed at motivating and mobilizing Christians and churches to work together to solve societal problems, address crises, and work toward a common agenda for the good of others.

This kind of working together is not uncommon in the urban ministry world due to the overwhelming needs that exist in our communities, but it remains a tremendous challenge to sustain effective Kingdom partnerships and collaboration over the long haul.

In this chapter, I would like to explore the mandate that our triune God has given us to live out a Christ-centered unity in the world and in our cities and communities. We'll examine practical principles and examples for how to establish and maintain effective partnerships that address the needs of our neighborhoods, and more important that demonstrate to the world the unity that Christ-followers can have because of our common faith.

Human beings have incredible capacity to accomplish impressive feats by working together. We can use that capacity to accomplish God's purposes or we can use it for our own benefit. When I reflect on this, I immediately think about the great human-initiated building project found in Genesis 11.

UNGODLY COLLABORATION

In Genesis 11:1–4, we read that the human race was at a unique place in the history of our existence; all of the inhabitants of the earth were united by one language and a common speech, or a common vocabulary. They were also all gathered together in one location, in a plain called Shinar, when they verbalized a bold plan to build a city with a tower reaching into the heavens that would be sure to make a name for themselves as a people. They would be famous all over the world for their great accomplishment, and would be united as a civilization, able to tackle any challenge that came their way. The fear of being scattered throughout the earth might have pushed them to work together, but their principal motivation seems to have been an intense pride and arrogance and desire to be famous.

The people possessed the capacity, the ingenuity, and the willingness to work together to build this great tower in their new world-class city. What they lacked was an understanding that they should have been about making God famous, submitting to His authority and leading, instead of striving to make a name for themselves. It is striking to me the action that God was willing to take in order to correct mankind's sinful efforts to establish their greatness apart from Himself.

> *"Come, let us go down and confuse their language so they will not understand each other." So the Lord scattered them from there over all the earth, and they stopped building the city. That is why it was called Babel— because there the Lord confused the language of the whole world. From there the Lord scattered them over the face of the whole earth. (Gen. 11:7–9)*

Great unity and collaboration already existed in Genesis 11 at the Tower of Babel. But it was not pleasing to God in that it was about us, and our purposes and our greatness, and not about Him and His greatness.

So, what does it mean to be about Kingdom partnership and cooperation in our world and in our communities? How do we deal with the challenge of working together now that we not only have to crucify our human, sinful nature, but we have to do it in the midst of so much diversity of cultures, classes, and political and theological allegiances?

A BIBLICAL VIEW OF COLLABORATION

To answer that extreme challenge, we must root all of our efforts to work together in a solid biblical theology of unity, cooperation, and community. When I say *community* I am not speaking of neighborhoods, but of the fellowship that we can experience as human beings in relationship to one another, and more important, as followers of Christ.

The Scriptures are full of references to the reality that we are a people created for relationship and community. After the creation of Adam, God declared that it was not good for man to be alone (Gen. 2:18), and then He created woman to be his partner and co-steward of the earth. Together, Adam and Eve were empowered by a loving God (who by very nature is an example of perfect unity and community in the Trinity) to live life in perfect harmony, to care for all of creation, and to work together to fill the earth with new life as they reproduced.

Adam and Eve's devastating act of rebellion and disobedience in the garden changed all of that. Their rebellion infected all of mankind with a propensity toward sin in every pore of our being, leaving us estranged from God and from one another. As Adam and Eve hid from God in their shame, we too consistently find ourselves hiding from our Creator and from each other, while desperately yearning for the fellowship and community we were created to live in.

The Good News of God's biblical revelation is that God never abandoned His prize creation, but in fact orchestrated a dramatic intervention plan that would lead not only to the redemption of sinners, but to a restoration of all of creation, through Jesus Christ.

So, the God who declared, "Let *us* make man in *our* image" (Gen. 1:26, the Triune God working together to accomplish His purposes), is the same God who enters our sinful world in the incarnate Christ, sent by His heavenly Father, to accomplish the works of the Holy Spirit. What an amazing picture of biblical unity and cooperation that should inform our own views of what it means to work together in the name of Christ.

The Original "One Campaign"

The original "One Campaign" has nothing to do with international funding but was initiated by Jesus Christ in John 17. As Christ-followers, we cannot read Jesus' great priestly prayer without realizing that Christian unity is an essential consequence of being reconciled to God through Christ. When we were made right with God, we became a part of His new family regardless of our class, culture, or gender, and we were sent on a mission into a world still unaware of His amazing love and plan for redemption.

The reality of His redeemed community working together in unity was to be a tangible demonstration of God's actual power to change hearts, and to bring about not just individual change, but a total transformation of society and creation. Notice the power of Jesus' prayer:

> *My prayer is not for them alone. I pray also for those who will believe in me through their message, that all of them may be one, Father, just as you are in me and I am in you. May they also be in us so that the world may believe that you have sent me. I have given them the glory that you gave me, that they may be one as we are one: I in them and you in me. May they be brought to complete unity to let the world know that you sent me and have loved them even as you have loved me. (John 17:20–23)*

Clearly, God's intention for us as His followers is that we be united in purpose and commitment to Christ and His Kingdom.

The Body

One of the most powerful and important truths about unity and collaboration in the Bible is communicated in 1 Corinthians 12, using the human body as an example of our need for one another as Christians. Traditionally, we refer to this passage to examine the priesthood of all believers in a local congregation, which helps us to understand how important it is for each one of us to use his time, talents, and treasures to advance God's Kingdom and to build up the local church. While this is a very important application, it is equally compelling for us as we consider the call that we have as Christ-followers to work together in cities and in neighborhoods as an expression of our unity in Christ. Read this familiar passage with collaboration in mind:

> *The body is a unit, though it is made up of many parts; and though all its parts are many, they form one body. So it is with Christ. For we were all baptized by one Spirit into one body—whether Jews or Greeks, slave or free—and we were all given the one Spirit to drink.*
>
> *Now the body is not made up of one part but of many. If the foot should say, "Because I am not a hand, I do not belong to the body," it would not for that reason cease to be part of the body. And if the ear should say, "Because I am not an eye, I do not belong to the body," it would not for that reason cease to be part of the body. If the whole body were an eye, where would the sense of hearing be? If the whole body were an ear, where would the sense of smell be? But in fact God has arranged the parts in the body, every one of them, just as he wanted them to be. If they were all one part, where would the body be? As it is, there are many parts, but one body.*
>
> *The eye cannot say to the hand, "I don't need you!" And the head cannot say to the feet, "I don't need you!" ... If one part suffers, every part suffers with it; if one part is honored, every part rejoices with it. (1 Cor. 12:12–21, 26)*

Nowhere is the example of the diversity of the body, made up of so many different parts and functions, so important to embrace as in a city like Chicago, which is made up of seventy-seven distinct neighborhoods, with unique histories, ethnic makeup, and challenges. Each community is filled with people from a multitude of religious traditions, and no one single congregation can boast that it has the ability to reach everybody in the entire city for Christ.

If we understand this passage correctly, we have to confess that a big suburban congregation, with a multitude of mostly affluent white members, cannot say to an inner-city congregation, located in a very poor Latino barrio, "We don't need you," or "We are more important than you because of where we are located or because of our size."

Or, a small storefront church in an African-American community cannot say to a congregation on the North Side that worships in the Polish language, that it does not care about that ministry because it caters to a different culture.

If we really took this passage seriously, it would dramatically affect the way we viewed others in the body of Christ. We would celebrate the fact that not all church congregations have the same gifts. We would celebrate the fact that diverse denominations help us to understand different aspects of our faith (even areas where we may be weak).

Not all congregations have the exact same vision or calling. Some will be called to work with the sexually abused. Some will be anointed to work with addicts. Some will have a special ability to engage politicians and businesspeople. Some will be passionate about reaching children, and others will be especially effective in working with the elderly. But all are essential members of the Church with a capital C in a given city. The question that we must ask ourselves is this: Are we more concerned about everyone being like us, or the residents of our city and neighborhood becoming like Jesus?

CHALLENGES OF COLLABORATION

Theological Challenges

The Bible speaks very strongly about our call to maintain and even cultivate Christian unity—but what are the essential Christian beliefs that we must agree on in order to fully engage in partnership? Am I compromising the gospel if I work with a church or ministry that has divergent theological views from my own? These are the "rubber meets the road" kind of realities we must face when considering working with others, even to do something good.

When I first moved to Chicago's La Villita neighborhood on the Southwest Side, I immediately began to visit all of the churches in our community, Protestant and Roman Catholic alike. I wanted to meet all of the religious leaders of our barrio and let them know I was eager to learn about their experiences in the community. I must admit, as an evangelical with a deep commitment to social justice and community development, I met a lot of leaders whom I knew I did not agree with theologically, but I was committed to finding common ground.

Crossing denominational and theological lines can be very controversial and risky, and we must learn to discern when and where it is OK to partner with others. When I get frustrated about the complexity of working with others, I remind myself that the disciples struggled with similar issues as they set out to preach the Good News:

"Master," said John, "we saw a man driving out demons in your name and we tried to stop him, because he is not one of us."

"Do not stop him," Jesus said, "for whoever is not against you is for you." (Luke 9:49–50)

Practically, that is not bad advice for us today as well, as we navigate the challenges of working in very diverse metropolitan contexts like Chicago. If people and organizations are not against the purposes of Christ, maybe it would be of greater harm to the Kingdom if we did not try to work in collaboration in ministry.

Self-Sufficiency

Unfortunately, another major barrier to Christian unity and collaboration in our communities is a spirit of self-sufficiency and non-cooperation. Ironically, in many cases, this kind of isolation or non-engagement is the result of ministry success and growth. As in the Tower of Babel account, churches with good intentions can get so caught up in doing great things, and making a huge impact for God, that their kingdom building becomes more important than building the Kingdom of God.

Few of us would admit to this kind of arrogance or self-absorption—thinking that our church, our ministry, or our organization is the only game in town, or feeling like we don't need to interface with the rest of the body of Christ in our city—but too often this is how we act and this is how we are perceived. Our independence can easily turn to spiritual pride, and we do nothing to cultivate our connection to other churches or ministries right in our own backyards.

Sadly, we must admit that the church is not exempt from the sin of pride and arrogance, and these attitudes always make working together almost impossible, even for the sake of Christ. Competition and even jealousy are the negative consequences that result when we Christian leaders neglect the biblical mandate to live out our connectedness to others in the body of Christ.

Busyness

A legitimate barrier to effective collaboration is the incredible busyness that most church leaders experience on a daily basis. Christian leaders are being pulled from all directions: too much to do, too many demands, too many opportunities and needs. The thought of fitting in one more "non-essential" meeting seems impossible.

How do we discern whether we should join a community coalition that is forming to combat gang violence, or whether to chair an upcoming evangelistic or prayer gathering? The more leaders are rooted in a community, the more they are connected to the people's walk with God, and the more they are listening to the Holy Spirit's promptings related to their own calling, the easier it will be to know what efforts to get involved in.

It is essential to figure out what giants are threatening the well-being of our city, and to determine what role you should play in addressing those needs. Often, it will require working with other organizations and ministries to tackle the issues that really need to be addressed in a community. While we cannot do everything and meet every need, we are called to pray for the city and to seek its welfare (Jer. 29:7). To do so in the midst of planning weekly church services and weekend camps will take a new willingness to not do everything ourselves, but to look for ways to partner with others who can share our load of community outreach.

EXAMPLES OF COLLABORATION

One of the greatest privileges I have in my role with the Christian Community Development Association based here in Chicago is to regularly connect and network with other leaders in the city. Chicago is full of inspiring examples of what can happen in a city when leaders are willing to lay down their differences, make time to invest in relationships, and find creative ways to support and partner together for the sake of the Kingdom.

A number of years ago, the Extension Ministries Director of Willow Creek Community Church, Alvin Bibbs, helped to establish the Chicago Pastors' Alliance to provide a forum where pastors and leaders in the city could come together to communicate with one another, and to continue their own growth as leaders by bringing in top-notch urban ministry pastors and experts to provide training on various topics. Because of the learning these gatherings offered, leaders have . made time to invest in this monthly meeting.

River City Community Church and New Life Covenant Assemblies of God Church work together to advance the impact of the gospel in the Humboldt Park community. New Life outgrew the building where they worshiped on Sunday mornings. After moving their gatherings to a local high school, they made the decision to rent their building to River City for their Sunday worship services.

While this may not seem like a huge sacrifice, these two ministries are ministering in the same neighborhood and could have pitted themselves against each other. Instead, recognizing the need to reach more people in the community, and acknowledging the fact that both ministries have distinct ministry focuses and philosophies, their sharing of resources is a Kingdom gain.

A good friend, Tony Danhelka, who has pioneered Christian community development work in the suburbs of Chicago, moved on a vision to network area pastors. Tony and his wife, Donna, were burdened to see pastors pray together and work together to express our unity in Christ.

With a bit of apprehension, this couple began to dream about gathering the key spiritual leaders, or gatekeepers, of the Chicagoland area together to build relationships and to pray. Miraculously, what has resulted is a regular gathering of these very influential leaders who are looking for ways to work together, and to use their influence to mobilize the churches in the city to pray and do good works in the name of Christ.

Another exciting new movement in Chicago is a growing network of urban youth workers spearheaded by the Nehemiah Project and its director, Brian Dye. Along with providing online communication and resources for the area's youth workers, they help to lead learning groups in partnership with a national youth movement called Urban Youth Workers Institute, and sponsor local training opportunities for the next generation of urban leaders.

Brian also works closely with leaders like Pastor Phil Jackson of the House Hip Hop Church to informally guide and mentor young youth pastors in need of support. Increasingly, these young leaders are building strong relationships, greater ministry skills, and more effective youth ministries because of their willingness to work together and collaborate.

All throughout the city, ministries are finding ways to partner and work together. They follow the legacy of ministry giants from the past. Dr. Ray Bakke, who has gone on to become a worldwide expert in city ministry, started out in Chicago ministry where he never met a leader or an organization that he could not partner with, if it meant seeking the peace of his city. Dr. Bill Leslie, who was the founding pastor of La Salle Street Church, was always looking for creative ways to work with others for the sake of Christ. Dr. Verley Sangster, who was one of the first missionaries to urban kids in Chicago through the work of Urban Young Life, was always challenging the church to work together to reach young people for Christ. Dr. Daniel Alvarez founded one of the largest Latino social service agencies in Chicago, Casa Central, and was a pioneer in working with local government to bring services to the poor. With such a fantastic legacy of leaders who have gone before us and understood the need to collaborate and work together as a sign of the Kingdom, we are inspired to carry on this great tradition to really bring about change in our communities.

Restoring Our Neighborhoods Together

When many of us think about the idea of collaboration, we don't get too fired up! In fact, what comes to our minds may be images of boring, drawn-out meetings, with leaders trying their best to find an ounce of common ground to be able to stay in the same room together, let alone take the city for God.

In the twenty-five years I have worked in urban ministry, some of the most dynamic and effective collaboration has been addressing the needs of the city or of our community. Often, when crisis comes, the residents of our community expect church leaders to respond in some tangible way. I believe we have an unprecedented opportunity today to show our communities that the church is willing to roll up its sleeves to address the real-world issues and problems of our day, instead of staying on the sidelines, paralyzed by our denominational divisions and minor theological disagreements.

Frankly, the very people who need Christ the most care the least about this kind of Christianity, and are looking for a group of people who are marked instead by the love and passion of Christ Himself. Community leaders, parents, children and youth, the police, and our neighbors are expecting us as people of faith to offer something different.

Addressing Youth Violence

In Chicago, churches and pastors have often been called to rally around the issue of youth violence. Sadly, it is after a child has been killed in a drive-by shooting that we often see images of community leaders and parents standing at the crime scene pleading for the violence to stop. In my neighborhood of La Villita, we established a community organization called Neighbors Against Gang Violence to address the out-of-control gang activity in our community. We worked with the police, schools, parents, the social science department of the University of Chicago, and gang members themselves to make our streets safer for our children.

In the Humboldt Park neighborhood of Chicago, the YMCA has initiated a gang intervention program with churches as vital partners in helping young people. The director of this outreach has established a partnership with a Baptist church that has been actively praying for the community and that mobilizes its people to take ownership by being a visible presence on the streets. They have made T-shirts to bring attention to their efforts, and other neighbors have started to take a greater interest in the youth in the community. They have tried to get to the root problem of these young people's issues and concerns as they pray for them and build relationships with them.

The fact is, in every metropolitan urban area of our nation today, the issue of youth violence is an ever-present reality. Churches can unite to start alternative youth programs focused on mentoring, education, employment, and spiritual development.

Looking at Education

Traditionally, churches have shown two approaches to addressing the educational deficiencies in the city. One approach has been to supplement our children's education by establishing after-school programs and tutoring centers, and getting involved in supporting under-resourced neighborhood schools. The other approach has been to provide alternatives: to begin Christian schools, to lobby for the establishment of public charter schools in their communities, or to provide families with vouchers to attend existing private schools. Both approaches often require that churches partner with others, as they step out of the four walls of their buildings and move into active involvement in the community.

On the West Side of Chicago, in the Austin neighborhood, Circle Urban Ministries lives on both sides of the public-private education controversy. For twenty-five years, the organization has sponsored youth programs, supplemental education classes, tutoring courses, and after-school activities—all serving public education students. After many years of serving the educational needs of their kids, they realized that their efforts were not having the impact they had hoped.

"The greatest need in our community is indigenous leaders," says executive director Glen Kehrein. "We asked ourselves, 'How many leaders have we developed over all these years from all these programs, and what is the prospect for the future as far as developing the next generation of leaders?' The demonstrated results were more anecdotal than real."

Because the ministry had the children an average of only ten hours a week, Kehrein says Circle decided to take a comprehensive approach to investing in the children—realizing they faced problems ranging from poverty to gangs. In 1995, Circle Urban Ministries, in partnership with Rock of Our Salvation Church, opened Circle Rock Preparatory School. Recently, they have entered into a partnership with a Catholic-based educational organization to increase the quality of education their children are receiving.

Whether in creating these kinds of alternative schools or working to reform our current public educational system, we cannot address the serious educational needs and issues in our cities without working with others.

Health Care for the Poor

Twenty years ago, Dr. Art Jones worked closely with pastor Wayne "Coach" Gordon to establish a health clinic in the African-American community of Lawndale. When Dr. Jones began his work, Lawndale was one of the most medically underserved communities in Chicago. With a deep passion to serve the poor and the uninsured, the clinic began to meet the medical needs of the local residents in partnership with Lawndale Community Church.

61

At the start, some area doctors volunteered some time, and suburban churches provided some support, but it was the local members of the church who really took ownership of the clinic's outreach. As the clinic grew in impact, it established partnerships with local hospitals, local schools, and other local churches to make certain that as many residents as possible received much-needed medical services.

Many Spanish-speaking residents in the neighboring community of La Villita also began to come to take advantage of the clinic's services, so it became necessary to work in collaboration with an entirely different community. The clinic has grown to such a degree, with more than 100,000 patient visits a year, that it now works closely with the state and federal governments, receiving funding to provide better care for the poorest of the poor. The Lawndale Christian Health Center could not do what it does without a willingness to work with a variety of organizations, agencies, and churches to accomplish its mission. With the lack of quality health care being one of the huge issues affecting the poor, imagine what would happen if clinics like this were opened all over our nation.

KEYS TO EFFECTIVE KINGDOM COLLABORATION

As I reflect on the reasons that some collaborative efforts succeed and some fail, I would like to suggest a few key factors that are essential for working together.

Relationships

In my opinion, personal relationships are the key to establishing any kind of meaningful and sustained partnerships in the city. In most urban communities, it is not common to work with others we do not know, or with whom we have established some kind of relationship. Very few of us respond well to impersonal pitches requesting our time and resources. We are more receptive to the requests of a peer or friend who takes the time to ask for our help, support, or involvement regarding an issue of concern.

The best advice I could give a young pastor or leader who desires to make a difference in the community, and wants to work with other ministry leaders, is to invest in building relationships first, before asking anybody to do anything, especially when you suspect the request may be outside of their comfort zone.

Notice the high value Robert Linthicum, author of *Transforming Power: Biblical Strategies for Making a Difference in Your Community*, places on relationship building in ministry:

Perhaps the biblical person most skilled in building relationships was

Jesus. He built relationships intentionally and firmly. In fact one can argue that this was an essential and unique work of Jesus (along with his atoning death). In order to work toward the realization of the Kingdom of God, Jesus needed to build a permanent organization. It would be the strength of that organization (first, a disciple band, then a church) that would perpetuate the effort to realize God's Kingdom after Jesus had returned to the Father. And no such permanent organization could be built and sustained unless it was built on firm relationships.[1]

Kingdom Perspective

When we seek to build the Kingdom of God, instead of only being concerned with our own kingdom and organization, good things happen. Others will perceive pretty quickly when a leader is only concerned with what will benefit that leader, and will resist working together.

When our true motivation is for God to be glorified, it becomes less important that our name is mentioned, or that we get credit for some joint effort. The important thing is that people's lives are touched, that Christ is proclaimed, and that a strong witness to the Lordship of Christ is demonstrated.

Common Concerns

An important key to coming together in the city is to find common causes that we can agree to work on together. Because of diverse philosophical and theological beliefs, it really becomes essential that church leaders and Christians work to identify the things that unite us and to build on that common ground.

Although some churches may never be able to host a joint evangelistic campaign, they can work together to address homelessness in a neighborhood. While we might not agree on every aspect of our faith, we can learn to love and respect leaders and ministries that are different from us.

Historically, Christians from many denominations have come together to advocate for the unborn, work for human rights, fight for the needs of the poor, and pray for the safety of our neighborhoods, all because they have been willing to find common ground.

CONCLUSION: MAKING GOD FAMOUS IN OUR COMMUNITIES

Rick Warren's P.E.A.C.E. plan seems to be getting a lot of traction these days. It is an ambitious attempt to get Christians to work together to address what Pastor Warren calls some of "the giants of our day": spiritual emptiness, self-serving leadership, extreme poverty, pandemic diseases, and rampant illiteracy. He is banking on Christians coming to realize that we have a purpose as the church that is way beyond our own happiness or even way beyond the numerical growth of our own churches or ministries.

It is clear that even a megachurch the size of Saddleback Community Church cannot accomplish this vision on its own. Thousands of churches and millions of Christians need to come together to work for the Kingdom of God. We may not necessarily jump on board with any one particular plan to influence our world or community for Christ, but we are being challenged today to stop living as lone ranger Christians, and lone ranger ministries, and to start working and praying and dreaming about how we might honor Christ by being the united body of Christ that He came to establish on this earth.

REFLECTION QUESTIONS

1. Evaluate your ministry honestly and prayerfully. Are you more motivated by the idea of making a name for your church, your group, or even yourself, or by the idea of seeing the community transformed for Christ?

2. Prayerfully determine the essential Christian beliefs that you must agree on in order to fully engage in a partnership with another church or ministry to advance the kingdom. Ask the Holy Spirit to reveal which ministries in your area fit those criteria.

3. Based on 1 Corinthians 12:12–31, what are three personal steps you can take to begin developing the mind-set that others very different from you are just as valuable and just as integral to helping the residents of your city or neighborhood become like Jesus?

4. With no holds barred, dream about some outcomes that could take place in your neighborhood, town, or city if you committed to working together with other churches, ministries, or community organizations to address the serious issues in your midst.

JOHN FUDER received his Ph.D. from Biola University and has been a professor since 1994 at Moody Bible Institute's Graduate School in the heart of Chicago. He spent twelve years with CityTeam Ministries in San Jose, California, and two years with Impact Ministries in Chicago. For his doctoral research he worked with people on skid row in Los Angeles. Doc Fuder lives in Chicago's Edgewater community, is married to Nel, and has three children and one grandchild. He is the author of *Training Students for Urban Ministry* and the general editor of *A Heart for the City*.

CHAPTER 3

"EXEGETING" YOUR COMMUNITY:

Using Ethnography to Diagnose Needs

John Fuder

Introduction: We're Not in Kansas Anymore!

"Hey, Doc! I'd never been in a bar before until I came to Moody!" reflected a Moody graduate student after one of our many urban excursions in Chicago—a gay bar in Boystown on the North Side of the city. Other ministry forays find us in Little India, a Hindu and Muslim community, with signs saying, "Ask us anything!"

We had a recent adventure on a street corner near an el (elevated) train stop. Armed with poster boards and felt-tip markers, we encouraged passersby to write their thoughts in response to the question, "What do you want to say to the church?"

Taking the classroom to the streets includes learning experiences with immigrants in Chinatown, incarcerated youth at the Cook County Temporary Juvenile Detention Center, and homeless men and women at the Pacific Garden Mission. A highlight of the school year includes the annual day, Service in the City, in which hundreds of graduate students and all of the faculty partner with local churches and explore and minister in as many as a dozen ethnic and minority communities.

THE LABORATORY OF THE STREETS

Dr. Ray Bakke has been reminding us for years that "mission is no longer about crossing the oceans, jungles and deserts, but about crossing the streets of the world's cities."[1] MBI sits strategically in just such a setting. An article in the *Chicago Tribune* cited Illinois as the most religiously pluralistic state in America.[2] Chicago is at the heart of that diversity.[3]

In addition to hands-on ministry experiences, every graduate student, regardless of his or her major, takes a course in Community Analysis. A recent class of about twenty-five students conducted interviews in more than a dozen cultures. These included African (Togo, Ghana), Japanese, Korean, Chinese, Mexican, Brazilian, Pakistani, Turkish, Polish, German, Assyrian, and African-American.

These cross-cultural contacts instigated dialogue about Buddhism, Taoism, Communism, Islam, Judaism, Catholicism, and the New Age Movement. The lifestyles of those interviewed varied widely, from gang members, pimps, and prostitutes to immigrants (legal and illegal) and homosexuals. It was a snapshot of the world, and all within a few miles of our campus.[4]

A Historic Training Ground

Recently, on the eve of the Moody Bible Institute's annual Founder's Week conference, the headline of *M.B.I. Today* announced, "Little Hell: The Training Ground for D. L. Moody."[5] The article states, "When D. L. Moody arrived in Chicago . . . he was warned to stay away from an area of town known as 'Little Hell.' Few Chicagoans ventured into this area characterized by gambling, fighting, prostitution, and drug addiction. Even the police had little presence there."[6]

Dr. Lyle Dorsett, in his extraordinary biography on the life of D. L. Moody, *A Passion for Souls,* reiterates, "Moody was one of the few who had the audacity and courage to go into the worst district of Chicago, 'the Sands.' Sometimes called 'Little Hell,' this is where Moody went to rescue souls."[7]

The *Chicago Tribune* had characterized the area as "decidedly the vilest and most dangerous place in Chicago . . . the resort or hiding place of all sorts of criminals. . . . The most beastly sensuality and darkest crimes had their homes in 'the Sands.'"[8] Dorsett continues, "The Sands, located just north of the Chicago River on Lake Michigan's shore, was a place where children . . . were emotionally and physically wounded. Often beaten, sexually abused . . . these youngsters were discarded and treated like the rats and other vermin that roamed their . . . tenement hovels."[9]

So immersed was Mr. Moody in this world of need that his contemporaries called him "Crazy Moody."[10] But these early experiences and exposure to need "changed the course of his life" and became "the legacy of the ministries that he founded." He later reflected, "I don't believe I should be in ministry now if it had not been for that experience. God kindled a fire in my soul that has never gone out."[11]

These encounters formed the theoretical framework that was intentionally embedded in the original Chicago Evangelization Society, precursor to the
Moody Bible Institute. Its initial focus was to "offer classes and practicums on
how to reach the unchurched in the poorest neighborhoods." This "fire in my
bones" that Moody expressed was for workers to "learn how to get hold of the
masses . . . to reach these newcomers to the cities . . . in ways that were experi-
mental and practical—not merely academic." One of the school's earliest objectives for its students was a "knowledge of the Word of God and a knowledge of
man."[12]

A TOOL IN MY TOOLBOX

It was the early 1990s, and I was engrossed in Ph.D. studies at Biola University in Los Angeles. I had spent the prior twelve years with CityTeam Ministries
in the San Francisco Bay Area. The city was my calling, and I was headed to teach
urban ministry at Moody Graduate School in Chicago.

My coursework was in Biola's School of Intercultural Studies (SICS), under
the capable mentorship of Dr. Sherwood and Judy Lingenfelter. My first class,
Social Organization, had one major assignment—to build a relationship with
a non-Christian from a different culture than my own and develop a ministry
strategy to reach that individual for Christ. In more than twenty years of formal
education, it was the most profound learning experience of my life.[13]

I was introduced to Charles Lindsey (aka "Green Eyes") by some dear friends
who were living in community and doing ministry on the edge of skid row in
downtown Los Angeles.[14] Green Eyes was an African-American, homeless, disabled crack-cocaine addict living in a dilapidated refrigerator box ("cardboard
condo") on a nearby sidewalk.[15]

The "tool" in my ministry toolbox, taught to me by the Lingenfelters, is
ethnography.[16] *Ethnos* means people group, and *graphe* is description; in essence
ethnography is the skill set of collecting case studies of diverse ethnic cultures. I
was introduced to basic categories or criteria with which to collect and organize
data, including life history, family/relationships, friendships/networks, interests/
activities, and beliefs/values.[17]

Dr. and Mrs. Lingenfelter's experiences and writing on culture and ethnography were a huge help to me.[18] They also pointed me toward the work of cultural anthropologists like James Spradley,[19] who is in many ways the "guru" of
ethnography. That initial course set in motion my doctoral dissertation.[20] With
the blessing of the Lingenfelters, the "mentoring" of Green Eyes, and the help of
a handful of graduate and undergraduate Biola students, we immersed ourselves

in ethnographic research among the homeless, gangs, prostitutes, and illegal immigrants in skid row.

Theoretical Foundation

In addition to this collage of cultures, my journey was also to explore the literature to discover helpful resources in the area of ethnology (the study of ethnic peoples). I found numerous ethnographies, which greatly informed my own research.[21] But I was really after materials written from a Christian worldview, those with a more missional, gospel-centered focus, through which I could filter my experiences and better equip Moody students in the years ahead.

Meanwhile, back in Chicago, a young man named Mark Van Houten was ministering to people roaming the streets on the city's North Side. He had written two books describing his exploits. Concurrent with my intercultural classes at Biola's SICS was coursework on the same campus at Talbot School of Theology. Integral to that curriculum (as is the case at Moody and almost any seminary) is Hermeneutics, how to study the Scripture.

The first chapter of Van Houten's initial book is entitled "The Exegesis of a Community." In it he states,

> *The exegesis of a community can pay big dividends to all ministers and missionaries . . . to the community residents . . . to God. To "exegete" literally means "to lead out," to work toward understanding. One usually hears the word in connection with the study of the Scripture. . . . No matter how adept an exegete a theologian is, however, it is all for naught if he does not also understand his contemporary audience.[22]*

Dr. Ray Bakke had also been influencing the city of Chicago for more than two decades, modeling and teaching a similar paradigm. He writes,

> *How do you interpret a neighborhood? . . . How do you interpret Scripture? Most of us have been taught to look at a text in context. The passage may communicate powerfully . . . by itself, but it usually helps us to relate it to the chapter and the book . . . to know something about who wrote it and when and why. We need to apply the same principle to our neighborhood. We can regard it as a specific text, or we can work to find out what makes the city tick and how that affects our community.[23]*

Another voice that echoed loudly in my heart during that season of preparation and learning was that of Dr. Leith Anderson, pastor of Wooddale Church in a suburb of Minneapolis. In a lectureship series at Dallas Theological Seminary, he stated, "Effective practitioners of ministry for the 21st century should be as adept at the hermeneutics of culture as they are at the hermeneutics of the Scriptures." His appeal was "to combine ethnography with exegesis," particularly in North America, "an encyclopedia of every ethnic group in the world."[24] His succinct challenge to the body of Christ has been the central focus of my activities with Moody students since the mid-1990s.

Helpful Resources

During these years in Chicago, additional resources have highlighted the significance of ethnography for ministry purposes. Greenway and Monsma's *Cities: Missions' New Frontier* is one such example.[25] But the works of the late Dr. Harvie Conn have been of particular help. Serving as the editor of *Planting and Growing Urban Churches,* Conn appeals for "a more balanced hermeneutic" in the training of ministry practitioners, musing over "the proper mix" of the biblical text with the contemporary needs of the city and its people.[26]

One of the most practical chapters in Conn's anthology is the third, written by John Holzmann. It chronicles the efforts of the Caleb Project Research Expeditions (CPRE), whose focus is to "engage in ethnographic surveys of urban centers . . . to determine the sociological realities of those cities." CPRE combines classroom instruction and "ethnographic practice trips" in various cities for "mobilizing and training Christians to become strategically involved in church planting efforts."[27] Some of our own graduate students did extensive ethnographic research with CPRE and are now immersed in church planting in the Muslim world.[28]

But Conn's most thorough work, co-authored with Dr. Manny Ortiz, is entitled *Urban Ministry.* A major section of this exhaustive primer is devoted to ethnography, anthropology, and the social sciences. The authors join with Dr. Chuck Kraft in a challenge "to consider the work of anthropology as a significant tool for mission."[29] Conn and Ortiz emphatically state that "the church needs to learn the appropriate language to use" in ministering cross-culturally, and that "case studies [ethnography] can increase our learning curve and our skills."[30] They remind us that "the use of the social sciences does not in any way compromise our commitment to Scripture and the Sovereign Lord who holds all of life and history together. Rather they help us recognize that God uses concrete, social realities to bring His redemptive message home."[31]

WHAT DOES THE BIBLE SAY?

Waymire and Townsend, in their excellent book, *Discovering Your City,*[32] prompted my thinking about the biblical basis of community analysis. Could we be so bold as to suggest a theology of research for the church? I believe we can! Nehemiah is generally portrayed as the "poster child" of this methodology. Dr. Bob Lupton does a thorough, practical study of his life and work, with numerous insights, in his book *Renewing the City*.[33]

In essence, when Nehemiah gets the news about the state of disrepair of Jerusalem, he goes out and conducts research, thoroughly "inspecting the walls" (Neh. 2:13, 15). He then builds community (remainder of chapter 2), assembles a team around a common vision (chapter 3), and gets to work despite persistent opposition (chapters 4–6), until the job is done and the celebration begins (chapters 7–8).

This same "investigative" approach was also required by Moses, in Deuteronomy 13:14. He exhorted the leaders to "investigate and search out and inquire thoroughly" about the reports of idolatry among the people of Israel. The apostle Paul, in Acts 17, models a similar strategy in the city of Athens. Initially "observing the city full of idols" (v. 16), he takes a closer look in verses 22–23, observing "that [they] are very religious in all respects" and "examining the objects of [their] worship." As Dr. Leith Anderson adeptly states, "Paul should be seen as a skilled ethnologist who understood cultures while communicating truth."[34]

But one of the most explicit biblical blueprints of community analysis is in Numbers 13–14, where the spies are sent out to "exegete" the land of Canaan. Selected leaders are chosen to form the survey team (13:1–16), and they are given specific research criteria (13:17–20). After an extensive forty days of analysis (13:21–25) they return and report their findings (share the data) "to all the congregation" (13:26–33).

The response is less than enthusiastic (14:1–4). Could this have been the first recorded instance of that infamous mantra of a timid church, "It's never been done that way before"? As is often the case in our ministry endeavors, the needs were too great, the opposition too strong, the people too incorrigible . . . in short, it was just too risky.

Godly leadership steps up to stem the tide of negativity (14:5–21), as Caleb and Joshua join with Moses and Aaron in crying out to God to forgive their hesitance, redeem His reputation among them, and take the land as the ultimate preview of the gospel to the nations (v. 21—"all the earth will be filled with the glory of the Lord"). (Scripture quotes on this page are from the NASB.)

SO HOW DO YOU EXEGETE A WHOLE CITY?

The process starts one neighborhood at a time, or even just a few streets at a time in a community. In the years of training graduate students in this methodology, we have focused our efforts in one third of Chicago's seventy-seven neighborhoods, from Uptown and Rogers Park on the North Side to Englewood and Washington Park on the South Side and Austin and Humboldt Park on the West Side. Recent classes have also analyzed some of the surrounding suburban communities including: Waukegan, Evanston, South Barrington, Wheaton, Aurora, Elgin, Bellwood, Maywood, Dolton, and South Holland.

But the best way to start is one life at a time. In the last five years, Moody Graduate School students have collected well over three hundred ethnographies of an array of beliefs and cultures surrounding our campus.[35] A plethora of ethnic groups represents every continent, ranging from Albanian to Vietnamese, Guatemalan to Kenyan, Native American to Iranian, and dozens in between. We have engaged scores of lifestyles and activities, from AIDS patients to Wiccans, skateboarders to Holocaust survivors, push-cart operators and tattoo artists, gangbangers and refugees, panhandlers and runaways.

But that parade of needs and nations all have "a face and a name," a great cast of characters such as Two Bills and Mr. Big; Blackhawk and Peace Dove; Shorty, Speedy, and Smiley; Muhammad and Swamy; Oscar and Rosie; Igor and Natasha; Sylvester and Chester; Bert, Barney, and Ralph; Agnes and Legs; Omar and Tito; Ming Lee and Zita; MG, Rubio, Winston, Fong, Mushcat, Zona . . . In the words of one of our students, each one "has a story to tell that is worth hearing."[36]

LESSONS LEARNED ALONG THE WAY

The take away from these experiences is extensive; for some, even life changing. I like to call it "the hidden curriculum" of the Moody Graduate School. The same could be said for any church or ministry endeavor adapting the same methodology. The following excerpts are drawn from dozens of pages of students' reflections, grouped into similar learning patterns, and presented as transferable principles from the laboratory of the city.

Value of Relationships

- "There is no way to measure what I have gained from this experience. . . . What started as an assignment has become a friendship and a chance for me to show the love of Christ to someone who has not seen it before."

- "The biggest lesson I have learned from this assignment is how little it takes to become involved in someone else's life. . . . It is a permanent bridge to talking about matters of faith."

- "The process of doing ethnography is, in and of itself, a means of initiating relationships with potential longer-term contacts."

- "This ethnography proved to be a perfect vehicle for some good neighborliness."
- "We have met week after week and have built a relationship . . . our friendship has made a difference."
- "I trust Christians" (comment of a Russian Jewish immigrant).

Growing in Compassion

- "I truly believe that if we are to have any voice in the community we need to first love the community. We need to show them that we care."
- "As a seminary student in the big city for five years, one might assume that compassion would have developed for the less fortunate. . . . Compassion has been born in my heart for another whom I would have continued to overlook had I not been prompted in that direction."
- "I have a heart for the lost, somehow. . . . It breaks me completely apart and I feel like a total mess before the Lord. . . . I hurt and ache. . . . I see my Maker in these broken people."
- "Thanks for the opportunity to learn from this assignment. May I continue to grow toward being 'messed up' for all of God's people."
- "The Cross cries out for those marginalized and forgotten. . . . We are so concerned about the black-and-white, right-or-wrong, sin-or-no-sin approach that we easily miss the heart of compassion Jesus would have toward the individuals involved."

Local Mission Field

- "This exercise stretched me. I found that beyond my customary boundaries there is a mission field. The images of which will not soon leave my mind. The words of which will not soon stop ringing in my ears."
- "I learned that there is so much I do not know about other cultures that are right here in Chicago. I had no idea the extent of the hostility."
- "I'm happy that heaven is going to be better than Chicago. Chicago is a violent city. I was born in Chicago. I hate it that some people are prejudiced and that we can't get along with people . . ." (an African-American teen on the West Side whose father and siblings are all either incarcerated, gang-banging, or drug-dealing).
- "I'm grateful for this assignment that helped me to get out of my comfort zone and pursue hearing someone's story that is totally different from my own."

- "I am a pagan . . . my family hates me . . . my life is hell on earth . . ." (a Goth who is a practicing Wiccan).

- "It made me realize that though I may think I am seeing and, therefore, knowing what is going on around me, I really have no idea at all."

- My informant "has opened my eyes to a world of poverty, physical limitations, prejudice, loneliness, violence, substance abuse, and the cry for human dignity. This would have passed me by."

- "God has called us to go out into our communities. . . . We need to start in the places where we live. Our mission field can be our own neighborhood, among the Muslims, Buddhists, Catholics, and all the other religions out there."

Overcoming Fear, Prejudice, Complacency

- "I was extremely nervous to interview someone. . . . I couldn't imagine what I would say. . . . I dreaded the whole thing. God knew all about my fears and hesitations. . . . He provided."

- "I learned that I should help myself to overcome the overwhelming feeling of fear and distress after being exposed to the front line of lost souls. . . . I debrief my experience by prayer."

- "I learned that we need to be ready at all times for relationships that God might bring into our lives. I need to cast that initial fear I feel to the Cross in order to pursue the work of God unencumbered. . . . I need to be braver than I have been. . . . I need to weigh that fear with the seriousness of the other person spending eternity in hell."

- "It is human nature to be judgmental of other people. . . . If we don't take time to understand where a person has come from, what they are going through, and where they are headed, it is difficult to relate and withhold judgmental attitudes, even when we do not intend to do so."

- "It makes me feel horrible that I do not make more of an effort to reach out to hurting people, and I sit idly by and allow them to be damaged by others when I could be showing them the unconditional love of God through me and protecting them."

- "Honestly, I never prayed before, intentionally, for people in the city of Chicago. It is a conviction for me to start with prayer today for the broken, needy people in the city."

Bridge to the Gospel

- "The friendships built through the ethnographic process—getting to know a person on their own terms and on their own turf—provide ideal starting points for sharing the gospel."

- "What an excellent witnessing opportunity ethnographies can be. It allows you to begin a friendship, ask questions that can get to the heart of the matter, and receive a deeper passion for the unsaved."

- "The value of ethnographic research in developing a clear and effective ministry strategy cannot be overstated no matter what ethnic or religious group one is seeking to minister to. . . . [My informant] was more than willing to listen to a brief presentation of the gospel message."

- "Here is something I learned about the people in the city through this ethnography. People who are lost don't know they are lost. . . . I learned that as a Christian, it is our job, our mission, and our purpose in life to reach lost people and bring them into a relationship with God."

- Reflecting on a homosexual informant, struggling with depression and suicide, whose quest in life had become to find true love and acceptance from a man: "We are eager to share Christ with him, but how? . . . We are still pondering. Right now we are concentrating most on meeting him at the well [a local Starbucks]. . . . How do we make every moment count? . . . We will pray and we will love."

Skills for Future Ministry

- My informant "has taught me to be 'street smart.'"

- "I'm very happy for this project. . . . I'm going to use this strategy, and will teach other Christians to do so. . . . This is exactly what should be done to diagnose those who are spiritually sick, before offering the right and effective solution."

- "By going through the ethnographic process . . . I have been able to hone the skill for future application in my own ministry. I understand the value of waiting and watching as we gather knowledge and resources that will help us meet the needs of those we are ministering to."

- "One thing I realized is that I need to make an effort to make eye contact, and show by my body language that I am interested in what someone is saying. . . . I need to be transparent and ready to talk as well as listen."

- "This was a valuable experience as it reminds me how important it is to be fully engaged in listening. It is the only way to enter into another person's world. Ministry is so much about listening to a person's story and how they have interpreted their experiences."

- "I see that there is a richness of sharing life with those who have been in some way cast out. I see the value in team, being able to work together with others who share a similar calling of compassion."

- "One thing is for sure, the value of doing ethnography is immeasurable. . . . The complaint often lodged against Christians is that people can 'hear' what we're saying, but they can't 'see' it. One sure way of avoiding this is by doing ethnography. Taking the time to learn from other people's life experiences is not only essential to ministry, but it should be foundational."

Burden for the Church

- "I would like to see a greater missionary mind-set amongst Christians. . . . But I would also like to see a heightened sense of seeing ourselves as missionaries and our churches as mission base-camps."

- "Churches in the neighborhood can use this type of research to introduce themselves and understand how the community is changing. . . . Local churches can become more effective as they exegete their community."

- "I learned that it is so much more exciting to be swimming in the river of faith [being a witness in the world] where the action is, than sitting in the hot tub of faith where things are comfortable. I had been in the hot tub way too long."

- "We need to raise up a new generation within the church that is willing to actively love sinners in a way that gets our hands dirty, puts us in uncomfortable places, and causes some people in the body of Christ to grimace and turn the other way." (Reflection of a graduate student now ministering to AIDS orphans in Africa.)

- "I have learned that the real issue is not the difficulty of the task, but the willingness of God's people to take timely action. . . . But it will take commitment, time, and money."

- "Our churches need to be fighting for justice and exuding mercy all with a humble heart. . . . If we can motivate our church members to get actively involved in the lives of these people, it gives us great opportunities to share the gospel with them."

Disillusionment with American Values

- "Meeting [my informant] challenged the way I think of life. Even though I don't consider myself the 'white picket fence' dreamer, I think there are a lot of American values that I hold. . . . What I considered to be necessities of the world did not seem to matter to him [a homeless man]. It was a topsy-turvy idea for me."

- "It truly is a sad state of affairs that the Western church flourishes financially while those like [my informant] pedal on by. . . . We, the affluent church, are so blinded by our prosperity that we fail to see the superficial nature of our focus on self. Perhaps it is we who are enslaved to addictions as much as or more than [informant—a street person]."

- "Among the many other things I have learned through cross-cultural involvement, I see the absurdity of having a selfish love that denies others the experience of acceptance, happiness, and material possessions."

- "We must . . . give up the American dream as an idol. I believe that one of the biggest obstacles we have in the United States in the 21st century is we have been conditioned to comfort."

TOP TEN TIPS TO EXEGETE A CULTURE

Here are ten summary principles, suggested as a blueprint or strategy, for diagnosing a community:

1. Go as a Learner

This requires humility and persistence, and the courage to push past your fears. An accepting and inquisitive posture, while bathing everything you do in prayer, can open doors into another culture. Betty-Sue Brewster's model of culture learning is very helpful here: learner, servant, friend, story teller, intercessor.[37]

2. Seek Out an "Informant"

Find an individual who is a gatekeeper, an insider, a "person of peace" (Luke 10:6). Someone who will let you in to his lifestyle or subculture. An expert who can teach you about his or her journey as "lived experience." One who is a model (albeit imperfect!) of another belief or practice and can "hook you up" in that world.

3. Build a Relationship

As much as you can, be a "participant observer"[38] in that person's life, culture, and activities. A relationship, growing into a friendship, is key because in it a "trust-bond" is formed,[39] and trust is the collateral of cross-cultural ministry. In the process, God is at work to break your heart for that community (Matt. 9:13; Luke 13:34).

4. Use an Interview Guide

You may not always "stay on script," but it is helpful to work from an outline. You could apply the same categories used by our students (page 67), and then adapt questions within them to meet your specific needs.

5. Analyze Your Data

Depending on the formality of your community analysis, you will in all likelihood end up with some form of "field notes." A crucial step, often neglected, is to examine your data for holes, patterns, hooks. What missing pieces could your informant fill in? What interests, activities, or values are recurrent themes? Is there anything you could use to enter your informant's world more deeply?

6. Filter Through a Biblical Worldview

What Scriptures speak to the information that you are discovering? What does the Bible say about the activities, lifestyles, and beliefs you are exegeting in your neighborhood? What would Jesus do, or have you do, in response to the needs? A biblical framework is your strongest platform on which to mobilize your church/ministry/school to action.

7. Expand into the Broader Community

Your informant can act as a "culture-broker" to give you entrée into the additional lifestyles and subcultures within the broader community. As you learn to "read your audience" (become "street-wise") and develop credibility ("cred") in the neighborhood, you can leverage those relational contacts into greater exposure and deeper familiarity with the needs in your area.

8. Network Available Resources

As your awareness of the community grows, you will invariably feel overwhelmed by all there is to do, missionally speaking! You do not have to reinvent the wheel. Is anyone else working with that audience? Can you partner with another church or ministry or agency? With whom can you share and gather resources and information?

9. Determine What God Is Calling You to Do

With your newly acquired knowledge about your community, what do you do now? Plant a church? Start a new ministry? Refocus your current programs? Much of your response will depend upon your personnel and resources. But you are now poised to do relevant, Kingdom-building work in your community.

10. Continually Evaluate, Study, Explore

Ours hope in Christ is firm, but everything and everyone around us in our world is in constant motion. Is your neighborhood changing (again)? Who is God bringing to your community now? Is your church or ministry responsive to those opportunities? Are you winsome, relevant, engaging? We must always ask these questions, in every generation, in order to "serve the purposes of God" (see Acts 13:36).

CONCLUSION: WHAT DID THEY SAY?

At the start of this chapter, I referenced an outreach on the streets with our students conducting some initial exegesis of a community. The neighborhood is Boystown, the playground of thousands of homosexuals. The answers to our question: "What do you want to say to the Church?" were extraordinary. People waited in line to write their comments. They filled six two-by-three-foot sheets of paper.

In addition to the usual references about God's existence, wars, hatred, evil, racism, and the afterlife, some of the comments were heartbreaking. Here are a few of those pleas for help:

- "God needs to advertise better!"
- "You only love those who are like you."
- "Why don't you practice what you preach?"
- "I wish you had a better answer for this community!"

That last response is haunting. It illustrates the reason for this chapter. Oswald Chambers, in his classic work, *My Utmost for His Highest*, captures the essence of what should be our response:

> *Jesus has some extraordinarily peculiar sheep: some that are unkempt and dirty, some that are awkward or pushy, and some that have gone astray. But it is impossible to exhaust God's love, and it is impossible to exhaust my love if it flows from the Spirit of God within me. The love of God pays no attention to my prejudices. . . . If I love my Lord, I have no business being guided by natural emotions. I have to feed his sheep.*[40]

Ethnography with a Kingdom focus, applied by Christ-followers in churches and ministries, can help us find those sheep.

REFLECTION QUESTIONS

1. How informed are you and/or your church about the needs in your neighborhood? What are you doing to "exegete" your audience (become "street-wise")?

2. Do you have relationships with the "gate keepers" (informants) in your community? Who are these "people of peace" (Luke 10)?

3. Can you and/or your organization identify the significant lifestyles/beliefs/ ethnicity in your ministry area? How can ethnography help you do that?

4. Are you actively partnering with other churches/ministries/agencies to impact lives locally? What networks can you tap into for greater effectiveness?

Recommended Reading List

Bernard, Daniel. *City Impact*. Grand Rapids, MI: Chosen, 2004.

Chiseri- Strater, Elizabeth and Bonnie Stone Sunstein. *Field working*. Upper Saddle River, NJ: Prentice Hall, 1997.

Claiborne, Shane. *The Irresistable Revolution*. Grand Rapids, MI: Zondervan, 2006.

Dorrell, Jimmy and Janet. *Plunge 2 Poverty*. Birmingham, AL: New Hope, 2006.

Fetterman, David M. *Ethnography*. Thousand Oaks, CA: Sage, 1998.

Field, Taylor. *Mercy Streets*. Nashville, TN: Broadman and Holman, 2003.

George, Timothy and John Woodbridge. *The Mark of Jesus*. Chicago, IL: Moody, 2005.

Hall, Ron and Denver Moore. *Same Kind of Different As Me*. Nashville, TN: W Publishing, 2006.

Paul, Greg. *God in the Alley*. Colorado Springs: Shaw, 2004.

Pillar, Rajendra K. *Reaching the World in Our Own Backyard*. Colorado Springs: CO, Waterbrook, 2003.

Sider, Ronald J., Philip N. Olson and Heidi Rolland Unruh. *Churches That Make a Difference*. Grand Rapids, MI: Baker, 2002.

Sullivan, Barbara. *God's Ground Force*. Minneapolis, MN: Bethany, 2006.

JUANITA IRIZARRY currently serves the Christian Community Development Association (CCDA) as its Institute Director, coordinating trainings across the country to educate CCDA members in the key principles of Christian Community Development. She also teaches nonprofit management at DePaul University and urban studies at Eastern University and does nonprofit strategic planning consulting through Najera Consulting Group. She has a Master of Public Administration from Harvard University, a Bachelor's degree in history/political science and Spanish from Greenville College, and has completed sixty hours of graduate study in urban planning and policy with concentrations in housing and community development at the University of Illinois at Chicago.

CHAPTER 4

THE BORDER, THE BARRIO, AND THE 'BURBS:

Ministry Among America's Biggest Minority

Juanita Irizarry

Introduction: Latino Immigration Issues and the Church

I met Patricia Sobalvarro while I was a graduate student in Boston. A mutual friend from Emmanuel Gospel Center asked me to help Patricia prepare for a panel discussion in which she would talk about immigration policy from her faith perspective. Patricia is a member of Congregación León de Judá, a bilingual Baptist church in Boston's Dorchester neighborhood—one of a handful of churches that I visited while studying in that city. I had attended there one Sunday morning when it was announced that folks from that congregation were organizing through their Agencia ALPHA ministry to take a busload of people to Washington, D.C. to rally in favor of comprehensive immigration reform. It turns out that Patricia is the founder of Agencia ALPHA.

Patricia was born in Guatemala and brought to the United States without documents when she was eleven years old. Availing themselves of the opportunity to work hard and sustain themselves economically, the Sobalvarros eventually got the opportunity to legalize their status in the U.S. through the 1986 immigration legislation signed into law by President Ronald Reagan. Patricia was the second in her family to graduate from college, studying economics and international relations on a full-ride scholarship at Boston University. Since then, she has worked for more than a decade with prestigious financial firms.

FROM ILLEGAL IMMIGRANT TO INDIGENOUS LEADER

Patricia feels very blessed that she has had the opportunity to grow up and succeed in the U.S., achieving the "American Dream." But she grew increasingly conscious of the plight of others who did not have the same opportunity. So she returned to school to receive a Master's in Nonprofit Management so she could pursue a new dream developing inside her. She wanted to give something back. That vision would eventually lead her to cut back on her hours at her high-paying job to establish and oversee a nonprofit, immigrant-focused ministry through her church:

> ... to transform lives and both socio-political and economic structures based on solid Christian values. To integrate immigrants in the social, economic, and political aspects of society to improve our living conditions in the United States as well as in our countries of origin. To educate, equip, and empower new leadership committed to seeking social justice on behalf of immigrants who live, work, and strengthen this nation.[1]

That generous spirit also led her to assist me in a class assignment at Harvard's Kennedy School of Government, where she testified in a mock legislative hearing on comprehensive immigration reform. My classmates in "U.S. Congress and Lawmaking" spoke later of how impressed they were with her as she shared her perspective on what a just, comprehensive immigration reform proposal might look like, integrating her personal immigration and faith journeys. She bravely included her own genuine reflection on her struggle as a Christian wanting to honor the laws of the land while also seeking to honor God's commands to love our neighbor and the alien among us. She emphasized the Christian's duty to care for the poor and oppressed.

> Many immigrants live as second class citizens. Because of their legal status, many of them are exploited in the workforce, denied of certain civil liberties, stripped from their self-esteem, and constantly living in fear of being deported. Given this context, ALPHA Agency was born.... For the past 5 years we have met innocent people whose only crime has been wanting to put food on the table of their children.[2]

Today, Agencia ALPHA serves immigrants from all over Central and South America. Its website quotes Jeremiah 22:3, "This is what the Lord says: Do what is just and right. Rescue from the hand of his oppressor the one who has been robbed. Do no wrong or violence to the alien, the fatherless or the widow, and do not shed innocent blood in this place."[3]

My first encounters with Patricia and Congregación Leon de Judá had come during the height of the 2006 immigration debate, sparked by Congressman Sensenbrenner's controversial bill that included provisions to penalize people providing services to those who were in this country illegally. A wave of protest marches took place across the country. Many churches and other service providers tried to figure out how to respond.

THE BATTLE AT THE BORDER

A few hours from the Mexico-Arizona border, Kit and Ian Danley of Neighborhood Ministries in Phoenix struggled with different segments of their support base as the organization's Christian community development work began to encompass advocacy on behalf of their undocumented clientele. The ministry had moved in this direction as it had been confronted with the grim realities of providing housing services to residents and loan funds to entrepreneurs without the proper paperwork. Their church's traditional youth group trips to San Diego were complicated by the dangers of taking the congregation's kids in vans past checkpoints along U.S. state highways, where border patrol agents regularly seek to root out the undocumented by stopping vehicles traveling in the Southwest near the border. In light of the organization's focus on incarnational ministry, Neighborhood Ministries folks on the front lines came to understand intimately the needs of their most vulnerable neighbors as they related to them in their daily lives.[4]

I had just recently come to understand some of those struggles a little bit better myself. Though I know undocumented people in my neighborhood and church, the harshness of the immigration struggle had hit me hard on a recent trip to Arizona. Just after taking an "American Immigration Policy" course, I visited Nogales with Maria Gomez-Murphy, the director of Way of the Heart, a nonprofit organization serving low-income residents on both sides of the border. As we walked past the checkpoint to have lunch in Nogales, Mexico, Maria told me of the advocacy work she has done on behalf of U.S. citizens of Mexican descent, like herself, who have been picked up by border patrol agents looking for "illegals." She explained the dehumanization that everyone with brown skin (and no badge) is prone to experience in that environment.

I was particularly taken aback by the context as we literally stepped past the wall. The other times I had crossed the border I had driven across a long bridge over the Rio Grande. This time, I looked up to see humble houses on the Mexico side, just footsteps from a sheet of metal stretching across the hillside. Those who live higher up the hill have a full view of the affluence and opportunity of the U.S.; I couldn't imagine the alienation and pain those families must feel.

As the Danley mother-and-son team considered appropriate responses to such realities, they referenced Jesus' words from Matthew 25:34–40.

> *Come, you who are blessed by my Father; take your inheritance, the kingdom prepared for you since the creation of the world. For ... I was a stranger and you invited me in. ... Then the righteous will answer him, "Lord ... when did we see you a stranger and invite you in?" ... The King will reply, "I tell you the truth, whatever you did for one of the least of these brothers of mine, you did for me."*

Reflecting on the realities around them, they wrote in the Christian Community Development Association's *Restorer* newsletter:

> *We see you Jesus in the face of our undocumented brother paying university level tuition for a community college education. We see you Jesus in the face of the worker who after long, tired days still finds time to organize and coach a soccer league for our kids in the neighborhood. We see you Jesus in the face of a battered mom who is afraid to call the police after her husband has abused her in an ugly drunken moment.[5]*

But as the Danleys' church processed such issues together, some members threatened to leave the congregation in response to preaching about caring for the stranger in God's name, which the members saw as "political" and not as justice issues. Meanwhile, another congregation was taking the call to care quite literally. This one happens to be in my neighborhood in Chicago.

SANCTUARY IN THE CITY

Lately there has been talk in my community and the media about Flor Crisostomo, an undocumented immigrant who was taken in by Adalberto United Methodist Church in Chicago's Humboldt Park neighborhood.[6] The church is providing sanctuary for her in a city declared by Mayor Richard M. Daley as a "Sanctuary City"—where the city's resources are not used to help immigration officials carry out their duties. Flor is the second such immigrant avoiding deportation by taking refuge in this church.[7]

Adalberto Church is located in Chicago along what neighborhood residents proudly refer to as *Paseo Boricua* (The Puerto Rican Way). Down the street from two gargantuan, sculptural renditions of Puerto Rico's flag, the church is right smack in the heart of the cultural hub of Chicago's Puerto Rican community—whose people are born with U.S. citizenship whether they are native of the island or the mainland; who are technically considered migrants rather than immigrants;

who sometimes resent the presence of "illegal aliens" who are perceived to represent competition for jobs. They also feel resentment when raiding immigration officials mistakenly detain Puerto Ricans. Yet Adalberto Church's pro-immigrant stances in the name of social justice have been bolstered by local Puerto Rican leaders who have a sense of solidarity with other Latinos and their struggles.

Near the intersection of Chicago's officially designated community areas of West Town, Humboldt Park, and Logan Square, this neighborhood was mostly Puerto Rican when I was a child. Some Mexicans were around at the time, but now they seem to be everywhere, even though the Humboldt Park *barrio* is still the cultural heart of Chicago's Puerto Rican community. As I was growing up, Logan Square was the hub of the city's Cuban community. Since my grandmother lived in Puerto Rico, a Cuban neighbor and good friend of my mother served as my surrogate *abuela*. Although we lived in the shadows of the St. Sylvester Catholic Church with its English and jam-packed Spanish and Polish masses, my family attended a Plymouth Brethren church where my dad was one of the preachers. In addition to people from Puerto Rico, Cuba, and Mexico, our Spanish-language congregation included families from the Dominican Republic, Colombia, Ecuador, Guatemala, Paraguay, and that distant land of Texas. I distinctly remember the amazing potluck dinners we had, replete with dishes from across Latin America.

LOVE YOUR (LATINO) NEIGHBOR?

These stories surely stir up much controversy about the church's role. Many Christians would argue against the law-breaking activity and posture of the church and Flor. Flor characterizes her actions as civil disobedience in the face of the failures of both the U.S. and Mexican governments to craft relevant and just trade and immigration procedures and policies that reflect economic realities in both countries.[8] Some might denounce a church that harbors them. Yet others would focus on Leviticus 19:33–34, "When an alien lives with you in your land, do not mistreat him. The alien living with you must be treated as one of your native-born. Love him as yourself, for you were aliens in Egypt. I am the Lord your God."

Regardless of one's political perspective on the issues, when ministering within the Latino community one cannot avoid addressing the immigration issue and the related challenges referenced in each of these stories. Documented or not, many poor Latinos live in constant fear and insecurity as they are confronted on a daily basis with exploitation and abuse and lack of access to food, shelter, health care, and economic resources.

The Diverse Latino Community

Also key to ministry among this diverse community of people is an understanding of the distinctions among Latino nationalities and the different demographic realities in distinct geographies. Chicago is a particularly excellent laboratory for examining and experiencing Latino diversity in this country. With significant numbers of Mexicans and Puerto Ricans, along with a smattering of Cubans and others, Chicago's Latino community is quite representative of the overall mix of Latino nationalities in the U.S.

Hispanic or Latino?

As I visited Family and Children Faith Coalition in Miami recently, and sipped a delicious cup of *café con leche*, the strong Cuban influence in the neighborhood, the ministry, and city politics was plain to see. The staff there pointed out that in their minds the term "Latino" referred to Mexicans whereas the term "Hispanic" felt more relevant to them. Meanwhile, my studies have taught me that Cubans have a special immigration policy just for them, so the plight of Mexicans without papers (or Dominicans or Haitians or others) may or may not be of concern to South Florida's dominant ethnic group.

Back home in my neighborhood, a short walk from *Paseo Boricua* and Adalberto Church, *Latino* is the more politically correct term for all of us these days, especially for those who choose not to favor our Spanish heritage over our indigenous roots. Yet my father, a "Nuyorican" (Puerto Rican from New York) born during the Depression, comfortably calls himself Hispanic as many of those of his generation and geography did, long before the U.S. government chose the term as the official U.S. Census category for those of us of Spanish-speaking descent from the Americas.

Amidst all of this diversity, the 2000 U.S. Census says that the three largest Hispanic nationalities in the U.S. are Mexicans, with 63.9 percent of the Hispanic population; Puerto Ricans, which comprise 9.1 percent; and Cubans, who make up 3.5 percent.[9] Hispanics have distinct histories in their homelands and in the U.S. Their immigration, refugee, and naturalization status varies from ethnic group to ethnic group and among groups and generations. Their economic conditions and political views differ as well. Accordingly, ministry among this complex group requires attention to a wide variety of needs, attitudes, values, and orientations as well as an awareness of Hispanic inter-group relations issues.

THE BURGEONING LATINO COMMUNITY

Whether one immediately grasps the nuances of the different nationality groups or not, it is hard to miss the Hispanic community in the U.S. today. As of the 2000 U.S. Census, Hispanics are now the second-largest group in the U.S., after whites, with more than 34 million people. Of course, Hispanics have been here for a long time, but the dominant culture has just begun to wake up in this new millennium to the reality of the presence and explosive growth of the Hispanic community. While Hispanic pop stars were drawing the public's attention in the first part of the decade, Hispanic population growth in the U.S. was surpassing all projections. By 2005, the Hispanic population had already grown to 42 million—more than 20 percent growth since 2000. Of these, the native born now number more than 25 million, and the foreign born are nearly 17 million.[10] Meanwhile, as of 2000, one-third of all Hispanic U.S. citizens were age seventeen and under.[11]

Misnomers and Myths

This Latino population growth on the national level is reflected in many of our communities. In some neighborhoods that have decades of firsthand experience with high Latino birth rates and extended families, it comes as no surprise that Latinos are now the largest "minority" in their community or across the country. In other states and municipalities where not too long ago Latinos were still few and far between, the rapidly expanding number of Latinos in the U.S. may seem quite unexpected, confusing, even threatening. In their lack of awareness and experience, many people lump all Latinos into the same category. Some refer to the entire ethnic group as immigrants or assume most of them are undocumented. Again, the Chicago area is a microcosm of the national scene, with local attitudes mirroring those of much of the nation. The *Chicago Sun-Times* points out:

> *Ask a typical Chicagoan where most new Latinos in the area are coming from, and they'll probably describe some illegal border crossing. But they'd be wrong. The source of 72 percent of the group's recent population growth is actually the maternity ward, where Latino children are being born to proud parents who have achieved or are still pursuing the American Dream.[12]*

Primarily due to the growth of the Latino community, Chicago's population expanded in the last decade of the last century after years of population decline. Meanwhile, the size of the Latino community in the suburbs also exploded, such that more than half of all Latinos (55 percent) in the Chicago region now live outside the city limits.[13] The resulting shift in the ethnic makeup of many communities has surprised many residents and leaders who were not accustomed to

Latinos living in their neighborhood.

Many imagine that this bold appearance of Latinos on the suburban scene follows the historic pattern. Previously, successive waves of former city-dwellers, including various racial and ethnic groups, have climbed the ladder of success and moved from the city to the suburbs. But in the case of Chicagoland's Latinos, in recent decades many have moved directly to the suburbs from Mexico. It is a common joke that after one person relocates from Mexico to a particular municipality in the Chicago region, soon his whole extended family and eventually his whole town from Mexico will follow. But Mayor Donald Peloquin of southwest suburban Blue Island, Illinois, contends that it is no joke. Intimately in touch with his community, this colleague who sat with me on the Chicago Council on Global Affairs Mexican American Task Force confidently identifies the town in Mexico to which the majority of his Latino constituents trace their roots. Similarly, he identifies the town in Italy from whence the other dominant Blue Island ethnic group came in previous generations.

Burden or Blessing?

Latinos are strong in number, and they are probably here to stay—in the city as well as the suburbs. The Latino community itself is quite diverse, and plenty of Latinos fit in the middle class. Yet many of the typical urban woes that befall the poor in the inner city also appear in suburban pockets as low- and moderate-income immigrants and their U.S. citizen children struggle to survive and thrive, often in isolated, under-resourced communities throughout the metropolitan region. But needy Latinos are sometimes especially left out in the cold. Local schools, businesses, social service agencies, and churches are not quick enough to adjust to the specific realities of these new community members. Even as well-intentioned service providers and advocates begin to grasp the suburbanization of poverty, in some regions there is too little awareness and understanding of the Latino community. Furthermore, much of the government and nonprofit sector infrastructure is ill-equipped to deal with Spanish-dominant clients and with poverty and discrimination issues that are manifested differently than in the African-American community.

Despite the reality that native-born Hispanics outnumber the foreign-born, the fact that many of our country's new suburban neighbors are recent immigrants has many implications. Although two-thirds of Chicagoland's Hispanics are citizens and more than three-quarters of the region's Hispanic households are bilingual,[14] the significant number of recent arrivals with language barriers and cultural differences is strongly felt by receiving communities. Unfortunately, too few residents and leaders understand the benefits these newcomers bring to the table.

> *This influx of Latinos, mostly from Mexico, into the region's*
> *municipalities has not always been an easy transition. At best, some*
> *municipalities have welcomed the assets that Latinos bring and embraced*
> *the creation of a diverse society. At worst, the region has seen episodes of*
> *outright hostility. Overall, there is an uneasy acknowledgment that the local*
> *community has changed, resulting in varying degrees of both ethnic tension*
> *and acceptance of new neighbors.*[15]

To combat misunderstanding and promote the economic integration of Mexicans, who comprise 80 percent of Latinos in the Chicago region,[16] the local Mexican American Task Force noted a number of important recent statistics. The group highlights the contributions of the highly entrepreneurial and hard-working Mexican immigrant community and other Latinos. At the time of the task force's study, just past the midpoint of this decade, Latinos accounted for almost 10 percent of the region's total household income. They made up nearly 15 percent of the Illinois workforce. The expansion of the Latino labor pool was very closely aligned with the total number of new job opportunities that were created in the area. Latinos accounted for almost half of the growth in owner-occupied homes in the region.[17] Understanding these data, Mayor Peloquin says that he is counting on the energy of the Mexican community to revitalize his town.

Similarly, other local officials are trying to address reality and lead their communities through an adjustment process. Many municipal mayors in the Chicago region have come together to learn and discuss ways to promote inclusion and positive relations among community members of varying backgrounds. The complexities of this type of process are summarized in "Forging the Tools for Unity: A Report on Metro Chicago's Mayors Roundtables on Latino Integration," which wisely acknowledges that "each setting is unique. The regional economy, local labor needs, attitudes of native population, and perceived strain of the undocumented population on local resources all require that each community consider its own way of developing a plan for local immigrant integration."[18]

Some Latino-Specific Examples

While communities and congregations need to respond to the new reality of Hispanic neighbors, cultural competence tends to be severely lacking in the Church, the government, and business. Many in urban ministry think of poverty in African-American terms and do not imagine that the needs among other populations might not be quite the same. In addition, most models are developed within an inner-city framework and do not account for the transportation dilemmas and extreme isolation the poor face in many outer-ring municipalities.

This disconnection became clear to me as I directed Latinos United, a Hispanic-focused policy and advocacy organization in the Chicago region. Fortunately, my colleagues and collaborators regularly joined me in expressing concern about the lack of human services infrastructure and leadership within suburban Latino communities. But I often felt like a lone, broken record as I sat on advisory councils and steering committees, reciting the list of ways in which familiar problems manifested themselves differently among the Latino population. Sometimes blank faces stared back at me. Other times I saw lightbulbs go off in people's heads as they began to understand. They realized that homelessness in the Hispanic community less often means that people are sleeping on the street and more often means that they are overcrowded—and thus do not qualify for federal homeless-assistance dollars, as people in that situation once did according to federal housing policy, while being set up for unique abuses.

Unwelcome Neighbors

More recently there have been intentional efforts on the part of local elected officials to find ways to promote smooth transitions. But this comes on the heels of a very bumpy decade as various municipalities throughout the region responded quite harshly to earlier waves of out-migration from the city and immigration from Latin America. From the mid-1990s to the middle of the first decade of the twenty-first century, the Chicago metropolitan region was a hotbed of municipal discrimination against Latinos. Some suburbs used selective enforcement of the occupancy standards in their building codes to root out Latinos and combat overcrowding. For example, if authorities found twelve Latinos living in a home intended for only ten, they cracked down on that household, whereas they did not apply the same standards to households of other racial and ethnic groups.

Another town used an urban planning mechanism to justify demolishing a Latino neighborhood, deeming as blighted a rental housing complex full of Hispanic families even though there was little rationale for such a determination. Yet another tightened its occupancy standards in order to make it harder for Latinos to move in while grandfathering in the large households of white ethnic groups that had lived in the municipality since an earlier generation. During that period, the U.S. Department of Justice sued seven municipalities nationwide for housing discrimination against Latinos. Five of those municipalities, including the examples highlighted above, were in the Chicago suburbs. Since then, in a wave of anti-immigrant sentiment, the U.S. has seen a number of towns and cities across the country challenging federal fair housing law by attempting to institute local regulations that would keep landlords from renting to undocumented immigrants.

Meanwhile, individual landlords across the country were also increasingly reacting to their discomfort with the presence of Hispanics by denying housing to Hispanics at alarming rates. In 2003, the U.S. Department of Housing and Urban Development (HUD) determined that for the first time, Hispanics had surpassed African-Americans as the group that most often face housing discrimination.[19] In a similar vein, in 2001 and 2002, Latinos United conducted a study with Interfaith Housing Center of the Northern Suburbs, which found that one in four Hispanics looking for rental housing were discriminated against. Meanwhile, predatory lending practices (which have contributed to the current foreclosure crisis) were of major concern as vulnerable immigrants and other Hispanics pursuing the American Dream of home ownership were targeted for scam loans and unwise deals. Despite facing high levels of abuse, however, Hispanics are the least likely to report instances of discrimination, according to the HUD study. Especially if they are immigrants, they are not likely to be aware of their rights. Also, they may not be culturally inclined to challenge an authority figure such as a landlord, a banker, or a real estate agent. Or their documentation status may make them afraid to speak out.

I tested some of what I learned in my personal search for housing. A home owner considering selling my town house, one day I left a message at a real estate office to find out more about a house that was on the market in my gentrifying neighborhood. No one returned my call. I called again a few days later using an anglicized version of my name. I was attended to immediately. I cannot prove that it was discrimination that led that company to respond to one call but not the other, and I never reported it. But the more one knows about the realities of discrimination, the more it makes one wonder.

Pushing the Poverty Around

For most of my life, my parents have lived within blocks of where I live today. They never had the money to buy a house, but we lived in the same apartment for the majority of my years living at home. Then rising prices and deteriorating conditions led my parents to move a number of times within a relatively short span of years. They had settled in a decent apartment on a beautiful boulevard, only two blocks from my town house in the same architecturally significant sector of our community. But the allure of those gorgeous greystones, the proximity to good transportation corridors, and the presence of recreational and other amenities eventually attracted urban "pioneers," speculators, and upscale urban professionals. One day the two-flat where my parents lived in the upstairs apartment sold for $350,000. The new owners moved in downstairs and soon announced that my parents' $550 rent would jump to $1,200. With my mom's salary from a

Christian school and my dad's semi-retirement status, there was no way they could afford that.

Fortunately for my parents, I had enough room for them in my town house. Fortunately for me, they agreed it would be a temporary situation. But when my parents finally found a suitable new living situation a year later, they had to leave the neighborhood they had long called home. Though we were thrilled that a Latino former colleague of mine was generous enough to provide them an apartment for a cheaper price than he would offer to a total stranger, my parents were paying more than they had paid before to live in a building that was in worse condition.

Though the new place was only a few miles away, they were disconnected from their friends and familiar places. My elderly father, who does not drive anymore, no longer lived within walking distance of the church where he still plays leadership roles. Nor was he steps away from the train station to get downtown to the part-time teaching job he has held at Moody Bible Institute for years. They no longer lived within the boundaries of the community group with which my mom had been a committed volunteer, nor within the limits of the city ward where they had helped on the campaign of the local alderman. They moved much farther from *Paseo Boricua,* where Puerto Rican music plays from storefronts, neighbors set up portable tables on the sidewalk to play dominoes, and my parents enjoy Sunday brunch at Nellie's, whose namesake was a beloved neighborhood activist and friend from church.

My mom now had to drive out of her way to pick up her needy friends whom she would often take with her on trips to the grocery store. Neighbors who had been ministered to by my parents for years could no longer drop by for a cup of *café con leche* and some comforting words unless they had a car. My parents no longer were likely to run into friendly faces on the street—kids who had once been in my mom's kindergarten class or former playmates of mine who still remember the way my parents opened our home to them.

This story has a happy ending so far. My parents are among the unusual ones who eventually found a way to move back to the neighborhood, thanks to a generous Christian friend who provided an apartment at below market rate. Mom and Dad's "love your neighbor" lifestyle is more fulfilling now that they have reconnected with those members of our community who are still able to live here, and their retirement years are more convenient and enjoyable, even as they squeak by on a very low income, as they have regained access to local amenities and their support system. I am grateful that my parents are nearby as I begin to contemplate child care needs and as they need more elder care from me.

In this day of high housing prices, Latinos are not the only people whose community fabric is torn by the unaffordability of housing and residential displacement. But for immigrants and other marginalized groups who often feel a need to cling to one another for dear life as they struggle with uprootedness, social isolation, or discrimination, forcible relocation can be particularly disorienting and can add to the sense of oppression and systemic injustice. Some argue for development that displaces the poor in the name of beautifying the physical space of a neighborhood and getting rid of the "bad element." It is a well-worn strategy for mayors who need more property tax revenues and a reputation for urban revitalization, police commanders who need to be able to claim improved crime statistics, and the real estate industry folks who just want to make a quick buck. But these strategies do very little to fix the problem. Just pushing the vulnerable around does not address the social ills that come with poverty and oppression.

Residents Respond

My Puerto Rican community, whose people have been pushed from one Chicago neighborhood to another more than once, is pushing back. "We Shall Not Be Moved" is a common refrain as community residents organize. They work to ensure that developers do not get special treatment that makes more high-end housing development possible. They actively point out the problems when our police officers participate in racial profiling. In some of the suburbs where municipal housing discrimination has been so rampant or where school districts have wittingly or unwittingly defied the law by requesting social security numbers to enroll Latino children in school, local Latino leadership has blossomed as a result. Residents organized and fought for their futures in the face of such challenges. In some cases, new community organizations have formed or existing ones have reached beyond their previous boundaries to address new needs.

HOW DOES THE CHURCH RESPOND?

Unfortunately, too seldom has that aid come from the Protestant church. Some of my friends in the Puerto Rican community have been surprised about my engagement with local cultural activities, community development, and political endeavors. Their experiences with the church have led them to believe that one has to choose between loving God and loving one's culture and community. Many Latino congregations understand individual socioeconomic needs from firsthand experience but lack a theological foundation for holistic ministry and social justice. Meanwhile, most dominant-culture congregations are underprepared to reach out to new neighbors across cultural, class, and language barriers.

There are not enough Agencia ALPHAs, Adalberto churches, and neighborhood ministries.

For a number of years I served on the leadership team of a small congregation that had been in my neighborhood for years, since European immigrants had founded the church more than a century before. Having already been through a racial split, when Puerto Rican and white styles clashed, a couple of decades later the church was trying again to be culturally sensitive to its largely Latino environment. But in the end, the congregation wanted the Latinos (and African, Haitian, and Chinese immigrants) who worshipped there to assimilate into the dominant white culture. Ultimately, that congregation withered down to a handful of folks before merging with another church.

Today I am active in a young church plant in my lifelong neighborhood. Still a largely Latino community, our context also includes African-Americans and newcomer white neighbors. Our congregation claims the long list of Latinos mentioned above, plus folks from Venezuela, Honduras, Costa Rica, and more. We have members who are documented and not, from first generation to third, with entrepreneurs, engineers, and ex-cons among them. Yet our congregation is struggling with what it means to be community-focused and social justice–oriented. Many of our members want to evangelize, but they personally want to escape the challenges of the tough neighborhoods where they were raised rather than live incarnationally among gangs or drugs or to challenge gentrification and systemic oppression. But some have marched in Chicago's immigration rallies, and the pastor challenges the congregation not to dismiss biblical teaching on justice as mere politics. Recently, a large number approached the altar, responding to a challenge to commit to embracing the community.

CONCLUSION: CRISIS OR OPPORTUNITY?

In the midst of the immigration debate, a housing crisis, and the dearth of appropriate services for a vulnerable population, the church must consider how to respond. The current gaps in responsiveness and leadership development pose a great opportunity for the church to live out the whole gospel. Craig Wong, Executive Director of Grace Urban Ministries in San Francisco's Mission District, poignantly reflects on the challenge in Evangelicals for Social Action's *PRISM* magazine:

> *Over 27,000 immigrants in detention facilities last year. 4,000 workplace arrests. 5,000 reported border deaths (since 1994). Over 220,000 deportations. Social vilification. Separation of families.*

Withholding of health services. Physical abuse. We are being told to accept, essentially, that this is just what happens to those who "don't play by the rules." God's people, however, are called to live by a different set of rules. The current immigration crisis, therefore, represents a moral "third rail" for the American church: how we engage it can be the difference between life and death.[20]

REFLECTION QUESTIONS

1. How can your church actively engage in education, reflection, and action about the moral issues related to undocumented immigration?

2. Do you understand the systemic challenges that make life harder for the poor? What are you doing to become better informed?

3. In what practical ways can you learn about the specific assets and needs of the Latinos and immigrants in your community?

4. What are the churches in your area doing to develop cultural awareness to effectively receive and serve Spanish-dominant newcomer neighbors, or newcomers from other areas?

Recommended Reading List

Bean, Frank D., and Gillian Stevens, *America's Newcomers and the Dynamics of Diversity* (New York: Russell Sage Foundation, 2003).

Carroll R., Daniel, *Christians at the Border: Immigration, the Church, and the Bible* (Grand Rapids, Mich.: Baker, 2007).

Christian Reflection: A Series in Faith and Ethics 28: "Immigration" (Waco, Tex.: The Center for Christian Ethics at Baylor University, 2008), http://www.baylor.edu/christianethics/index.php?id=14715.

Massey, Douglas S., Jorge Durand, and Nolan J. Malone, *Beyond Smoke and Mirrors: Mexican Immigration in an Era of Economic Integration* (New York: Russell Sage Foundation, 2002).

Tichenor, Daniel J., *Dividing Lines: The Politics of Immigration Control in America* (Princeton: Princeton University Press, 2002).

SAM NAAMAN and a group of missionaries started the South Asian Friendship Center in the heart of the Indian Marketplace in Chicago. His wife, a doctor, also serves at the center. This is the first center of its kind to reach Muslims and Hindus in North America. He teaches at the Moody Bible Institute in the department of World Missions. Sam and his wife, Debbie, have two sons, Blaise and David.

CHAPTER 5

A SPECIAL BLESSING FROM THE LORD?

Muslims Among Us

Sam Naaman

Introduction: Islam in America

Muslims are coming to America, highly concentrated in our urban centers. You may meet them when you take a cab, in convenience stores and donut shops, etc. They represent a mosaic of different cultures, languages, and ethnic groups, and their numbers are growing in the United States. According to some estimates, they number from 6 to 8 million.[1] You may see them with their beards and white or black caps. Muslim women could be seen in head coverings (hijab) on our streets and college campuses.

How do we respond to the growth of Islam in our country? Some suggest that they may be a threat; for others they present a wonderful opportunity to share Christ and invite them to be part of the Kingdom of heaven. The following pages will review my journey of seeking to love Muslims for Christ and highlight a model of ministry to Muslims that has been active in Chicago since 1997. My hope is that we will look at our Muslim population as Jesus would, with love and compassion.

THE STORY OF GHULAM[2]

The Second World War was at its peak in the mid-1940s. Up in the hills of Kashmir, India, Ghulam Rasul was a young man with big dreams. Coming from a military family—his father had served in WWI—it was natural for Ghulam to get into the war. He wanted to keep the family tradition. War was attractive to him, it had action, and he wanted to serve his country, which at that time was ruled by the British. Ghulam came from a very religious Muslim family, where reading the Koran, going to the mosque for prayer, giving alms, and supporting the expansion of Islam were a duty, and there were no second thoughts to this routine.

When he joined the British Royal Air Force, he was posted in the northeast of India. There he met a British Army chaplain named Baxter. Ghulam and others called him "Whiteman" because of his color. Baxter had an unusually caring heart compared to many other British officers. When the Japanese Air Force raided their unit, Baxter invited the young men to follow him to the chapel, which was a simple tent in the middle of the army unit. Baxter then prayed, "Lord Jesus, these young men do not know You. Please give them another chance to live so that they may come to know You." Everyone wanted to live and so they said "Amen" after Baxter prayed. Ghulam remembered that the whole unit was destroyed, but the chapel remained intact. This made him consider that the Jesus of the white man had power to save. It was his first encounter with Christ.

Shortly thereafter Ghulam was severely injured by an explosion, and his whole right side was badly burned. At the medical unit, the doctor looked at him and said, "This soldier is so badly wounded, we cannot treat him here. How about we send him down to Calcutta?" As the doctor was talking to his staff, two nurses came forward and said, "He may not make it to Calcutta. If you do not mind, put him outside our living quarters and we will take extra care of him. Maybe he will make it." The doctor was pleased with these words and treated Ghulam with the help of these two nurses. They went out of their way to care for him. They fed him, talked to him, and tried to cheer him as the healing began.

After about twenty days, Ghulam was well enough to be released. The doctor and his staff were at his bedside. They were not sure whether he could see because the blast and the injuries were so severe. To lighten his spirits, the doctor asked Ghulam as he prepared to remove his bandages, "Young man, whom would you like to see first?"

Ghulam replied, "If possible, I would like to see the two nurses who treated me."

The doctor said, "They are right in front of you."

His vision was blurry, but he recognized their voices. He asked them, "Why did you care for me so much? I am a stranger, a simple soldier. If you had not taken care of me, maybe I would have died."

They were able to say, "We cared for you because of Jesus Christ. We are Christ followers, and He commands us to care for the hurting."

Ghulam was so overwhelmed by their kindness and compassion that he began to weep with gratitude. They told him, "Ghulam, your eye wounds are still fresh. Please do not cry."

Partition of India

Life went on. India and Pakistan were gaining independence. India was divided; Muslims migrated to West Pakistan and Hindus fled from there. This was by no means a peaceful division. Thousands of Muslims and Hindus were killed in this migration. By this time Ghulam had returned to his home in Jammu, Kashmir, which became part of India since the ruler was a Hindu, though the majority population was Muslim. Muslims rebelled against this decision. Guerilla warfare broke out against the captor Indian army by the Muslims, and an open call for "Jihad" (holy war) was declared by Muslim clerics all over Kashmir. Since Ghulam came from a strong Muslim family, he gladly joined the Jihad in the name of Allah. He was the leader of a platoon whose primary objective was to ambush the Indian army and kill the Hindus fleeing from Kashmir. This was in retaliation for the Muslims who were being killed by the Hindus. Ghulam and his platoon killed many Hindus without mercy.

During this time they were on a mission and they came across a village. They inquired if there were any Hindus left there. They learned that all Hindus had fled, but a Christian family remained. Ghulam and his soldiers proceeded to their house. They knocked on the door and two elderly men answered. Ghulam gave them the ultimatum to become Muslims. If they refused, they would be killed. The two men started pleading for their lives.

In the meantime a small girl came out of hiding and told Ghulam that he was welcome to do anything to them, but first allow them to pray. She said, "I want to pray to Jesus because I believe that my Jesus can save us."

Ghulam laughed at this small girl, and said, "Listen, girl, I have killed many Hindus with my own hands, and have seen many Muslims being killed by Hindus. None of their gods came to save them. But if this is your last wish, you may pray." He continued, "We will kill your father and uncle, and take you as a prisoner and exchange you to get our Muslim girls back from the Hindus."

These three people knelt in the room and started to pray. When they finished praying, Ghulam saw a very bright light come toward him. He was so afraid that he started to back away from the door. His army did not see anything. Then Ghulam said to his soldiers, "Let us go back, we will not kill these people."

His comrades replied, "Why are we not killing them? Let us finish the job and be done with it."

Ghulam then told the girl and her father and uncle, "Please forgive us, and we will not kill you."

They responded, "We forgive you in the name of Jesus." This was his third encounter with Christ.

Muslim Extremist

A few days later, Ghulam and his soldiers were passing a field where they saw a young Hindu woman with a newborn child. She put the child in Ghulam's arms and said, "I have a last request for you. I know my fate; you will kill me, or I will be raped and killed by you. But please before you take any steps, kill this child in your arms, because your Allah commands you to kill the infidels, and this child and I are Hindu and infidels."

As she finished her plea, Ghulam took a look at the child sleeping calmly in his arms. He asked himself, *What am I doing? What wrong has this child done to be killed by me? How can God create life on one hand and then ask me to take life on the other hand? How and why am I killing in the name of Allah?* He gave that child back to the Hindu lady and escorted her safely across the border to India.

The Jesus of Baxter, the Jesus of two Indian nurses, and the Jesus of a small girl. Who is this Jesus? Isa (Jesus) is a great prophet of Islam. Ghulam had some knowledge of Isa, but there was much more to Jesus than he knew. He was becoming disillusioned with Islam, so his brother took him to the local Muslim cleric to answer his questions. One major issue for him was why he was killing innocent people in the name of Allah and Islam. No cleric in his hometown of Jammu satisfied him, so he stopped reading the Koran and praying at the local mosque. He got more disturbed and left his house in search of truth. He thought to himself that he could not bow before 300 million gods of Hinduism, and he was not willing to pray in the mosque. He remembered Jesus, and started asking Him that if He is the Truth to appear and speak to him, and that he was willing to give his life for truth.

After several days of desperation, he told God that if He would not answer his prayers, he would kill himself by lying on the railway line. If God told him to go to hell, he would refuse because he was desperate to follow the truth. During this time, he heard a clear voice say "My grace is sufficient for you" in Urdu, Ghulam's language. He started reciting this phrase, and began to feel more peaceful. One morning a janitor at a railway station overheard him and asked, "Young man, are you a Christian?"

Ghulam responded, "No, I am a Muslim."

The man continued, "Then why are you reciting these words, and how do you know them?"

Ghulam told him the whole story.

The man replied, "I am an illiterate man, but I know these are the words of

Christ Jesus. Maybe He spoke to you as you sought for Him; you better meet my pastor." With that, he bought him a ticket and Ghulam went and met this pastor, who later adopted Ghulam as his son and led him to faith in Christ.

After his conversion, Ghulam went back to his Muslim family and tried to share Christ with them, but they did not accept him or his message. They disowned him, and poisoned him, but he survived. Then they beat him and told him that if he did not recant his faith in Christ they would kill him. Ghulam prayed that if God gave him another chance, his family would see His power. He was locked in a room to be killed the next morning and that same night he heard a gentle voice say, "Run." He thought to himself, *The door is locked.* He pushed on it, it opened, and he ran for his life. He moved to another province in Pakistan, got married, and had three children. For the next fifteen years he had no contact with his Muslim family.

Ghulam was my father.

I LOVE MUSLIMS

My love for Muslims grew when I saw the desperate need to reach them, and that not many Christians were serving among them in Pakistan. The Lord gave me a wonderful opportunity to serve with Operation Mobilization (OM) and Campus Crusade for Christ, specifically, starting the *Jesus* film ministry in Pakistan. Our home was the OM base. We were very active in reaching Muslims; several came to Christ in these years. I went to Korea for theological studies, and was due to return the end of 1990.

On June 2 of that year, my only brother, Obed, was gunned down outside our church in Pakistan. A single bullet took his life. This was a great shock to me far from home. I was not able to attend his funeral. My father, Ghulam, preached at Obed's funeral and said, "I forgive the people who shot my son, and if I meet them I am willing to kiss the very hands that shot my son." In our country kissing of hands is only offered to someone you dearly love.

Seventy-five percent of the people at Obed's funeral were Muslims, and they were shocked to hear this. People commented, "Maybe Ghulam has lost his mind. How can you forgive killers of your own son?"

Ghulam responded, "I have preached on forgiveness for the past thirty years. This is the time to testify to what I preach and believe in."

This was a turning point in our lives. We became refugees. When I went home from Korea, there was no longer a home. We moved to another city and tried to start our lives again. I became even more devoted to share Christ with Muslims. Loving and reaching Muslims became the passion of my life. I was accepted for my doctoral studies at Asbury Theological Seminary, and I came to the United States in 1992, the same year the Islamic Shariah Law[3] was enforced in Pakistan. My academic advisor and mentor suggested that I seek some other opportunity to serve Christ, as it was dangerous to return home. In the meantime, I finished all my coursework and was invited to be an intern with the Christian and Missionary Alliance Midwest district in Chicago, serving among South Asians. I met several people who had served in South Asia among Muslims and were now reaching them in Chicago. Through much prayer and the counsel of many, I settled in Chicago and started reaching Muslims.

Chicago is home to more than one hundred mosques, several Muslim bookstores, Islamic high schools, an Islamic university, and several Muslim publications. Some estimate there are close to 500,000 Muslims in Chicagoland.[4] Chicago is also famous for its North Side "Little India" marketplace on Devon Avenue. Devon has South Asian newspapers, grocery stores offering special "halal" meat, Muslim bookstores, South Asian restaurants, offices of many Muslim organizations, and jewelry and clothing stores all catering to the needs of South Asians. This marketplace attracts people from neighboring states like Michigan, Indiana, and Wisconsin, and sometimes cars of its customers carry license plates from as far away as Minnesota.

THE SOUTH ASIAN FRIENDSHIP CENTER (SAFC)

In the summer of 1993, a team of North Americans and South Asians from different denominations came together to reach Muslims in Chicago. We prayed and felt the Lord clearly guiding us to start a ministry center in the heart of Devon Avenue to reach South Asians. Devon, like neighboring Albany Park, is the Ellis Island of Chicago. Many are attracted to this area because it feels like home: the people, the marketplace, the food, and more. Urdu, Bengali, Hindi, Nepali, Punjabi, and many other major South Asian languages can be heard in this area. Besides the shops, the area is full of many apartment buildings that house South Asians.

We targeted this neighborhood for our team, showing an incarnational model of ministry to Muslims. We started sharing this vision with local churches and other Christians in the area who had a burden to reach Muslims. The Christian and Missionary Alliance, Assemblies of God, the Evangelical Free Church of America, International Teams, Christar, and other independent churches and mission organizations joined our efforts. We opened the South Asian Fiendship Center in the fall of 1997 as a faith ministry. We do not receive any government grants and by God's grace we are still serving the community.

The SAFC team is multilingual and multicultural. North Americans, Indians, and Pakistanis all work together. In Christ we are all one, agents of peace and reconciliation, as a testimony to many in the neighborhood, since India and Pakistan are archenemies. We also have many area college students who come and serve with us from Moody Bible Institute, Wheaton College, Trinity International University, and some local volunteers. As we were beginning the center we met with many Indian Christian churches. The India Evangelical Free Church has been faithful in sending its members to volunteer at the center on a weekly basis. This church consistently prayed for more than thirteen years for a ministry like the SAFC to start in the Devon area.

The ministry started in a small, humble place. Our former landlord was an Indian Muslim. We were very open with him about who we are and what we do to serve the community. We started a bookstore that has books and the Scriptures in South Asian languages, audio and video tapes, and other attractive reading materials from South Asia. We offer Internet, fax, and copy services. We also have a lending library for our videos and books, a major attraction for English-speaking children, who check out VeggieTales, Adventures in Odyssey, and other materials. We also offer *Jesus* videos and DVDs in different languages.

SAFC also attracts people who come to watch cricket matches brought directly by satellite connection from anywhere in the world. Most of the games are on from 9 P.M. to 6 A.M. This brings many men to the store. Indians and Pakistanis sit in the same place, drink tea, and chat. This helps break down the prejudice and animosity that exists between these cultures. It is amazing to see and feel the tension when India and Pakistan are playing as we cheer them on from a neutral place!

A Safe Place

SAFC also attracts women who want to learn English. Many have basic knowledge, but struggle with conversational English. We offer one-on-one English tutoring. This is primarily done by our student volunteers. In the process of English tutoring, we minister to numerous women who open up and share their hurts, struggles, and challenges of life in America as a Muslim. Many of these women cannot drive, so our staff often takes them to John Stroger (Cook County) Hospital when they need medical care. We also serve them by being a liaison for the area schools and an advocate for them in times of crisis, such as marital difficulties. At times we have to mediate on their behalf, reminding their husbands to treat them with love and respect. Occasionally the children, who have grown up here, call and report wife-beating. Painfully we have to remind them that spousal abuse can cause the police to intervene.

Women's ministry is one of the major outreaches of SAFC. Women come here because they feel accepted and because it is a safe place for them to share their hurts and sorrows. In one incident recently, a lady approached us about phone harassment on some family issue by a male in the community. She went to the local mosque with this problem and it was not addressed to her satisfaction. She did not want to involve the police, so she approached our women's director to mediate the conflict. We invited her to come and meet this person at our center. They talked and the issue was resolved. It was a great relief for this Muslim lady to know that we cared for her, even though her own people had shown little interest in her dilemma. All of this builds our credibility in the community.

Very early in our ministry to Muslims in Chicago, we focused on compassion. We meet people at their point of need spiritually, emotionally, and physically. Our mission statement clearly states that we exist to proclaim the uniqueness of Jesus Christ among the predominantly Muslim and Hindu marketplace of Devon Avenue. People who come to us are amazed by many things. First they are shocked that Indians and Pakistanis are working together under one roof. Then they see South Asians and Americans working together. Furthermore, they are surprised by the fact that all who serve at the center are volunteers. Finally, they observe the many students who on a weekly basis sacrifice their time, talent, and money to come and teach English, tutor children, play chess, go on outings, etc. All this is done in love for them unconditionally, without any strings attached. The daily sacrifice of our staff and volunteers is a blessing to them. When they ask us why and how we do this, our response is always because of the love of Christ.

The kindness and care that Muslim women and children receive at SAFC stands in contrast to the opposition many experience from their families and the community. Over the years we have had incidents of blatant resistance from some of the local Muslims. Many tell us that they are counseled by the local mosque not to come to SAFC. Some women have been humiliated by their husbands for coming to a Christian place. Many are verbally abused, and a few have been physically assaulted. Still they come because the love of Christ draws them and is clearly shown by our staff at the center.

Meet Aisha

The testimony of a woman I will call Aisha demonstrates the impact of SAFC. Aisha's marriage was arranged by her parents to a Pakistani Muslim man living in Chicago. She arrived here from Pakistan, only to discover that her husband was already living with a European woman. She tried to confront him, and complained to her in-laws that he was cheating on her. If their son already had a woman, why was she deceived into marrying him? Her husband plainly told Aisha that he married her under pressure from his parents, that he does not love her, and that she can live with and serve his parents.

Aisha was extremely depressed and had no place to go. She started working in a local jewelry shop and saw our advertisement for ESL at the center. She signed up to be tutored in English. As time went by, she confided her situation to our staff, and they encouraged her. One day she came by the center with her plane ticket to Pakistan, mentioning that her husband was taking her back for a vacation. Our staff made copies of all her papers and kept them, suspicious of this sudden love of her husband.

On Christmas Eve, our staff received a frantic phone call from Aisha in Pakistan. She was very distressed and said that her husband had taken her passport, her return plane ticket, and all of her money, and had divorced her over the phone from another city. We mobilized many of our staff and volunteers for prayer. For the next six months we worked with some attorneys who offered their services and sent Aisha all the necessary papers for her to return to the United States as she desired. As she was coming, her former husband threatened that he would harm her when she returned.

One of our staff members opened her home to Aisha and tried to find her a job. We also helped her in the courts to finalize her divorce as her husband had insisted. In the course of a year, the love, care, and constant prayer shown by the center's staff melted Aisha's heart and she started asking questions about Islam and Christianity. Through a series of Bible studies, apologetic ministry, and Christian love she gave her life to Christ. Now she is a bold witness for the Lord.

WHAT ABOUT A CHURCH?

After about two years of ministry on Devon, people started asking us to take them to a church. We looked around and found it difficult to bring Muslims to area churches. After much prayer the staff felt a clear indication from the Lord to plant a church. South Asian Fellowship is the result of that effort. It is a contextualized worship service in Urdu/Hindi and English. The main focus is South Asian seekers, but it also is attended by some who are preparing to go as missionaries to South Asia. The fellowship is led by a Pakistani pastor.

One person who attends this fellowship is Amina (not her real name). Twenty years ago she came to America from Pakistan with her husband in search of a better life. After enduring much abuse, she left him and with her two children moved to Chicago. She says:

I was from the Ismaili sect of Islam so I became involved in the Ismaili community to make friends, but instead I became lonelier. One lady where I worked became my friend. She would listen to my struggles and pray for me. She was a true Christian and would tell me about Jesus. But I rejected what she said because I was taught as a Muslim that Jesus was not the Son of God and that He did not die on the cross. Years later I was invited to church by another friend. This time I was ready to listen. After a few weeks, I accepted Christ as my Savior and Lord.

Amina has since led her two children to faith, and others among her relatives and friends are responding. Amina is a bold evangelist and shares her faith wherever she goes.

South Asian Fellowship also attracts and serves others from a Muslim background, like Nuri. This is her story in her own words.

My name is Nuri. I am from Somalia. Because of the war in my country, I had to go to a refugee camp in Kenya. I was a Muslim surrounded by Christian Ethiopians who befriended me and led me to faith in Christ. God has blessed me with a wonderful Christian Ethiopian husband. When my Muslim family in Somalia found this out, they sent my brother to kill me and my husband. When he came, my husband wasn't home so he pulled out a concealed knife and stabbed me many times in the chest. Also he poured boiling water on me. God mercifully spared my life. My new Christian Ethiopian family in the refugee camp surrounded me with love and cared for me in the hospital. My love for Jesus has grown through this experience.

Abdul is a former Muslim and is also a part of South Asian Fellowship. He shares:

I am from a Muslim village in Liberia. I was raised as a Muslim and I thought that the religion of Islam was the true religion. When the civil war broke out in my country, I saw how Muslims delighted in torturing and killing innocent people in the name of Allah. Even my village, a Muslim village, was attacked by Muslims. They killed men, women, and children and burned my village to the ground because we did not support the rebel cause. I escaped with my daughters by running into the jungle, but my wife who was in another part of the village was killed by the rebels. We were taken in by Christians who protected us and cared for us and brought us to a refugee camp. The Christians also suffered much from Muslims, but they helped us even though we were Muslims. Because of this love, I began to

*attend Christian worship in the refugee camp. Then I came to reject Islam
as a false religion and to believe in Jesus as the Son of God who loved me and
died for me.*

South Asian Fellowship, in the heart of Chicago, is a place of refuge, care,
and love for many Muslims who are hurting.

We have endured much opposition from a small segment of Muslim extrem-
ists in Chicago. On the other hand, many moderate Muslims appreciate what we
do. The leadership of the Pakistani Muslim community has nominated SAFC
staff members on two separate occasions to be recognized by the mayor of Chicago for our center's exceptional services to the South Asian community. All this
is possible because we focus on building bridges of better understanding, and we
seek to minister faithfully in this area, patiently trusting the Lord to reward our
efforts as He chooses to do so.

In the last three years, we have been invited to meet and minister in a North-
shore nursing home that has a whole wing of South Asians. Initially, it surprised
us to find elderly South Asians in an American nursing home because the family
is a strong unit in South Asia. Our teams go to this facility to speak with the Asian
seniors and hold worship services in Hindi/Urdu and English. In doing so we
demonstrate the love and care that can only happen because of Christ. A few have
come to know Him and we also have an opportunity to minister to their family
members.

SAFC also serves as a place of vision-casting for local churches. Many church
groups come for mission trips. Typically this includes an overview of SAFC and a
visit to a local mosque where they observe the prayers. They eat an Indian meal in
a Devon restaurant followed by a debriefing session at SAFC. This gives them an
exposure and a vision to reach their Muslim neighbors.

We have recently started a New Year's party, called Milan, in the Urdu language. This is to welcome the New Year with prayers for peace and harmony
among different ethnic and religious groups in the Devon area. It has grown into
a very popular yearly event, and has been attended by more than three hundred
people annually. Community leaders address the people, then we sing Christian
songs, followed by a clear message on Christ as the Eternal Prince of Peace (Isaiah
9:6). We also offer Bibles, other Christian literature, and *Jesus* DVDs on this
occasion. Many Muslims have commented that this is the best way to welcome
a new year. They long to be accepted by Americans. Some have said, "Why can't
we live in harmony here? We left war and strife back home. We do not need these
things here."

The common sentiment among Muslims is a sense of longing to be accepted by the majority population. Many have never met a true follower of Christ. Their eyes are blinded by their distorted, judgmental picture of Christianity. When they meet us, the veil falls off and they see the attractive beauty of Christ. This New Year's party has also enabled our American friends to come and meet with Muslims. For some this may be the first time to engage with a Muslim family. They sit at a table, chat, and eat a meal together. Many walls are brought down and a new understanding is created between Muslims and Christians. Relationships are furthered when these same Muslim leaders invite our staff to participate in their functions.

In recent years SAFC's model of ministry has been adopted by other mission organizations serving among Muslims overseas. These centers are very effective in reaching Muslims in cities and are building bridges of better understanding for sharing Christ.

CONCLUSION: TOWARD THE HARVEST

God determines the times and the exact places where people should live. He does this "so that men would seek him and perhaps reach out for him and find him" (Acts 17:26–27). "How, then, can they call on the one they have not believed in? And how can they believe in the one of whom they have not heard? And how can they hear without someone preaching to them?" (Rom. 10:14). It is my deep desire and prayer that many will be called to reach Muslims among us. Our dream is to have these kinds of centers in all the major metro areas of America. Pray that God will allow this to happen. "The harvest is plentiful but the workers are few. Ask the Lord of the harvest, therefore, to send out workers into his harvest field" (Matt. 9:37–38).

REFLECTION QUESTIONS

1. What practical ways could you support those who are reaching out to Muslims in your community?

2. What would it take for you to start your own prayer and support group for Hindus or Muslims in your area? How might your church be involved?

3. How can you share the gospel, the love of Christ, with Muslims in our postmodern world?

MARY NELSON is President Emeritus of Bethel New Life,
where she served for twenty-six years. Bethel pioneered
in faith-based creative community-based efforts to build
healthier, sustainable, and equitable communities on
Chicago's West Side. She serves on the Boards of Sojourners
and Christian Community Development Association. Mary
has her Ph.D. from Union Graduate School and six honorary
Ph.D.'s, and is now doing consulting, writing, and teaching in
faith-based community development. Mary lives, works, and
worships on the West Side of Chicago. She is on the faculty
of ABCD Institute (Northwestern University), CCDA Institute,
and SCUPE.

CHAPTER 6

ECONOMIC DEVELOPMENT IN THE HOOD:

The Church's Role in Creating Jobs

Mary Nelson

Introduction: Needs and Opportunities

Bethel Church, on Chicago's West Side, was holding an all-night prayer vigil in front of the church, seeking to highlight the need to put away guns and reduce violence in our community. The church building was lined with crosses with the names of young people recently killed in violence. In the early hours of the morning, only a few people were brave enough to be praying outside, the echoes of gunshots and voices not far away. Some tough young men sauntered by, pausing as they looked at the crosses. "But Cinque's name is missing," said one.

We put Cinque's name on a wooden cross. Then our leader said, "Can we pray together that you're not the next name on a cross?" Embarrassed, the young men consented and we stood in a circle praying that God would open doors of new possibilities, that God would touch their hearts, that God would walk with them. Tears slid down the faces of the young men and they sauntered away. The next morning, as the prayer group was disbanding, one of the young men came back and said, "God touched me last night; I want a different life. Will you help?"

Walking down the road with unemployed, undereducated, or formerly incarcerated people is not easy. God touches people's lives and transforms them, and as agents of God, we are but helpers. As we work with people we quickly bump up against their challenges and struggles. A job or a business is one of the most important aspects in that journey of transformation, but helping people in such a way often moves us into "uncharted territory."

We are called to be concerned about our low-income neighbors and communities. Creating and linking people with jobs and developing businesses is one of the challenges. The marketplace does not focus on those left out of the system, nor on creating jobs in under-resourced neighborhoods. But the need and opportunity are there:

- Over 3 million in the United States are in prison or on probation at any one time, with a 66 percent recidivism rate. America has the highest rate of incarceration of the developed world. A job upon re-entry is critical to staying out of prison.[1]

- More than 2.5 million working families, with 6 million children, earn less than the official poverty level for a family of four (2002), and 9.2 million American working families (one in four) earn less than two times the official poverty level.[2] This is a sharp indication of underemployment and the lack of living wage jobs.

We must use the insights of the marketplace and God's enabling to creatively make a difference. One of the original R's of Christian Community Development Association (CCDA) is redistribution (along with relocation and reconciliation), the economic well-being of people who are often left out of the economy. CCDA's understanding of redistribution includes the just distribution of resources, in place of unjust lack of resources. Just redistribution brings new skills, relationships, and resources into communities of need to empower residents of a given community to bring about healthy transformation.[3]

This chapter is about the tools and principles of Christian community economic development. The focus is local communities and the local economy. People of faith, through congregations and organizations, have the opportunity to be catalysts for transformation. It is an exciting journey to experience the hope that comes when someone gets a job, is able to support a family, and makes plans for the future. In being part of this journey we move toward God's plan for people living full lives in healthy, sustainable communities.

IN PERSPECTIVE

As Christians seeking to be about God's work, we need to keep our efforts in perspective. It is God who transforms, God who calls us to be about the work, and God's will that we seek to discern in the people and communities where we focus. God has a vision for individuals and communities (Isa. 65:17–25): for people who "build houses and get to live in them, … plant vineyards and enjoy the wine, … fully enjoy the things they have worked for. The work they do will be successful." But in case we become too focused on our own well-being, God cautions in Amos 5:10–11, "You people hate anyone who challenges injustice and speaks the whole truth in court. You have oppressed the poor and robbed them of their grain. And so you will not live in the fine stone houses you build or drink wine from the beautiful vineyards you plant." As we plan economic development initiatives, we seek a balance between individual wealth creation with "community good"; we seek justice and fairness; we seek community. This is the value-added aspect of our faith, the community context of our efforts.

I share the insights and experiences of more than twenty-five years as a part of Bethel New Life, a faith-based community development corporation on Chicago's West Side. Bethel Lutheran Church started Bethel New Life, focusing on its riot-torn low-income community with a commitment to affordable housing and development without displacement. It was a daunting task in a 98 percent minority community, with 36 percent of the residents living in poverty (compared to a national average of 11.3 percent).[4] Starting with affordable housing led to people needing decent wage jobs. So began the evolution of Bethel into a holistic community development approach, developing more than 1,200 units of affordable housing, employment services, services for the elderly, child development centers, and a host of related programs. Isaiah 58:9–12 became the framework of Bethel's efforts to create an affordable, livable, just community. The way to a healthy community is through the combination of justice and compassion.

STARTING OUT—JOBS, JOBS, JOBS

When Bethel was just getting started, we focused on affordable housing, but soon found out that even the most inexpensive housing is not affordable if people do not have jobs, living wage jobs. We did not know how to take the next steps and did not have the resources. We prayed, seeking God's guidance. We talked to many people and visited programs to find out what others were doing. We also spent time clarifying what our goals and desired outcomes were, keeping in mind God's calling. This turned out to be a good three-step process for any group seeking to move into uncharted territory:

1. Pray about it as a group.

2. Talk to people and find out what others are doing. Much information can be gathered on the Internet, but there is no substitute for getting a group of people together to visit other places.

3. Clarify goals and desired outcomes. It is important to identify, both for your group and the community, how many "loaves and fishes" you possess. What are the strengths, people skills, resources, opportunities in your group/congregation? In the community?

The study of the feeding of the five thousand (Mark 6:33–44) from this perspective is a way to get a group thinking about resources and acting on Jesus' command to "feed them."

Out of this process, Bethel focused on three strategies for dealing with jobs: starting an employment center and linking people with existing jobs, bringing companies into the community with first-source hiring agreements to prioritize neighborhood hiring for available jobs, and creating new jobs and businesses in the community for community residents.

Employment Services

Bethel Church and community residents were out on the streets of our low-income West Side Chicago community, walking with signs and shouting, "Down with Dope, Up with Hope." We approached young people standing by waiting to resume their drug sales. Many of them said, "Man, we need jobs, jobs that pay enough to live on."

Employment services is most often a good starting place. Often services start small in church basements, but are best done in coalitions with others. There may be such services already in place in your community, and you may just need to connect with them. Other situations call for starting up employment services. Usually this includes some kind of pre-employment training and job referral services. There are several noteworthy models in place across the country:

1. Jubilee Jobs: Work for sustenance, dignity, and hope in Washington, D.C. (www.jubileejobs.org) is a Church of the Saviour model.

2. Jobs for Life (www.jobsforlife.com) started out of some local churches, with the help of a committed businessman, and linked up with community colleges in Raleigh, North Carolina. Now there are related sites all over the country and twelve international sites. Training and curriculum are available for this model.

3. Joe Holland, a Harvard graduate, spends his major energies with the homeless and addicts in Harlem, New York, and has developed a process: Holistic Hardware: Tools that Build Lives, faith-based Life and Job Skills for Restoring Lives in Crisis.

We do not need to reinvent the wheel when focusing on employment initiatives. Use the resources available. (See the list of resources at the end of this chapter for other suggestions.) Here are some lessons we learned at Bethel:

1. Employment services lead to developing specific job skill training. Make sure you have researched employer needs for those skills, what other employment programs are nearby, and have thought about what you can do well. Community colleges are often better at doing these things, and you can link up with them.

2. The intake process should be a strengths-based approach, identifying first the skills, experiences, hopes, and dreams of people, not a litany of deficits.

3. When we understand people's life experiences and the failures and unfairness of many of our societal institutions (public education, prison, etc.), we will need to prayerfully consider joining advocacy and action groups to address these wider issues.

4. Not all jobs are "good jobs." Often entry-level jobs are minimum wage, and one has to work for wage progression, and join others in advocacy around unfair labor practices. One such advocacy group is Interfaith Worker Justice (www.iwj.org), which "calls upon religious values to educate, organize and mobilize the religious community on campaigns to improve wages, benefits and conditions for workers, giving voice to workers, especially low-wage workers."

Bringing in the Jobs

Vacant industrial buildings and an underused industrial park at the edge of our community proved to be important assets and opportunities. Bethel decided to market opportunities for companies, and offer our assistance in relocating into our community. We were especially interested in bringing in companies that would be (a) good to the employees (fair wages, e.g.), (b) good for the environment, and (c) good to the community. Some organizations focus on bringing in and retaining companies. Bethel cleaned up an environmentally dirty site and began marketing it. After several missed opportunities, Bethel attracted a moving and storage company to the site. There were a lot of jobs in truck driving and moving people, not many in storage. We negotiated a good price for the land with the owner and required a covenant of "first source" hiring, that jobs first be made available to community residents. (See the Resources list for Good Jobs First materials.) Talking with the owner, we discovered a willingness to do more to create a training program for drivers and helpers. With our help, he was able to obtain some City of Chicago training funds and build a training school. Such marketing of community opportunities can be around commercial development as well. Michael Porter of Harvard has identified the potential for good business opportunities for many of our low-income, minority communities.[5]

Creating Jobs/Businesses in Community

Initial efforts often start with developing an employment center, a daycare center, etc. We can make such efforts be more than merely a social service by intentionally turning them into opportunities for community economic development as well. For example, starting a daycare center to provide affordable, accessible child care for working parents provides opportunity to (a) hire from the community (creating jobs); (b) develop career ladders by connecting with community colleges for training; (c) contract locally for services (bus transportation, catering, supplies, maintenance, etc.); (d) connect underemployed parents with employment services, financial literacy, and income tax preparation; and (e) train and empower parents through involvement in decision making at the center, listening and working with them in advocacy around the issues that challenge the community. It is a matter of being intentional about goals and outcomes greater than the direct service. Sometimes you start with one thing, and it leads to a lot of other opportunities and/or challenges.

Many years ago Bethel was part of a major welfare-to-work project. As we were working to train and place people into jobs, one of the greatest obstacles was the lack of affordable, accessible child care in the community. After struggling with the issue, we decided to create our own solution. We identified a number of participants interested in working with children, and cajoled the community colleges to provide training for people in the community to be licensed child care home providers. Training included not only child care, but also the rudiments of being self-employed. Then we worked with the now certified graduates in getting their apartments licensed for operation. Landlords were reluctant to have inspectors come in, so we had to find another alternative.

Checking into affordable new home construction, we discovered minor modifications would make the homes licenseable. But how to make the connection? Home ownership meant immediate cutoff from welfare, and banks were reluctant to provide mortgages to former welfare recipients newly self-employed as home daycare providers. We involved five banks and split up the twenty-six graduates into groups. Then, in conjunction with the State of Illinois, we devised a lease-purchase program that allowed a gradual diminution of welfare assistance, and Bethel became the fallback on the loans. Out of this effort, then, came twenty-five former welfare recipients now self-employed as home daycare providers; twenty-five formerly garbage-strewn, vacant lots in the community, now homes of ownership and pride; and affordable, accessible child care available to most mothers in the community.

Social Entrepreneurship

A whole new field of social entrepreneurship has developed: not-for-profits, which are adopting for-profit business approaches to provide revenues, focus, and effectiveness, and which combine the passion of a social mission with a business approach. A number of years ago, Bethel looked at the community opportunities, identifying the large number of seniors in the area, and numerous neighborhood residents who were natural caregivers. At the same time, the State realized that it was cheaper to care for the elderly in the community than in nursing homes. After researching the economic market and future of services for the elderly, contacting the State, and a lot of prayer and discernment, Bethel determined to start in-home services for the elderly, hiring and training community residents to care for their senior neighbors.

Because the State's rate of payment did not provide a livable wage, Bethel brought in community colleges to train workers on a career ladder so they could advance in salary, and in many cases move out of Bethel to higher-paying jobs. These included jobs as certified nurse's aides, licensed practical nurses, and registered nurses. Low staff turnover was the result of our commitment to the workers. Twenty years later, the initiative still exists, with more than two hundred people employed providing home care services. While it has not been a major moneymaker, it has supported the expansion and stability of Bethel while meeting our community goals.

One of the most famous examples of social entrepreneurship is Manchester Craftsmen's Guild/Bidwell Training Center in Pittsburgh (www.manchester bidwell.org), which evolved as a result of Bill Strickland's creative response in a low-income community. For example, art and recording studios work with artists and recording engineers; catering training provides airline food; and a greenhouse grows food and spices.

Another model that is almost totally supported from the earned income on the social enterprises it operates for formerly homeless, addicted people is Pioneer Human Services in Seattle (www.pioneerhumanservices.org), a forty-three-year-old conglomerate of ten social enterprises including assembling, packaging, catering, and sheet metal fabrication. Most of its contracts are with large corporations.

Youth entrepreneurship initiatives are another outgrowth of the social enterprise movement. Vocational education embraces youth entrepreneurship. Many faith-based groups have experimented with this, such as youth printing and selling T-shirts or selling services, the sort of Junior Achievement approach. One of the most famous youth entrepreneur efforts is National Foundation for Teaching Entrepreneurship (NFTE; www.nfte.com). NFTE has a proven youth-training program and curriculum. Since 1987, NFTE has provided entrepreneurship education programs for young people from low-income communities.

IN SEARCH OF PROFITS: A CAUTIONARY TALE

Some faith-based organizations have started for-profit businesses (social enterprises) with hopes of creating income from the business to support unfunded service programs and initiatives. As are other small business start-ups, fewer than half of such start-ups are successful. Here is our experience.[6]

With high hopes, Bethel New Life opened a $1.25 million Material Recovery Facility (MRF) in the midst of our community. The recyclable waste processing plant created at least thirty-five new jobs; our feasibility study showed that it should at least break even in a year and ultimately produce profits to help our programs. Our priority was creating jobs for currently unemployed neighborhood people, especially people coming out of prison and desperate for beginning work. The MRF was an outgrowth of the recycling buyback center, which took an "asset" of our community (lots of garbage) and turned that into an opportunity. We had paid more than $1 million in cash to community residents for the garbage in the prior two years. Seeking to create more stable jobs through processing up to 100 tons of garbage a day, we struggled with operational problems of high turnover, downtime, lack of a good mechanic, and high repair costs. Some unemployed young men we had hired left, saying the work was too dirty for them. Some days ten garbage trucks appeared at our gates at 6:30 A.M. and we were not ready for them. Other days we had employees standing around (money down the drain).

After seeking to address these problems and losing hard-to-come-by funds, and doing a lot of prayer and searching, we determined that we were not good at operating a specific business, but we were good at identifying the opportunities and putting things together. We sold the business (and later the building) to a firm operating MRFs in other locations, on condition that they keep the existing employees and that they hire local future employees. This is not the first nor the last enterprise that we initiated. Others have spun off or been outsourced. Some have continued successfully (but not without challenges), such as our in-home care for the elderly noted earlier in this chapter.

HARD-LEARNED BUSINESS LESSONS

As you consider developing and operating an economic enterprise, be prepared for a lot of hard work. Business requires willingness to risk, prayer, and sometimes a long time before the profits appear. Here are some of Bethel's discoveries.

1. **Be clear about your goals for the enterprise.** The more Christian/community good you seek, the slimmer you shave the potential profits. It is hard to do it all.

2. **Take time to research what you intend to do.** Do thorough preparation, a feasibility study (visiting similar businesses, looking at the competition), and a good business plan with conservative operation projections. Think through the organizational structure most appropriate to carry out your goals (for-profit, not-for-profit, cooperative, profit sharing, employee stock ownership, etc.).

3. **Be creative in putting together the initial capital to reduce the burden of debt.** Allow enough funds for sufficient working capital, especially in the start-up years. For example, we used "sweat equity" of eighty hours of work as the buy-in on a co-op enterprise, and it helped to minimize working capital needs by delaying the first cash payday for two weeks. We leased machinery, rather than buying it.

4. **Have some of your own resources at risk.** This will give more energy to ensure good management. If you do an employee-management profit-sharing plan, for example, then your manager should have something at risk as well.

5. **Identify the management skills and experiences needed.** Hire the right people from the start, with the right skills and experience, not some relative or church member who is a nice person. You can always build in on-the-job training programs for others that you groom for better things.

6. **Continue to learn from others.** Visit other places, search the Internet, seek connections with trade organizations—whatever areas you need to develop, pursue the resources for educating yourself in those areas.

Building Assets

"Smart Savers helped me see a brighter future for myself."
   —Participant in a financial education and individual development account program

Another aspect of community economic development focuses on individuals and their financial well-being. Financial education, laced with the values of our faith, is taught in numerous settings. Low-income people are often stuck in a cycle of debt (including usurious payday loans and credit card debt) and no savings to fall back on. They can be guided to a better future through financial education or home ownership. Bethel has operated a Smart Savers Program (eight weeks of financial education and Individual Development Accounts—IDA) for a number of years. Bethel first used *Faith and Finances* as curriculum, and currently uses Thrivent Financial for Lutherans free curriculum, *Your Values, Your Choices, Your Money*. Such training includes the values of our faith (stewardship, giving back, and people over things) as a critical component to financial education.

Very often such training is coupled with IDA accounts, matched savings accounts that usually can be used for further education, a down payment on a house, or starting a business. Federal funds have been available for matching funds through the Assets for Independence Program (U.S. Dept. of Health and Human Services). Going through the group training is most often an uplifting, helpful, and often life-changing experience, with strong peer group support and an ongoing relationship with the organization.

Another economic activity in this vein is income tax preparation provided free for lower-income participants. Such efforts use volunteers and tax software and assist people in obtaining not only the Earned Income Tax Credit (EITC), but also other tax rebates and credits. Bethel does this at its site in partnership with the Center for Economic Progress (www.centerforprogress.org), a national organization that sets up volunteer tax assistance. Bethel has a local bank available, opening savings accounts for direct electronic deposit of tax refunds while also providing an opportunity to move people into the financial mainstream. The interaction time while doing the tax preparation also allows for relationships and encouragement for people. In 2007, the Bethel site helped community residents receive more than $1 million back in tax refunds, a major impact in our more than two-square-mile Garfield Park community.

Many low-income people have been victims of unscrupulous lending practices associated with payday lending and subprime mortgages, or have gotten involved in credit-card arrangements without reading or understanding the fine print, and find themselves with bad credit and major financial challenges. Assisting people to get credit cleared, refinancing, and other such efforts goes a long way toward enabling financial stability.

Advocacy Counts

"Speak out for those who cannot speak for themselves, for the rights of all the destitute."
(Prov. 31:8–9)

"Learn to do good, seek justice, aid the oppressed."
(Isa. 1:17)

When we as the family of God get involved with people struggling for a decent life, hear their stories, and experience some of their challenges, we understand that often their personal efforts and programs do not overcome the injustices and barriers in our society that hinder full citizenship and a full life. Inferior public schools in low-income communities, lack of public transportation to where the jobs are, and millions of uninsured people without adequate access to health care are just a few examples. Isaiah talks bluntly about the kind of action God is looking for: "Break the chains of injustice, get rid of exploitation in the workplace, free the oppressed, cancel debts" (Isaiah 58:6 THE MESSAGE).

People of faith are taking the lead in advocacy efforts around living wages and worker abuse, such as the Interfaith Worker Justice (www.iwj.org). Payday loans, subprime lending/predatory lending, consumer fraud, and credit card usury practices challenge our positive efforts and compel joining with others in getting the facts, hearing the stories and experiences of affected people, identifying colleagues in advocacy, and using our voices, the ballot, and our relationships to seek better and fairer ways of dealing with these issues.

Real Estate Development

"At last we're going to do something we can see," said a Bethel Church member at the vote to start a housing ministry focusing on the square mile around the church, the origins of Bethel New Life. Housing around the church was crumbling and abandoned. We did not have any money and did not have the know-how to do it, but we felt God's push to be "restorers" (Isaiah 58) of the community, starting with affordable housing. Low-income congregants put in five dollars a week each until we had five thousand dollars, and that was how it all got started. Today, Bethel has developed more than 1,200 units of affordable housing and brought more than $125 million of new investments into a once credit-starved community.

Real estate development, especially as a catalyst for community restoration, can be economic development, too. Home ownership is the surest way to build assets. Marketplace developers are looking for "location, location, location" and most often our communities are not locations that attract the marketplace. It is best to find others who are experienced in housing and work with them at the start. Congregations often work on special-needs housing (elderly, homeless, single parents, etc.) or work with social service organizations to sponsor housing.

Bethel got help in developing affordable housing in the community through partnering with experienced, faith-motivated suburban builders who helped us develop lower cost, energy efficient housing. It is not enough to do low cost construction; in today's efforts, one must create housing that is energy efficient (small size, insulation, caulking, solar roof tiles, etc.), and involve community contractors or ensure local hiring as part of a larger contract. On a large project, Bethel got a landscaper to hire some formerly incarcerated people to do the work, added some training, and got the landscaping done and jobs created at the same time. Some groups have also done commercial and industrial developments that are major catalysts in community turnarounds. Abyssinian Baptist Church in Harlem, New York, is one such national model, developing affordable housing, a Pathmark grocery store (with more than two hundred employees), Thurgood Marshall Academy, and much more (www.adcorp.org).

Five Loaves and Two Fishes

Frequently we have big ideas and then stop short, thinking we have too few resources. It is important to start with what we have, such as people, skills, real estate, and opportunity, and not wait until everything is in place. Putting resources together is a journey of connecting. We must start with our own equity (money, sweat, property, etc.), and then we can approach others to join with us. Luther Snow's book, *The Power of Asset Mapping: How Your Congregation Can Act on Its Gifts,* is a great tool for discovering the abundance of what is in your midst.[7]

Share a vision, the specific outcomes, and small first steps with individuals, other churches, and foundations. Identify the city, county, and state resources that are available. Look at the annual reports of those working in that field to see where their funds came from. Get to know the people who handle these funds and share the idea, the feasibility study, and the small beginnings. Check out the relationships in your congregation, denomination, or circle of supporters. Follow up, be persistent, and share the vision. God makes a way, often very different from what we plan. We should turn over every stone and not be discouraged.[8]

CONCLUSION: JUST DO IT!

Here are some final thoughts learned from experience in the exciting God-given journey as people of faith in building lives and community. Most important, all along the way, undergird your thinking and plans with prayer. Pray for discernment, for new eyes to see the possibilities, for God to bring partners to the table.

Avoid the do-gooder framework. Seek out, listen to, and involve the community from the very beginning.[9] Be clear about goals and hoped-for outcomes, what the people of faith bring to the process. Keep your eyes on the prize so that you do not get sidetracked into doing relief work rather than development.

Do not try to do it all yourself. Seek out partners, other congregations, and for-profit organizations with shared values. Start small with six- to twelve-month time spans and winnable first efforts. Then celebrate what God is doing in your midst. For example, Bethel did a job fair before starting an employment center.

Be about the work of advocacy for long-term impact and justice all along the journey, and involve those most affected by the injustice.

Do not be afraid to build the road as you travel. Be flexible, and try different approaches. Keep exploring other alternatives.

The journey of partnering with congregants and neighborhood residents to make a difference in people's lives and build community is exciting and challenging, not for the faint of heart. Surround it all with prayer, celebrate the little successes, and weep over the disappointments. We call it the "agony and the ecstasy." When one experiences the God-given nudge, the new eyeglasses of opportunity, the sense of community, just do it. God will make a way.

REFLECTION QUESTIONS

1. What are the God-given opportunities in your setting to help bring about the "fullness of life" for individuals and the community? Ask God to give you a new perspective. Walk around the community, and talk to the people.

2. What strengths, capacities, and resources are in the group or the community to build on? Do an "asset map" of your resources. Pray for discernment.

3. Share ideas for the next steps. Visit other groups that are doing things in your area. Determine a short-term plan (six months) and move forward.

Resources

Jobs for Life (www.jobsforlife.com) mobilizes churches and community-based organizations as training sites, providing the curriculum and processes necessary to provide job training and support for low-income people.

Annie E. Casey Foundation (www.aecf.org/MajorInitiatives/FamilyEconomicSuccess.aspx) provides free materials and videos and examples of family economic success, which includes workforce development and family economic supports (EITC, etc.).

Good Jobs First (www.goodjobsfirst.org) works on accountable development and smart growth for working families. Especially helpful is their publication on Community Benefits Agreements, which gives examples and documents for seeking local hiring from large companies and developments.

Larson, Rolfe. *Venture Forth! The Essential Guide to Starting a Money-making Business in Your Nonprofit Organization* (St. Paul, Minn.: Fieldstone Alliance, 2002).

The National Foundation for Teaching Entrepreneurship (NFTE) (www.nfte.com) helps low-income young people build skills and entrepreneurial creativity through curriculum and training tools to improve academic, business, and life skills. NFTE partners with schools and community groups, uses volunteer mentors, and helps youth actually develop small businesses. Training and curriculum materials for high school, middle school, and advanced levels are available.

Nederveld, Gary, and Erica Chung. *Faith and Finances* (Grand Rapids, Mich.: CRC Publications, 2000).

Your Values, Your Choices, Your Money by Thrivent Financial for Lutherans. A teachers guide, a participants workbook, and PowerPoint aids downloadable free on the Internet (www.thrivent.com). Go to Programs & Outreach, then Financial Education.

SCOTT CLIFTON was born and raised on the East Coast. He has been married to Linda for seventeen years and together they have three adventurous boys, Ben, Danny, and Jonathan. He and his family lived in west London for about four years prior to coming to the Windy City. They are proud owners of a registered bungalow in the Mayfair neighborhood in north Chicago. He received his undergraduate degree at the University of Delaware and his master's degree at Westminster Theological Seminary.

JACKSON CRUM is the lead pastor of Park Community Church. Park is located in the city of Chicago with one of their campuses in a changing area that was previously part of Cabrini-Green. Jackson is married to Donna and they have two sons.

CHAPTER 7

NEW WINESKINS:
Paradigm Shifts for the Church

Scott Clifton and Jackson Crum

Introduction: A Call to the City

Jackson and I (Scott) are cut from the same ministry cloth. We both grew up in white, affluent suburbs of major cities, both were engaged in church ministry for fifteen to twenty years in the suburbs, both graduated from a conservative evangelical seminary, and both are on a steep learning curve about urban ministry!

Our ministry stories have followed a similar pattern, and while we understood, appreciated, and even enjoyed life in the suburbs, we knew that God was challenging us to do life and ministry in a different context. The Lord led us to the same city, Chicago, but along different paths. Jackson tells how he was "nudged" to answer a call to the city.

JACKSON'S STORY

I was on staff at a church in the suburbs of Philadelphia for close to twenty years, having left for three years to plant a church only to return with no intention of leaving again. When the time came I thought they could just bury me in the back field. My wife, Donna, and I loved the church, the people, and the area. But God was up to something.

For the last year I was at Church of the Saviour, I sensed God asking me every couple of weeks, "Jackson, are you willing to go anywhere or do anything for Me?"

Being alone at the time I would answer out loud, "Yes, God, I will go anywhere and do anything . . . but can I stay here? I love what You are doing here, I love what You are up to, and I love the people." That went on for about a year until one night in March 2003.

Our church was hosting a missions conference, and that evening God stirred me once again. As I was driving home alone and passing my boys' elementary school, God asked me, "Are you willing to go anywhere and do anything for Me?"

The question was the same, and my reply started the same way, "God, I will do anything and go anywhere." This time I held out one hand with my palm turned up toward God, "And I give You Church of the Saviour."

For the first time, my reply to God did not add a loophole with the word *but*. I felt a weight lifted from my shoulders, and it scared me! It finally registered that I had not been answering "yes" without question, but had been really responding "no."

I arrived home and told Donna, my wife, about my prayer. She almost fell over! She had been sensing God's leading for a while, and in retrospect I could see that the Lord had used her to nudge me several times. One of these times came while we were staying in New York City. She wondered aloud if the day would come when we would end up living in the city. I declared to her at that time, "There is no way on God's green earth I will ever live in the city!"

The Plot Thickens

God certainly has a sense of humor. It was about two months after I made that emphatic statement that I received an informational packet from Park Community Church in Chicago about their job opening for the lead pastor position. I was not looking to leave, but I kept it in the stack of DVDs I received from churches for friends who might be "feeling a nudge" to move elsewhere in ministry.

A week later, a "while you were out" slip appeared announcing a call from Park Community Church. After a moment or two I realized it was the same church from which I had received the informational packet and DVD. I felt an overwhelming urge to call. I desired to find out more. I was not mad, unhappy, or even looking to leave my current church. I was content.

As I sat down to make the phone call I picked up the DVD and watched it. The scene of the yearly baptism in Lake Michigan caused me to pause. I thought, *Whoa! What is this church in Chicago that would do a baptism service on the beach with several hundred people in attendance?* The rest is history: The process went great; I was thoroughly impressed with the church and its vision to reach an urban context of 2.9 million people. Both Donna and I knew that God was calling us to do church and life in Chicago.

Joining the Team

About a year and half later Linda (my wife) and I (Scott) joined the staff at Park Community Church. We had already begun the urban journey four years prior via London, and God's call to the city was still alive and well in our hearts. No matter how much we enjoy white picket fences, rolling hills, and free parking, there is still nothing better than to be right in the middle of where the masses of humanity meet: Chicago!

A CALL TO CHANGE

Park Community Church's ambition has always been to minister in the shadow of the skyline,[1] and for twenty years it has continued to be faithful to the vision: "We exist to be a biblical community where the gospel of Jesus Christ transforms lives, renews the city and impacts the world."

In the early years, Park was more of a neighborhood church, attracting and ministering to people from the North Side Lincoln Park and Lakeview neighborhoods. Over those years, Park grew into a regional church reaching north into Rogers Park, south to Roosevelt Road, and west to Humboldt Park. However, there was never a particular long-term strategy of transformational community development into any of these neighborhoods.

For twenty years, Park has been known as the "church that serves." Any month you could find more than 350 volunteers serving in about a dozen partner ministries throughout the city. Park has rarely begun new works, but rather has lent muscle to existing ministries such as Breakthrough Urban Ministries on the West Side, Liberty in Christ Ministries on the South Side, and Good News Community Kitchen on the North Side. The criteria for past partnerships were based on ministry effectiveness, relationships, and volunteer opportunities, not geography.

In March 2004, Park made a bold and defining move when it decided to buy and gut-rehab a hundred-year-old dry goods warehouse right in the heart of the Cabrini-Green low-income redevelopment project. For the first time we could develop a clear "Jerusalem, Judea, Samaria" strategy for our ministry in Chicago (Acts 1:8). We needed to "laser in" on one community and understand how real transformation takes place. We needed to learn how to listen to a community, reflect on what we are hearing, and then respond to how the Spirit is leading.

Central to Park's vision has always been to "renew the city," yet how that was going to happen was ambiguous at best. We had no accurate system to quantify or qualify whether our ministry resources (people, finances, and prayer) were having significant impact to renew any Chicago neighborhood, street, or block. Individual lives and maybe families were being transformed through the gospel, but we had no measurement tool to determine if an entire neighborhood was being changed.

Dramatic changes had already taken place through gentrification in the Cabrini-Green housing project. The broad-sweeping plan for redevelopment is to be completed in three phases encompassing the William Green Homes, Francis Cabrini Extension North and South,[2] and the Francis Cabrini Rowhouses. The rowhouses are currently being used as temporary housing for families in the process of being relocated. Because of their significant architectural and historical value, the plan is for them to be rehabbed and kept.[3] The concept is to create a mixed income community, where 50 percent of the housing stock (condos and townhomes) are at market rate, 30 percent are for public housing, and 20 percent are discounted for "working folks of modest means."[4]

New Skin

Jesus told us that "no one pours new wine into old wineskins. If he does, the new wine will burst the skins, the wine will run out and the wineskins will be ruined. No, new wine must be poured into new wineskins" (Luke 5:37–38). The gospel (new wine) of Jesus Christ demands new wineskins because the gospel not only saves you, but it also changes you.

That is why Paul can make his climactic pronouncement, "Therefore, if anyone is in Christ, he is a new creation; the old has gone, the new has come!" (2 Cor. 5:17). The gospel declares that those who believe by faith in Jesus Christ become righteous in God's sight and are seated already in the heavenly places; yet practically, our feet are still firmly planted on earth. This paradoxical positional truth of the "already, not yet" is foundational toward our understanding of adoption into God's family. What if we elevated this truth to a community level—God is pouring out His transforming gospel, not just on individuals but on whole communities? What effect would we anticipate seeing?

The added challenge facing the Cabrini-Green area are two distinct cultures living literally side by side; there is no "other side of the tracks," technically, in this neighborhood. They all share the same streets. This is witnessed dramatically in the local Dominick's supermarket; *Chicago Tribune* reporter Mary Schmich comments,

> *Walk through the store's doors—with Cabrini and the downtown skyline at your back—and you're also walking into a social test kitchen. Rich people, poor people, black people, white people—from produce to poultry to pantyhose, this is a collection of classes and colors rarely seen in Chicago.*[5]

Extreme wealth and extreme poverty shop the same aisles, yet are not engaged in forming real community.

The gospel crosses all cultures and economic classes and calls people to form a new community based on their "one hope . . . one Lord, one faith, one baptism; one God and Father of all, who is over all and through all and in all" (Eph. 4:4–6). The gospel is still the power today to restore people back to God and reconcile people to one another. Since the gospel is able and God is desirous for communities to come together, the question remains, What should be the Church's first steps to help bring these two polar-opposite socioeconomic communities together to form one community?

Directly to the west of the church is a new development that is made up of 90 percent economically advantaged people. Directly to the east and just one-half block south are 100 percent economically disadvantaged people. What should be Park's first steps in helping to bridge these two communities?

The View from My Chair

As I look out my office window, this disparity currently exists. The question that aligns my thinking is, How will Park act as a bridge and not a *buffer* between these two communities? Will we through our programming and direction of resources face either east or west? Or, will we take on the challenge of bridging these two communities together in partnership with the other local churches?

God has raised up His Church for such a time as this, and how this group of churches responds in faith will potentially dictate whether this housing experiment ever becomes a true community. Social engineering can never accomplish what Christ has done on the cross, and we affirm that the Church is the God-ordained representation of that work to the world.

We firmly believe that God is calling the local churches to invest their time, talent, and treasures into the development of this community. These are resources that no alderman, condo association, or park district could ever muster. We believe and need to keep on believing that the real win is not for our individual churches to grow, no matter how wonderful that would be. Rather it is partaking in the Kingdom development of this community. It is partnering with God to see His wholeness, wellness, and goodness come to transform the community in which we live.

I have recently been thumbing through Vincent Donovan's classic *Christianity Rediscovered*, which gives his account of bringing the gospel to the Masai tribe of East Africa. He quotes a comment made by a student that gives great insight into what Park is currently facing:

In working with young people in America, do not try to call them back to where they were, and do not try to call them to where you are, as beautiful as that place might seem to you. You must have the courage to go with them to a place that neither you nor they have ever been before.[6]

What is needed is the courage to take people to a place they have always longed for but never found. What if, in the process, these two communities discovered unity, forgiveness, sacrifice, and joy?

Both sides are cut off from the real community they were always meant to experience. They suffer under the same wandering that Leslie Newbigin calls "a strong sense of moral and spiritual exhaustion. Having constructed a society of unprecedented sophistication, convenience and prosperity, nobody can remember what it was supposed to be for."[7]

What if, when the gospel is pronounced, it will not seem or feel strange to them? In a sense reaching out to unbelievers is putting some pieces of discipleship (at the community level) in place before salvation. They have already been living out, in part, its truths; and now they come to encounter its source and power.

In a conversation with Bob Lupton of Family Counseling Services in Atlanta a couple of years ago, he told us that the redevelopment of Cabrini-Green is the grand social housing project experiment in America. If it succeeds it could possibly become the model for other urban centers to imitate. He added that no one has written the "how to" book on ministry into that type of community. This underscores Donovan's point. We need the courage today to step out into unknown territory, yet with our feet firmly planted on the truth that God will do "immeasurably more than all we ask or imagine" (Eph. 3:20).

ADVENTURES IN MISSING THE PLOT

Often the Church's approach to solving problems is to create programs. Yet rarely do programs get to the systemic issues that created the problems. They act more like a bandage that covers a wound instead of a scalpel that will heal it. Jackson and I have been on the "inside" of church ministry for a combined fifty years and have created more programs than we care to recall. Programs have their place, but too often they are a quick solution to an issue that runs much deeper.

Jesus' method of changing the world was to be devoted to a few good men. Robert Coleman says, "His concern was not with programs to reach the multitudes, but with men whom the multitudes would follow."[8] By choosing programs over people, the Church continues to miss the plot of how Jesus meant His gospel to be demonstrated and proclaimed.

A principle that missionaries use when pioneering new fields is to locate a "person of peace" based on Luke 10:6. A "person of peace" may be defined as "a person sovereignly prepared by God to receive the gospel, before you arrive."[9] Cornelius, Lydia, and the Philippian jailer are common examples from the New Testament of a "person of peace" (Acts 10; 16). We are just in the beginning stages of looking for those people who are influencers in the community, the people who are willing to engage in relationship with us and, more important, embrace the goal of creating unity in diversity.

What is instructive from Scripture is that the "person of peace" may start off as being noteworthy for destructive rather than constructive behavior (the Gerasene demoniac, Mark 5) yet, through encountering Jesus, he may become a great community asset. In a recent community meeting, Alderman Burnett encouraged the local clergy, school, and community officials not to expect the kids who are already coming out to programs to lead the necessary change, but rather, to reach out to those still on the fringe or beyond the current scope of the programs. From those kids the leaders may emerge.

It would be all too easy to enter into this changing neighborhood and either "face west" and engage with the culture we understand or "face east" and throw together a number of programs that in reality will never change this community. We have taken to heart the *One-Minute Manager* slogan, "When I slow down, I go faster."[10] We are following a simple three-step process: Listen, Reflect, and Respond in developing a strategy to help change the community.

Listen

We are intentionally asking questions of seasoned urban practitioners and long-time residents of Cabrini-Green to discover what they believe this community still needs. We are establishing these dialogues across denominational lines, from faith-based to city-based organizations, and including those involved in civil and law-enforcement roles.

What is going well that we can add value to? What is not going well that we might be able to support? Listening has meant slowing down and reorganizing priorities to engage in the existing faith community in our new neighborhood.

Listening to the community is the fifth component of the Christian Community Development Association (CCDA) strategy for a church or ministry to engage a community.[11] Often well-meaning Christians charge into the inner city with a "messiah complex" ready to save the day. It would serve the community well if we followed Jesus' example, "The Son can do nothing by himself; he can do only what he sees his Father doing, because whatever the Father does the Son also does" (John 5:19). Jesus said this because He knew that "my Father is always at his work to this very day" (v. 17). God's work does not begin when we show up; it is already well underway. A big part of our job is to slow down and observe where He is already at work and join Him there.[12]

Every community, no matter how outwardly desperate, has assets and contributions. CCDA teaches an eight-step approach toward community development. One of its basic premises is to approach a community like a coach rather than like a consultant. "Coaching is the process of coming alongside a person or team to help them discover God's agenda for their life and ministry, and then cooperating with the Holy Spirit to see that agenda become a reality."[13] On the other hand, consultants just tell you what to do.

CCDA's philosophy

> *believes that the people with the problem have the best solutions and opportunities to solve those problems. Christian Community Development affirms the dignity of individuals and encourages the engagement of the community to use their own resources and assets to bring about sustainable change.*[14]

In order to listen well, we have intentionally developed friendships with other clergy who are based in the community, yet have some opposing theological views. It is often arrogance or abundance of ministries that inhibits pastors from crossing over doctrinal boundaries and thus causes them to miss the richness of God's diverse community. Also, we will be using our new facility for community meetings and "listening stations" so we can know and better appreciate what the Lord is already doing in our midst.

Reflect

We are fighting against our natural tendency to be a "get it done," hard-charging church. As we listen to the advice given, we need to take time and pray and ask God, "How are You calling us to respond to these needs?" What God-given gifts, abilities, passions, and resources can we use in a God-honoring and community-edifying way?

We are keenly aware that Park may be perceived as part of the group that tore down Cabrini-Green, so it is not just doing things, but doing the right things in the right way at the right time. God's Church has been here since the beginning of this community, engaged with effective, long-haul urban ministry. We are the "new kids on the block" with a steep learning curve. Therefore we heed Solomon's advice, "Plans fail for lack of counsel, but with many advisers they succeed" (Prov. 15:22).

Respond

We are trying to respond only after first listening and reflecting on what we believe God and the community are calling us to. It has not been easy, yet pastors and parachurch leaders are telling us that we have approached this move the best way possible. It is critical that we respond with the time, talent, and treasures the Lord has given us to steward and that we stay engaged until the gospel has brought about lasting change.

From the myriad of good approaches a church can undertake to address community development, Park has decided to channel its financial, prayer, and human resources toward enhancing both youth and adult education in our new neighborhood. Our initial three-prong approach includes middle/high school tutoring, adult continuing education, and financial scholarships for at-risk kids in the low-income projects. At the time of this writing, we are in the process of developing teams of volunteers who will lead these projects with the end goal of seeing a reduction of the number of working poor in our community along with an increase in selective school enrollment and graduating high school students.

We are hoping that through supporting a stronger educational base, the church will be more fully engaged with community transformation. Our desire is to be involved in ministries that develop people's God-given abilities so they will be able to provide for themselves and contribute to their communities.[15]

The underlying question is, How does a church discover its role beyond programs and begin to leverage real economic, social, and political capital to bring transformation to a community? To what lengths are we willing to go to associate with those of different doctrinal camps in order for the gospel to be demonstrated and proclaimed? Are we ready to be more Kingdom-minded than church-focused? Donovan notes:

> *The gospel is not progress or development. It is not nation building. It is not adult education. It is not a school system. It is not a health campaign. It is not a five-year plan. It is not an economic program. . . . Our business as Christians is the establishment of the kingdom. It is a kingdom that takes its beginnings here in this real world, and aims at the fulfillings of this world, of bringing this world to its destiny.[16]*

We can no longer afford to miss the plot, especially with the opportunity that God has graciously given to all His Church in the Near North Side of Chicago. Donovan drives home that our business is not the establishment of programs but the furtherance of the Kingdom. We are to live out Kingdom values, developing friendships and partnerships based on these values and when necessary employing resources to create programs that will promote these values.

Yet, only when Kingdom values such as justice and mercy begin to challenge and change city systems and city structures can we expect lasting change to occur in our community. The call is to truly incarnate ourselves into the reality of this changing neighborhood.

LESSONS ALONG THE WAY (SO FAR)

People Need Mentors

Jackson and I both recognize that our learning curve is about as steep as Mount Everest! Yet we learned along the way that by asking simple and honest questions, such as, "What does it mean to do ministry in the city?" our learning curve has shortened. God has also provided mentors who had already been investing in the city and understood what ministry looked like: men like Dr. John Fuder of Moody Graduate School, Pastor Daniel Hill of River City Community Church, and Pastor Victor Rodriguez from La Villita Community Church have been generous with their time and we have developed friendships in the process.

Live Among Them

We learned the value of living in the city rather than just doing ministry in the city. Our congregation needs to know that we are in it with them, facing the same issues that they face: housing costs, public schools, traffic and parking problems. Living in Chicago is great, but there is a very real level of stress in doing life here. We are learning to embrace life in the city, stress and all, the same way they have.

Travel As They Do

One great lesson I (Jackson) learned was when I came to Chicago and survived my first three months without a car. I learned the public transportation system, which ended up being a priceless experience. When you take the bus, you can sit next to a business executive in a three-piece suit on one side and on the other, let's say, a person with different hygiene standards! It is a snapshot of the city. Taking public transportation, for some of the passengers, is a choice because it is the easiest or most convenient way to get around. However, for others, it is their only mode of transportation. I spent those bus rides asking, *O God, how do we reach these people?*

Service Is the City's Apologetic

A helpful diagram found in *The Externally Focused Church* unpacks how "service is only location that encompasses the needs and dreams of the city, the mandates and desires of God, and the calling and capacity of the church."[17]

The church is able at the same time to fulfill the needs of the city and be obedient to the desires of God when it engages in sacrificial service to the city. We have been called by God to invest in the peace and prosperity of the city (Jer. 29:7).

A friend may not come out to church with me on Sunday, but if I invite him to volunteer at a homeless shelter, repair a senior citizen's garage door, or help clean out a vacant lot, he will more than likely say, "Sure, I have time for that." Why? Because those who live in the city understand the need to get involved in the "mess of humanity." When that happens, you are inviting that person into God's redemptive work for the city and allowing him to see that as a follower of Christ you are actively engaged in helping to make the city a better place to live.

Service is critical for the Christ follower because of the example that Jesus set for us. Paul records of Jesus, "Who, being in very nature God, did not consider equality with God something to be grasped, but made himself nothing, taking the very nature of a servant" (Phil. 2:6–7a). Jesus was not just a leader who served, but a servant who led. His very nature was that of a servant. There is a striking difference between serving and taking the nature of a servant, the difference between outward conformity and inward transformation.

Ministers Need to Pause

City ministry is tough. The burnout rate is considerable. For five years I (Jackson) have watched as pastors come and eventually leave because of the difficulty and the drain of urban ministry and the constant demands. What does it take to thrive in an urban area for an extended period of time? You must be spiritually filled. Sabbath breaks ensure you retain the ability to stay committed for the long haul, and engage in activities that are spiritually refreshing.

Even Jesus took breaks, sometimes with His men (Matt. 16:13) and sometimes alone (Mark 1:35). We need time to be refreshed from God's Word, prayer, and quiet, because ministry happens in the wake of pursuing Jesus. Dan Webster brings out another incredibly important truth as he makes a case for being quiet: "In quiet I am reminded that I am a child of God first and a servant of God second."[18] Quietness aligns my call to serve with my position as a son of God.

CONCLUSION: THE ROAD AHEAD

God is always doing new things. The cities of this country are changing dramatically, and the time is coming when there will be fewer places where a city church will be able to specialize in one type of economic subgroup. The same is true for the suburban church as they encounter the suburbanization of the poor.

We have to relearn how to have a dealer in purple be in fellowship with a jail warden (Acts 10 and 16). We have to rediscover the purpose and real potential of the gospel: to break down all dividing lines and stop the subtle nonsense that reconciliation just cannot happen in our lifetime. We need courage to say no to the "quick fix" mentality of programs that never get at the root issues separating God from people and people from people.

It will take boldness to step out, make mistakes along the way, and keep our eyes fixed on Jesus (Hebrews 12:2). With confidence that God is orchestrating both the means and the ends to His glory, we should proclaim His gospel in word and deed, bold and unhindered (Acts 28:31), expecting that the cities of man will become the city of our God.

REFLECTION QUESTIONS

1. Do you have open hands toward God with the ministry you are currently involved in? Are you able to pray, "God, I will do anything and go anywhere"?

2. What is a greater win for your church: community development or church numerical growth? How do you support that answer through allocation of the church's time, talent, and treasures?

3. What social markers would need to change in your community for you to be able to say it is being transformed? How is your church allocating resources to get after those markers?

In 2001, **AL TOLEDO** sensed the Lord leading him and his family to leave New York, where he was an Associate Pastor at the Brooklyn Tabernacle, and begin a work in the city of Chicago. In January 2002, the Chicago Tabernacle, a multi-racial church of about four hundred, was birthed.

CHAPTER 8

GROWING A CHURCH THROUGH PRAYER:

The Story of Chicago Tabernacle

Al Toledo

Introduction: A Firm Foundation

There is nothing like a good upbringing. Rearing children in a good home has endless benefits: building in all the right things that they need to know when they grow up and are out on their own and providing an important living example for them not only to hear but also to experience. If a picture is worth a thousand words, then a good model is worth either a thousand lectures from a parent or lifetimes of living without a teacher. A good example gives context to what is important and how important things should be handled or honored. Crucial intangibles are more often caught in a home rather than taught.

This principle is especially true of the church, which God calls His "house." We pastors are given the huge responsibility of helping to build a house where Jesus is the foundation and head. He is honored and revered as Lord when the priorities and culture of the household of faith revolve around seeking Him. The Bible is clear that the most important thing that takes place in God's house is prayer (Matt. 21:13).

As my wife and I embarked upon a call from God to pioneer a church in Chicago, we were blessed in being the benefactors of a good spiritual upbringing. Coming from the Brooklyn Tabernacle, for years we both heard, possibly thousands of times, an invitation to "the most important meeting of the week"—the weekly prayer meeting. We not only heard it, but we saw it play out in our own spiritual home. Our church family gathered once a week with all of our pastors leading the way as we cried out to God for all of our needs and the needs of others around the world. We saw God answer requests that were humanly impossible. We experienced His presence in a personal and intimate way, but most of all, we learned how the household of faith should function here on earth. After all, Christ did say, "My house will be called a house of prayer for all nations" (Mark 11:17).

God's family is on the right track when it prays. Getting on the right track is what we desperately wanted as we came to Chicago. We came with the firm conviction that if we built our church on the foundation of prayer, nothing would be impossible; but if we did not, then our efforts would be in vain. Despite the fact that praying in faith has always been a great challenge to His people, it is still the great priority of God's house. We firmly believed that we were meant, as Andrew Murray stated, "to dwell often in the private place, with the door shut against the world, your work, your responsibilities. There the Father waits for you."[1]

THE IMPORTANCE OF PRAYER

Although many churches have moved away from the prayer meeting, we knew that we would have to make the sacrifice to teach our people the importance of prayer. Home fellowship groups and midweek Bible studies seem to be far more popular in our city, but we were convinced that prayer would be our only hope if we were to become who God wanted us to be as a church family. God's family should consist of a people who are fluent in the language of prayer. Prayer is the language spoken by the earth-bound citizens of heaven. Fluency in that language makes them efficient in all the spiritual transactions of God's Kingdom. In the same way that language barriers often hinder communication, we wanted to make sure we were growing believers who had no struggle communicating with their Father. This foundation of prayer in the house of God is a mandate of Scripture that has been tried and tested by His people throughout history. Prayer has always brought about deliverance and direction from above. All revivals were ignited and sustained by the humble servants of God seeking His face.

What is wonderful about the declaration concerning "His house" is that it contains the great priorities that one needs to be focused on in the ministry. Since God is love, we know that His house should be a place that is characterized by people experiencing and expressing their love for God. Those who seek Him always grow to love Him. The main reason God wants us to pray is that when we pray we fall in love with Him. His presence is liberating and transforming (2 Cor. 3:17–18). Who would not want to be free and liberated?

"To know him is to love him" might be a cliché, but it is still especially true of

Jesus. A prayerful people become a passionate people. As a pastor, there is nothing I want more than to lead a people that passionately love Him. The main problem is that teaching alone falls short. In just a few years we have had the privilege of watching many brothers and sisters become more Christ-centered and passionate about their walk with God as they learned how to pray.

Impacting a Life

A member of our church named Jamie was raised in a church in the Midwest. She left college heading for Los Angeles with stars in her eyes, deciding she was going to be a rich and famous actress. Living and working in Beverly Hills, Jamie spent most of her days partying with Hollywood's stars. She became immersed in the world and anything it had to offer. While Jamie was in Los Angeles, on a downward spiral to destruction—exhausted and lonely—a childhood friend who attended our fellowship began praying earnestly for her. She shared her burden for Jamie with others who began calling on the Lord for her.

One night, while Jamie was at a very elite party, God miraculously opened her eyes to see how sad and empty everyone around her was. When she got home, she got on her knees and seriously repented. God started doing a beautiful work in this woman's life. He began drawing her close and removed her desire for many of the things that consumed her.

She decided to visit Chicago and attended our Thursday night prayer meeting, the very place where her friend lifted her up to God. I quote her as she shares her experience of that night: "I was amazed at the passion these people had while calling on the Lord, the faith and assurance they had that God would answer them, and the hope and expectancy they had because they had prayed. Three months later I moved to Chicago. I had to know the Lord the way these people knew the Lord!"

Watching Jamie over the past year, it is evident that she has fallen in love with Jesus. She inspires us to seek Him more. Now, Jamie is mightily used in our church, attends Bible college, and aspires to be in full-time ministry. Prayer is the only answer for someone who is seeking "more."

The People of His Presence

Praying people become the people of His presence. The Bible records that the unschooled fishermen who were Jesus' disciples distinguished themselves because they had been with Jesus (Acts 4:13). Moses pleaded with God not to allow Israel to go forward without His presence. Otherwise, there would be no distinguishing quality to the children of God. This love for God, this "distinguishing quality," only comes from time spent in the presence of the Lord. Rhonda

Hughey states:

> *When the presence of Jesus is not manifest in the church in a tangible way and we continue our programs, we are inviting the religious spirit to set up her throne in our congregations and ministries. This spirit is more than happy to become a substitute for Jesus; in fact, it has been the goal of the enemy all along. Eventually, as the church grows more and more compromised and disconnected from Jesus and her ministry in the world, two things happen: true believers will leave the empty institutionalized church in pursuit of life and intimacy with Jesus, and others will remain, determined to shape and mold it after their own image.*[2]

The Bible promises times of refreshing in the presence of the Lord (Acts 3:19), and only the presence of God can truly restore the "burning realities of eternity" in the people of the Chicago Tabernacle. Only seeking His face can help us overcome the downward pull of the world. The first church was born in a prayer meeting and progressed as a result of prayer meetings (Acts 2; 4). Fresh energy, conviction, and leading from above was required for the difficult times the apostolic fathers lived in, and it was supplied to the people seeking God. Although our times have changed, our spiritual needs have never changed. Talking to the Father is the greatest need of our lives.

DIVERSITY THROUGH PRAYER

Another priority emphasized by the Lord's statement, "My house will be called a house of prayer for all nations" (Mark 11:17), is the issue of diversity. Our country and churches are always grappling with unity in the midst of our diversity. There is a scar on our nation's history because of the atrocities of slavery and segregation. Although this struggle remains in our city, God does have a solution for the problem of racism. Certainly, racism and prejudice should not have a hold on His Church! As Dr. King said, "Should not the moral guardian of our communities live above the degrading elements of this world?"[3] When my wife and I were moving to Chicago in 2002, we were surprised by the numerous reports we heard depicting Chicago as one of the most segregated cities in America. What a challenge to someone who just wanted to start a church with doors open to everyone! How would we build a church for all people? The Lord made it real to us that to *try* to be diverse would be in vain.

There are issues of the heart that only God can reach, while human efforts continually fall short. The spiritual answer—God's answer—is prayer. When people engage in spiritual battles for one another, walls are torn down and bonds of love are created that surpass human or earthly understanding. When a sister prays for another sister's sick baby or a marriage that seems to be hanging by a thread, a union of love is formed that can only take place in the presence of God (Col. 3:12–14).

The love of God does not see skin colors or socioeconomic backgrounds—His love simply loves. When we fervently pray with someone, we become blind to the things of the flesh. I often marvel at the unique friendships that exist in our church family. We have a young professional named Lindsey, who grew up in a very well-to-do family from Connecticut. Many of her new friends would never be found in her Connecticut neighborhood—but what does that matter to love? After being at the church for only a short time, a precious friendship was formed between her and a Puerto Rican young lady. She tells us of how, on one occasion, Cicely said to Lindsey, "I never thought I would be friends with a white girl!"

Lindsey answered, "To tell you the truth I never thought that I would be friends with somebody who was Puerto Rican." These women have entered into the trenches of prayer together, calling on the Lord for each other's needs.

This story is the picture of what happens when people pray together. Issues such as skin color, race, and social status cease to be obstacles when one realizes the common bond every human has—the need for God. The more we get people interceding for one another, the closer they become. I do not believe in formulas for obtaining diversity in a church. However, if there was a "formula," prayer would be it.

Our choir has now grown to about fifty members, and diversity is definitely one of its salient features. The goal of diversity, however, has never played a role in any of our deliberations; we just experience the beauty of diversity and the blessing of unity as we pray. The first thing our choir does before every rehearsal is spend time worshiping and seeking the Lord. Praying brings about a love and unity that is needed to minister, despite how different we are.

THE SOURCE OF POWER

When God stated that His house is a house of prayer, He was emphasizing that His power would be available to meet the needs and solve the problems of His people. Dutch Sheets said that "we can run our churches and ministries from the board room or the prayer room. The first produces the works of man. The other births a move from God."[4]

What is so special about the prayer meeting to my wife and me is that prayer has given us our own miracle stories to boast about in the Lord. Coming from a prayer ministry as powerful as the Brooklyn Tabernacle's is a wonderful heritage, but we needed God to move in Chicago for a small band of believers the same way that we saw Him move on behalf of the cry of more than two thousand in Brooklyn. One of the first things I learned as a senior pastor was that the few can always secure the blessing for the many when His people begin to pray. Prayer does not require large numbers, and yet it gives one personal access and authority. The mightiness of God is revealed for small numbers just as it is for large.

We began our work on Chicago's North Side by renting the basement of a church whose sanctuary use had been prohibited by the city of Chicago. We knew that we needed a building, but the problem was that as a three-month-old church, we only had two thousand dollars in the bank. No lending institution would even give us an application for a mortgage. Despite the obvious, we decided to start looking and believe God for a building.

We found an old church for sale that needed a couple hundred thousand dollars' worth of repairs, but our hearts felt like God was truly in this situation. We needed a down payment, a mortgage, and a reasonable purchase price. We told our real estate agent that we would have to bid at least $100,000 below the asking price and she said, "That'll never happen." We said that we would first take this to God at our prayer meeting before we made the offer.

The "Seven-Day Miracle"

That Thursday night prayer meeting was the beginning of our "seven-day miracle." I presented the situation to a group of about fifteen people who had gathered to pray, and one of our deacons took the microphone and cried out to God. He prayed, "Lord, we need a building and we need the right price; we need a mortgage; and Lord, we need these now." The next day we put in our ridiculous bid and God began to move. The sellers accepted our offer! Sunday we showed pictures to our small congregation and took pledges in hopes to raise another three to four thousand dollars. By the end of that meeting our small congregation of about forty people miraculously pledged $27,000. We were stunned by the outpouring of faith on our congregation.

That same day I was scheduled to fly to Springfield, Missouri, to preach and share about our vision for the Chicago Tabernacle. After I presented the work God had set before us, the pastor collected an offering. It was the largest offering ever collected on a Sunday evening in the history of the church! We went back to Chicago with a check for $40,000. Little did we know that God had placed the president of a lending institution in the service that evening. We received a call from his office and were told that not only would they give us a mortgage but that we would not have to make payments for the entire first year! God had done in seven days everything we asked for and launched our church in just three months.

Although the call to prayer is an obvious emphasis of the Bible, I fully understand why prayer meetings are not as popular as midweek Bible studies or home fellowship groups. As Charles Finney said, "Prayer meetings are the most difficult meetings to sustain—as, indeed, they ought to be. They are so spiritual that unless the leader is especially prepared both in heart and mind, they will dwindle."[5]

THE WORK OF PRAYER

Running a prayer meeting is definitely the hardest thing I have ever done in ministry. Our flesh resists it and our hearts seem to find intercession very difficult. One would think that doing God's will in this area would be filled with ease, but I liken it to driving a car with square wheels. After the initial excitement of praying wore off for our young congregation, we began to experience one tough meeting after another.

There were many discouraging rides home from a meeting that was supposed to be accomplishing so much. Not only did we struggle with fatigue, but we often could not seem to garner a real sense of unity in prayer. The Lord put it on our hearts to persevere, and after a while the grace to pray began to fall upon our church. The hard edges started to soften and soon we were leaving the prayer services full of joy and the assurance that we had really reached the throne of God.

Since then, God's undeniable power has manifested itself in the lives and difficult circumstances of many of the people we have prayed for. Drug addicts have been delivered, marriages have been restored, and several backsliders have returned to the Lord. The enemy has never ceased to resist our meetings, but we have found a new confidence that when we call upon Him, He will answer. A friend of mine who pastors a church in the Midwest has recently turned his midweek Bible study into a prayer meeting and has been met with great opposition. Even some of his key leaders are refusing to attend. There is nothing the Devil resists more vehemently than a serious effort to pray.

The more popular alternatives to prayer seem to be easier today. The myth that belonging is the same as believing has firmly taken hold and greatly influenced churches to employ methods that are more geared toward making visitors—and eventually church members—feel comfortable, rather than grow strong in their walk with God.[6] However, a very influential church in our country has recently done a study on its own members concluding that many of these methods have not managed to create strong Christ-centered believers.[7]

If God says that His house should be called a house of prayer, is it not logical to conclude that He will determine how fruitful our ministries are by what kind of diligent seekers we produce (Hebrews 11:6)? The Lord knew that prayer in the church would be a great battle. He even warned us that we wrestle not against flesh and blood but against principalities and powers (Eph. 6:12). My pastor always said, "If you beat the devil in the place of prayer you can beat him everywhere. But if you don't then he always has a trump card on you."[8]

One of the things that seemed to plague the people of Israel was the fact that God's great deeds continually withered from fact to distant memory, to fiction, to myth (Psalm 78:1–11). Perhaps this is why each generation struggles with becoming a praying people. For example, Scripture says, "The effectual, fervent prayer of a righteous man availeth much" (James 5:16 KJV). As a pastor, I am challenged by what the average Christian in my church thinks when hearing the phrase "effectual, fervent prayer." This is one of those crucial points when one's belief must be shown in experience. Theology that descends from the heart of God is always living and vibrant. As we minister in the city of Chicago, the great needs of our people are not affected by passionless intellectualism. A knowledgeable people is good, but God seems to say that a learned, praying people is better.

Modeling Prayer

One of the greatest gifts my pastoral leaders gave me was a living example of an "effectual, fervent prayer." I had read Paul's words, "I am again in the pains of childbirth until Christ is formed in you" (Gal. 4:19). I also read that Jesus, during His days on the earth, offered up loud cries and tears (Heb. 5:7). But if I had not seen it in the lives of my leaders, then these truths could have easily just become words on a page. I suspect that I would not have the conviction that God wants prayer to be the main priority if I had not experienced it myself.

I believe the main reason people do not like going to prayer meetings is that people are not used to hearing living prayers. Charles Finney said that cold prayers, lacking the "unction of God, will freeze a meeting to the point of death."[9] If the leaders cannot pray passionate prayers, then how can the followers? My heart trembles at the thought that a person would come to my church and never hear or see anyone in leadership cry out to God. Great sermons do not mean anything if they do not inspire great responses of prayer. Only prayer produces the true fire of God upon His people. We have watched so many people change despite the fact that we have a simple ministry. That is because a powerful transformation takes place when people come face-to-face with the Master.

SUGGESTIONS FOR RUNNING A PRAYER MEETING

1. Have all leadership in attendance.

The priority of prayer must be demonstrated by the leaders in order for the burden to be caught by the people. Without this display of the priority of prayer by the leadership, prayer will easily fall by the wayside in the minds of the people. If the senior leadership does not attend the prayer meeting, then it remains an important but secondary focus of God's house. The leaders must lead in this area in order to create a house of prayer.

2. A few is all it takes.

Do not worry about the attendance as long as you are encouraging the body that the prayer meeting is the most important meeting of the week. Over time the spirit of prayer will start to fall on the rest of the congregation. My pastor taught that prayer is a grace that falls, and when it does, God's Spirit begins to affect the entire congregation.

3. Pass around the microphone.

One of the best ways to teach and encourage people to pray is by passing around the mic. Although you want to be sure to choose those with proven grace in the area of public prayer, after a short season it is good to have the members of the congregation lead in prayer for the different requests being tackled that evening. The people tend to feel more engaged in the meeting and they also come more prepared to seek God. This corporate participation creates a greater sense of unity and focus.

4. Use prayer cards.

Prayer cards are an excellent tool to help the people take on the burdens of others in the congregation and around the world. They also give the people in the congregation a confidence that we will pray for them when they need it. This sharing of burdens is another form of advertisement for attending the prayer meeting. People are always drawn to places where they know they will be prayed for.

5. Include altar calls.

A great way to teach people to become strong prayers is to allow response times of prayer to a brief faith-building message in the meeting. Immediate responses to a word take place when the truth is freshest in their hearts and therefore can lead to truly inspired prayers. All the patriarchs responded to words of promise from God by building altars. True prayer is most often a faith response and can be developed by the practice of prayer for a truth that the Lord has made real in the meeting.

6. Encourage team praying.

The Bible encourages us to "pray for each other" (James 5:16) during our times of need. Team praying and responding creates a unity of heart and purpose. It also helps people break free of an unholy self-consciousness that hinders the spirit of prayer. It practically teaches them that prayer is not a show or about self, but rather speaking to God, and interceding for someone in desperate need of God's help. Team praying aids in breaking through in the area of public prayer and fosters the special fellowship that people experience when they share intimate times of prayer.

7. Do not overschedule.

Prayer is such a relational and heart-oriented activity that it is best when we follow the leading of the Spirit rather than a planned outline. The Bible says, "We do not know what we ought to pray for, but the Spirit himself intercedes for us with groans that words cannot express. And he who searches our hearts knows the mind of the Spirit, because the Spirit intercedes for the saints in accordance with God's will" (Rom. 8:26–27). It is better to trust God to handle the agenda of the meeting than quench the direction that the Spirit wants to lead us in.

CONCLUSION: THE PRIORITY OF PRAYER

Biblically speaking, the priority of prayer in God's house is irrefutable. The role that prayer plays in the Kingdom of God, from Genesis to Revelation, stands out as the main instrument for taking ground in the spiritual kingdom. The simplicity of "ye have not, because ye ask not" (James 4:2 KJV) shouts at every person who has been called to lead in the church. I thank God that I learned about the priority of prayer through the example set by my leaders. I have learned that the only way for a ministry to experience the love, life, and power of God is to lay down a firm foundation of prayer. The programs, activities, and tasks of our ministries will only go as far as our prayer altars. "Lord, teach us to pray" (Luke 11:1).

REFLECTION QUESTIONS

1. What are the God-ordained priorities of the church? How does your church show prayer as one of its top priorities?

2. How does a leader inspire true passion in the fellowship of believers?

3. When does God stretch out His hand of power, and why? In what ways have you experienced God's power in your life?

4. How can God use you to ignite a ministry of prayer in your church?

Recommended Reading List

Bounds, E. M. *Powerful and Prayerful Pulpits.* Grand Rapids: Baker Book House, 1993.

———. *The Weapon of Prayer.* Goodyear, Ariz.: Diggory Press, 2007.

Chadwick, Samuel. *God Listens.* Westchester, Ill.: Good News Publishers, 1973.

Cymbala, Jim. *Fresh Wind, Fresh Fire.* Grand Rapids, Mich.: Zondervan, 1997.

Finney, Charles. *Revivals of Religion.* Virginia Beach, Va.: CBN Univ. Press, 1978.

Myers, Joseph R. *The Search to Belong: Rethinking Intimacy, Community, and Small Groups.* Grand Rapids, Mich.: Zondervan, 2003.

Phelps, Austin. *The Still Hour.* Homewood, Ala.: Solid Ground Christian Books, 2005.

Prime, Samuel. *The Power of Prayer: The New York Revival of 1858.* Carlisle, Pa.: The Banner of Truth Trust, 1998.

Part Two

CHURCH-PLANTING
MODELS

NOEL CASTELLANOS has worked in full-time ministry in urban communities since 1982. He has served in youth ministry, church planting, and community development in San Francisco, San Jose, and Chicago. Noel is a highly sought after speaker, motivator, and mentor to young leaders throughout the USA, and has a deep passion to serve and invest in the lives of emerging leaders. After serving on the Board of the Christian Community Development Association for many years, he has established the new CCDA Institute, which is working to equip emerging church leaders in the philosophy of Christian Community Development, and currently serves as the Chief Executive Officer of CCDA. He and his wife, Marianne, have three children, Noel Luis, Stefan, and Anna, and make their home in the barrio of La Villita in Chicago.

Introduction to Church-Planting Models

Noel Castellanos

HOW NEW CHURCHES ARE UNLEASHING GOD'S LOVE IN OUR COMMUNITIES

U rban church planting is not for people who are afraid of failure or adventure. I have attempted two church plants in the last twenty years in Chicago, and my experiences have been some of the best of times and some of the most challenging of times.

In 1990, after being exposed to the teaching of Dr. John Perkins while leading an urban youth ministry in San Jose, California, my wife and I were compelled to move from sunny and shaky California to the freezing tundra of Chicago to establish a new Christian community development (CCD) type ministry with a church at its center. Our youth ministry had always struggled with the challenge of bringing new, raw, streetwise converts to Christ, into an already established church setting designed to protect and nurture the children and youth of its members. No question that these kids were not perfect and mature in their faith, but they were so much further along than our newly evangelized kids. This pushed us to think about starting a new church congregation for these youths and their families. Dr. Perkins' teaching confirmed our growing conviction about the need for new wineskin churches in the heart of the *barrio* or "hood."

The other reality that moved my wife and me to consider the possibility of moving into church planting with a CCD twist was the realization that simply having a new church in the community was not enough, but that it had to be a church of and for the community as well. Again, the philosophy of CCD became relevant as we worked to formulate our own ministry philosophy. We began to understand that to be a community church that was contextually relevant, and that was totally open to minister to folks who were unchurched or slightly churched, we had to be concerned about the whole needs of youth and their parents, and we also had to be concerned about the environment of the neighborhood. That is, we had to embrace our need and our responsibility to change the dysfunctional aspects of how our neighborhood worked for our neighbors to truly thrive.

To make a long story short, our small family moved to an inner-city neighborhood in Chicago called La Villita to establish this new kind of work. Twenty years ago, the church planting movement was not where it is today, and I hardly ever thought of myself as a church planter. Instead, as we partnered with Lawndale Community Church to begin this new work in our Mexican barrio, we sought to establish a community-based, Christ-centered ministry that would produce disciples who loved God and loved their neighborhood. To do so, we reached out to the children in the community, taught them about the love of Jesus, helped them with their homework, taught them to read, provided mentors, ran summer programs for them to keep them out of trouble, and tried to engage their parents in everything we did with the kids. Out of this simple strategy, a worshiping community—yes, a new local church—was birthed. Almost twenty years later, La Villita Community Church continues to minister to our community in the name of Christ.

I am convinced that every neighborhood needs community-focused churches to minister to its neighbors. I also believe that even though many church congregations already exist in every city in America, the birth of new churches almost always breathes new life and new vitality into the body of Christ, in that it creates a new and renewed commitment to reach out and to find new people to love in the name of Christ as its mission.

In this section of *A Heart for the Community*, you will have an opportunity to read about some of the most exciting church planting efforts in the Chicago area. Many of these leaders are close friends who have forsaken much easier occupations and less risky endeavors to jump into the front lines of church ministry. Some have hooked up with denominations, some are independent efforts, some are efforts built on the foundations of long-standing church ministries, and some are a combination of two or more of these. What they all have in common is that they demonstrate the impact that new churches, established with a clear mission to reach out to those who are far away from God, and with a heart to meet the real, practical felt needs that people have, can have for the advancement of God's Kingdom.

I will never forget the first conversation I had with Isaías Mercado, the founding pastor of La Casa del Carpintero (The Carpenter's House) in Humboldt Park. He was an elder in a good church with a growing ministry, but he and his wife felt a deep burden to reach people in their neighborhood who may never attend their present church. This burden could not be ignored, and finally, with no denominational support, no staff, no big donor, and no building, they launched out to establish this new church to build people and to build the community. Five years later, through many highs and some lows, this new church is making a difference in the lives of people in that neighborhood, and Isaías has been able to use his gifts of leadership and teaching to establish a solid, growing ministry that is drawing people to Christ.

On the Near South Side of Chicago, I recently preached at an African-American church that has been in existence for many years. Today, it is being led and pastored by a young, dynamic man named Jonathan Brooks. This ministry is being revitalized by new leadership and by a huge number of young people mixed with some adults who have been there for a long while. I have great hope that this church will do some serious "Kingdom damage" in that neighborhood!

Megachurches, multi-site churches, denominations, individual congregations, and already established churches are all changing the church-planting landscape of the Chicagoland area. In the urban core and in the surrounding suburbs, committed leaders and their families are creating teams, extending their faith, and putting their lives on the line as they invest in reaching people for Christ through these new churches that are focused on the poor, the rich, the educated, the broken, and everyone in between.

Imagine the church getting to the place where it feels content with its impact in a city. Imagine the spiritual leaders of a city declaring that "no more churches are needed here." This kind of church would die within a short period of time! As a living organism, the fellowship of Christ and His bride, the church, are by nature always growing and expanding, like a healthy body.

With all of the good efforts that are emerging around the city of Chicago and around the country, we still need to see new church efforts invigorate the church at large. In Miami, a group of young Moody graduates is establishing a new work in a gentrifying community on the edges of downtown. In Orlando, a young Puerto Rican leader is dreaming about reaching young people through a church planting effort designed just for them. In San Diego, young, dynamic leaders are blazing a new trail through church planting efforts that are focused on meeting community needs. In Long Beach, California, a young Korean leader is reaching out to Latino and African-American college-aged students and equipping them to make a difference in their community.

All of these efforts are breathing new life into the church, and we must find ways to support and sustain these pioneering works. In Oklahoma City I recently encountered a young church plant working to establish a church committed to the poor, meeting downtown, just a few blocks from the site of the Oklahoma City bombing memorial. A few years earlier, a committed businessman made a significant Kingdom investment to help launch this church. He became so excited about the impact the church was having that he also committed to funding a new church planting initiative to start as many new churches as possible in their city. Can you imagine the impact this kind of vision and commitment will have?

I love church planters, because they are a bit crazy! They are a different breed, with great courage and with a thick skin to deal with intense challenges and constant rejection on their way to establishing a healthy, growing church. These leaders encourage and challenge my faith, and they push me to consider if I am doing all I can to live out my Christian faith. In this way, they are a gift to the entire body of Christ.

Finally, if what Bill Hybels says is true, that "the local church is the hope of the world," then Chicago has some good days to look forward to in regard to Kingdom impact, as new churches are bringing hope and new life to some of our neediest communities.

PHIL JACKSON has more than twenty years of experience working with youth and young adults. He currently serves as Pastor for The House Covenant Church, Chicago's first all teen and young adult hip hop church, and is an Associate Pastor for Lawndale Community Church. He is an author of *The Hip-Hop Church* and is also a contributing author of chapters for various other books, as well as an editor for Crossway Publishing's *Urban Devotional Bible*. Phil and his wife, Kim, have been married since 1985 and have three children.

CHAPTER 9

JESUS ON THE MIC:
The Hip Hop Church

Pastor Phil Jackson

Introduction: Where It All Started

There I sat in my friend's car, frustrated, angry, hurt, emotionally bankrupt, and not knowing how to express my emotions over the murder of a close friend. All I could think about was retaliating. I wanted to get the feelings of hopelessness and powerlessness out of my system, and the only way that seemed possible was to put someone else in the grave. All of a sudden, the radio played one of the most powerful rap songs of the 1980s, "The Message" by Grand Master Flash and the Furious Five. The song stimulated a sense of hope, as if we were in church worshiping God, or listening to a choir singing a powerful gospel song that stirred up the soul. It was then that I knew I needed hip hop; it was then that I realized that hip hop was more than cleverly skilled emcees speaking rhythmically over tight beats.

The history of hip hop is an organic one: no artificial flavors from mainstream society, a history that comes from the people, by the people, for the people. Hip hop culture is an important force in the lives of young people today, in that it shows them that someone understands their world. Young people who both love Jesus Christ and are influenced by hip hop culture and rap music are often perplexed about the place they have in the church and the body of Christ overall.

This is where our dilemma starts as Christ followers who are seeking to bridge the gap; this same dilemma is also the connecting point toward change. Jesus Christ came from heaven to earth to live among us. He walked with those no one would have ever walked with. He did life with common, everyday hurting people, and as He did, people were never the same. I believe today Christ would walk with the dope dealers, people living with HIV (modern-day lepers), drug addicts, gangbangers, and even the hip hop culture.

The question is, What does incarnational ministry look like when seeking to reach those influenced by the music or lifestyle pressure of the hip hop culture?

Our journey is to first examine hip hop through its history to understand the root of its influence. We then must see where Christ is already working in hip hop culture and join in along with Him. It is not as if this culture caught Jesus off guard and now we must bring Jesus to "them." When we see a community as Christ does, we will see how and where the truth of Christ is seeping in and join Him there. To do this we must put on a different pair of glasses and see the needs of the people and the value of the community within the culture before writing it off as something demonic or unworthy. "Jesus is on the mic," spittin' or teaching truth to all who would hear! In order to reach people no one else is reaching, you must do things no one else is doing.

A LOOK AT HIP HOP CULTURE

Many people confuse rap with hip hop and dismiss the culture of hip hop because of the negative messages rappers give. This, however, is missing the bigger picture of the cultural impact of hip hop. Simply, rap is what you do while hip hop is who you are. Hip hop culture demands authenticity. Not all rappers qualify to be part of hip hop culture.

Rap music is the visual expression of a larger community that is broader, more diverse, and less obligated to be solely defined by some rap songs that send sexual and/or violent messages. No one rap song can define hip hop culture.

Bakari Kitwana states in his book *The Hip Hop Generation* that hip hop was trying to find itself or define itself while six major phenomena were shaping the worldview of this hip hop generation during the 1980s and '90s.

1. Worldview influenced by black youth visibility in popular culture

2. Worldview influenced by globalization of their culture

3. Worldview influenced by persisting segregation in America

4. Worldview influenced by public policy regarding criminal justice

5. Black youth culture influenced by the media representation of young blacks

6. Worldview affected by overall shift in quality of life for young blacks

As all of this was going on in the lives of young blacks and Latinos, these disenfranchised young people finally felt heard and that they counted. Yet the Church was generally silent and not receptive to this community's concerns. On the whole, the Church became more antagonistic. The need being met by hip hop is that of being validated as worthy, valued while still living in a culture that the whole world has labeled negative, no good, a waste. When someone does well from this community it is seen as a surprise. The need to belong is the deepest need that we humans have, and hip hop met that need and still does today for many people.

When everyone else says you don't count (because of the lack of quality education, poor housing, and poor living conditions), you will do everything to defend yourself. The church being so hard against hip hop and rap became just another affirmation that our young people don't count. Within the most holy place in the inner city, the church, there was (and at times still is) no real sanctuary for the hip hop culture. Instead of reaching out, the church has pushed away this community.

The initial frustration of course will be with the music, lyrics, and clothes that don't seem to match what is common to worship. The black church has better understood R&B (rhythm and blues) as music that crosses over from the holy to the secular. The soloist in the church worshiping on Sunday even while singing at the club throughout the week seemed more understandable.

The hurdle we must overcome is the mind-set that keeps us from experiencing new ways of expressing faith in Christ. We remain comfortable in the traditional evangelical paradigm even when it means rejecting those outside it. When others' ways become a little harder to understand, fear sets in, and we often turn toward demonizing others. Efforts to communicate the gospel to those alienated people become more difficult.

The Church's Response to Change

The story of what happened to Thomas A. Dorsey (considered to be the father of gospel music) is a perfect example of the typical church response toward this type of change. Dorsey came from Georgia to Chicago and brought the blues style of music into the church. As soon as he started to play, the church declared Dorsey's brand of gospel music unworthy of a hearing within the sanctuary. The church responded much the same way to the rock 'n' roll Jesus Movement that swept the country in the early 1970s. In both instances, the traditional church failed to see the positive influence contemporary music could have, blessing its listeners and encouraging them to draw nearer to God.

The intense quality in blues music can lift up gospel music beyond its mere form, a quality that most preachers in Dorsey's day failed to understand.[1] Dorsey was demonized and his songs were not played in African-American churches for years. Dorsey continued to press on with his vision of music, and as he did so a generation found its way back to Christ and the church. Because of his belief in this message, eventually things changed and now you cannot go to an African-American worship service without seeing one of Dorsey's songs in the hymnal or hearing the choir singing "Precious Lord" during the service.

Hip Hop Birthed from Injustice

Hip hop culture did not start out as an intentional effort to make money or exploit women, which is what most people see it doing. Rather, it set out to communicate pain, hurt, joy, and love from a disenfranchised community of people trying desperately to be heard.

Hip hop's story started in the early 1950s with a man named Robert Moses who was not a rapper at all. He was hired by the city of New York to build the Cross Bronx Expressway, a seven-mile, six-lane stretch of road that went from Queens to downtown Manhattan. This new "urban revitalization" destroyed parts of the South Bronx where families had lived for generations in communities that thrived in multicultural relationships. Jobs were lost as companies sold and moved, leaving more and more buildings vacant.

When this type of urban revitalization happens and areas are left to "fend for themselves," they become traumatrigenic communities. Traumatrigenic means living with the constant pressure of violence, poverty, drugs, death, and powerlessness as a daily way of life.

As I talk about hip hop's inception, it is important to note that it came out of the pain and anguish of those trapped in poor communities in the South Bronx and other areas. It is not a victim mentality but a survivalist mentality that birthed hip hop and has taken it to where it is now. The current reality of hip hop's authority and influence in people's lives goes from the wealthiest suburbs to the poorest neighborhoods. It now has shown its influence in all ethnic groups in every type of community. But the message of hip hop still comes from the street.

When traumatrigenic communities have fewer and fewer options in managing the everyday stress and strain of life, the need to release this tension becomes unbearable. Communities living with this pressure often will explode over built-up frustrations from the injustices happening to them over the years. The most recent examples would be the 1992 Los Angeles riots and the 1991 Cincinnati race riots. It would be as if you lived in a war zone and every day bombs dropped all around you, to the point where this had become normal. Yet, under this stress people either will choose to fight and deal with it or take off in flight and leave it.

Within traumatrigenic communities, most of the time people are left with three ineffective methods to try to maintain their sanity: daily drug use, sex, and violence. Hip hop came at just the right time to provide a positive alternative survival tool in the midst of these negative reactions.

For example, after all the construction in the South Bronx of New York, while hip hop was being shaped and developed as a culture in the 1970s, houses and communities were burning. The people from within their own community were burning it down. When you constantly see and live in a country that promises so much prosperity while you are walking around broken glass and abandoned buildings everywhere, your hope of this "American Dream" becomes a nightmare. Thus, the irony is that hatred turns inward and often is expressed through self-destruction as was evident in the South Bronx and in urban communities today.

In a ten-year span of time, more than 4,300 blocks were burned. Homes, apartments, and businesses vanished from those neighborhoods, leaving them in ruins. What happens to the psyche of a teenager, a young adult, or a parent when their neighborhood is literally on fire? The landlords, during that time, would pay a youth fifty dollars to set his building on fire when it was empty; they called them "rent-a-thugs."

The landlord would get a settlement of $150,000 from the insurance company, and then the insurance companies would raise their rates. A senator from New York at that time was quoted as saying, "If the people in the South Bronx wanted to live there, they would stop burning it down!" It was out of this type of injustice that the culture of hip hop was born. Hip hop became a positive alternative to build sustainability.

The Man Behind It All

It all started around 1973, with a man named Kool Herc (short for Hercules because he was big and carried big speakers) who came from Kingston, Jamaica. He had parties in the park and in the clubhouses for everyone in the community. Kool Herc would DJ at these parties, spinning records and mixing rhythms from different records. He used the record itself as an instrument; as he reversed the rotation of the record, it sounded like the record was scratched.

The more creative he could be with the records, the better the event was. As he was DJing, he would start speaking on the microphone to get people moving back and forth, called "mocking." From this mocking, rap was born. During a party someone would grab the microphone and mimic Kool Herc and start to rap. From there, the other elements of hip hop such as breaking (where dancers spin on their backs, hands, and head, moving to the break beat in the record) was born.

Graffiti brought the voice from the spray can, which gave a visual image to the culture. Dance brought out the movement of the culture. All of this came from a community of hopelessness similar to other times of despair in black history when new methods for coping were created for survival. For example, it was against the law for slaves to marry, so those who got married signified that by jumping over a broom.

When the master would come and take the ham out of the pig and think that the pig was finished, slaves found bacon, chitterlings, pigs' feet, and ribs, and made something out of what looked like nothing. Hip hop was likewise created out of the necessity to survive and to make sense out of a senseless situation.

THE ELEMENTS OF HIP HOP

Four key elements are observed in the culture and visible in most hip hop videos:

1. The DJ

2. The emcee

3. The B-Girl or B-Boy (breaker girl or breaker boy or Bronx girl or boy)

4. Graffiti or taggers

Most people limit hip hop to these four elements. What is often missed when talking about hip hop is the fifth element, knowledge.

This element of knowledge is where we can see Christ working in the culture. Ecclesiastes 3:11 says God has put "eternity in the hearts of men." He has put this hole in our hearts that can only be filled with Him. But most of us fill this void with everything else but Christ, until it all falls apart.

The knowledge that hip hop talks about is getting your mind right and living up to your purpose. This is our contact point. Here we can sit at the table and talk about real issues, which is why we must not just write this community off. The additional components of hip hop, which are birthed from the others, are:

- Street fashion

- Street language

- Street knowledge

- Beat box

- Street entrepreneurship

The Spirituality of Hip Hop

I need to detour for a moment to set up the reason we as Christ followers need to be at the table. How far will we go to meet people and take them from where they are to where Jesus would have them to be? Hip hop culture is in need of real people with a real faith in a real God who can bring about real deliverance! The yoke of this temporary illusion of satisfaction from materialism, violence, hatred, sex, lust, and envy that seems to be adopted by young people through the music of rap has to be stopped.

Second Kings 6:26–29 tells of a woman who, when asked by the king why she was crying, told him that a woman came to her and said, "Let's eat your baby today, and we will eat my baby tomorrow." So she gave her baby to the woman. When she showed back up at the same place the next day, expecting the woman to bring her baby, she never showed. The woman had sacrificed her baby for a temporary fix. She had a legitimate need, food, but she fulfilled it illegitimately, by sacrificing her child. The culture shows the same thing; the heart that is not filled with Christ is lost. Hip hop just turns the volume up loud so that everyone can see how much they need. The temporary stuff the culture desires and the pseudo power it seeks are only a substitute for Christ. The culture doesn't know about sin; they just know something hurts. They know something is missing, but not that it is a relationship with Christ.

The body of Christ must present the message of Jesus Christ in a way that is culturally sensitive while remaining biblically accurate, being wise as serpents yet gentle as doves (Matt. 10:16). We need to be at the table engaging this culture about who Jesus is.

Participant Observation

When Paul went into Athens, Acts 17:16 tells us, "He was greatly distressed to see that the city was full of idols." That distress must burden us as we look throughout our cities and see the idols. Hip hop to some is an idol, and we must come into the culture as an I.P.O. (Involved Participant Observer). Participant observation is a research method that puts you right in the middle of what or who you are studying.[2] In this research process, you make no assumptions or judgments; you just observe and listen and learn. You are with the people daily as life is happening.

The difference is that an Involved Christian Participant Observer puts on the flesh of the culture while maintaining a strong belief that "Christ will use me as I do life within this community." This was Paul's example as he spoke to the "religious people" and told them he represented this "unknown god" (Acts 17:22–23). We represent this unknown God to this culture, yet how will He be made known? Through harsh judgments, or with love that is able to press through their issues until they can see Christ?

Oral Communication

One bridge that must be crossed first, in order to understand hip hop spirituality, is the communication breakdown. If a person cannot read, then telling him where to find something in the Bible is an exercise in miscommunication. Hip hop's foundational style starts with oral communication. In most urban communities conflict and communication coexist. Just because we were fussing a few seconds ago doesn't mean we are not going to talk; when we are arguing we are finally talking. The key that confuses the older non–hip hop influenced generation is that our communication style is linear, straight up and down; don't add anything to it or we are lost. Most of the hip hop culture is all over the place, sometimes using web thinking where people talk like they are surfing on the web, one random half conversation to the next. This is frustrating to the linear thinker or communicator.

The other way of communicating in hip hop is spiral, where a person starts somewhere and ultimately finishes someplace that makes sense for the listener. It is both sender and receiver friendly. In other words, when I am speaking to you, I am also receiving. Most communication in church is from the preacher and is only sender friendly. The spirituality of hip hop is an underlying force that we as followers of Christ can connect with. It is observed in the same tension that birthed hip hop, the need for freedom from the oppressor, which is rooted in liberation theology, that salvation comes from freedom from the oppressor.

Black and Latino liberation theologians James Cone and Gustavo Gutiérrez observe that the depth of liberation theology is birthed out of the pain people have gone through.[3] The need for freedom from that pain in a holistic way means justice for the poor, and other social sicknesses overcome. The role Jesus plays in some liberation theologies can be elusive at best, yet it is Christ, the true liberator, who is calling this culture to Himself. Therefore, justice becomes a bridge toward a community often hostile to the message of the gospel and the institution of the Church.

AN AUTHENTIC GOSPEL

The hip hop culture needs fewer definitions of the gospel and more demonstrations of the gospel. Not signs and wonders but a Christian community that is serious about living for Jesus Christ in every facet of life in such a way that lives are changed. Instead, they see too many hypocritical messages from churches of wealth and prosperity while many in their own churches' communities continue to suffer. The gospel according to hip hop is justice, but this message really started with God. Hip hop needs to see before they hear when it comes to any type of spiritual reality.

Hip hop only sees justice from a natural, worldly perspective, not as Jesus sees it. Christ sees the natural injustices stemming from a disconnect with Him. His desire to redeem humanity is the first move; when our relationship with God is right, all things will be addressed from this. This is another entry point for us to connect with the culture through conversations.

Hip hop lives with a postmodern mind-set, which is skeptical of explanations that claim to be valid for all groups, cultures, traditions, or races, and instead focuses on relative truths believed by each person. In the postmodern understanding, interpretation is everything; reality only comes into being through our interpretations of what the world means to us individually.

THE CHURCH'S RESPONSE TO THE CULTURE

Rather than seeking to understand why rap musicians were saying what they were saying, what needs this music and this lifestyle was presenting, and looking for ways to show Christ, pastors were trying to arrest the artists, smashing the tapes, protesting in front of music stores and concerts. This response only validated to the hip hop community the disconnect of the church and its relevance to them. As a pastor, I can understand the reasons for this response, but if the music is a reflection of the heart, then it is the heart that must change before the music will. When the heart is not anchored in Christ, it will turn everything it can toward satisfying itself.

The hip hop community has heard about Christ, but the problem is that they rarely see the Messiah in the lives of people in the church. We must commit to be part of helping this generation of hip hop–influenced young people discover that their identity is found in their rebirth in Christ, not in their performance.

Psalm 11:3 says, "When the foundations are being destroyed, what can the righteous do?" We are responsible for those foundations to be built into the lives of the least of these. Sometimes it is hard to break the soil so that you can build the foundation.

Hip hop culture strives to uplift people with self-awareness. This can only go so far without Christ, but it is a gateway for us to connect, helping to move people from whatever state they are in. Rap music is driven by revenue and tends to be blown by the wind of the hip hop industry. The hip hop industry has done major damage to the culture because it is only interested in record sales. If the wind is blowing booty and snap rap songs, that is what will be played.

Hip hop record labels are not in the business of cultural empowerment. Whatever can keep young black and Latinos buying their artists' music they will sell, no matter how degrading it may be to the culture of their consumers. This is why the body of Christ needs to be intentionally engaged in the hip hop community. We should be working to purposefully create alternatives that will speak truth into their lives.

We understand John 1:14, where it is said of Jesus that "the Word became flesh and made his dwelling among us," but the test is how we live out this "dwelling among" in ministry to those we serve and more specifically, to the hip hop culture.

People often see the church as hypocritical, not truly living up to the One we say we are following, Jesus Christ. A hypocritical testimony is what we call churchianity. That is all the visible elements of what happens on a Sunday morning: the preaching, singing, the jumping up and shouting, high emotions, and of course the giving. But if this is all you see in the church, and in the meantime the surrounding neighborhood is going to hell in a handbasket, people will continue to be confused about the real purpose and value of church.

WELCOME TO THE HOUSE

This is one of the main reasons we started the House Covenant Church, Chicago's first all teen and young adult hip hop worship experience. We gathered for several months in the summer of 2003 to create a vision about an idea I believed God was leading me to, that there could be a real community of people who love Christ, love hip hop, and are committed to seeing Christ glorified in the culture.

On Saturday October 4, 2003, we started our hip hop worship services. Each week four to five hundred high school and college students come out to "rock the mic" with us as we represent Christ to the fullest through hip hop. We met every first Saturday for eight months, and then we went to every first and second Saturday. Now we are meeting every Saturday in North Lawndale at our parent church, Lawndale Community Church.

Psalm 127:1 says, "Unless the Lord builds the house, its builders labor in vain. Unless the Lord watches over the city, the watchmen stand guard in vain." So we have as our axiom "Unless the Lord builds the house . . ." See, if Christ is not building our lives, then we must stop and surrender to Christ. We were created by Him and for Him in order to give Him glory. This is our focus at The House, to expose young people to the hope that Christ has for them through our unique Christ-centered hip hop service.

Through the leadership of Wayne "Coach" Gordon, Lawndale provides everything from our offices and money for part of my salary to our meeting rooms and of course our worship area. We would not be able to do what God has called us to do if we did not have the two partnerships of Lawndale Community Church and the Evangelical Covenant Church denomination.

I serve as one of the associate pastors of Lawndale as well as the senior pastor of the House Covenant Church. I was the youth pastor for Lawndale Community Church from 1994 until 2001, then I moved to the East Coast to serve with Compassion USA before God moved us back to Chicago to start The House.

The Evangelical Covenant Church is our denomination, and they guide and lead us in how to sustain a viable church that impacts the community in important and meaningful ways. We are a Covenant Church and Lawndale community church plant, and from their openness to the Spirit, God is helping us all figure out how to build this unique church. The House Covenant Church states in its vision to communicate the gospel in a real, relational, and relevant way to teens and young adults influenced by the hip hop culture.

We believe in the local church's role to draw people to Christ in a very direct and personal way within a community that the hip hop culture can relate to. We call it a "hip hop worship experience" because we know that there is only one church, not a black church, Latino church, or Asian church, but each ethnic group or cultural community has a cultural style of worship that is specific to it. Helping our hip hop culture see that gets them to become receptive again, or for the first time, to Christ.

CONCLUSION: THE ATMOSPHERE

A typical hip hop worship experience would go as follows. Videos are playing as you come in the building, and the lights are dim. As the videos finish, the "House emcees" jump onstage and spit lyrics that get everyone into the worship for the night. We see worship and the service as a whole, taking the community in the direction it should go as one; therefore everything flows toward that end. We have poets, drama, dancers, video clips, preaching, and a call to make a decision for Jesus. We have seen lives changed over and over again, moved toward following Christ. In order to grow what you are seeking to plant, you have to have the right atmosphere. We must continue to evaluate what we are seeking to grow in Christ and see if our atmosphere is matching.

REFLECTION QUESTIONS

1. What is the difference between hip hop culture and the hip hop industry? What are the elements in hip hop culture that are visible?

2. Where is Jesus Christ already working in the culture of hip hop? How is the fifth element of Knowledge a potential doorway for the gospel?

3. Why is hip hop an important influence today? Can a church reach this generation without having to have a hip hop worship experience?

Recommended Reading List

Dyson, Michael Eric. *Holler if You Hear Me*. New York: Basic Civitas Books, 2006.

George, Nelson. *Hip Hop America*. New York: Penguin, 2005.

Kitwana, Bakari. *The Hip Hop Generation*. New York: Basic Civitas Books, 2002.

―――. *Why White Kids Love Hip Hop: Wankstas, Wiggers, Wannabes, and the New Reality of Race in America*. New York: Basic Civitas Books, 2006.

Kyllonen, Tommy (aka Urban D.). *Un.orthodox: Church. Hip-Hop. Culture.* Grand Rapids, Mich.: Zondervan, 2007.

Smith, Efrem, and Phil Jackson. *The Hip-Hop Church: Connecting with the Movement Shaping Our Culture*. Downers Grove, Ill.: InterVarsity, 2006.

Chang, Jeff, and D. J. Kool Herc. *Can't Stop Won't Stop: A History of the Hip Hop Generation*. New York: Picador, 2005.

VHS Movie, *Wild Style*

DVD, *The Spook Who Sat by the Door*

ISAÍAS MERCADO is a graduate from McCormick Seminary in Chicago with a Master of Divinity and a Doctorate of Ministry degree with an urban ministry concentration. He is the Founding and Senior Pastor of The Carpenter's House, a thriving bilingual church in the Near Northwest Side of Chicago. Rev. Mercado also serves as the Vice President of the Latino Leadership Foundation, a non-profit ministry that supports Latino Christian leaders in their efforts to impact the barrios of our nation with the gospel. He has been married to Lucrecia for twenty years and has three children, Alexis, Isaías, and Emmanuel.

CHAPTER 10

THE VOLCANIC MODEL:
An Eruption Within the Latino Community

Isaías Mercado

Introduction: "It's Time, Daddy"

n the fall of 2002, while having dinner as a family, my daughter unexpectedly said those prophetic words: "It's time, Daddy." My heart began to race—I knew that a decision was imminent. As a family, we were discussing the possibility of church planting in our neighborhood. I had sensed that God was leading us in this endeavor but struggled for the past year and a half on how it would become reality. With no financial support, no core team, and no facilities, I struggled to comprehend whether this was what God really wanted us to do. As silence filled the dining room, we were suddenly aware of the calling that God had placed not just on my life, but on our lives as a family.

My wife said, "She is right. It is time to leave, begin, and trust God." The eruption (adventure) began.

THE "VOLCANIC" MODEL: STIRRING THE LAVA

My grandfather planted a new church in Chicago in 1972 (Alpha and Omega Church), and I spent much of my childhood hanging out at the rear of that sanctuary. Without my knowledge, the DNA of a church planter was being formed in me. At age seventeen, in the middle of a Thursday night youth service, I felt God's Spirit drawing me in a merciful and inviting manner. It was at that moment that I first began to sense the call of God upon my life. When I was eighteen, I was leading a puppet ministry that served children in the *barrio*.

I was exposed to many different ministerial capacities within the church. I was a musician and Sunday school teacher who became Sunday school superintendent, youth teacher, adult teacher, and eventually an associate pastor. All of these roles helped to expose me to God's provision in ministry. I witnessed a history of God providing and sustaining a local initiative.

In 2002, when I became a chaplain at a drug rehab center, I was exposed to some dark, challenging realities. I started to think that we needed a church that could embrace people "where they're at" and provide them with tools that could empower and awaken them into a more healthy and significant reality.

In this rehab clinic I was leading spirituality groups. In a way, it was like having a small church. Some of the participants would ask, "Pastor, where is your church?" I realized that few congregations were receptive and accepting of people with these kinds of needs. This began to shape the image of the kind of church I wanted to plant, a church that would be responsive to these individuals. I wanted it to be a place where people could find hope and restoration, regardless of their present struggles; a place where people would be given an opportunity to live a life that reflects God's power to take the marginalized and rejected and turn them into a living testimony of His love, mercy, power, and glory; and a place where people would be embraced and assisted as they discovered their own divine purpose.

I knew that such a church would not be conventional, but volcanic, like a powerful volcano ready to explode with great force, power, and unpredictability. I am convinced that God "shows up" and demonstrates His power to transform lives, and to establish vibrant churches in some of the neediest places on our planet—in places like inner-city Chicago.

HUMBOLDT PARK: *MI CASA* (MY HOUSE)

Humboldt Park is located on the Northwest Side of Chicago. The name can be used to describe the community or the 207-acre park. A community is defined by its people. Geographical boundaries in urban settings are constantly changing, mainly due to the gentrification process and the displacement of the poor. Nevertheless, the residents are still strongly connected to what their areas represent to them.

Most of the neighborhood was annexed into the city in 1869, the year the park was laid out, but the area stood just beyond the city's fire code jurisdiction (as set out after the 1871 Chicago fire), which made inexpensively built housing possible.

Beginning in the 1950s, Puerto Ricans settled the area. The infamous Division Street Riots in 1966 led to a push for Puerto Rican rights. In a fire at Our Lady of the Angels School in December 1958 in the Humboldt Park community, the school lost ninety-two students and three nuns in five classrooms on the second floor.[1]

In the 1970s gang activity, crime, and violence were strong in the area. The neighborhood continues to be economically depressed, with housing values below the citywide average, and overcrowding remains a serious problem. However, the neighborhood's Puerto Rican population, in the face of gentrification, remains insistent on keeping and expanding a community through many housing, political, social, and economic initiatives. One example is the *Paseo Boricua* (Boricua Walkway) business corridor on Division Street between Western and California Avenues, where two fifty-nine-foot steel gateway-like Puerto Rican flags are planted.

The Need for a Barrio Theology

When you are raised in the midst of violence, unemployment, drugs, and gang influence, survival becomes a way of life, a mind-set. We felt God moving us to serve within this barrio context we call home, helping our neighbors to move beyond this "survival mode" through the life-changing power of Jesus Christ. We believed that our community needed to hear the Good News that transforms every aspect of people's lives. Storefront churches are the ones in the trenches in our barrios, but we must seek to increase their effectiveness in reaching people beyond the soul. The church has to be an agent of holistic change and a beacon of hope that also begins to transform our dysfunctional communities.

Why has the church failed to live up to its redemptive potential in our communities? From my vantage as a Latino pastor from the barrio, I believe we often fail because of our inability to integrate our theology with our barrio reality. Not to say that our theology is incorrect, as much as that it is incomplete. We were taught to "come out from among them" (2 Cor. 6:17 KJV) but never to return. (One example would be having so many church services that we end up competing with Jesus' agenda to "go to them" not "make them come to us.") Second, we have not fully developed a social ethic that would enable us to influence our communities. We must continually strive to sharpen our biblical/theological vision to do more effective ministry in our communities. Dr. Martin Luther King said,

> *The gospel at its best deals with the whole man, not only his soul but also his body, not only his spiritual well-being but also his material well-being. A religion that professes a concern for the souls of men and is not equally concerned about the slums that damn them, the economic conditions that strangle them, and the social conditions that cripple them is a spiritually moribund religion.*[2]

179

Contextualized Theology

We must find ways to apply theology ourselves, in our own context. As Peruvian theologian and Dominican priest Gustavo Gutiérrez said, "To drink from your well is to live your own life in the Spirit of Jesus as you have encountered Him in your concrete historical reality. This has nothing to do with abstract opinions, convictions, or ideas, but it has everything to do with the tangible, audible and visible experience of God, an experience so real that it can become the foundation of a life project." [3]

Historically we have transplanted different theological paradigms into our context without taking into account their serious implications in our communities. For example, taking a European individualistic manner of observing salvation and applying or importing it to a communal-oriented society is detrimental. This "imported theology" undermines our inherent communal values and traits. Therefore it is imperative that we develop a theology that rises from Scripture and addresses our own experience and context. What is that Latino experience? Professor Harold Recinos of Southern Methodist University in Texas put it bluntly: "Latinos in the barrio experience life between suffering and death in a society that negates their right to exist with human dignity." [4]

It is unfortunate but true that many sermons on Sunday have nothing to do with our neighborhood reality on Monday. We must demand a church that notices how life is being lived daily by persons existing in conditions of oppression and misery.

It is of immense importance for the Church to "have church" as it is often expressed in the barrio and to "be the church." That is, to be separate from the world in order to seek the wisdom, guidance, and face of God, renewing our weary spirit in the shadow of the Almighty. On the flip side, many believers have lost their usefulness to the world and to their community because they rarely leave the church building. The church that keeps too full a schedule of meetings and expects full attendance holds its members or parishioners hostage, and impedes them from developing their gifts and making an impact in their barrios.

We must also call into question church traditions that become so involved, active, and consumed by the needs of their communities that they lose their prophetic and priestly zest, as well as their dependence on the Spirit of God. We must retreat as a church and replenish our souls and then return to our community to empty ourselves, leaving deposits of hope and seeds of a better tomorrow.

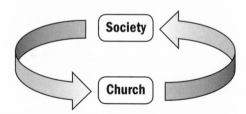

Facing Overwhelming Needs

Confronted with the harsh realities of barrio life, it is easy to become overwhelmed. In order to serve this type of community effectively, we must be keenly aware of our own brokenness and of the real needs of our neighbors. The more we identify with our neighbors, the more we become acutely aware of their struggles, which often include abuse, violence, and addiction.

Now, people who are constantly exposed to a life without purpose, surrounded by poverty and exploitation, usually confess faith in God. But this faith often expresses itself as a coping mechanism that allows them to escape reality in order to dream of a future where pain and suffering no longer exist.

Others seek an escape by finding comfort in drugs, alcohol, sex, and even a temporary feeling of power by the use of violence. As we are exposed to these complex issues, it is very easy to believe that not much can be done. Sometimes we end up with a "paralysis of analysis." Instead, the church is called to offer the hope of a different kind of life, filled with hope, love, and forgiveness.

Our task, therefore, is to develop a mind-set within the church that recognizes the bondages from which we have been set free, and use that recognition to summon up enough courage and compassion to involve ourselves in freeing others from the very reality they wish they could forget.

ELEMENTS OF THE LA CASA DEL CARPINTERO MODEL

In establishing The Carpenter's House Church, we have sought to use a three-step approach that we have found to effectively address the realities of the barrio in which we minister. First, we must be *sensitive and spontaneous* (Spirit led into solidarity); second, we must constantly *embrace and envision* the residents in our community; and lastly, we must continually seek to *empower and equip* new church members who have become followers of Christ.

Sensitive and Spontaneous

In my work as a chaplain at El Rincon, a drug rehabilitation center in our community, I was often devastated by the brokenness and devastation I encountered in the lives of my clients. The more sensitive I remained to the needs of these individuals, the more I sensed the Holy Spirit was able to empower me to minister effectively to their lives. Often, I had to pray to God, asking Him to protect the lives of women who were about to go sell their bodies for money to survive. I felt a sympathy and compassion for them that could only come from Christ.

This kind of "incarnational ministry" is exemplified by Christ, who entered our broken humanity in order to demonstrate solidarity with a sinful and lost humankind. A sensitive and tender heart can only be maintained by being in the presence of a loving and merciful God. When our ministry is fueled and motivated by our intimacy with Christ, instead of being repulsed by the weakness and frailty of humanity, we are drawn together in solidarity as we offer God's restoration and healing, not as perfect people, but as broken and wounded healers.

Spontaneity is also a key value in our barrio ministry. We have discovered it is essential to be flexible in our approach to ministry and not be so concerned to predetermine our every move and program. For many, spontaneity might hold a negative connotation because it is perceived as being disorganized, impulsive, and unfocused. However, spontaneity is directly connected to sensitivity when it provides the flexibility and adaptability to respond to people's needs whenever and wherever they arise. Another key benefit of this approach is that spontaneity facilitates an environment that promotes the development of indigenous leaders in more informal ways. By refusing to be bound by traditional or formal patterns of organization, this model frees the leader and the potential leader from the rigid structures that normally restrict and restrain creativity. Spontaneity can also foster a strong faith that is completely dependent on the guidance and provision of the Spirit of God.

Here's an example of spontaneity in action. One day, taking a drive, I noticed the YMCA gym within walking distance from my house. After speaking to my pastor, I called the director of the gym and asked if he would consider renting it so we could open a church. Within a few months, we had rented the gym with no lease and opened a church in the middle of our community. At this point we were not concerned about how we would pay and support our ministry—the calling was so strong that it almost replaced any fears or hindrances with boldness and hope. As Abraham was called to leave his people by faith, trusting that God would be faithful to the promise He gave, spontaneity allowed us the space to experience God's provision in such a powerful manner. This confirmed to us the fact that God was concerned with our situation and that He was leading us every step of the way.

Embracing and Accepting

We also seek to be a community that is inclusive—accepting people where they are, with the expectation that the redemptive work of Jesus Christ will transform them. Many churches cause people to feel that they must change *before* they become a part of community. Thus, people feel as though they don't measure up to the doctrinal and relational expectations of the church and they don't fit the profile of a believer. Instead, we emphasize the value and importance of embracing people where they are.

As Jesus approached the woman at the well in John 4, we are exposed to a prime example of embracing and accepting. Jesus broke the paradigm of division and invited this woman to worship the Father in spirit and truth, despite her race, religion, or past sins, and by doing so He empowered her to become one of the first evangelists of the New Testament. Being present in people's reality, whatever that might be, frees you from having to invent ways to gather people. You are surrounded by the needs, and these needs constantly create opportunities for ministry. Accepting broken and sinful individuals seemed to be very central to Jesus' ministry, and we believe it is a key element to effectively and biblically minister to our neighbors in our barrio.

Envisioning and Equipping

Envisioning and equipping is helping people see themselves as God sees them, created in His image. Though the Fall has distorted and marred this image in all of our lives, we still carry it. I am reminded of an interesting passage found in Judges 6. Here we read of a man (Gideon) hiding, fearing for his life, and simply trying to survive. Yet when the angel of the Lord addressed him He called him "mighty man of valor" (KJV). At first this almost sounds funny, ironic, maybe even sarcastic, but God has a way of reminding us of our true potential. He lifts up the broken and creates new hope and opportunity out of ashes; this is the same hope that many in our barrios need to have infused. This hope is not based on their abilities, but on His ability to love, mold, and use them. The challenge our people face is rediscovering God's purposes and plan for those who believe that they are no longer worthy and useful in society.

Empowering

Empowering seeks to provide an atmosphere and environment for people to explore their giftedness and ministerial passions. When people who are important to God are not able to see this reality because of sin in their own lives, or because they have been sinned against time and time again, then we must be passionate about creating an atmosphere where they can make mistakes and make strides in their leadership. A person's healthy maturity, then, can be measured by an ability to dream (to try to attain God-given goals), rejoice in success, and reflect on failure in order to continuously learn and move forward. When Jesus called Peter the rock upon which the Church would stand, He knew that Peter was impetuous, had anger issues, and still had many faith hurdles to overcome. Yet, even after Peter denied Christ three times, Christ still gave him the call to feed His sheep.

At a retreat I recently led for our church members, I ministered to a young man with a horrid relationship with his father. When he was a small child, his father would humiliate him by smearing his hands with his own urine as a punishment for soiling his pants. Led by the Lord's Spirit, I kissed his hands and told him that God loved him and that his heavenly Father had a wonderful plan for his life. At that moment, this young man experienced healing and a sense of self-worth that was lacking in his life because of the abuse of his earthly father. Our barrios are filled with men and women in need of this same kind of restoration.

STRENGTHS AND WEAKNESSES OF THE MODEL

Our volcanic experience of church planting (very intense and heavily dependent on God's power and leading) in no way assumes that our approach and values are relevant in every context. This model was birthed from and for our urban community, and does not pretend to be a general church model for the twenty-first century. As Walter Brueggemann challenges us, "There is no single or normative model of church life. It is dangerous and distorting for the church to opt for an absolutist model that insists upon conformity in every circumstance." Rather, this model seeks to present a more spontaneous and flexible approach to urban ministry. [5]

One of the strengths of the volcanic model is evident in its connection to people's needs in the midst of their rawness and their brokenness. This compassion cannot be taught; it can only be developed and cultivated within the landscape of pain and suffering. Only hearts open to these realities and receptive to the notion of the Kingdom of God can experience a sympathetic consciousness of others' distress.

Another strength of this model is that it fosters the development of indigenous leaders. It operates from within the community it is serving. This type of leadership springs up from our contextual soil. It affirms and validates our invitation to work with God in collaboration, as active agents of change in our own history. The pastor following this model seeks to use the leadership, resources, structure, and style found within a community to advance that community.

Some of the weaknesses of the volcanic model include financial pressures, lack of emphasis on organizational structure, uncontrollable variables, personal and ministerial isolation, and a strong propensity to burnout. There has to be a balance between spontaneity and planning. At some point, the organization must establish clear goals and missions, yet at the same time it must remain sensitive enough to avoid becoming irrelevant.

CONCLUSION: FOLLOWING ABRAHAM

As we began our ministry, we were aware that the major impulse behind our action was "response," first to faith in God's power and His alternative reality for our community, and second, to the needs that we witness and experience daily. Desiring to contribute to change in our community, we often felt the church models that already existed were deficient in one way or another. This is one of the reasons we chose to be nondenominational. However, the downside to this choice is that we are experiencing church planting almost as if we are "lone rangers."

Being committed to offering a prophetic voice in the community, while at the same time seeking to engage with those who are most in need, causes many traditional pastors to view our work with skepticism and often contempt. Thus, a real sense of loneliness and isolation results, and this helps lead to burnout.

In reflecting on all of this, I realize that this model is truly connected to the Abrahamic model of faith. It is only sustained by a friendship with and trust in a God who is in relationship with His children—a God who is very present and active in the world, and a God who is seeking to use His new creation in order to help bring about justice, love, and mercy.

If a church plant is going to be successful within our urban setting, it must be rooted in the belief that God empowers us to be faithful witnesses within the messiness of our human experience.

REFLECTION QUESTIONS

1. What does it mean for your ministry to follow Jesus and love people sensitively and spontaneously?

2. What vision do you see for the residents in your community? How can you empower and equip them?

3. Do you tend to lean more toward organization and structure, or spontaneity? How can you begin to lean toward the other side in ministry to people?

LUKE DUDENHOFER is Pastor at the Bridgeport location
of New Life Community Church, a multi-site church in
Chicagoland. Serving in this role since 2002, Luke desires to
be used of God to lead a reconciling church, where spiritually
lost people are united to God through faith in Jesus and
culturally diverse people are united to one another as a
community in mission for Jesus. Luke is a graduate of Moody
Graduate School. He and his wife, Melissa, have three
adopted children and live in the Bridgeport neighborhood.

CHAPTER 11

BECOMING A CHINESE NEIGHBOR:

Pursuing a Church with Yellow and White

Luke Dudenhofer

Introduction: Beyond Smiles and Head Nods

Though it seems strange for a gregarious pastor to admit, I have found myself speechless on numerous occasions when it comes to connecting with the Chinese residents of my neighborhood. I greet my Chinese friend with a hearty "Hello" and he responds with an accented echo. Continuing the conversation with a question about his well-being or a comment about the weather all brings the same result: a smile and a head nod. Not giving up, I begin pointing to things, speaking the word in English and asking him to identify the object in Chinese. Despite my creative and fervent gesturing, all attempts at dialogue are met yet again with a silent smile and a friendly head nod. Communication has ceased. The potential relational connection is short-circuited. We both say good-bye and walk our separate ways. How could I be stuck like this? What was the problem?

The problem was not exclusively a language gap. Most of my neighbors would be able to carry on some conversation in English. The problem was not that I was too busy, self-absorbed, or unconcerned with the lives of people around me. I had been ministering in the South Side Bridgeport neighborhood for more than five years, I was intentionally investing time and effort to connect with my neighbors, and I really cared about their spiritual condition.

I did not want to buy into the false idea that certain friendships, especially cross-cultural friendships, are just hard to establish and perhaps should not be pursued. I did not believe that the homogeneous growth principle[1] was God's direction for ministry in our neighborhood. I needed to see my frustration through a different set of eyes. I needed God's perspective, His lens. I came to learn that getting beyond smiles and head nods required seeing our Chinese neighbors as God does.

UNDERSTANDING OUR CONTEXT

Our ministry is nestled in a Chicago neighborhood called Bridgeport. First settled by Irish canal laborers who were given land contracts instead of cash, many European ethnic groups developed a strong presence in this South Side community.[2] The Irish, Italian, Polish, Lithuanian, and Croatian communities each built its own Roman Catholic house of worship. Of the Europeans who settled in Bridgeport, the only Protestant group was the Germans, who established the first and largest Lutheran church in the neighborhood. The Hispanic and Chinese immigrants who arrived later added their respective beliefs. Today, only six small Protestant congregations are present in our neighborhood of 35,000 people.

Bridgeport is known as a place of political connections, producing many key players in Chicago's machine politics.[3] The Irish immigrants who first settled here came to hold offices of leadership in law enforcement, the priesthood, and city government. The traditions of political "insider privilege" and getting things done according to who you know continue to this day. To date, five Chicago mayors have claimed Bridgeport as their home.

Bridgeport is also known to be family friendly. Many extended families live in close proximity throughout the neighborhood. Rent is still affordable and shopping is nearby. Public transportation is convenient and crime is relatively low. Public schools are decent; private schools are plentiful and still teach the languages of European ancestry. City parks and social organizations offer year-round activities for the children. The weekly *Bridgeport News* prides itself on running "Only the Good News about Your Family, Your School, Your Club, Your Neighborhood . . . Your Community in Your Newspaper."[4]

But Bridgeport residents are stereotyped around the city as being keenly protective of their heritage (translation: territorial and racially prejudiced). In 1919, a horrific race riot between ethnic whites and residents of Chicago's black community (just east of Bridgeport) claimed the lives of many from each group. Many men from Bridgeport traveled east just to start trouble during those days.[5] In the 1960s, African-American students attempted to move into the neighborhood. They faced such hostility that they were forced to move out.[6] As recently as 1997, a group of white teens mercilessly beat two young African-American boys who were riding their bikes through the neighborhood. One boy was seriously injured.[7]

So Bridgeport is not a neighborhood known for welcoming diversity, though it has always been a diverse place. In the 1970s, Hispanics began to move into Bridgeport's affordable housing, quickly becoming a significant portion of the population. In the 1980s, Chinese neighbors began to move in, most relocating from the nearby Chinatown neighborhood. Today, Bridgeport is comprised of nearly one-third Chinese, one-third Hispanic, and one-third white residents of various ethnic backgrounds.[8] Add to that a growing number of African-Americans who work, shop, and live here, and this is a neighborhood with great potential for the reconciling gospel of Jesus Christ.

In Bridgeport, residents are good at co-existing but not really sharing life together. Friendships across racial lines seem to be limited to settings where a report card or paycheck is involved. Voluntary integration is quite rare and, unfortunately, this trend seems to be no different among God's people. The snare of segregated lives, self-serving thinking, and a lack of understanding our neighbors still holds many Christ followers captive in their homogeneous groups. Many churches prioritize ministries that are effective at reaching "their own" people and quietly ignore "those other people." As we recognized that we were guilty of the same wrong thinking, our church decided to make some changes.

We began to act on the truth that God is glorified when His church is multiracial and multicultural, and that churches located in diverse areas should pursue this vision of being communities of reconciliation.[9] New Life Community Church in Bridgeport was at that time predominantly white and Hispanic. We committed to becoming intentional about reaching all people with the gospel of Christ, especially our growing number of Chinese neighbors. This chapter is a summary of our continuing journey to love the people of Bridgeport and become neighbors to all in the vineyard of Chicago.

HOW CAN WE BE NEIGHBORS?

In Luke 10:25–37, Jesus teaches a powerful truth through the radical story we know as the parable of the good Samaritan. In this strong rebuke to the religious culture of that day, Jesus switches the question from "Who is my neighbor?" (verse 29) to "Which of these three do you think was a neighbor?" (verse 36). The law expert who asked the question wanted to justify his own behavior (verse 29). In effect, he was asking Jesus, "In order to stay in God's favor, whom am I responsible to love, and whom can I legitimately ignore?" Through the example of the Samaritan, Jesus shows that loving your neighbor is about *being a neighbor* to all, regardless of earthly labels, race, or social status.

Neighbors Who Care

Our church began to ask God for sensitivity to the people around us. We began to ask God to give us a holy discontent with being a largely homogenous church in a very diverse neighborhood. We acknowledged that our past efforts to reach the Chinese population had not been very fruitful. We asked God for wisdom to know how to build meaningful relationships and clearly proclaim the gospel. We asked Him to humble us and make us servant-learners. Our attitude began to change, growing in Christlike love and a sincere burden for the spiritual destiny of those different from us.

Neighbors Who Share God's Multicultural Heart

We knew in our heads that God loves all people, but our lives and our worship community did not reflect that truth. Our long-held understanding of worship needed to be expanded. I recall one significant Sunday, while preaching a sermon on worship, we placed ourselves in Revelation 4 and 5, joining the elders who worship around the throne. We paused to experience John's grief when he found that no one was worthy to open the scroll of God's future plan for mankind (Rev. 5:1–4). We reminded ourselves of the complete and utter hopelessness of mankind without God (Rom. 3:9–20). The future without God is a terrifying thought.

But then we were reminded of the good news. The slain Lamb seated on the throne of heaven is worthy because He shed His divine blood for the diversity of humanity, purchasing some people for God "from every tribe and language and people and nation" (Rev. 5:9). In response to this, we began to worship in song, just like in heaven, but now with our new understanding of God's plan of multicultural redemption (Rev. 5:11–14). That day we sang in English and Spanish and, for the first time, in Mandarin, the national language of China. It was a beautiful worship celebration; I did not want to stop singing that day!

We have now incorporated these languages into our worship on a regular basis. Everyone has been edified by the beauty of singing in Mandarin. We are equipping our people to worship with God's heart and also teaching them a few words to speak to their neighbors. "*Sheng di hen hao*" (God is so good) is bound to get a response when spoken to a Chinese friend. This emphasis on multicultural worship, based on our future in heaven, helps us know what we are pursuing.

Neighbors Who Really See

One of the key terms in the parable of the good Samaritan is *saw* (Luke 10:31–33). The word literally means "to be aware of, to have knowledge of, or to perceive."[10] In the story, all three travelers saw the wounded man, but only one stopped to help. As we learn how to be neighbors, we are learning to truly see our community and seek God for ways to take appropriate compassionate action.

COMMON VALUES OF OUR CHINESE NEIGHBORS

Risking overgeneralizations, it would be helpful to paint a picture of what we are learning about the common values of our Chinese neighbors. This is meant to be a broad picture of an East Asian/Chinese mind-set with a few brief comments about the Church's response for ministry.

Priority of Family

Our Chinese neighbors have a deep love of family. Many families include multiple children, a blessing that parents could not experience while living in China. Because parents work late hours, schedules are often structured so that preschool-aged children can be awake when parents come home from work. On our block, it is not uncommon for these young children and their parents to be outside playing at 10 or 11 P.M. Grandparents often live with their adult children and assume the caregiver role for young grandchildren. Inviting grandparents into the home and including them in the life of the family demonstrates a strong respect and honor for the elderly.

As another sign of family commitment, I have often heard of family groups working together to prosper in the neighborhood. Extended families pool re-sources and submit large down payments for property, making it easier for all in the family to purchase their own home. Working together in this way allows families to have long-term economic stability and support one another by living in proximity.

Communal Versus Individual

Our Chinese neighbors tend to have a communal mind-set, in contrast to the American value of individualism. The Chinese mind-set does not see life first through the personal lens but through the community lens. They can be more at ease being part of a community without distinctly individual rights or a high degree of privacy. In Eastern thinking, the aim is to honor the past by conforming one's life to the family and community.[11] This means individuals will consider plans by first examining whether their decision will bring shame or honor to the family.[12] Only if the decision avoids harm for the family will they ask themselves, "What will this accomplish for me?"

Seeing through a community lens also means that our Chinese neighbors do not need the personal space that Americans hold so dear. Sociologists note that the mind is what most Eastern-thinking people value as private space. If one's thoughts are private space, then everyday life, even in overcrowded settings, can be accomplished without a great deal of personal space.[13]

American neighbors are sometimes puzzled by this lack of individual space. In Western thinking, a strong emphasis is placed on personal identity and not conforming to the wishes of others around you. An American often thinks *What will I gain?* as a basis for making decisions. In this system the individual is free to choose and emphasis is placed on self.[14]

A tension arises here when it comes to calling people to trust in Jesus for salvation. The Chinese person views himself as one small part of a historic community with established traditions and beliefs, and does not feel freedom to choose what to believe. The decision is made for the individual based on what the group believes, and to choose otherwise would be to dishonor your heritage and bring shame upon your ancestors.[15] Scripture calls people to personal repentance and faith in Jesus, yet we also gain a communal identity in the body of Christ (1 Cor. 12:12–13). The Church needs to be a strong relational community for Chinese believers so it can support them when they are faced with the need to respectfully choose Jesus over family (Matt. 10:37–39).

People Versus Programs

The Chinese are regarded as good neighbors in our community. They care for their property and seem to enjoy stable families. Even with a language barrier, they are polite and accommodating to those around them. This reflects the strong Eastern value of relationships above programs. In everyday dealings, nurturing relationships and keeping things in harmony reign supreme. Relational conflict is strongly avoided. Any kind of ministry to this culture must therefore be strong in relationships. In contrast, an American mind-set can view people as tools to achievement, and often prioritizes successful programs more than people.[16] Only practical and authentic Christlike love, demonstrated in good deeds, will convince our neighbors of Jesus' love for them (Matt. 5:16; 1 John 3:18). The Church needs to emphasize relationships as the basis of everything it does.

Dealing with Shame

In order to understand the need for salvation, all people need to first be confronted with their sin. Eastern minds view sin as having bad manners.

When the Eastern mind is convicted of sin, a person thinks in categories of shame and dishonor. This condition can be horrifying for the Chinese perpetrator because in his mind the offense is committed against the entire community and its traditions, and recovery can seem impossible.[17] The Western mind thinks of sin in categories of guilt. When one breaks a law and is caught, he is tried and found guilty of that specific act. The Western mind views this guilt as a serious burden, but one that can be removed. Our legal systems allow people to "do the time" and get on with life. Western thinkers believe they can redeem themselves after a fall by doing something to regain a right standing.[18]

When the Bible speaks of sin it includes aspects of shame (Isa. 50:7) and guilt (Psalm 32:5). Neither can be removed through human effort. The result of sin is a heavy burden that can only be removed through divine intervention. Only the sinless God-man Jesus Christ, who became a sin offering in our place, can make us righteous and give us right standing with God (2 Cor. 5:21). The Church needs to emphasize that Jesus not only erased our guilt, but He took our shame upon Himself and absorbed it forever (Heb. 12:2; 1 Peter 2:6). Believers can be free from shame and walk in the righteousness of Christ! When a Chinese neighbor understands his sinfulness and hears that Jesus takes away his shame, he will agree that the gospel is good news indeed.[19]

When invited to speak at a Chinese student outreach event, I taught from the parable of the lost son in Luke 15:11–32. Seeking to apply what I had learned in this area of sin being an issue of shame, I emphasized all that the younger son had done to dishonor his father and family. The climax of that story is the Father's forgiveness, acceptance, and replacing shame with a robe of honor although the son clearly was undeserving. This is a powerful picture of the cross of Christ removing our shame.

Priority of Education

In the traditional Eastern view of education, the teacher is of greater importance than the student; therefore, the student must not question what is taught. The student's role is to learn the subject, excel, and thereby show honor to the teacher. In Western thinking, the teacher is important as a conveyor of ideas, but not necessarily an expert on the subject. Teachers in a Western setting are respected, but in recent years they are progressively seen as facilitators for the student to begin thinking independently.[20]

On weeknights during the school year, Chinese school-aged children are not seen playing in our neighborhood. Most Chinese youth are at home studying because they know the importance of excelling academically. Our community has a few specialized tutoring programs that cater to this high value of education and that seem to be successful businesses. The best public elementary school in the neighborhood is majority Chinese. The less than average district high school for our area has very few Chinese students; they are attending the higher standard magnet high schools in the system. In the past, our church has attracted Chinese students with an after-school outreach that included an emphasis on tutoring and homework help.

In light of this Chinese mentality concerning education and the role of the teacher, the Church needs to be careful about appointing Bible teachers. It is imperative that the Church train up people of integrity whose life, as well as their teaching, is viewed as an authoritative presentation of the truth. A missionary training book states that there are three requirements for a Western teacher in a Chinese ministry setting: "(1) He represents his Christ, not his culture; (2) he really knows Christ and the Bible; and (3) he is schooled in religious matters."[21] It will also be important to equip Chinese believers to become like the "Bereans," examining the Scriptures for themselves, investigating if what has been taught is truly the Word of God (Acts 17:11).

OUR CHINESE NEIGHBORS

The Chinese in our neighborhood are a unique mix of students, newly arrived immigrants, and American-born Chinese residents whose family immigrated here at least one generation ago.

The International Student

There are several prominent colleges near our church, and many Chinese international students live in our neighborhood. The vast majority of these students speak Mandarin, the national and majority language in China. These students, undergrad and graduate level, are the future leaders of China. Many have been sent here through government jobs, and will return to those leadership positions after studying abroad. Others seek to become professors in universities. These students desire to be leaders, influencers, and change agents in the world.

The Church has a wonderful opportunity to reach the entire nation of China by influencing its future leaders with the gospel. A great way to minister to these students is to provide a "home away from home" and invite them to share life with your family. Students are not in a situation of distress but are pursuing educational and vocational advancement. They are relatively strong English speakers and usually have an interest in experiencing American culture. They seem much more open to an English-speaking ministry because of this "educational" mind-set.

We have been able to partner with a Chinese student ministry in our neighborhood and have seen the sincere questions that many students have about Christianity. This ministry shares home-cooked Chinese food, gathers for singing and testimonies, then splits into Bible studies for seekers (evangelistic) and believers (discipleship). I was encouraged at this ministry recently when one young woman told me she was not yet a believer, knew nothing about the Bible or Jesus Christ, but was impressed with the lives of those who profess to follow Him. What a field of souls God has made ready for harvest (John 4:35)!

We praise God for the opportunity to reach and disciple international students at our church. Several have trusted Christ through parachurch ministries and then joined our fellowship to be mentored to baptism and grounded in the Word of God. Our entire congregation has been enriched through those who have stayed and become part of the committed core.

The New Immigrant

Immigrants are what the Scriptures call "aliens," those who are traveling from one country and culture to another.

God Himself loves and defends the cause of aliens (Deut. 10:18). He is personally concerned about their well-being. He watches over them (Psalm 146:9) and treats the one who seeks membership among His people just like one of His people (Numbers 15:15).

God commanded the Israelites to love aliens as they love themselves (Lev. 19:34). Israel, having been an alien nation in Egypt, knew how it felt to desperately need the mercy of God (Exodus 23:9; Deut. 10:19).

God's heart is clearly for the inclusion of aliens in the life of the community of believers. They became partakers of the covenant with God (Deut. 29:10–12), and therefore were held responsible to keep the commands of God and learn the fear of the Lord (Deut. 31:12).

Love and inclusion involve sustaining aliens until they can sustain themselves. God commanded the Israelites to provide for aliens so they could continue to live in the land (Lev. 25:35). Farmers were to leave any missed grain, fallen fruit, or olives so that the poor and the aliens could glean from the fields (Lev. 19:10; Deut. 24:19–21). Through the Israelites' obedience in bringing tithes into the storehouses, the fatherless, widow, poor, and alien would eat and be satisfied (Deut. 14:28–29; 26:12). Job recalls for his friends that one way He feared the Lord was by housing the stranger who was new to the land (Job 31:32). Jesus Himself reinforced this command by teaching that when we invite strangers into our home, we are ministering to Him (Matt. 25:35).

God commanded that His people not mistreat or oppress the alien among them (Exodus 22:21). The Israelites were not to take advantage of (Deut. 24:14) or act violently against aliens (Jer. 22:3). God rebukes His people harshly for oppressing the alien in their community (Ezekiel 22).

Finally, God commands that there be justice for the aliens among His people. The cases of aliens are to be heard without bias (Deut. 1:16). God's judgment comes when His people deprive aliens of justice (Mal. 3:5).

To understand the new immigrants in our community, we took several weeks to craft a survey that would help us find information we could act on. We wanted to learn about the "average" Chinese resident in our neighborhood, if such a person existed. Targeting Chinese residents, the survey was written in traditional Chinese characters. We asked questions like "Where were you born? What is your native tongue? How long have you lived in the Bridgeport community? Do you live with extended family? Are you interested in learning English? How else could you be helped to become established in this new place?"[22]

Our survey revealed that most immigrants in our neighborhood primarily speak Cantonese (a minority Chinese language), they have been here less than five years, they work in factories or restaurants, and they live with extended family. Almost all are interested in learning English. Many valued earning more money and were interested in learning how to manage their money. Observation has revealed that immigrants seem especially vulnerable to gambling, sadly evidenced by the long lines for the shuttle buses to area casinos. Respondents noted that programs to help with parenting in America would also be helpful.[23]

Another round of survey questions would be a wise next step. We want to learn the deeper needs of immigrants, what pushed them out of China, and what pulled them to this country and neighborhood. We want to hear their dreams and the burdens they carry. In short, we want to know their felt needs so we can build bridges to their spiritual needs.[24] This information can only come through relationship.

The Complex ABC

The final subgroup of Chinese friends in our neighborhood is the American-born Chinese (ABC). This group holds many of the values of their immigrant parents or grandparents, but they are more American-minded in their view of Chinese traditions. Our ABC neighbors are grounded in respect for elders, honoring their families, emphasizing education, and carving out a more prosperous material life. Most in this group do not personally believe in many of the practices of ancestor worship,[25] like offering food to small idols or displaying charms on cars, but they do not stop participation out of respect for their elders. American-born Chinese individuals live in two worlds, navigating through competing ways of thinking, and can struggle with a sense of personal identity and finding out where they fit in this culture as a Chinese-American.

Consider my twenty-two-year-old neighbor. His parents left China to establish a better life in America. When they first arrived, both parents worked and took English classes in their spare time. My neighbor was born in Chicago and has lived his entire life in Bridgeport. As soon as possible, my neighbor went to day care while both parents went to work. Cantonese was always spoken at home, but the rest of his world was in English.

My neighbor recalls the first years of elementary school as being very difficult because of the need to read and write in English. He spent a few years in a bilingual classroom before being immersed in English teaching all day. He successfully graduated from high school and enrolled for one semester at a community college. He worked full-time at a local grocery store for more than three years, and now he is a teller at a bank in Chinatown. He enjoys improving his sports car, playing basketball with friends, and eating BBQ in the alley behind his house (where we often talk). Though his physical appearance is clearly Asian, he has the lifestyle of a lifelong American citizen. That is precisely because he *is* a lifelong American citizen.

My neighbor does not shy away from speaking of his parents' values and traditions, but he has told me that they are not for him. He will participate when required, but he puts no faith in those rituals. Religiously my neighbor considers himself an atheist, not convinced that there is a God or that he needs one. He is comfortable with his material prosperity and does not see his spiritual need. In this respect, he reflects much of the thinking of the average lost soul in America today.

I believe my neighbor's story is quite typical of the ABCs in our community. He is immersed in American culture, yet needs to honor family and cultural values that seem to hinder being "American." Being so close to Chinatown, immigrants in our area can sustain a very traditional Chinese home because the strong cultural center supports and encourages that practice. Overall, it seems that our Chinese neighbors choose not to assimilate into the larger melting pot of American culture. I do not sense any bitter feelings toward American culture, but they are simply proud of who they are as Chinese and do not want to lose that sense of identity. So it seems to me that the older generation (forty and over) will only become as "American" as they absolutely have to. The younger generations are very integrated during school years, but after college tend to return to a more Chinese-centered life with their new family.

We, as the Church, need to teach that Christ must reign above culture. But to communicate that, we need to know and engage the culture of those God is seeking to save. The message of Christ is unchanging, but the method of communication must change in order to be rightly understood.

Our church began to consider whether our ABC neighbors know they are wanted and welcome. If not, how can we pursue friendships with them so they can see Christ in us? Are we not connecting with the Chinese immigrants because of the language barrier? If so, what ministries can we start or support that do speak their heart language? Are we kind, gracious, and intentionally hospitable to curious students? Are our homes and family lives open to them? Are we willing to become all things to all people so that some can come to salvation (1 Cor. 9:22)? The answers to these questions will continue to shape our ministry efforts in the years to come.

NEIGHBORS WITH A PURSE (READY TO HELP)

Believers need to view all that they possess as healing resources, ready to be used whenever God presents an opportunity.

Salvation

The gift of salvation is our greatest resource. The saints need to be trained to share the hope of the gospel of Christ with those at home, at work, and on the streets of the community (Col. 4:2–6; 1 Peter 3:15–16). Though it is good to invite the unsaved to church, that is not evangelism. At New Life Community Church we try to strike a balance between "Come to Sunday Celebration" and "Come to Jesus." Our evangelism training incorporates the meat of the Word of God with some cultural understanding of different groups in our area so the gospel can be packaged in a relevant way. Our training is intended to help members become aware of their multicultural neighborhood and become effective disciple-makers in it.

Hospitality

As people of God, we are commanded to offer an oasis to people and say "Come to our house!" (see 1 Peter 4:9). Inviting people inside can quickly break down barriers and communicate acceptance and belonging. Many in our congregation have started building relationships through simply inviting Chinese neighbors into their homes for a meal.

Acts of Kindness

Every believer has a prepared list of good works that are resources to help others (Eph. 2:10). Jesus said it is our good deeds that will cause people to give glory to the Father in heaven (Matt. 5:16). On my block I have practiced "community service" by mowing (summer) and shoveling (winter) the yards and walkways of neighbors. This is a simple gesture, but it has opened doors for greater friendship with everyone, especially the Chinese families on my block. Like every other culture in the world, the Chinese respond to love in action.

Welcoming the Alien

In our context, it is important to remember that many Chinese immigrants are completely new to our language, economy, traffic system, food, and overall way of life. The shock of so many new challenges can take months or years to wear off. During this transition, we must not shun our new neighbors or make them feel inferior.

Cultural tutoring is perhaps the first and best step to letting newcomers know that God's love extends to them. One ministry of this kind matches Chinese immigrants with an English-speaking "tutor" to practice conversational English and learn about American culture. The time commitment for this ministry is minimally two hours per week, with room for extra time that both parties agree to. The key is to be involved in the assimilation process of new neighbors by helping meet needs that are unique to their situation.

Perhaps equally important in helping immigrants is offering English language classes. In America, knowing English is absolutely essential for those who want to prosper in business, be equipped with education, and participate in the education of their children. Our congregation has members involved in a nearby ESL ministry, and we are considering hosting classes and tutoring at our location in the future.

The Church needs to find ways to support and strengthen the Chinese family. Children's ministries should be clean, well-organized, and loving. Teachers should be well trained and excellent. Marriage classes, marriage counseling, and parenting classes should be offered to encourage the family. In these ways we can communicate the holistic love of God, which has answers and hope for every aspect of life.

NEIGHBORS WHO COOPERATE

In hopes to build our network of ministry cooperation, our church began Kingdom inquiry in the neighborhood. Where are the other life-giving churches in this area? Who else is reaching our Chinese neighbors with the gospel? We learned more about the historic Chinese Christian Union Church in nearby Chinatown and their more recent church plant only two blocks away in our Bridgeport neighborhood. This church has a strong tradition of reaching and establishing Chinese immigrants in the faith. Part of that ministry is the Pui Tak (Higher Values) Center, which offers English classes, cultural tutoring, and a Christian school that minister to thousands of Chinese residents each year.

We started meeting with leaders of churches and ministries, seeking to build relationships and foster a spirit of cooperation among God's people. We understand that believers are called to minister as members of the Kingdom of God, not representatives of local church kingdoms (Eph. 4:3–6). There are enough lost souls to overflow every church building ever erected. Only by working together, collaborating on the Great Commission, can we see God bring about renewal and revival in our midst. We need to be able to point people to Jesus and the Church even when it means they attend somewhere other than our local assembly.

Our friendship with one neighborhood Chinese church began when a few from our assembly attended their new building dedication. We were the only non-Chinese speakers in attendance, but we were received with tremendous grace and warmth. God opened the door for another partnership when I was invited to give the evangelistic message for a Chinese student outreach. As these gospel partnerships have grown, we have found a common burden for unity among God's people combined with a greater understanding of each ministry's special purpose. We have started to participate together in community-wide prayer, evangelism training, and sports outreach events. So far five churches with African-American, Chinese, white, and Hispanic members, ranging in tradition from Pentecostal to Lutheran, have begun to work together to reach our community. We sense that God is very pleased with this spirit of cooperation for the Kingdom.

NEIGHBORS WHO PRIORITIZE

We prioritized our resources. Instead of filling a parsonage with the more traditional staff member, we looked for someone who could equip us to be a neighbor and better share the gospel in our diverse community. We asked him to facilitate partnering relationships with neighborhood churches and equip us all in evangelism. He quickly found work as an ESL teacher in Chinatown, which multiplied our connections in the Chinese community.

We hope to start a Chinese-speaking small group, and perhaps provide translation for our Sunday celebrations. Some leaders of our church are meeting regularly with the leaders of other ministries for prayer, support, and collaboration. A few of our leaders have enrolled in classes to learn Mandarin, enabling them to connect more effectively with the international students. Because this is bigger than a growth technique or passing fad, we are convinced God will enable us to keep this "every nation" focus in our ministry.

CONCLUSION: JUST DO IT!

As Jesus concluded His shocking story about the Good Samaritan, He sent everyone out with the command, "Go and do likewise" (Luke 10:37). So we are pressing ahead to be like the Good Samaritan, who reflected the heart of God. We are reaching a small and growing group of Chinese neighbors who live in the area. We are legitimate and active gospel partners with the Chinese-speaking congregations in the neighborhood. More of our members have significant roles in the Chinese immigrant community. Lord willing, we will one day be a snapshot of that multicultural worship celebration in heaven. If God can do it here, He can do it through His Church in your location too.

REFLECTION QUESTIONS

1. In what ways does your congregation need to grow to embrace God's vision for multicultural worship? In what ways will your church culture need to change?

2. How is your church actively being a neighbor to the hurting in your community? Are there any neighborhood issues or people groups that it would be easier to just ignore? How will you equip your church to stop and help these neighbors?

3. Do you have an updated knowledge of the population of your area? What are the cultural characteristics of the different groups in your community?

4. How can your church collaborate with other ministries to more effectively minister to the neighborhood? How can you begin to expose your congregation to the cultures you seek to reach?

Recommended Reading List

Anderson, David. *Gracism: The Art of Inclusion*. Downers Grove, Ill.: InterVarsity, 2007.

Fong, Ken Uyeda. *Pursuing the Pearl: A Comprehensive Resource for Multi-Asian Ministry*. Valley Forge, Pa.: Judson Press, 1999.

Lin, Tom. *Losing Face and Finding Grace: 12 Bible Studies for Asian-Americans*. Downers Grove, Ill.: InterVarsity, 1996.

Lingenfelter, Judith E., and Sherwood G. Lingenfelter. *Teaching Cross-Culturally: An Incarnational Model for Learning and Teaching*. Grand Rapids, Mich.: Baker Academic, 2004.

DANIEL HILL is the Founding and Senior Pastor of River City Community Church, located in the Humboldt Park neighborhood of Chicago. Prior to starting River City, Daniel launched a dot-com in the nineties before serving five years on the staff of Willow Creek Community Church in the suburbs of Chicago. Daniel has his B.S. in business from Purdue University, his M.A. in Biblical Studies from Moody Graduate School, and his certificate in church-based community and economic development from Harvard Divinity School. Daniel is married to Elizabeth, who is a Professor of Psychology at Chicago State University.

CHAPTER 12

CHURCH IN EMERGING CULTURE:

Ezra, Nehemiah, and Esther Ministry

Daniel Hill

Introduction: A New Way to Think

"How do you measure the success of a church?"

This penetrating question was posed by Dr. John Perkins, founder of the Christian Community Development Association (CCDA). I was sitting at our midweek service as I did any other Wednesday in the late 1990s, but little did I know that this seemingly innocuous question would lead me on a journey that would forever change my life.

I was a pastor's kid, and it seemed in the moment that a response should be coming to me more quickly than it was. Yet I could not find a cogent answer that seemed complete enough.

Dr. Perkins continued to poke at us. He began to list potential answers to his question. "Is success determined by your Sunday service attendance?" This was always the first item on a pastor's résumé, yet we were pretty sure this was not the answer. "How about the size of the church budget? Maybe success should be measured by how many staff the church employs? Maybe success is determined by how many periodicals write stories on your church. How do you measure the success of a church?"

When he was satisfied with the uneasiness in the room, he finally offered his own perspective on what the answer should be. "The success of a local church should be directly tied to the degree that it holistically transforms its immediate neighborhood. Any other success factor is secondary."

RECALIBRATING A WORLDVIEW

The timing of this question from Dr. Perkins was divine. I had been contemplating the possibility of planting a next-generation church in the heart of Chicago, and this question (and answer) caused me to take a step back and re-evaluate true success in a church.

For the two to three years leading up to this moment, I had been steeped in the national conversation around reaching young adults, the age demographic most missing from the American church at the time.[1]

At the time I was working in the Axis ministry at Willow Creek, which was a ministry designed to reach the twenty-something generation. In addition I worked a part-time job at Starbucks. I considered it quite an opportunity to be able to interact with secular-minded postmodern folks during the early morning hours, and then spend the rest of my day with the Axis staff trying to figure out how to most effectively engage this generation. Part of the joy and struggle of our ministry was trying to define success as we reached out to this generation.

Since this next generation had dropped out of church in record numbers, success was largely measured in terms of re-engaging them with the local church. Therefore, whatever shifts needed to be made—teaching style, worship style, candles, incense—were all considered if it might get them back into the doors of the church.

But here was Dr. Perkins giving a much broader vision of the church's impact in society, and it was a picture that compelled me to rethink success. This image called for much more than a return to the institution of the church—it called for a holistic understanding of the Kingdom of God and of the gospel of Jesus Christ. He painted a picture of church that was on mission; church that would address the needs of the poor and vulnerable of society; church that would tackle head-on the issues of race, poverty, and economics that had become such key problems of our generation.

After hearing Dr. Perkins preach, I realized I was at a crossroads. I had to ask myself an honest question: Did I have a theology big enough to reflect these dimensions of God's heart? Was my theological understanding of God and mission broad enough to include evangelism, emerging generation distinctives, racial reconciliation, social justice, and community development? I was pretty sure it did not.

I decided that before I ever planted a new church I needed an expanded theology.

Rediscovering Jesus

I spent the next couple of years becoming a student all over again. On paper I was armed with an undergrad degree in Business, a graduate degree in Biblical Studies from Moody Graduate School, and a number of years of practical experience at Willow Creek. But I quickly realized that nothing on that résumé had fully prepared me to take on the task of doing holistic ministry in an urban context. I would need a serious amount of training to be ready for this task.

The next two years were marked by one discovery after another. As I read the works of great authors,[2] visited dozens of inner-city ministries, and sat under many incredible mentors, I realized that I had somehow closed my eyes to a whole dimension of the gospel. There was another dimension to the life and message of Jesus Christ that I had somehow missed. I was humbled by numerous ministries that displayed the love of God to a hurting world, and was amazed at how little fanfare they received. I was challenged to form a more biblical worldview that connected me to God's heart for the lost, the last, and the least of these.

A BIBLICAL VISION

This proved to be an elusive task. I found myself doing a lot of copying and pasting, where I would grab certain parts of one church's mission, another part of a book I liked, and then add something from a great sermon I heard. It was not until I came across Dr. Ray Bakke's book *A Theology as Big as the City*[3] that I finally found a single framework that I felt captured the heart of what we wanted our church to be about. Almost immediately I knew that this would be the way I would communicate our church's vision.

The thesis of the book is that God has always cared about the city, and that He is consistently raising up leaders to join His mission of holistic urban renewal. In one chapter he says that if you want a cohesive model for holistic urban ministry, you should look to the story of three intriguing missionaries: Ezra, Nehemiah, and Esther. Though their stories are usually told individually, Bakke helped me discover that the real magic comes when you read these as a single story of urban transformation. If you want to know the full breadth of the ministry of Jesus, you read all four accounts of His life in the New Testament beside each other. In the same way, if you want to watch God rebuild the city of Jerusalem in its post-exile state, you have to read all three of these together. Here is a quick summary of each, through the lens of holistic urban ministry.

Ezra: Spiritual Renewal

Ezra was a priest—the only clergy of the three. Ezra was grieved by the fact that in their post-exile despair the people of Jerusalem had turned to foreign gods and had completely lost their way. He was committed to seeing the souls of the Jewish community renewed and restored, for without that level of spiritual renewal all else would fail. So Ezra dedicated himself to ministry that in today's terminology might be called spiritual renewal. This might traditionally encompass evangelism, discipleship, and church planting.

Ezra was a Bible teacher. (He once preached an all-day sermon that people actually stayed for!) He was a prayer warrior, interceding for revival in the land. He focused on discipleship ministries that would reform the Hebrew people and bring them back to their moral compass. Spiritual renewal is both crucial and central to the holistic ministry of a city, but the story of Ezra reminds us that it was not enough to rebuild the city. Ezra the priest was going to need some help.

Nehemiah: Socioeconomic Renewal

While Ezra had been trained in formal ministry, Nehemiah was a businessman who worked in the royal court. But what Nehemiah lacked in formal Christian education he made up for with a passion for the heart of God. The walls of Jerusalem had been destroyed by Nebuchadnezzar, and had remained in ruins for almost a century and a half. Nehemiah knew that this grieved the heart of God, and he became motivated to assemble a team and participate in God's urban renewal project.

Nehemiah risked his well-being and reputation when he went to the king and asked for a leave of absence so that he could go mobilize the Hebrew people to rebuild their city. When he arrived in Jerusalem he became what today in urban ministry might be called a community developer, or someone engaged in socioeconomic renewal. Nehemiah was concerned for the safety and protection of the people, the economic well-being of the city, and the capacity to raise healthy families.

The other crucial component of Nehemiah's ministry that I discovered through Bakke's commentary was the keen sense of awareness he had about the dangers that so many Christian community organizers fall into, paternalism and/or colonialism. This is when a Christian, coming from a position of privilege, arrives in an at-risk area with a plan of how he or she is going to save the community for the people. Though these community developers are usually sincere in their motives, they unknowingly strip the local people of their dignity and pride, and actually create more resentment and hopelessness.

This was a foundational discovery for me. If our church was going to be holistic in its approach, we needed more than trained clergy. We needed emerging community development leaders to be part of our mission. They could do things I could not do, and I could do things they could not do. We needed each other in order to catalyze socioeconomic renewal.

Esther: Cultural Renewal

After exploring the implications of the spiritual renewal that Ezra represented for the city of Jerusalem and the socioeconomic renewal that Nehemiah orchestrated, Ray Bakke encouraged his readers to look at the story of Esther through the lens of the two previous books.[4]

Nehemiah is now building up the community and restoring the walls of Jerusalem. Ezra is preaching and teaching and rebuilding the spiritual fiber of the community. But now they face an extraordinary barrier to their efforts that neither is capable of overcoming. A villain named Haman wants to exterminate the Jewish community, and he has convinced the king to legislate this dastardly plan. The government has passed a bill that legalizes the killing of all the Jews.

Ezra and Nehemiah each brought nonnegotiable elements to the mix, but as evil made its way into the system, neither of them had the cultural power to do anything about it. For the final element of Christian urban renewal to take place, God was going to have to ordain a leader to go into realms that neither Ezra nor Nehemiah was trained or equipped for. Here is how Bakke says it:

> *Somebody has to move off the map of the godly into the godless structure and change the law. . . . Someone has to go into the black holes of the city where God's name is not known. They need to access power and change law. Esther teaches us that it's not enough just to repent for sin. Charity dollars won't make up the difference. It's systemic, and the law has to change. You cannot save the city on the streets alone. We need advocacy in the courts and legislatures because on the world's scale and on the city scale the systems are not fair. You cannot just repent and go on.[5]*

The story of Esther shows how God accomplished His plan of justice and renewal through a queen who had divinely acquired enough cultural power to make systemic change in the structures of society.

From a local church perspective, I believe Esther's ministry represents cultural renewal in the city. Cultural renewal deals with systemic changes in society. It involves reconciliation not just at a personal level, but at a corporate level. Cultural renewal moves people toward an integration of Christian faith with vocation. The book of Esther chronicles a woman who was growing equally in her spiritual maturity and impact in society. Esther is an incredible model for leaders in the professional/business realm, arts and media realm, and the political realm for making an impact in society.

A COHESIVE FRAMEWORK

Reading these thoughts from Dr. Bakke was a revelation for me. My hope to reach the emerging generation; to experience the reconciliation work of Christ across racial, cultural, class, and gender lines; to be involved with holistic community development and caring for the poor; to live as a community of people joining the mission of God—it was all embedded in this framework.

When we launched River City Community Church, this would be the framework that we built our theological house around. It would take time for us to grow into that space as a church, but it would always live there before us. We would not be rigid or draw artificial lines between an Ezra, Nehemiah, and Esther ministry, but their lives and experiences would create the parameters of our vision in Chicago.

Like unfurnished rooms, Ezra, Nehemiah, and Esther represented our vision. Now it was time to flesh out some of the core components in each room for us as a church.

EZRA MINISTRY

Like Ezra, we believed that the most critical and central piece to holistic urban transformation was spiritual renewal. Connecting people back to their Creator was of utmost importance, and like Ezra we wanted to see our people take discipleship seriously.

A Biblical Anchor

The writer of Hebrews reminds us that "the word of God is living and active. Sharper than any double-edged sword, it penetrates even to dividing soul and spirit, joints and marrow; it judges the thoughts and attitudes of the heart" (4:12). To continue the movement of Jesus to all of His people in the city, we knew that everything must be deeply rooted in biblical truth. From the beginning we have stressed that the Bible is the inspired Word of God; that it is good for correction and righteousness (2 Tim. 3:16); that it is the anchor for everything in a Christian's life. The Bible is what shapes us into the grace and knowledge needed to live the life He wants for us.

We believed from the beginning that it is the Holy Spirit, speaking through Scripture, who gives the power to convict people of their sins, and to lay down their idols and worship God. Scripture would be our handbook for life, our guide to a just community, and our portal into the presence of God. Scripture would be the force that would show us the way to defeating materialism, consumerism, individualism, racism, sexism, and classism.

Evangelism

Our desire to reach a broad cross-section of humanity immediately brought to the surface some difficult evangelism challenges. The problem at River City was that our non-Christian friends represented too wide of a spectrum to cleanly fit into any one program. We had everything from antagonists to curious seekers; from younger brothers (dramatic sinners) to older brothers (moral, yet lost); from followers of other world religions to melting pot, spiritual types that had a little bit of everything. What type of program do you run for such a mix?

We realized that evangelism in our context was going to need to become more of an environment than a program. Instead of creating seeker-specific programs, we began to focus on creating a certain texture in everything that the church did. We wanted our core believers to consistently assume that non-Christians were with us in *every* environment—whether that was Sunday service, small group, a serving experience, or even a Saturday night party—and that we expected them to be watching how we lived, talked, and interacted. We urged our core believers to welcome the questions, doubts, and difficulties of our non-Christian friends. We wanted the non-Christians to feel not only welcome, but intrigued and provoked about the message and person of Jesus. We intended River City to have as part of its mission the goal of processing people with worldviews that were very different from the gospel.

We regularly applied two tests to see if this climate was actually being formed. First, we would look to our non-Christian friends. We would observe and even ask if they felt welcomed and challenged by what they were seeing. Second, we looked to the attitude and conduct of our core believers in response to this challenge. The clear sign of success was when a core believer would come to the realization, "If I bring my unbelieving friends here, they are going to be surprised at how welcomed, embraced, and challenged they are by my Christian friends. And if they stay long enough, they are going to be surprised to see how attractive and compelling Jesus Christ is."

The Gospel

A side benefit to the numerous worldviews that came through our doors was the necessity to clearly articulate what a biblical worldview *should* encompass. This is when we clarified our understanding of the "gospel," the good news that through Christ the power of God's Kingdom has entered history to renew the whole world.

We realized that the beauty of the gospel is that it is not just a way to be saved from the penalty of sin, but is the fundamental dynamic for living the whole Christian life—individually and corporately, privately and publicly. In other words, it is not just a message of good news, but an entire worldview and way of life. It is a way of seeing the world, of interacting with Scripture and humanity, and of experiencing spiritual transformation. It is the dynamic of change for both the non-Christians and the Christians. It is not just the ABC's, but the A to Z of the Christian life.

We realized that too often we spoke of the gospel as the door you walk through to become a Christian, but that maturity was almost a separate path that involved trying hard to be moral and to live according to biblical principles. It was a big shift for us to begin to preach the gospel as a worldview that not only saves the non-Christian but also transforms every part of a Christian's mind, heart, and life as His truth and beauty penetrates more deeply. This became central to our preaching, as we insisted that the gospel needed to be the application of every sermon, whether the topic was sex, money, or racial reconciliation. It became the core of our discipleship strategies, as everything ultimately pointed back to building a gospel worldview into people. Finally, it became the focus of our evangelism, because every week our Christians learned how to more attractively and intelligibly communicate the way of Jesus to their friends who did not yet believe.

NEHEMIAH MINISTRY

When we started River City, our desire was to see increased social and economic justice in our geographic neighborhood. We hoped that the River City body would demonstrate compassion and the alleviation of poverty as tangible expressions of the Kingdom of God. We wanted to have the spirit of Nehemiah as we worked for socioeconomic renewal. To do this we knew that first we needed to learn both the history and soul of our neighborhood.[6] Second, we wanted to be sure to reflect some core convictions while doing so.

Theological Foundation

The life and teachings of Jesus regularly and directly connected a faith encounter with God to a lifestyle of caring for the poor. In Luke 10, the Great Commandment linked loving God with all of our heart, soul, mind, and strength with loving our neighbor as ourselves (and to be sure we didn't miss the point, Jesus tells the parable of the good Samaritan to explain who our neighbor is). When Jesus is asked to clarify His identity and role in Luke 4, He chooses to remind the people of the prophetic foreshadowing of the coming of the Messiah (Isaiah 61). Included was preaching good news to the poor, proclaiming freedom for prisoners, and setting the oppressed free. If this wasn't enough, in Matthew 25:31–46

Jesus listed different dimensions of serving the poor as perhaps the clearest sign of a gospel encounter.

If we were going to be a church defined by Nehemiah ministry, we realized it was crucial to draw this same theological connection between an experience of God's grace and a heart for the vulnerable of society. We needed to be a church of both proclamation and demonstration, of word and deed.

Racial Reconciliation

Typically Nehemiah ministry is going to require some level of racial reconciliation. The history of America has many wonderful parts, but it also has ugly chapters defined by economic-based racism. Whether you look at our exploitation of the first Americans, the slavery of Africans, the legacy of Jim Crow, or our country's chronic fear of non-white immigrants, we have a long and consistent history of race-based injustice.

At the core of River City, we believed that to engage in Nehemiah ministry was to first embrace the ministry of reconciliation. The apostle Paul reminds us, "All this is from God, who reconciled us to himself through Christ and gave us the ministry of reconciliation. . . . We are therefore Christ's ambassadors, as though God were making his appeal through us" (2 Cor. 5:18, 20). The ministry of reconciliation is a very difficult road that few would choose from a human perspective. Only a powerful encounter with the gospel and a renewed worldview gives someone the wisdom and endurance to knowingly swim into these chaotic waters.

Neighborhood Partnerships

Another critical dimension of Nehemiah ministry was to first become students who discovered the ways that God was already at work in our neighborhood. As a community that wanted to be thoughtful Christ followers, we knew that building *new* walls was a second priority; we had to first learn where people were already attempting to rebuild the walls. One of the clear examples of this was Breakthrough Urban Ministries. Founded by Dr. Arloa Sutter, Breakthrough was already doing marvelous work on the ground. Their rebuilding of the walls included ministry to the homeless, support groups, assisted housing, and after-school programming. We were extremely blessed to be able to partner with Breakthrough and join the rebuilding that they were already doing. This was just one example of multiple partnerships that we formed prior to launching anything directly through our church.

Community Organizing

We also wanted to follow in the footsteps of Nehemiah and listen to the cries

211

of the community residents and stakeholders. What walls still needed to go up? Where were the areas of vulnerability? How could we work in reciprocal relationship to begin rebuilding the walls?

The first cry we clearly heard from the people was from first-generation immigrants who needed access to English as a Second Language. We were told repeatedly that the only classes available were through community colleges, and that residents frequently could not afford the classes or make the limited time offerings work within their schedule. So in partnership with the community, we began to offer free ESL classes three days a week, engaging dozens of volunteers and hundreds of students.

The second cry we heard from the people was the need for educational opportunities for the youth of our neighborhood. Too often our community parents had only two educational options for their children: elite private schools that were financially inaccessible for the average family, or the neighborhood Chicago public schools, which were not preparing students well academically. Knowing that education is the passport to the future and perhaps the most dynamic factor in breaking out of a cycle of poverty, our church began to pray through this burden of the community. This became a central theme to our church body as we sought to join the invested community stakeholders in rebuilding the walls of education and creating a new future for our children and youth.

ESTHER MINISTRY

"Who knows but that you have come to royal position for such a time as this?" (Esther 4:14) were the divinely timed words that Mordecai passed on to Esther as part of her training. Mordecai was instrumental in helping this female, ethnic minority use her influence with the king to change an unjust law in the majority culture. It was our prayer that God would use River City Community Church as a Mordecai presence in the lives of emerging Esther leaders in our neighborhood as well. This meant at least three things.

Cultural Leaders

In the spirit of Esther, we began to use the term "cultural leader" to describe this aspect of our ministry. Our working definition of a cultural leader is someone who "creates, forms, or influences the cultural institutions and systems of society." We see cultural leaders as falling into three groups: creative types, professionals, and politicians.

We believe that if you work in one of these domains, you influence culture to some degree. The more influence or power you acquire within any of those specific areas, the more impact you have on society in general. Therefore, it was our desire to raise up a new generation of cultural leaders who could enter into the power structures of society representing the love, justice, and equality of Jesus Christ.

A Robust Understanding of Social Justice

The story of Esther's heroics takes place against the backdrop of racial injustice and oppression. The impetus for Haman's evil plan of genocide found its roots in his hatred for Mordecai and ultimately for the Jewish race. This has replayed throughout history. The justice associated with the Kingdom of God is opposed to racial and cultural chauvinism.

Reflecting the Kingdom of God on earth includes the tearing down of old systems and structures that protect privilege for the elite in society and bringing forth opportunity, justice, and equality for the vulnerable of the world. The apostle Paul reminds us, in Colossians 1:15, that Jesus is the "firstborn over all creation," and that the cross represents His desire to reconcile the systems of this world to Himself. Emerging cultural leaders must embrace this message. If they were raised in an environment without cultural influence or with a spirit of inferiority, they need the reconciling power of the cross to lift them from that. If they were raised in an environment of superiority or privilege, they need to be lifted from the damage done to them through that lifestyle (even if it is not as obvious due to the economic benefits that came with that status).

A document that has helped connect the journeys of both the oppressed and privileged to the heart of Jesus is the "Letter from Birmingham Jail," in which Dr. Martin Luther King Jr. writes in response to eight white clergymen who had actively denounced the civil rights movement:

> *I must confess that over the past few years I have been gravely disappointed with the white moderate. I have almost reached the regrettable conclusion that the Negro's great stumbling block in his stride toward freedom is not the white Citizen's Counciler or the Ku Klux Klanner, but the white moderate . . . who paternalistically believes he can set the timetable for another man's freedom. . . . Shallow understanding from people of good will is more frustrating than absolute misunderstanding from people of ill will. Lukewarm acceptance is much more bewildering than outright rejection. . . . Perhaps I was too optimistic; perhaps I expected too much. I suppose I should have realized that few members of the oppressor race can understand the deep groans and passionate yearnings of the oppressed race, and still fewer have the vision to see that injustice must be rooted out by strong, persistent and determined action.[7]*

This wonderful letter has helped us remember the heart of Jesus. Though it is a substantial step for people of privilege to grow in awareness of racial oppression and the struggle for freedom, it is not enough. Awareness without action leads to "lukewarm acceptance," and that can become more bewildering and even more damaging than absolute misunderstanding.

Instead, we remember that the Kingdom of God does not stop at awareness, but continues in a unified struggle toward the alleviation of injustice. It is a united body of believers coming around the "deep groans and passionate yearnings" of those who have been on the other end of oppression. It is through "strong, persistent and determined action" that we follow Jesus into the areas of society that most badly need the power of the gospel to shine in all of its beauty and grace.

Integration of Faith and Work

Too often Esther leaders are diminished in their influence due to the belief that the only way to truly serve God is through direct ministry. These potential cultural leaders often (and erroneously) believe that if you are truly sold out to God you will quit your job and go into full-time ministry. This too often sidetracks emerging cultural leaders, because they are unable to see how their vocation can be directly aligned with the mission of God. Instead of attempting to have Esther-like influence on society, they settle for just making money and building their own empires.

We realized that a key part of raising up cultural leaders would include theologically reshaping their understanding of faith, mission, and work. We also saw the need to go beyond an abstract understanding of this theology to creating places for people from specific vocational backgrounds to network and process together. Carrying out the mission of Jesus Christ takes on many different shapes depending on whether you are a schoolteacher in the public system, a real estate agent, an insurance salesperson, or a graphic designer. It was our desire to create specific training and nurture for both emerging and established cultural leaders so that they could learn how to better carry out the cause of Jesus in their specific sphere of influence.

CONCLUSION: TO SEE AS HE SEES

In John 5, we are told of an encounter between Jesus and a man who had been an invalid for thirty-eight years. When Jesus sees this man, His heart breaks, and Jesus heals him. This healing occurs on the Sabbath, which appalls the Jewish leaders. Instead of being able to see the wonder of God's heart for healing and salvation, they get caught up in the Jewish Sabbath regulations. Therefore they confront Jesus.

In hopes of extending to the Jewish leaders the same healing and salvation that the Father brought to the invalid, Jesus begins to explain both the heart of God and the anatomy of the miracle. He first tells these leaders, "My Father is always at his work to this very day" (John 5:16). With this Jesus tries to draw these men to the heart of God. The Father is a God of compassion, of healing, and of restoration. God is calling all people to Himself (including them) and wants to bring healing, salvation, and restoration to all who will come.

Second, Jesus says to these leaders, "I tell you the truth, the Son can do nothing by himself; he can do only what he sees his Father doing, because whatever the Father does the Son also does" (John 5:19). With this statement Jesus not only instructs the Jewish leaders on how to find God; He models for all of us how we can tap into the healing power of God. We do not recite some magic chant or break a blood vessel trying to summon enough faith. Instead, with a spirit of prayer and revelation, we search for what the Father is doing, and then join the redemptive adventure of God saving and healing the land.

The vision of River City is wrapped up in this quest. Our desire is to see what the Father is doing. We believe that part of this adventure requires people being smart—they need to know the things of God and understand what God is in the business of doing. We want people to have an intellectual understanding of the correlation between Ezra, Nehemiah, and Esther ministry. But we do not want this to stop at just an intellectual understanding. We want to be people who worship in "spirit and in truth" (John 4:24). We desire to be people of prayer and spiritual hunger—people who are transformed by the love of the Father, are built up by the Father, and then see in new ways what the Father is doing. We long to be swept up in the redemptive adventure of the Father and to see our neighborhood and city renewed spiritually, socially, and economically.

REFLECTION QUESTIONS

1. Do you believe that the way you use your material wealth is God-honoring in all respects? If no, in what areas is it not? What action are you taking to make changes?

2. Do you desire to participate in God's vision of economic renewal, particularly in the realm of caring and advocating for the poor? What experiences have you had with this in the past?

3. To what degree would you say you are currently an ambassador of reconciliation? What experiences have you had in regards to multicultural ministry or racial reconciliation?

4. In what ways would you say you are leveraging your vocation to further the cause of Christ or honor God?

CLIVE CRAIGEN has spent nearly twenty years of his life in urban ministry, both working with youth and in church planting. He received his B.A. from Grace College and his M.A. in inner-city studies education from Northeastern Illinois University. He is also a graduate of the DeVos Urban Leadership Initiative (Chicago 2000). He currently serves as Assistant Professor of Urban Ministry at Moody Bible Institute, co-shepherds a house church in Chicago, and works as a student mobilizer for Go2 Church Planting Ministries.

CHAPTER 13

HOUSE CHURCH:
Historical and Current Trends
Clive Craigen

Introduction: My Journey

How did I end up being involved in a "house church"? This journey started more than ten years ago while I was working in Chicago with Inner City Impact. I would not be where I am today if it were not for a number of people who significantly influenced my thinking and ideas about the church.[1] Above all, I would like to thank the young men and women in urban America who have taught and continue to teach me so much about loving Jesus. I dedicate this to those who have not yet become part of the family of God, but who so desperately need it.

Prior to getting involved in urban ministry, I never really gave much thought to the church. I grew up in the church and very much a part of conservative Christianity, but I do not remember hearing much discussion about what the church was and how it should express itself. Everyone seemed to assume that what we were experiencing was church as it was meant to be.

But when I began to work as a church planter, I quickly discovered that I was not prepared to answer the most basic questions about the nature and practice of the church. While I was struggling to answer these questions, I realized that I had been a part of "real" spiritual community three times.

The first experience occurred while I was in high school. I attended a boarding school for missionary kids in southwestern Germany, the Black Forest Academy. It was in this context that I discovered a group of believers who were a real community, a spiritual family. We studied together, lived together, played together, ate meals together, did ministry together, and gathered to worship as a corporate body. More than forty countries were represented and multiple denominational and church traditions present.

My second experience occurred in college. Upon returning to the United States after high school, I got involved in a local church, where the primary outlets for ministry were either working with children or serving as an usher. It seemed so tame and so comfortable.

Around the same time I got involved in an on-campus student ministry organization. Through this organization, students were mobilized to serve in three inner-city communities, to connect with athletes and students in local high schools, to do puppet shows, and more. Leaders were empowered and released to do ministry. A Halloween community activity was initiated that continues almost twenty years later. We did life together. We studied, served, cried, and laughed together. We studied the Bible, our lives were changed, and we gathered together formally and informally. I continued to be involved in the local church, but I had the nagging suspicion that something was missing. Back then, I did not know what it was.

The third experience came after college graduation, when my wife and I started working with Inner City Impact in Chicago. It was there that I encountered a real depth of biblical community with the staff who worked, lived, and worshiped together in the neighborhood. We lived Acts chapter 2. We ate meals together. We lived near each other. We shared in the joys and sorrows of urban youth ministry. We attended graduations, weddings, and funerals. We cared for each other and each other's kids. We even vacationed together. We made disciples, ran programs, and invested in youth and their families. We were devoted to the Word, prayer, fellowship, and an occasional communion service, like in the second chapter of the book of Acts. We were a real spiritual community, but we did not really know or appreciate it to the fullest extent.

Twice during this phase of life, the concept of beginning a new church was raised. My wife and I, along with two other couples, met several times to explore and pray about the possibility of starting a church. We concluded that it was too big and too complicated a task. I also met with a representative of a church planting organization; our conversation was about buildings, budgets, and bylaws.

Both of these incidents left me disturbed and uncomfortable. Something was not right. The conversations did not mesh with my reading of the early church in the book of Acts. This interest in church planting would not go away. Instead, it led to an ongoing internal conversation with God and His Word about the Church. I thought about it. I prayed about it. I read books. I debated with friends, coworkers, and mentors. But I could never fully come to terms with the basic question: What is the church?

Two stories gave me hope and encouragement as I pursued the answer to my questions. The first example was a local church in Chicago that had its origins in a young adult Bible study of an urban youth ministry. The second example was the story of a national urban ministry that eventually restructured itself to make the starting of new churches the goal of its urban ministry initiatives.

AN URBAN METAPHOR

By far the most profound insight I have had as it relates to the urban church came out of my interaction with young men immersed in street gangs. I worked for a ministry whose focus was prevention, and while we did not specifically engage in gang ministry, we regularly interfaced and worked with young men and women who were consumed by "the life."

I believe that street gangs are one of the clearest pictures in urban America of how the church ought to function and exist. Follow my reasoning before declaring me a heretic! The church requires a profession of faith. Street gangs require a declaration of allegiance. The church has an initiation called baptism. So do street gangs, but it is called a violation. The church studies the Bible, and street gangs have their literature and bylaws. People give money to the church. Street gangs require dues. The church exercises discipline with its members. So do street gangs, albeit in a harsher manner. The church (globally) suffers persecution and imprisonment. Street gangs are harassed by authorities, and spending time in prison is normal. The church makes disciples. So do street gangs.

One central concept rises out of this context: identity. If you are a member of the Latin Kings or Gangster Disciples, that membership defines who you are. Because it is your identity, this causes you to "represent." You "represent" on the corner, in school, on the bus, in the park, at home, and anywhere you go. Street gangs do not say they *go* to Latin Kings or Gangster Disciples. They *are* Latin Kings or Gangster Disciples. It is their identity.

We must recapture the idea of being a member of the body of Christ as our identity. We represent 24/7, 365 days a year, everywhere and anywhere. We must stop seeing the church as just a special place we go or a special meeting we attend. Meetings are important and have a necessary place, but they must be a means, not the end. Street gangs have meetings and gatherings, but that does not define their identity.

BIBLICAL EXAMPLES OF HOUSE CHURCHES

It is necessary at this point to take a step back and briefly review some biblical and historical data concerning the presence of house churches both in the New Testament and throughout the history of Christianity.[2]

The first disciples gathered in a house shortly after the ascension of Jesus. Acts 1:13–14 states that "when they arrived, they went upstairs to the room where they were staying. . . . They all joined together constantly in prayer, along with the women and Mary the Mother of Jesus, and with his brothers."

The early followers of Jesus received the Holy Spirit in a house. It started with the 120 and then apparently spread outside to the three thousand. Acts 2:1–4 says,

When the day of Pentecost came, they were all together in one place. Suddenly a sound like the blowing of a violent wind came from heaven and filled the whole house where they were sitting. They saw what seemed to be tongues of fire that separated and came to rest on each of them. All of them were filled with the Holy Spirit and began to speak in other tongues as the Spirit enabled them.

The first believers had communion and shared meals in homes. In Acts 2:46, the author says, "They broke bread in their homes and ate together with glad and sincere hearts." Also, Acts 5:42 reads, "Day after day, in the temple courts and from house to house, they never stopped teaching and proclaiming the good news that Jesus is the Christ."

Furthermore, when Saul (later Paul) wanted to put an end to the church, he went to the homes of those who followed Jesus (Acts 8:3, "Going from house to house, he [Saul] dragged off men and women . . ."). Then in Acts 12, after Peter escaped from prison, he went to a house and interrupted a prayer meeting, whose focus was his release.

During Paul's ministry in Ephesus, he and Silas stayed in the home of Lydia after she had believed the good news about Jesus Christ (Acts 16:14–15). It was Lydia's house where Paul and Silas came after they were freed from prison. In Acts 18:7, Paul left the synagogue and went next door to the house of Titius Justus. In Acts 20:20, in his address to the Ephesian elders, Paul says, "You know that I have not hesitated to preach anything that would be helpful to you but have taught you publicly and from house to house."

Romans 16:3–5 records a specific commendation of gratitude from all the churches of the Gentiles to Priscilla and Aquila. Paul specifically greets the church in their house in Ephesus. In a reference to Priscilla and Aquila in 1 Corinthians

16:19, Paul brings greetings from the church that meets in their house (in Ephesus). It is also worth noting that in Paul's letter to Philemon he includes the whole church that meets in his home as part of what he directs Philemon to do.

The early church engaged in the following activities in their houses: They broke bread (Acts 2:46), taught the good news (Acts 5:42), and prayed (Acts 12:12). In Paul's letter to the Roman church, he brings greetings from the church that enjoys the hospitality of Gaius's house (Rom. 16:23). In 1 Corinthians 1:11, there is an allusion to another possible house church, the one in "Chloe's household." Acts 20:5–12 also indicates that the church in Troas gathered in an apartment.

There were also house churches in Colosse: the church in Philemon's house (Philemon 1–2) and the church in Nympha's house (Col. 4:15). The bottom line is that the early church from Jerusalem to Rome and from Jewish families to Gentile ones predominantly met in homes and/or households.

BIBLICAL VALUES OF THE CHURCH

According to Acts 2, the early church was devoted to four things: prayer, the Word of God, the fellowship, and the breaking of bread. Healthy house churches and indeed all churches must manifest these four things. The house churches of which I have been a participant have demonstrated all of these. As a leader, I have consciously sought to make them a clear part of the house church practice. We have prayed together, we have studied the Word of God, we have gathered as a fellowship, and we have had a meal together and shared in communion.

A second biblical value driving the house church dynamic is drawn from the first epistle to the Corinthians. In 1 Corinthians 14:26, Paul says, "When you come together, everyone has a hymn, or a word of instruction, a revelation, a tongue or an interpretation." This provides an example of dynamic interaction and participation.[3] Most people seem to approach church as consumers, instead of coming with the express intention of edifying other believers. In truth, all believers must come with the commitment to contribute.

In most church expressions, there are few chances for anyone other than the pastor or senior leaders to share or respond to what is being learned. In many house churches, ample opportunity is given for sharing and interaction. There is time to pray together and in small groups. Participants can ask questions and respond to what is going on in the meeting. In addition to singing songs, the believers are invited to share what God is doing in their lives and also to exhort the rest of the body. Based upon the example of 1 Corinthians, the role of individuals to share must be included practically, not just representatively. The house church is usually done in a circle or semicircle fashion. This allows for face-to-face interaction with each other, rather than just between the individuals in the front and those attending. The gathering in households provides a natural setting for this type of interactive dynamic.

Furthermore, house churches were a living example of the Christian value of hospitality. They provided a natural context for identifying with one another. This became the basis for reaching out to others both locally and globally. Almost everyone could understand the household, as they were thus connected to an identifiable group.

In addition, house churches weaken the clergy/laity divide that has developed in the church going back to Constantine. House churches need leaders as do all churches. We know them as elders and deacons. But ordinary believers are also empowered and invited to influence and affect the group. House churches are an attempt to rediscover and practically demonstrate the priesthood of all believers.

Lastly, house churches provide an inherent cultural adaptability.[4] Based upon the regional location and/or the education and ethnic makeup of the area, the church is able to adapt and relate without compromising the essentials. It is also within the context of house churches that ethnic and socioeconomic distinctions were blurred and overcome as people built relationships and served each other. The relational and intimate setting for the house church provides a natural setting for the practicing of the twenty-seven or more "one anothers" listed in the New Testament.

HOUSE CHURCHES IN HISTORY

Not only were "house churches" prominent in the New Testament, they have been an essential part of Christianity around the world. This was the case until AD 313, when Constantine allowed Christians to meet legally. Once the union between the state and the church had been completed, by AD 381 it became illegal in the Roman empire for the church to meet in a setting outside the officially sanctioned church buildings.[5]

Furthermore, looking at the Radical Reformers of the Reformation, their churches were not in buildings, but small fellowships. Many gave their lives for what they believed, equally at the hands of the Catholic Church and the Protestant Reformers. While respect must be given to Luther, Calvin, and Zwingli for their contributions to Christianity, the reality is that their ecclesiology did not change much when they left the Catholic Church. Before the Radical Reformation, many, including the Celtic Missionary Movement and Waldensians,[6] the Lollards (John Wycliffe), and the Bohemian Brethren (John Hus)[7] gathered in small groups attempting to practice church as shown in the biblical accounts of the early church. After the Reformation, this pattern continued. The Anabaptists,[8] Quakers,[9] Pietists,[10] Moravians,[11] and Methodists,[12] among others, gathered in small groups, usually in homes practicing the art of making disciples.

Around the world, churches in places as varied as Latin America, Nepal, Burma, Kenya, Sri Lanka, and Mexico City are actively expressing their church life through house churches or equivalent forms.[13] David Garrison, in his book *Church Planting Movements,* documents and studies the dynamics and reality of church planting around the world.[14] It is not uncommon to discover churches using houses or similar contexts for the expression of their church life today.[15]

CURRENT TRENDS

According to a study by George Barna, 9 percent of adult American Christians are participating in a weekly house church.[16] Also, according to Barna's research, even more adult Americans, approximately 22 percent, are involved in some alternative expression of church life, either in the marketplace, workplace, or some other aspect of daily life.[17]

A word of clarification is needed at this point. The label "house church" is the most commonly used. But it is only one among many. The other terms include, but are not limited to, micro-church,[18] organic church,[19] simple church,[20] and intentional communities.[21] Each emphasizes something true about the house church. "House church" is the most limiting, because such a gathering does not have to, and does not always, meet in a home. A church can meet in a home and not be any different in its dynamic and structure from a larger conventional church. "Micro" speaks to the size. "Simple" refers to the interactive style and structure of the gathering. "Organic" identifies the exponential growth inherent in a small movement. "Intentional" highlights the intense and rich relational dynamic present in small gatherings. All of these terms are used in reference to the phenomenon of the house church movement.

In addition, not all house churches are equal. Many house churches are exemplary, but others are not to be recommended. Some have wandered into doctrinal heresy and others are orthodox. Some are charismatic; some are reformed. Some might be considered cults, while others are an attempt at isolation from the world and its problems. These have become ingrown and are not concerned for those outside the family of God. The truth is that conventional churches, both large and small, have also wandered into heresy and become unorthodox. Some are even cultic. Some have also become ingrown and rarely see visitors or conversions. Others are also secluding themselves from the world.

Just as each conventional church should be judged according to its doctrine and practice, so also the house church should be judged according to its doctrine and practice. We must not throw out the proverbial baby with the bathwater! The words of Gamaliel in Acts 5:38–39 are helpful here, "Leave these men alone! Let them go! For if their purpose or activity is of human origin, it will fail. But if it is from God, you will not be able to stop these men; you will only find yourselves fighting against God." The house church movement has scriptural roots, historical precedents, and modern-day examples.

DISCIPLE-MAKING REVISITED

The context for disciple-making is inherent in the structure of the house church. The prime directive of the Great Commission is the making of disciples. Matthew 28:16–20 communicates the command is to make disciples as we are going, baptizing them in the name of the Trinity and teaching them obedience to Jesus. The business of the church is to make disciples, corporately as well as individually. The making of disciples leads to the gathering of these followers into groups called churches.

This sequence has often been switched in the church. Churches gather crowds to eventually make disciples. Much effort is put into the meetings, infrastructure, and facilities of the church. Services and sermons are valuable, but they alone do not make disciples. Simply preaching on discipleship does not equate to the making of disciples. Disciples make disciples. A serious commitment to life-on-life relationships is essential. The need to be about disciple-making is emphasized by the relational, family dynamic of the house church. The needs of individuals are more apparent and the appropriate accountability can be made available. Obviously, disciple-making is not guaranteed in any setting, big or small, but it might be more natural in the context of a house church. Micro-size does not guarantee it, and mega-size does not prohibit it.

Furthermore, the commitment of parachurch organizations in urban America to making disciples has intensified this desire. Parachurch is "any spiritual ministry whose organization is not under the control or authority of a local congregation."[22] They have invested time and money in making contacts, sharing the gospel, and then making disciples. But because they were not the church, and because most parachurch ministries believe individual Christians need to be part of a local church, attendance at church became an important emphasis. Many organizations invest heavily in encouraging and assisting their disciples in becoming connected to a local church. The goal happens far too infrequently. In reality, what is a spiritual identity issue has become a spiritual discipline. A person becomes a Christian and then he/she is told to go to church rather than seeing herself as intimately part of the church.

What has developed is a fundamentally flawed model of making disciples and church integration. The commendable goals of making disciples and involving them in local churches actually work against each other, with involvement in church being seen as a "step" in the process of Christian growth rather than a basic identity. Some ministries have begun to recognize this and have taken steps to change. World Impact, a premier urban ministry in the USA, started out as an evangelistic ministry to children and youth. It transitioned to a holistic community ministry and now is committed to using its skill and expertise to start new churches.[23] Many college ministries have begun to describe their student groups as missional communities, witnessing communities, or something comparable.[24] These terms appear to be synonymous with church.

SOCIOLOGICAL PERSPECTIVES

The second influence on my journey to micro-church is a sociological one. There is a significant weakening of healthy families and communities in urban America. Compounding this is the absence of healthy male role models both within the family structure and outside of it in many neighborhoods. The single-female-headed household appears to be the norm. The ramifications upon the socioeconomic fabric and educational context of urban America are profound.[25]

It is here that house churches can have their greatest impact in urban America. They can provide a second family where spiritual fathers and mothers provide the shepherding and mentoring that individuals need to succeed in life. House churches are particularly structured to facilitate this. The reality is that large churches that want to be effective must also address this need for community or family. They must structure themselves small in order to accomplish this. As community in neighborhoods and families suffers under the weight of dysfunction, racism, and sin, the church is singularly positioned to *be* the answer, not just provide an answer. The sad truth is that in parts of urban America, the street gang is filling this void.[26] It is providing the support, identity, and purpose that families normally provide. Church buildings are prevalent across the landscape of urban America, but healthy families are conspicuous by their absence.

The demographics of urban centers contribute to increased loneliness and anonymity. People do not know each other and have become disconnected from everything but the Internet and entertainment culture. House churches provide a vehicle for intimacy and friendship within the context of a life purpose that is greater than the individual.

PRACTICAL SUGGESTIONS

Here is a list of practical things learned during my eight-plus years of being involved in a house church.

1. **Community starts at six and ends at fifteen.** A group that is smaller than six adults and participating teens will have a hard time sustaining itself and a group larger than fifteen (high school and up) will not allow for enough participation.

2. **Music is critical.** CDs can be used, but I would look for someone with a guitar or a keyboard. God has provided our groups over the years with many individuals capable of leading music.

3. **Participation is essential.** Intentionally plan activities that invite everyone to contribute something. Most people who have grown up in the church do not know how to participate. They are used to being spectators. Plan things that will require everyone to answer a question.

4. **Have a meal together if you can.** Most of our house churches have "broken bread" together, which provides a rich context for building relationships. Also, invite everyone to bring something for the meal. This creates ownership within the group.

5. **Create a menu of options** and then adjust and adapt as the meeting progresses. Here are suggestions for your menu list. (The basics of worship are the four biblical essentials addressed earlier, but this is part of how they are played out.)

   a. **Music:** Sing several songs, usually four or more. I recommend that you cluster them together versus scattering them among other activities. Another option is to split them into two sets. Occasionally, increase the number of songs by inviting others to do special music or make requests.

   b. **Teaching/Learning:** Choose a book of the Bible and then work through it in sections. You want this time to be as interactive as possible instead of a lecture by one person. Select a person to prepare and lead the study of Scriptures. Incorporate some group discussion about application to life. Encourage the other believers to read ahead in preparation for the next gathering.

   c. **Prayer:** Have the group pray in smaller groups, in twos or according to gender. Or have an individual share a request, and then have someone pray, and then have another person share a request, and so forth. Construct a prayer conversation as a group. Have someone pray and then have others build on what has been prayed. Use prayer to develop the thread of conversation. Prayer can be at the beginning, the middle, or the end. Vary the focus, from praise and thanksgiving to supplication. Sometimes, allow time at the end to specifically pray in response to what God has been speaking to your group. Do not be afraid to lay hands on specific individuals and pray in a concentrated manner.

d. Sharing: Invite the congregation to highlight or reflect on what they have read in the Scriptures that week. Limit commentary and allow the Word and the Spirit to speak. Allow for individuals to share what God has been teaching them. Incorporate a question relevant to the passage of Scripture to be studied. Ask for the reading of Scriptures with no comments.

e. Children: Include the children as much as possible. Provide at least one activity in which the children can participate. For example, have the group complete a phrase like, "I believe in Jesus because . . ." Have everyone do this. It also provides an opportunity for those not accustomed to participating.

CONCLUSION: WHERE WE ARE TODAY

Currently, I am shepherding a small house church on the North Side of Chicago. This group has met in a home since August of 2007. We are so recent, we do not have a name, beyond the church that meets in the "Family Name" home. Approximately twenty-five individuals meet weekly. This includes several families with children ranging in ages from four months to thirteen. Several high school students come regularly in addition to nine college students. The group includes Caucasians, Mexicans, Puerto Ricans, and an African-American.

The last year has been about laying a foundation, building identity, and becoming a spiritual family. The diversity of gifts, personality, and experience is being discovered. In addition to a weekly house church gathering, a number of individuals have led an outreach for youth at a nearby local school.

The next six months are critical for the growth and maturing of the house church. In the coming months, a monthly prayer meeting will start. Dialogue is happening within the house church body and with others outside for the purpose of birthing an additional group.

Starting in June of 2008 the group has met monthly in a larger celebration with two house churches in an adjacent neighborhood. Furthermore, over the summer, the leaders of several house churches in Chicago began meeting together for prayer, worship, and fraternity. During the course of the next year, a name will probably be chosen and legal status will be sought as well as affiliation with a national fellowship of churches.

Although I grew up in a Christian home that was unashamedly evangelical, I never understood the real nature of the church. I knew the church was important, but I did not really love it. It was not until I began my journey into the house church that I came to really love the church. In fact, I cannot have a conversation about ministry that does not lead to the church. Just as Neo took the red pill in the movie *The Matrix,* I have taken the "red pill" of organic church and would have a hard time going back.

REFLECTION QUESTIONS

1. What does the urban street gang have to say to the church?

2. Reflect on your journey with the church. Where have you found spiritual family, and where has it been absent?

3. House churches are present throughout the New Testament and the history of the church. What are the implications for the church now?

Recommended Reading List

Banks, Robert. *Paul's Idea of Community*. Rev. ed. Peabody, Mass.: Hendricksen, 2004.

Banks, Robert, and Julia Banks. *The Church Comes Home*. Peabody, Mass.: Hendricksen, 1998.

Barna, George. *Revolution*. Wheaton, Ill.: Tyndale, 2005.

Cole, Neil. *Organic Church*. San Francisco: Leadership Network Publication, 2005.

Cole, Neil, and Paul Kaak. *Organic Church Planter's Greenhouse*. Long Beach, Calif.: CMA Resources, 2003.

Garrison, David. *Church Planting Movements: How God Is Redeeming a Lost World*. Bangalore, Ind.: WIGTAKE Resources, 2004.

Guiles, Dave. *The ACTS Strategy*. Winona Lake, Ind.: Grace Brethren International Missions, 2000–2003.

Hirsch, Alan. *The Forgotten Ways*. Grand Rapids, Mich.: Brazos Press, 2006.

Lupton, Robert D. *Theirs Is the Kingdom.* San Francisco: HarperCollins, 1989.

Phillips, Keith. *Out of Ashes.* Los Angeles: World Impact Press, 1996.

Simson, Wolfgang. *Houses That Change the World.* Waynesboro, Ga.: Authentic Media, 2005.

Zdero, Rad, ed. *Nexus: The World House Church Movement Reader.* Pasadena, Calif.: William Carey Library, 2007.

DAVE AND ANGIE ARNOLD live in Albany Park, a neighborhood in Chicago's Northwest Side, which is the nation's third most ethnically diverse zip code and port of entry to immigrants and refugees. They were married in March 2000. Dave received his Bachelor of Science degree in pastoral ministry from Taylor University in 1998, and his Masters of Theological Studies degree from Michigan Theological Seminary in 2005. Angie received her Bachelor of Urban Ministry degree from Moody Bible Institute in 2009. Together, in 2005, they founded Bridge City Ministries, a vibrant, grass-roots ministry that focuses on planting ethnic house churches and organic churches in Albany Park, throughout Chicago, and the ends of the earth.

CHAPTER 14

HOSPITALITY IN THE CITY:
Reaching the Nations Through Neighborliness
Dave and Angie Arnold

Introduction: How Soccer Changed My Life

(Dave) have always been into sports, both watching and playing. When my wife, Angie, and I moved to the city, to the neighborhood of Albany Park on Chicago's Northwest Side, I prepared myself to play some serious basketball. After all, this is Chicago, the city of Michael Jordan and the Bulls dynasty. I assumed that basketball was the ultimate urban sport.

What I found out, however, is that in my neighborhood, soccer is the sport of choice, not basketball. *Oh great,* I said to myself. *Any sport but soccer.* You see, I once had a slightly embarrassing experience when it came to soccer. I was six years old and ready to take on the soccer world. All I knew about soccer was to dribble the ball as fast as I could downfield and then kick it hard into my opponent's net. Sounded simple enough.

Early on in the season, I had my big chance. All of us kids ran after the ball like mad dogs chasing a bone. When one kid got it, we all ran toward it, forming a blob of players all kicking at the ball frantically. There was no passing, no skill. Just running and kicking and yelling. Well, my big chance came . . . the ball was loose and I chased after it. This was my moment; my chance at sports stardom. All I remember was running—as fast as I could—kicking the ball in front of me toward the goal.

I heard the screams of the fans yelling my name. Then it dawned on me. The fans were not yelling my name because I had this super breakaway; they were yelling my name because I was going the *wrong way.* I was headed straight at

233

my goalie, winding up to kick into my own net. That about did it for my soccer career, and in later years I moved on to baseball and basketball.

So, here I was, twenty-some years later, starting a new church, and I found out that soccer is a major inroad to my community. I gritted my teeth and went on a search for a soccer ball. On that day, a friend and I headed out to the soccer field to meet people and (gulp!) try our hand at soccer.

To be expected, the players we met were great . . . amazing, really. They passed with such finesse and kicked the ball effortlessly. Not me. I passed the ball to the wrong players, tripped and fell down, and, well, let's just say I was sore the next day. But we kept coming back—week after week. My wife and some of the women of our church-planting team decided to make peanut butter and jelly sandwiches and provide us with a cooler of water. After an hour or so of playing, I would yell out, "Who wants a snack or drink?"

We had tons of players come enjoy the refreshments. One player commented, "We play here every Saturday and nobody's ever done this." Soccer, not basketball, opened the door to our community. Through playing every week, I developed relationships with people from all over the world: Africa, the Middle East, Eastern Europe, Asia, Latin America, and South America. You could say that I rediscovered soccer. And by rediscovering soccer I rediscovered something else—the importance of hospitality.

ALBANY PARK: A MICROCOSM OF THE WORLD

Chicago journalist and author of *Never a City So Real*, Alex Kotlowitz, wrote of Albany Park, "The world intersects at the corner of Lawrence and Kedzie Avenues, on the city's northwest side."[1] Albany Park is the Ellis Island of Chicago, the port of entry by which immigrants enter every year. It has been that way for years.

As early as 1912, German and Swedish immigrants started pouring into Albany Park. Shortly after them, Russian Jews settled here, making this neighborhood predominantly Jewish. In the 1970s, after the Jewish population moved out, Albany Park became predominantly Asian (mostly Korean) and Latin American. Lawrence Avenue, the main vein of Albany Park, was designated as "Seoul Drive." Although some of the Koreans have moved out, many of their shops and restaurants remain.[2] Albany Park is now home to between ninety and one hundred different nationalities, including many refugees who have been resettled here.[3] The principal of Roosevelt High School, Albany Park's main school, said, "Roosevelt High School represents a tapestry of hope where over 30 different language groups from 60 different countries are represented. We are a school that not only acknowledges but celebrates diversity!"[4]

Albany Park has the highest percentage of foreign-born residents in Chicago (more than 50 percent) and is located in the third most diverse zip code in the nation.[5] It is a microcosm of the world. So, as missionaries and church planters here, our vision is to make disciples of the nations in Albany Park. For us, the nations live side by side, across the street and down the block. However, because of the diversity here, and because of the large numbers of Muslim and Hindu people, not to mention Catholics and people of other religious backgrounds, Albany Park is very challenging to reach with the gospel.

THE IMPORTANCE OF HOSPITALITY

It was through soccer that I met refugees who had come to Chicago through World Relief, a refugee agency located in Albany Park. Next thing I knew, I was volunteering at World Relief twice a week and meeting different refugee families, both on the soccer field and in their homes. What I found was astonishing. Hospitality, sadly, is a lost art in our day. When you think of hospitality, what comes to mind? For many, hospitality is limited to concierges at hotels, Starbucks employees, or grandmothers who serve their grandkids chocolate chip cookies.

We believe, however, that hospitality is an essential part of church planting and reaching the city with the gospel. Bridge City Ministries (BCM), our church plant, uses hospitality as a main principle for reaching our community with the gospel.

The metaphor of a bridge fits well in a city like Chicago, with its many bridges over the branches of the Chicago River, which winds through the city. We want to be a bridge that connects people from all nations to Jesus.

Bridge City Ministries aims to "bridge" together the nations in a vibrant, healing community in Jesus. We desire to reflect diversity within unity. "For he himself is our peace, who has made the two one and has destroyed the barrier, the dividing wall of hostility. . . . His purpose was to create in himself one new man out of the two" (Eph. 2:14–15). One of the major ways we fulfill this vision is through using hospitality. The following principles are values BCM uses to accomplish our vision.

Eating Meals Together

One thing that is very clear in the Scriptures is the value of eating meals together. Jesus often ate with people, and according to the religious authorities, it was sometimes with the wrong people at the wrong time. Here are some of His meals with others:

Then Levi held a great banquet for Jesus at his house, and a large crowd of tax collectors and others were eating with them. But the Pharisees and the teachers of the law who belonged to their sect complained to his disciples, "Why do you eat and drink with tax collectors and 'sinners'?" (Luke 5:29–30)

When he was at the table with them, he took bread, gave thanks, broke it and began to give it to them. Then their eyes were opened and they recognized him, and he disappeared from their sight. (Luke 24:30–31)

Then Jesus entered a house, and again a crowd gathered, so that he and his disciples were not even able to eat. (Mark 3:20)

While they were eating, Jesus took bread, gave thanks and broke it, and gave it to his disciples, saying, "Take it, this is my body." (Mark 14:22)

The gospel writers gave special attention to Jesus eating with people, showing hospitality as a major thrust of His ministry. Moreover, Jesus told stories about how to throw a dinner banquet and the types of people who should be invited, which included the most unlikely and despised types of people in Jewish culture (see Matt. 22:1–14; Luke 14:1–24). Christine D. Pohl writes, "A shared meal is the activity most closely tied to the reality of God's Kingdom, just as it is the most basic expression of hospitality."[6] Think about it: when we share a meal with others, sitting around a dinner table, eating, drinking, laughing, a special bond is shared. It is not a coincidence that heaven, as depicted in Revelation 19:9, is a wedding feast.

Some of the ways that this is practically lived out at BCM is every Tuesday night, when a group of us who are committed to ministering in the neighborhood meet together to eat. Over the meal we talk about how God has been working in our lives, ways in which we have poured our lives into others (discipleship), and where we have seen Jesus at work—what we call "Jesus sightings." Henry Blackaby says it like this, "Find out where God is at work and join Him there."[7]

Not only do we value spending time in each other's homes and sharing meals together on Tuesday nights, but we also value spending time and eating in the homes of other people (specifically refugee families) in the neighborhood. An example of this is when a family of five from Krasnodar, Russia, came to Chicago as refugees. The family are Meskhetian Turks (originally from a region in the country of Georgia), and had lived in Russia for fifteen years. The family came through World Relief and settled in an apartment a few blocks from where we live. Ironically, a month before the Meskhetian family settled in Albany Park, a group of us from Bridge City went to Russia on a mission trip and learned about the people, the culture, and ways to reach them with the gospel. Because of this, we had an instant connection with this family, whose primary language is Russian.

One blustery January day, we stopped by their place to see if they needed anything. They invited us in, and the wife began serving us Russian tea and brought us soup and bread . . . just like being in Russia! Although our ability to speak Russian was limited—and so was their English—we had the best time eating, laughing, and attempting to communicate. Through spending time with them in their home and having them in ours, this family is extremely open to the gospel, even though they are Muslim.

A group of us also began to visit a family from Mongolia on a regular basis. We will never forget our first visit to their home. They seemed to be surprised that we came to visit and stayed to have tea and cookies with them. Before we left, we joined hands and prayed together. After that, as we prepared to leave, the lady of the home said, "When you leave, I am going to call my mother right away. She told me that no one would ever visit me in America! I am going to tell her that six people came and stayed for tea!"

Lastly, I (Angie) use cooking as a way to offer "strangers" hospitality as soon as they enter the country. I have a passion to serve and love people—and the major way I do this is through food. One of my favorite ways of using food for hospitality is preparing a meal for new refugee families.

Every time Dave goes to the airport to pick up a new refugee family, I prepare a meal to give them, a meal that fits their culture. I make Burmese food, Malaysian food, African food, and more. I wait in anticipation until Dave returns home to tell me what their reaction to the meal was. The fact that someone took the time to cook food from their own country leaves them feeling very welcomed. I have learned that food, as a part of hospitality, is a universal language.

Finding Persons of Peace in the City

Our church plant has one simple strategy—hospitality. Jesus sent His disciples in twos and said, "When you enter a house, first say, 'Peace to this house.' If a man of peace is there, your peace will rest on him; if not, it will return to you. Stay in that house, eating and drinking whatever they give you. . . . Do not move around from house to house" (Luke 10:5–7).

This is more of a natural approach of discipleship that gets you into people's homes and lives. Michael Frost and Alan Hirsch, authors of *The Shaping of Things to Come,* say it this way:

> *Finding a person of peace and basing our ministry there seems like a less effective method in the short term. But in the long term, a church-planting project that emerges out of the households of local, indigenous leaders will*

be much richer and more effective. . . . People of peace are key people who are spiritually open, have good reputations and have influence in the community.[8]

Brian and Inna, leaders of our church plant, frequently visit the home of the Meskhetian Turk family. But they also have the family in their home. The Turks are a family of peace because they are open and comfortable with Brian and Inna. Not only that, but our team has met their extended networks—other Meskhetian Turks who live in the neighborhood—which has resulted in Brian and Inna becoming "insiders" with this unique unreached people group.[9]

In the early 1990s, Inna came from the Ukraine as a refugee through World Relief. She and her husband, Brian, have a strong connection with the Meskhetian Turks because of her culture and experience. They are "the gospel" to this community; that is, they live out the message of Jesus in words and actions—and hospitality is a huge way they do that. The hope is, then, to see this family come to faith and start to reach out to their Meskhetian relatives and friends (their networks) and start house churches. Because of their involvement with this family and others, Brian and Inna are preparing to go to Russia someday as missionaries and plant churches. Here in Chicago, they are getting plenty of training.

Incarnational Living: Being "Sent" on Mission

One of the values that our church plant has committed to is living in the community that we are serving. Because we are based here, a group of us at BCM are intentionally living in Albany Park. As God calls us to plant "out," that will require disciples to relocate as needed. Relocation, which is a key value of CCDA (Christian Community Development Association), is a value we live by as well. That value is "to intentionally re-locate to the community you feel called to."[10]

One of the words we use in our context is the word *apostolic*. In its purest sense, the word "apostle" means "the one who is sent."[11] We feel that we are "sent" into Albany Park as mission-agents of Christ, seeking to make disciples by living out hospitality. Michael Frost, a missiologist out of Sydney, Australia, says it this way: "We see our daily life as an expression of our sent-ness by God into this world."[12]

Jesus saw Himself as sent on a mission, as did Paul and other writers of the New Testament:

Jesus said to them, "If God were your Father, you would love me, for I came from God and now am here. I have not come on my own; but he sent me." (John 8:42)

"For I did not speak of my own accord, but the Father who sent me commanded me what to say and how to say it." (John 12:49)

Again Jesus said, "Peace be with you! As the Father has sent me, I am sending you." (John 20:21)

Paul, an apostle—sent not from men nor by man, but by Jesus Christ and God the Father, who raised him from the dead. (Gal. 1:1)

In the same way, we who follow Jesus are sent on mission. The term *missional* has become quite popular today. Being missional means that we live on-mission—that is, we live as mission agents of Christ to this world. Jesus sends us into the harvest fields as laborers, and that harvest is plentiful and the need for workers is great (see Matt. 9:37–38).

BUFFET OF THE NATIONS

Dave has offered us the biblical appetizer for practicing hospitality and I (Angie) would like to offer you the buffet. (You see, I am Sicilian-Italian and offering a buffet is my specialty.) Part of what I do at Bridge City Ministries is coordinating the food at any of our particular gatherings. As time has gone by, our food has evolved into a buffet of the nations. Since our friends and neighbors are from all over the world, our food has reflected our diversity.

Picture what this looked like one summer afternoon. Each weekend during the summer months, Bridge City Ministries hosts a gathering at Foster Beach, on Chicago's North Side. All of the members of our church planting team load up their cars with friends from the neighborhood and head to the beach. One sunny June day, two Assyrian ladies came and brought some very tasty tea. Also, our Turkish-Russian friend brought homemade Turkish bread and piroshkis (dumplings with the most delicious fillings). This particular day was probably our biggest crowd, and at least a dozen countries were represented. The day was full of soccer and volleyball games and plenty of people mingling and minding the food table.

In the middle of this fun, storm clouds rolled in and it began to pour. Everyone ran together under a tree, using umbrellas, towels, blankets, and anything they could find that would shelter them from the storm. Turks and Somalis, Iraqis and Ethiopians, Americans and Assyrians, all huddled and muddled together. As the rain began to let up, we came out from our coverings and someone shouted, "A rainbow!" There it was, not only one, but *two* full, huge, vibrant rainbows crossing one end of Lake Michigan to the other.

Mohammed (not his real name), a twelve-year-old Somali refugee who frequents our house to eat with us, said, "Angie, what does a rainbow mean?" I told him it is God's promise to us. He yelled out several times at the top of his lungs, "A rainbow means God's promise!"

On the way home that day, Abdi (who is a Muslim but open to Jesus) said to me, "Angie, you do so many nice things for so many people. God is happy with you." That melted and pierced my heart.

Of Rice and Men

When I first started cooking for our international friends, culturally I automatically thought I should make pasta, bread, and meat! But after serving pasta and several different types of food, I soon learned that the G's (our nickname for our refugee friends) *love* rice. So I cooked it up really well (and lots of it) with plenty of tomatoes, onions, and seasoning. Inevitably it was devoured, without a grain to spare! Rice was their mainstay in the refugee camps and you would think they would be tired of it. But rice is what they know, and when I cook it up, I add all the extra love I can muster. They know that too. I think that is why it tastes so good to them.

One day Ali (not his real name), a Sudanese refugee boy who is thirteen years old, asked me if I would teach him to cook when he turns eighteen. I said, "I'll teach you to cook now!" How funny . . . I knew hospitality through food would be part of my ministry, life, and love here in the city, but I thought I would be teaching women and little girls to cook. Ali's desire to learn is an example of what God is doing through our ministry and His affirmation of one of my dreams for Bridge City Ministries.

A Very Sweet Dream (On the Back Burner)

Bridge City Bakery and International Café is my dream. This bakery and café is to be a place where people are welcomed with open arms and served delicious, affordable international food; a place where "everyone knows your name" and which serves as a bridge of reconciliation: nation to nation, and nations to the Lord. Also, I dream for it to be a place that will offer a natural setting for communities of faith, and discussions of faith, to develop. Recently I felt the Lord was prompting me to take the first, very small step to beginning this endeavor, so I did. I put together a menu and circulated it throughout my circles of friends and their businesses. Soon orders came flooding in, and so did the rave reviews! I now spend hours at a time baking out of the small kitchen in my home, and I know this is the beginning of the entire dream becoming a reality.

I love cooking and baking. I love being on my feet for hours straight doing it. I love the feeling of hard work and accomplishment. One time Dave asked me what my favorite part is. I thought for a second and told him it was pulling the baked goods out of the oven and seeing how beautiful they are, but even more when I can serve them and watch how food brings people of all nationalities and faiths together with some sort of commonness. This, then, becomes the bridge of reconciliation.

I also greatly enjoy having the neighborhood kids (all of whom are Muslim) over for a meal. This is one of my favorite parts of living in this mission field. I feel that I was created to cook and created to love. When the kids come for dinner, they gobble up the food, but I have noticed what they find most irresistible is being loved. They thrive on our love and acceptance of them. Through our many meals together they have come to know that we truly love them.

One day we were walking the kids home and another neighborhood boy came out onto his second-floor balcony and yelled, "Hey Ali! Is that your sister?"

Ali hollered back, "Yeah! This is my sister Angie." Now obviously we are not blood related, as Ali is a beautiful chocolate brown and I am a light cinnamon at best. But the others in the neighborhood recognize that bond we have as family. This speaks volumes to the kids and to the rest of the neighbors of the love of Christ in our hearts.

It is a beautiful thing that God uses hospitality through food and my passion for people to reflect the life of our Lord. Oftentimes around the dinner table, or just sitting on the floor eating rice and fruit, spiritual conversations will arise. My prayer is this: "Father, guide my hands as I cook, my mouth as I speak, and my heart as I love."

ANGIE'S BANANA BREAD

2 cups flour	Preheat oven to 350 degrees. Grease and flour a 9x5-inch
1 tsp. baking powder	loaf pan. Stir together the flour, baking powder, baking soda,
1 tsp. baking soda	salt, cinnamon, and nutmeg. Set aside. With an electric mixer,
¼ tsp. salt	beat the peeled bananas at moderate speed until mashed.
½ tsp. cinnamon	Beat in the egg, sugar, and oil. Then add the dry ingredients
¼ tsp. ground nutmeg	and beat in gradually, on low speed. Mix just until blended.
4 large ripe bananas	Stir in the chocolate chips and walnuts. Fill the prepared
1 egg	loaf pan and spread level. Bake 50 to 60 minutes. Let stand
¼ cup vegetable oil	10 minutes before transferring to cooling rack.
⅓ cup dark brown sugar	
½ cup chocolate chips	
½ cup chopped walnuts	

REFLECTIONS ON HOSPITALITY

God is doing something extraordinary in our day. He is bringing the nations to the cities, and many of those nations are from parts of the world where hospitality is practiced every day.[13] America is known for individualism and private spaces—living our own lives, in our private homes, often unaware of the people around us. But when you go to Africa, or the Middle East, or Latin America, hospitality and shared spaces are a part of the DNA of the people—it is in their blood.

These cultures and many more are coming to cities like Chicago. This should cause us to reexamine how we reach the city and make disciples of these nations, calling us to involve and invest our lives by contextualizing the gospel to reach the different people groups of the city. Hospitality is universal and crosses any language or cultural barrier. Here are a few reflections on hospitality and how it can be practiced:

• Everyone wants to be loved and valued. Look for a family (such as a refugee family or immigrant family) and "adopt" them. Take them to dinner; invite them to your home; teach them ESL or how to use a computer.

• Learn people's stories. Everyone has one, whether they live in a high-rise building downtown or on the streets. Hospitality is about learning people's stories.

• Get to know your neighbors. Find out if there is a widow or an immigrant family that lives near you and have them over. Look for the lonely, the hurting, the broken; get to know them and find out what their needs are.

• Search for "Jesus sightings" in your community. This can happen by doing a prayer walk and asking God to lead you to a person of peace (Luke 10:6). He will direct you and guide you to the right people.

• Attempt to learn a new language, or even just a few phrases. Find someone who speaks that language and try to speak to him. Watch how that will make an impact!

• Adopt an ethnic restaurant in your area. Get to know the waiters, the cooks, and the regular customers. Learn about their food (which will give you insight into the heart of their culture).

• Bring food to a neighbor or a person of peace in your community.

CONCLUSION: A CALL FOR HOSPITALITY

Hospitality must be relearned and activated if we are going to reach the nations in our cities. Although it is risky, challenging, and time-consuming, the end results are amazing. Ultimately discipleship is all about love and friendship. People are looking for life and life to the full.

In a powerful scene in the riveting film *Les Miserables,* based on Victor Hugo's epic novel, Jean Valjean (played by Liam Neeson) falls in love with Fantine, a former employee of his who ends up prostituting herself to provide for her daughter.[14] Fantine becomes very ill and is growing weaker as the days go on. Valjean begins to care for Fantine by visiting her every day. One day, Valjean decides to eat lunch with Fantine, so he sets up a table outside, complete with cheese, bread, meat, and a flask of wine. He then very tenderly picks up the weak Fantine in his arms and gently seats her at the table, wrapping a blanket around her.

Although no words are exchanged during this scene, you can see the joy and hope in the eyes of Fantine—that feeling that she is loved, cherished, and accepted by another. The power of hospitality changed this lonely, sickly prostitute into a woman of hope and dignity. Hospitality does this. It makes you feel like you are special, like you have value and worth . . . and it changes people.

The city is a place where hospitality must be practiced if we are to "seek the peace and prosperity of the city" (Jer. 29:7). Our prayer is that we, the church of Christ, would rediscover the beauty of hospitality—through soccer, eating a meal with a refugee, baking or cooking rice, finding people of peace, and simply loving. All it takes is love and faith the size of a grain of rice . . . I mean mustard seed.

REFLECTION QUESTIONS

1. Why do you think hospitality is important in the city? Is hospitality something you see in your life? If not, why?

2. Why was hospitality so important in Jesus' ministry? What does that say about our "strategies" today? How is hospitality a key component to discipleship?

3. How is food important as it relates to the Kingdom of God and to hospitality?

4. What are some practical ways you can practice hospitality in your own life? Is there a refugee or low-income family or an international student you can begin to reach out to?

Recommended Reading List

Frost, Michael. *Exiles: Living Missionally in a Post-Christian Culture* (Peabody, Mass.: Hendrickson, 2006. The chapter entitled "Exiles at the Table" alone makes this thought-provoking book worthwhile.

Oldenburg, Ray. *The Great Good Place: Cafes, Coffee Shops, Bookstores, Bars, Hair Salons and Other Hangouts at the Heart of a Community* (New York: Marlowe and Company, 1999). This book, written by a well-known sociologist, really captures places of hospitality (like Starbucks and other venues) that are at the heart of a community. He coined the term "third place"—which is that place people go where they are most themselves, open to new ideas, and looking for community. (First place is the home and second place is your work.)

Pohl, Christine D. *Making Room: Recovering Hospitality as a Christian Tradition.* Grand Rapids, Mich.: Eerdmans, 1999. This is a good start on understanding hospitality. The author gives good practical examples of ministries that use hospitality.

Schaeffer, Edith. *L'Abri.* Wheaton, Ill.: Tyndale, 1969. This book is filled with great stories of how God used Francis and Edith Schaeffer, who opened up a hospitality house in the mountains of Switzerland.

Simson, Wolfgang. *Houses That Change the World.* Waynesboro, Ga.: Authentic, 1998. This is an excellent book on the nature of house churches and how God is using house churches throughout the world, including ways hospitality is practiced.

WILFREDO DE JESUS is Senior Pastor of New Life Covenant Ministries, one of the fastest growing churches in Chicago. New Life is a vibrant and caring church that is reaching out to the community. Wilfredo De Jesus received a Bachelor's degree in Communications from Trinity University and a Master's degree in Christian Ministries from North Park Theological Seminary. Wilfredo resides in Chicago with his wife Elizabeth and their three children, Alexandria, Yesenia, and Wilfredo, Jr.

PAMELA TOUSSAINT is a graduate of Fordham University with a BA in communications/journalism. She has written extensively for numerous periodicals such as *Decision*, *Discipleship Journal*, *Spirit-Led Woman*, and *Black Enterprise*. Pamela has authored and coauthored many books to literary acclaim, including *Signs of Hope in the City*, *Boys into Men*, and *Great Books for African-American Children*. She has been featured in *Charisma* magazine, on *Joni*, *Paula White Today*, and *Focus on the Family Weekend*.

CHAPTER 15

HEALING THE HURTING IN HUMBOLDT PARK:
Church Rebirth

Wilfredo De Jesus
Interview by Pamela Toussaint

Introduction: Home in the Hood

t was once said that if you walked into parts of Chicago's Humboldt Park neighborhood at night, you might not come out. Pastor Wilfredo De Jesus, who was raised there during the 1970s, agreed. "I saw a lot of despair and abandoned buildings growing up," he recalls. "Gangs were prevalent, but this has been my home." It still is. But today, Pastor De Jesus walks around Humboldt Park pretty freely, as one of the most influential local pastors in the area. He has been senior pastor of New Life Covenant Church (NLC) since 2000, taking over the helm from his father-in-law, Reverend Ignacio Marrero, who founded it as Palestine Christian Temple in 1965. New Life Covenant holds five services on a Sunday, including one in Spanish. It provides a church home for more than four thousand people, and steadily growing, within the neighborhood of roughly seventy thousand residents.

The church's demographics reflect the diversity of its Humboldt Park environs. NLC attracts not only Latinos, who comprise most of the congregation, but a healthy number of African-Americans, Anglo-Americans, and a smattering of Polish, Russian, and Asian-Americans too. Indeed, Reverend Marrero took seriously the commandment of the Lord to "go into all the world and preach the good news to all creation" (Mark 16:15). It seems "all creation" has now come to Humboldt Park.

GROWING PAINS

Passion and conviction notwithstanding, the journey of church-building in a rough-and-tumble environment has not been an easy one, for father-in-law or son-in-law. After a few moves to buildings in the Humboldt Park area, in 1976 NLC settled into its current facility, affectionately known to NLCers as the "Mother Church Campus," at 1665 North Mozart. "We were not exactly welcomed in the community," notes Pastor De Jesus.

> At that time it was not the neighbors but the gangs that ran this community. Many times after leaving church services or our Bible Institute, we came out to find that our car batteries had been stolen, our tires slashed, our windows smashed, etc. At other times, the surprise was when we arrived to church only to find that the windows in the building were broken, or even worse, our instruments and equipment had been stolen. It was a couple of rough years.[1]

To top that off, simply because the church had "Palestine" in its name, following a cultural tradition to name a Spanish church after a city, it was frequently called upon to comment on current political events in Israel. "We'd get calls from the [Chicago] *Tribune* and other papers wanting our ideas on the Palestinian crisis," says Pastor De Jesus with a laugh. "A lady on the block verified that people thought we were Palestinians. And I was saying, 'No, no, we're Puerto Rican!'"

Despite the obstacles inherent in growing an inner-city ministry, God was faithful to complete the mission He gave these men. When their new building needed extensive interior and exterior work in order to be suitable for broader ministry, financial resources were scarce. After much prayer, their plight came to the attention of the previous owners of the building. That congregation decided to bless NLC by canceling the debt on the property. Instead of taking years to pay off a mortgage, the church was now free to use those resources to do the much-needed renovations.

What's in a Name?

When he assumed leadership of the church in 2000, Pastor De Jesus decided to renovate the vision and the mission statement. Their stated vision is simply "to be a Christ-like congregation that transforms the community into a New Life." The new church covenant, which inspired its name change, is "to bring unbelievers to Jesus, to membership, to spiritual maturity, to training in ministry and to a passion for missions . . . for the glory of God."[2] The acronym of the name New Life spells out the church's values: **N**o Excuses, **E**xtra Mile, **W**ork, **L**ove,

Intercession, Family, Evangelism.

The name New Life also provides a constant reminder to Pastor De Jesus of the summer of '77—the year he stood in a church sanctuary and told the Lord, "If You're real, change my heart, change my life." God answered that prayer, but it was not because De Jesus had come to church looking for spiritual renewal. As a young man, he just wanted a job to help bring home some money for his mother. De Jesus's father, who struggled with alcoholism, left the family when De Jesus was eight. "Catholicism was all I knew," says Pastor De Jesus. "I remember seeing the priests drinking, and I couldn't understand how men of God could drink when I knew my dad drank, and was not a man of God."

The job young Wilfredo was hoping for—street cleaning—turned out to be a date with destiny, and key to unlocking his understanding of spiritual things.

Humble Beginnings

He was assigned to work at a little church called Palestine Christian Temple during their summer vacation Bible school. "The kids would come early to this program at this Pentecostal church and say, 'God bless you!' and go to the altar to pray," recalls Pastor De Jesus. "This was very different from my ritualistic Catholic Church experience. So I went to the supervisor and asked what these young people had, and they told me about Jesus and the sinner's prayer." He remembers being scared when the young people made a circle and began to pray for him—it seemed to him similar to what was done at a gang initiation, and that usually ended in a beating.

Though Pastor De Jesus admits he kept one eye open while they prayed, his conversion stuck. "I left with my sister, saying, 'I don't know what these people did to me,'" he recalls. "I felt supernatural." Today, NLC offers a summer jobs program to reach out to local young people for just that reason—so they too can have a supernatural experience with Jesus Christ, as he did back in 1977.

When Pastor De Jesus became born again in that little church, he never looked back. He went on to become Palestine's children's minister and youth leader, and after marrying Rev. Marrero's daughter Elizabeth in 1988, joined the church's denomination, Assemblies of God, as a minister. Later, he became the church's assistant pastor. "God said I needed to make a covenant to reach poor people in the city and around the world for Him," says Pastor De Jesus. But there was a caveat: "That the budget would not dictate my faith to reach the people."

Habla Espanol?

Every church planter knows that once you commit to your part of the Great Commission and are successful in reaching people for Christ, you will soon need more space to house and serve them. NLC has grown from two hundred to four thousand under Pastor De Jesus's skillful leadership over the past eight years.

Latinos make up almost 15 percent of the United States population and are expected to double their numbers by 2050.[3] Knowing that the younger generation of Hispanics would be bilingual, and have a preference for English, four of the five NLC services are offered in English. This approach is supported by the results of a recent Pew study that shows that "only 48 percent of those [Hispanics] born in the U.S. attend a Hispanic church, compared to 77 percent of those born outside the U.S."[4] This also worked well for Pastor De Jesus, whose preferred language was definitely English. He recalls, humorously, "So I get anointed as a pastor, but I don't speak Spanish well, and Spanish was our main language. But we have African-Americans and Anglos in our neighborhood. So I begin preaching in English, and second- and third-generation Hispanics, who prefer English, start coming in."

Those who prefer Spanish either attend NLC's Spanish service and midweek Bible study, or use headphones to receive translation during English services. "I had to come to the realization of what my strengths were," notes Pastor De Jesus, "and English was my strength. I was more Kingdom-minded than culture minded." Only one family left over the language issue, he says. The rest "understood that the vision was about people and they went with me."

As far as culture clashes go, Pastor De Jesus says there aren't many, even with the considerable diversity at NLC. "We are a welcoming people, so it's natural to us to welcome our neighbors," explains Pastor De Jesus, noting that his father-in-law's mainly Puerto Rican congregation had many Mexican, Honduran, and Guatemalan worshippers, who spoke with different Spanish dialects. "We already worshipped with people who were different from Puerto Rican culture, so we're used to it."

A Holistic Gospel

De Jesus's preaching style is dynamic and contextual, the worship described by attendees as "high energy." Sunday services are fairly short and sweet, with the sermon usually finished in less than thirty minutes, and the entire service running about ninety minutes. Sermon series entitled, "Lord, Change My Attitude (Before It's Too Late)," "Cheaters," and "The Gospel According to Star Wars" are standard fare at NLC, and like its programs, are geared to address exactly what members are going through.

For example, with 42 percent of the mothers among NLC's ranks being single moms, the church knew it had to be part of the solution for them. "When I did research and realized that the problems single moms faced were huge, I decided to address it. But with that comes dealing with the need for groceries, kids' issues, AIDS," says Pastor De Jesus. "I come from a single-mother home. Last year, I changed the oil in all of their [single moms'] cars, and gave each of their kids a book bag for school."

Another example is NLC's marriage ministry, which has within it a *remarriage ministry*—Blended in Him—that targets the needs of stepfamilies. "We contextualize that because that's what people are dealing with: divorce, blended families, family rights," says Pastor De Jesus.

Their motto is, "If we see a need, we fill it." To that end, Pastor De Jesus now oversees a mega ministry with more than one hundred programs and 501(c)(3)'s under its umbrella—something that would have made his father-in-law cringe. "He said if he knew twenty years ago that this much growth would happen, he'd have quit!" says Pastor De Jesus with a laugh. He had a portrait of his in-laws installed in the building's entrance. He notes, "The people have to know that this work didn't start with me." Honoring his father-in-law also means recalling the sacrifices he made to do ministry in Humboldt Park back then, including the death of his own child. His eighteen-year-old son was shot and killed in the neighborhood, on his way to get a pizza. Reverend Marrero himself was shot on another occasion. Still he stayed faithful to the calling. Today, the older pastor and his wife enjoy retirement in his native state of Puerto Rico. "We've also given them a lifetime of visits to Chicago anytime they want," says Pastor De Jesus. "We don't wait until people die to honor them."

Loving the Poor

With a baby boomer pastor educated at North Park Seminary, NLC could easily have joined the ranks of the growing number of middle-class megachurches that serve mostly white-collar "Christian commuters" who drive in from the 'burbs or from downtown once a week to attend services. Or, it could have become the haven church for those inbred, dyed-in-the-wool Christians in the Humboldt Park neighborhood for whom outreach was hardly top of mind. But another strong value Pastor De Jesus instituted when he took the helm is a deep desire to reach the poor and the unchurched in the surrounding area.

"The church hadn't done any type of outreach or social ministry in thirty years," notes Pastor De Jesus, recalling the reticence he met when he presented his agenda for the church to launch out into incarnational ministry, meeting the needs of the people in their blighted neighborhood. "I blocked the door and said, 'What kind of church are we? We have poor people around us!' I determined that every weekend we would be fishing—throwing lines and nets into the river to pull people out."[5] To this end, NLC is home to a full webpage of ministries, many of them geared to the hurting and to children.

Most notably, NLC incorporated New Life Family Services in 1998 as an extension of the church to serve the community. It is a not-for-profit agency located in the heart of Humboldt Park, and operates River of Life, a homeless shelter for women with children, and an after-school program. Other vital ministries under NLC include the Chicago Masters Commission, an intensive discipleship program that invites about twenty college-age students from all over the country to invest nine months to be trained as servants to youth. "It mimics the Mormon model where kids give two years of their lives to religious service," notes Pastor De Jesus. The students travel with him, conduct games and dramas, and teach abstinence and other issues relevant to young people. "When they go back home, they can be youth pastors."

Gangs to Grace is a ministry that's effective in reaching gang members for Christ. "Five percent of these kids are hard core," says Pastor De Jesus. "Ninety-five percent want out." He notes that he has had Thanksgiving dinner with Latin Kings and other gang members, sharing Christ's love with them. The ministry also held a seminar for parents, educating them about gang culture and warning signs to look for in their own kids. "Parents see their twelve- and thirteen-year-old kids with earrings and tattoos and are wondering if they are in gangs," notes Pastor De Jesus. Perhaps they are too scared to ask. The seminars NLC offers provide a safe place for parents to dialogue and learn about this issue that is becoming pervasive in inner cities and beyond.

We Are Family

The "F" in New Life, which stands for family, is a high priority. Each year, De Jesus has instituted "Family Week." It's not a week to bring in noted speakers offering clever tips on improving family life—it's a week when all evening services, church meetings, and activities are cancelled so families of both church and staff can simply spend time together. "We take care of our business in the home," explains Pastor De Jesus, regarding the annual week off. "We focus on the family. So everyone knows that family is very important here." Parents at NLC also have a wide range of choices for their children's spiritual growth. There is a dynamic children's church grouped by age, but also a kids' choir, Girls' Club, Leadership Training Academy, and a puppet and clown ministry that uses relevant skits to help children who face difficult decisions on a daily basis. The puppet team serves as a witness for Christ.[6]

Big Dreams Come True

Filling the need wherever it presented itself gave rise to the Chicago Dream Center (CDC), which opened its doors in 2007. It provides homeless women with food, shelter, and spiritual guidance. The clients who participate in this program are guided through a three-phase residential and recovery experience. Through funds raised entirely by church members, NLC purchased a farm for the rehabilitation of women who were struggling to overcome addiction and/or prostitution and who are part of CDC. The farm, New Life for Women, took in its first residents in August 2002. An annex was added to the farm in 2007 to accommodate even more women, and it now houses twenty-nine residents.

"We found out there was an epidemic of prostitutes, about six hundred, just in our area," explains Pastor De Jesus. "The city of Chicago came to us, a church, for help. And God placed in my heart to buy a farm." As God promised, He supplied. A member of NLC had an uncle pass away, and the church was able to purchase his fifteen-acre farm in Cambridge, Illinois. "When you can see a prostitute supernaturally changed in nine months, that's a revival!"

The Dream Center spawned Bread of Life, a ministry that feeds two hundred people two days a week. "We also adopted twenty blocks to clean through the Adopt a Block program, and we feed struggling families every Saturday, providing them grocery bags of food," says Pastor De Jesus. Their biblical framework is from Matthew 9:36–38: "When he saw the crowds, he had compassion on them, because they were harassed and helpless, like sheep without a shepherd. Then he said to his disciples, 'The harvest is plentiful but the workers are few. Ask the Lord of the harvest, therefore, to send out workers into his harvest field.'"

As stated in its covenant, NLC is also mission-minded and not lacking in laborers willing to give their time to the church's overseas evangelistic efforts. They have projects in Peru, Dominican Republic, and even Burkina Faso, West Africa, sending medicine, providing ambulances, running an orphanage and a widows' home, and building a cafeteria. "We went to the second-largest city in Peru, Chimbote, and found a desert," says Pastor De Jesus. "We planted a flag in a space the size of a football field, and declared it injustice." They also planted a church in Chimbote, and sent a mission team of volunteers to support that effort in 2008. A Christian school is planned for Burkina Faso, a mostly Muslim country.

Locally, the mother church has already spawned two satellite churches in the Chicago area, one in the West Side Pilsen community, and the other in Oakwood, on the South Side of the city. "We had to get rid of people because of lack of space," laughs Pastor De Jesus. The satellite churches were launched in 2003 and 2004, respectively.

PRINCIPLES OF CITY MINISTRY

Philosophically, Pastor De Jesus is influenced by the writings of Dietrich Bonhoeffer, especially *Letters and Papers from Prison* and *The Cost of Discipleship.* "He forced me to ask myself, 'Who am I?'" Partly in answer to that question, Pastor De Jesus offers four main principles he employs that help guide the success of NLC and its transformational work in Humboldt Park. Let's look at them.

Live in the City

"You cannot change a city from the suburbs."

"When I was eleven, there was a riot in my neighborhood during the Puerto Rican Day festival," recalls Pastor De Jesus. The riot turned into a two-day war between local gangs and the police department. "I decided to go into a store that was broken into, looking for a Pepsi. I went to the fridge, took the bottle." He made sure to close the fridge door. ("I was kind about saving the electricity.") Once outside the store, he remembers standing on the street with the Pepsi, feeling bothered. There was both a moral and a social dilemma within him, and a questioning of who he really was. "I walked back into the store, opened the case door, and put it back."

That dilemma kindled the fire that keeps Pastor De Jesus committed to bringing Christ to bear on the streets of Humboldt Park. He and his wife, Elizabeth, a main worship leader at NLC, and their three teenagers have always called this neighborhood home, and have no plans to leave. He notes that the family could easily move to the suburbs, which families often do for the sake of the kids. But in fact, all three of his children are involved in the ministry. "I want to eat and buy groceries where my people do. This is my hood," laughs Pastor De Jesus. He points out that many pastors come into a blighted neighborhood, preach, and then leave. "You have to be in the trenches, with the hurting and the pain. We don't need tokens; we need pastors who are called to be part of the change." He adds, "I say, 'If there's a fire in the hood, or a death, I can get up in the night, go to the fire, and attend to the family. That's being a pastor in the community. I see myself as the pastor of Humboldt Park."

Having his finger on the pulse of the neighborhood means knowing what the people need most. One of those needs is some stress relief, especially for single moms, at the start of the school year. Each September, NLC hosts an outreach, complete with back-to-school giveaways, free haircuts, and free groceries, that attracts five thousand–plus participants. Churches, nonprofit organizations, businesses, and city agencies all participate—and cooperate—to pull off the annual event that is run by more than six hundred volunteers. The 2007 HopeFest

Chicago was so successful it caught the attention of Mayor Richard Daley, who signed a resolution honoring NLC and the De Jesuses, and declaring it "A Day of Hope in Chicago." In order to expand the event's reach to ten thousand plus, the church now prepares packages for NLC members who desire to present Hope-Fest to their employers for possible corporate sponsorship.

Get Political (Outside of the Pulpit)

"God created the government, and we have to be available and involved."

De Jesus is fortunate to have had a relationship with former Chicago mayor Richard J. Daley since he was a young man. Well, in theory at least. The summer jobs program that placed him at Palestine Christian Temple—where his life was radically changed in 1977—was instituted by the mayor. He had the opportunity to relate that story to Richard M. Daley, Chicago's current mayor. "I told him what an impact his father had on my life," recalls Pastor De Jesus. "He asked me, 'Really? How?' I said, 'Because he helped introduce me to Jesus.'" A relationship ensued, and in 2005 De Jesus was appointed to be a Chicago city commissioner, recently meeting with the mayor regarding a rash of school killings. "He calls me to come and pray," says De Jesus, humbly. "We have a good relationship."

One benefit of De Jesus's background is that he has a working knowledge of the area's school system, and some built-in relationships. From 1998 to 2000 he held two positions, one as Assistant Pastor at Palestine, and the other as the Executive Assistant to the CEO of the Chicago Public Schools. This facilitated the arrangement NLC has now with Roberto Clemente High School on Western Avenue, where NLC meets for Sunday services while their new $20 million building is erected on seven acres nearby. "I'm an alumnus of the school. We came in and painted the classrooms and fixed up the auditorium. We have no church-and-state problems because of our outreach. We don't just talk, we do."

His work exposure, and no doubt his personal experience raising three teenagers, make De Jesus keenly aware of the issues school-age kids in his neighborhood face, including gang violence. De Jesus has been successful working with other churches to rally students from each of the area schools to march against violence. In 2007, after the shooting of a ten-year-old, he was able to orchestrate 120 churches to band together for a prayer vigil against violence. The overnight vigil and subsequent peace rally was themed "Exodus 20:13," and participants wore T-shirts that said, "Thou shalt not kill." The event garnered coverage by local television news. De Jesus knows that elected officials cannot do the job of keeping neighborhoods safe on their own, but need help from the affected communities, and from church leaders, to find real solutions. "We need to bring back a moral standard," states Pastor De Jesus. "No nation has ever survived where there has been a moral decay, and America is facing that."[7]

As Vice President of Social Justice for the National Hispanic Christian Leadership Conference, the largest Hispanic Christian organization in America, De Jesus also gets the opportunity to address his community's issues on a national stage. In 2008, he met with then-presidential candidate Senator Barack Obama, along with a host of Hispanic pastors and clergy, to discuss issues of concern to the Hispanic evangelical community. "The meeting went very well," says De Jesus. Obama "really understands the importance of justice issues such as healthcare, education, and immigration within the Hispanic faith community."[8] De Jesus also got the opportunity to pray for Mr. Obama at the conclusion of the meeting.

As part of his role on the NHCLC, which represents close to 15 million born-again Christians, De Jesus is able to influence immigration and education policies from a systemic standpoint. He also has the chance to address lawmakers on Capitol Hill regarding these two key issues for Hispanic communities. "Chicago is the sixth or seventh in the country in terms of the school dropout rate," notes De Jesus. To tackle this, he met with the U.S. Secretary of Education to help rally pastors in those cities with the highest dropout rates around this cause. De Jesus challenges inner-city pastors who balk at any political involvement. "Some pastors don't get so much involved with ministry," he observes. "Instead, they study ministry." He notes, "You have to be the tip of the spear as a leader, to give the church a voice."

Despite his considerable involvement in the political arena, De Jesus is quick to clarify that he keeps church and state separate within NLC. "I become politically involved when I'm off the pulpit. I never push a political agenda, never," clarifies De Jesus. "Off the pulpit, if you're going to get zoning or funding for your people, you have to get in there. The mayor calls me, and I have to be there to represent my people, and fight for their rights."

Empower the People, Manage the Growth

"The pastor cannot do everything."

"In the past two years I've done one wedding and a few funerals," says Pastor De Jesus, who believes in raising up church leaders—and putting them to work. "We have a system. Each minister has two months to serve 'on call,' and there are more than one hundred deacons who do hospital and home visits." De Jesus meets weekly with all ministerial staff, and is serious about them doing proper self-assessment and seeing measurable growth.

One interesting and pivotal experiment De Jesus did with his staff was called the "Gauge 08" survey, an extensive, in-house self-evaluation. "In seven years we experienced this explosive growth, but it was hard for us to do a self-examination," recalls De Jesus. "We had to ask ourselves, 'Is our foundation strong enough to sustain these thousands of people?'" Pastor De Jesus stopped the church for two weeks, brought in all of the leaders, and did extensive training. He got the title "Gauge 08" from the story of the Chernobyl reactor disaster—the malfunction of one gauge caused countless thousands of people to get cancer. "We have to make sure we're strong in the Word, so we surveyed them," notes De Jesus. What De Jesus's study and training time also uncovered was that NLC had a lack of servant leaders—the same people were doing two and three ministries each. The study showed that only five hundred of the four thousand members were serving in the ministry, so he started a recruitment campaign to address that and keep staff from burnout.

During the two weeks, leaders were also challenged about their willingness to embrace all of NLC's vision, particularly their commitment to the hurting and the broken. "Ninety percent said that the vision [of NLC] was clear to them, so my communication studies paid off," says De Jesus, who took the opportunity to speak frankly to his leaders. "We're in the ocean, and very few want to go that deep. But we are not to be particular about the fish we catch. We're not the Holy Spirit. He cleans them out, we catch them, and we love and welcome them."

After the survey was complete and the vision rehearsed, some church lay leaders had a choice to make: "I gave orders to the steam room to move forward, and told whoever wants out, to jump ship." As with any organization, large or small, the potential for misjudgment, indiscretion, or even criminal behavior among leaders also must be addressed. "We've experienced embarrassing moments with scandals, so we now scrutinize our volunteer base and do background checks," Pastor De Jesus says. "We were in the emotion of the growth and didn't handle that well."

As far as raising young leaders for NLC, the college students who participate in the Chicago Masters Commission represent one pool of potential future leadership. "I place the young adults in the community so they can get the heart education," says Pastor De Jesus. "For them to learn to have compassion for the inner city and the urban setting, their heart has to change. They have to live here, not go on a field trip." The true indigenous leaders—young people raised in the Humboldt Park area and church community who will take over the work of NLC—come through the ministry's Summer Jobs Program, just as Pastor De Jesus did years ago. But, he adds, "There is the lack of training for the Wilfredo De Jesuses of the future because of churches leaving the community."

The idea of a megachurch can conjure up for some the image of "sheep-stealing"—where a dynamic church comes into a community and deliberately attracts away faithful followers of smaller churches in the area. But the very make-up of NLC challenges that theory. "We have the people from under the bridge that nobody wants in our congregation," says Pastor De Jesus bluntly. "But if you'll go after them, God will send the people everyone wants." People visiting NLC have an opportunity to get plugged in through "Getting to Know You" evenings held there every three months. "My wife and I share our story, and introduce the entire staff, so no one feels disconnected."

Buy, Buy, Buy

"It tells the community you're invested."

Humboldt Park is an area undergoing major gentrification, a phenomenon that is hitting inner cities all over the country—but De Jesus notices a twist. "The issues back then at the start of NLC were in your face," assesses Pastor De Jesus. "The issues today exist, but are being thrown to the side due to gentrification. People are trying to paint a picture that this is not really happening," referring to how the change in socioeconomics and the rise in single-mother-headed households there, which is nearing 40 percent, is played down to attract certain buyers. "The façade is changing, but not the issues," offers De Jesus. "We bought three lots for $87,000 ten years ago," he notes, adding that today those lots would cost well over a million dollars. "Our position is, 'When are you moving out? We have eighteen lots in this area, and we're ready to buy!'" De Jesus has a word for well-intentioned pastors: "Keep one eye on the vision and the other on the finances of the church." He notes that oftentimes churches fail because they are not administratively astute about finances.

New Life Covenant's winning strategy has been to purchase drug-infested buildings and convert them—without putting the people out. "The more real estate you have, the more you begin to claim the land," explains Pastor De Jesus. "People see that and they glorify God when they see our banners saying, 'A Church for the Hurting.'" NLC bought all of their buildings with no money down, according to Pastor De Jesus. Buying property before prices rose helped De Jesus position the ministry to be financially healthy and prepared to handle the cost of future growth. "This way we can purchase things and not have to go to the people every week for money, always struggling to make it." As a result of NLC's buying efforts, the landscape in Humboldt Park is beginning to change. "We still see the poverty, the homelessness, the gangs," admits Pastor De Jesus, "but a little less."

CONCLUSION: "WE'RE NOT LEAVING THIS CITY!"

Notably, the administration building that became available to NLC housed the parachurch ministry Inner City Impact for several decades. The new five-thousand-seat facility will also sit on the same corner where Reverend Marrero housed his little church in 1965, on Chicago and Christiana streets. "I didn't even realize it, but we'd be returning to our covenant," notes Pastor De Jesus wistfully. "It was God's sovereignty that we will be housed there. And I don't care if I have to preach ten services, we're not leaving this city."

REFLECTION QUESTIONS

1. What does a holistic gospel look like in your community? What specific human needs can your church address?

2. Can you clearly articulate your church's/ministry's mission statement? Does it have a justice component? If not, how could God use you to strengthen that aspect of the ministry?

3. Do you have the staying power, with God's enabling, to purpose not to leave your city or community? What does it take for you to be at home in your area?

JON PENNINGTON is Coordinating Pastor of Chicagoland Community Church in the center-city Chicago neighborhood of Lakeview. He is a graduate with a Master of Divinity from Southwestern Baptist Theological Seminary in Ft. Worth, Texas, and has a B.A. in history from Morningside College in Sioux City, Iowa. Jon also serves as the next generation facilitator for the new work team of the Chicago Metropolitan Baptist Association. Jon is married to Alana, and is father of three children.

CHAPTER 16

"ALTERNATIVE" CELL CHURCH:

A Training Lab for Urban Missions

Jon R. Pennington

Introduction: The Promise

"Even in darkness light dawns for the upright, for the gracious and compassionate and righteous man" (Psalm 112:4).

Chicagoland Community Church (C3) meets in a small church facility it shares with another congregation in the Lakeview neighborhood on Chicago's North Side. The preceding verse is displayed on an artistic multimedia poster in the back of our sanctuary. Seven radiant yellow sunbeams violently tear through a deep navy background of splotched tissue paper. This work of art was designed by two of the many summer missionaries who serve in this neighborhood each year. The verse is taken from a psalm that was also the inspiration for an original song the C3 Praise Band has recorded. Many mission teams who have ministered in this neighborhood have spent time meditating on this verse. The church did not fixate on this text by accident. As with all Scripture, it expresses amazing truth. It is a simple yet wise poetic observation, as well as a beautiful promise from God to all who face intense challenges in spiritually dark places.

THE MISSION FIELD

C3 is in a neighborhood that perhaps Tim Keller, founding pastor of Church of the Redeemer in New York City, would define as "center city," but with unique aesthetic twists that make it both more interesting and more challenging than your common downtown scene.[1] It is one of those strategic places where the aggrandized and marginalized of our world negotiate America's culture on the street corner. But this "center city" has been raised to an art form and exaggerated beyond all sanity. Here the urban rhythm has become frenzied. A place like this is usually considered an irrational or impractical location for a new church. It can offer, however, an opportunity for strategically thinking far into the future.

There is really very little hope for an evangelical church in Lakeview, even less for a Southern Baptist one. Perhaps in a counterintuitive way, that in and of itself is enough of an argument to pursue it. Insanity and God's call often seem frighteningly similar to each other. The life and ministry of the Old Testament prophet Ezekiel demonstrates this clearly.

The challenges of Lakeview have nothing to do with the violent social justice issues most people face in urban ministry. Lakeview is not an "inner city" neighborhood, even though it is well within Chicago's city limits. The community does have its share of crime, and a few gangs do pass through, but nothing remotely like its less affluent neighboring communities. Lakeview's darkness cannot be defined to a particular type, but rather a montage of several facets. Street smarts are somewhat necessary in this neighborhood, but theological intelligence is actually far more valuable. Lakeview is not a place of physical danger, but rather of moral and spiritual dangers in a shocking variety. As many guests here have noticed, Lakeview is more like an Amsterdam neighborhood than a Midwestern city. Lakeview demonstrates Western Europe's coming to America. This reality has arrived with a certain kind of vengeance.

Our own non-scientific survey confirmed many of our church leadership team's conclusions, and a research project completed by Moody Bible Institute graduate students in our neighborhood a couple of years ago assisted as well. Prayer walks in the neighborhood and demographic statistics further support these observations.

The 2000 United States census points out that 60657, the primary postal code for the Lakeview neighborhood, is more Caucasian than the national average. The average household size in the neighborhood is 1.65, which is far smaller than the national average. Lakeview has a staggeringly high percentage of renters compared to homeowners. It has very few people below the poverty level, the median family income is nearly twice the norm, and the median cost of a home is $375,000. Almost half of its adult residents have achieved a bachelor's degree and more than a quarter have some kind of graduate degree. Only 28.3 percent of the adult population is currently married. These statistics are a brief snapshot of what it typically means to be a center city neighborhood. However, the distinctions between the alternative subcultures, poor transients, and other marginalized individuals is not generally reflected in the statistical analysis.[2]

The Precept group has updated this data for 2007 and has published a report with insights that give a deeper understanding of the neighborhood. The population is extremely dense, around 65,000 people, though it is declining slightly. The neighborhood rates statistically as "somewhat diverse," with "very high" ethnic diversity even though 83 percent of the Lakeview neighborhood is Caucasian. Most are in the "young and coming" lifestyle group, and it is considered a rather easy, low-stress area to live in, with residents' greatest concerns being pursuing their individual "hopes and dreams." That obviously does not include the homeless street kids to whom we minister. In a vast understatement, the report describes Lakeview families as "somewhat non-traditional." The median household income is a staggering $96,878. More than 60 percent of the neighborhood falls into the "Survivors" (Generation X) category; 48 percent of households have no "faith involvement" whatsoever, and their "faith receptivity level" is appropriately listed as "very low." But, if they are interested in faith, 73 percent of them look toward "historic Christian groups."[3]

Although these numbers paint a fairly accurate generalization of the Lakeview neighborhood, they miss much of the vibrant color you can only experience by being there yourself. Lakeview is a diverse place, and is primarily made up of the people group that marketing experts call the Bohemian mix. They are "a progressive, multiracial mix of students, executives, writers, and public interest activists . . . [and] can be described as the young and the restless."[4] Richard Lloyd, in his work *Neo-Bohemia*, traces the history and tendencies of this people group in the Wicker Park neighborhood of Chicago. This community to the west of us is similar to Lakeview in many ways. In discussing bohemian elements in modern Paris, Lloyd states that "Bohemia shared with these shadowy urbanites a culture of opportunism and a lust for experience in licentious sexual norms and the liberal use of drugs and alcohol."[5] This description applies well to the prevailing cultural trends in Lakeview. This hodgepodge of young urbanites is, however, augmented by a variety of other people groups all living in close proximity to each other. There is simply no description that can fully encompass the population of Lakeview.

THE MINISTRY STRATEGY

The very diversity of the neighborhood God called us to reach demands the use of some kind of creative strategy. The people groups in the neighborhood share two characteristics: They have specific felt needs and strongholds. These either need to be ministered to or opposed, respectively. From the beginning, we knew that we needed to do something to bring the gospel to people right where they were; however, we also wanted to see them drawn together as a unique people of God in this place. Desiring to be missional in our outreach and relational in our discipleship molded the development of our strategy.

The People

Lakeview is the home to one of the largest homosexual populations in the United States. An enormous gay-pride parade marches each summer only one block away from our church facility. Our church is committed to biblical standards for marriage and sexuality, which makes the advancement of the gospel very challenging among homosexuals. Most of our advances in this subsection of the community have come either through personal relationship building or as a by-product of one of our other outreach plans. We pray sincerely that God will show us a way to break through with the gospel into this people group. The fine arts community has provided some inroads for outreach.

The neighborhood also is the bedroom community for a large population of young urban professionals. They often work downtown in Chicago's Loop and take mass transit home every evening. They party at the many clubs in Lakeview, and they tend to be die-hard Chicago Cubs fans. This is convenient since Wrigley Field is also located in our neighborhood. Often they desire to find love and start a family, which usually means moving out to the suburbs. Sometimes, however, they settle their family into one of the expensive condos or townhomes that fill and surround the Lakeview community.

Relationship Builders

Outreach to this people group often is either pre-evangelistic or discipleship-based. Because of their interest in professional development, we are reaching out to them by hosting a speech club in our facility. Due to their devoted love for pets, last summer we offered our first ever "dog wash." We have a cell group that meets in the nearby Lincoln Park neighborhood, and this group has hosted outreach book discussions at the local Borders bookstore. Urban professionals often have had some kind of church experience. Some retain a kind of nominal faith, though many have replaced Christianity with a spiritual smorgasbord of beliefs. One person I am ministering to in evangelistic blog discussions was brought up Roman Catholic, left the church to pursue the Druid faith pluralistically, and is currently a practicing Buddhist.

Alternative Subcultures

The feel of the neighborhood is produced by the various alternative subcultures that either live there or spend their entertainment and relational time there. Lakeview is home to numerous theaters, clubs, and other venues. Add to that mix a wide variety of novelty and secondhand shops and you have the perfect destination for those bored with middle-class American culture. Goths, punks, the hard-core crowd, and many others are part of the multifaceted alternative subculture. Most are radically individualistic in style and dislike being placed into any one category, but they are very tribal in their relationships with their friends.

Each of the alternative subcultures has various cultural tendencies. Goths usually like things dark and old. They prefer wearing black clothes and listening to music that almost sounds like it comes from an eighties horror film. Those into hard core tend to have tattoos and piercings and listen to music that sounds angry. Kids in the punk scene tend to sport brightly colored mohawks and listen to very energetic music. Overall, they pride themselves in their individuality and style.

C3 offers various outreach concerts throughout the year to reach out to these diverse subcultural strands. We invite secular bands for a given culture who are willing to be "Jesus-friendly" and allow us to screen their lyrics and media displays. In that way, we gain an audience of non-Christians. We then invite appropriate Christian bands. We encourage some of our outreach-minded members to attend and build relationships with those who are there. During these events we also try other creative ways to communicate the gospel, such as video presentations and zeens (small magazines that deal with contemporary topics in almost a cartoon-book fashion). Much of this outreach is pre-evangelistic for cultures that have a very negative view of the Church and people who assume the Church dislikes them as well. I have seen many Goths come to our events who are surprised the church building did not collapse on them upon their arrival!

The neighborhood also has large numbers of the homeless, or those who are nearly so. This demographic basically has two segments in Lakeview: street kids and an older transient population. Street kids range in age from eleven to forty years old. They share the common experience of running away from or being kicked out of home. Many of the older "kids" grew up on the streets. Quite a few have serious drug issues. Some are transgender. Most survive through some combination of illegal activities such as squatting in condo construction sites, stealing, hustling, prostitution, and drug sales. The older homeless group either squats somewhere outdoors or they live in low-cost single-occupancy hotel rooms. Often they are dealing with long-term addiction or mental issues.

C3 reaches out to those in greatest financial straits in our community by networking with others who are also ministering to these individuals. We host a weekly fellowship time called Food & Friends for anyone who needs a warm dinner and a change of clothes, and we operate a weekly drop-in and meal for the youth in the neighborhood called Safe Haven. These are attempts to live out our discipleship by demonstrating compassion for those in the deepest need in our community.

A Cell Strategy

Much of our strategy has arisen from dealing with the specific issues inherent in such a culturally diverse and densely populated neighborhood. Even though it is generally felt that cell strategy can be problematic in North American urban contexts,[6] we chose to work with a cell strategy not unlike David (Paul) Yonggi Cho's strategy in Seoul, South Korea. Karen Hurston, in her work *Growing the World's Largest Church,* details many of Dr. Cho's strategies that we have attempted to use in our ministry. The "remarkable growth" of this amazing church was observed by Ms. Hurston firsthand in this "church in which I grew up."[7] Her analysis of his strategy proved pivotal to us as we developed ours, though other resources such as those provided by TOUCH ministries for the North American context helped as well.[8] In the end, we had to tailor and continue to alter these strategies to make sense in an intensely postmodern, urban environment.

Probably the best example of our ultimate vision can be seen in David Garrison's *Church Planting Movements,* which is a small book detailing the multiplication networks of cell churches and house churches in international missions. Garrison defines a church planting movement as "a rapid and exponential increase of indigenous churches planting churches within a given people group or population segment."[9] He also argues that either cell churches or house churches can accomplish this task based upon their ministry environment.[10] We have not yet figured out how to become sizable, but we have started to learn how to multiply. We hope that this multiplying tendency remains part of our permanent DNA.

Although it is clear that we will not have the same immediate impact described in these works, I am still convinced that this is one of the best ways to reach out to radically different people groups in Lakeview while still drawing God's people together toward a Kingdom vision. It is amazing to see how God is beginning to use this new people, Chicagoland Community Church, to impact both our community and the world.

The beautiful thing about a cell group strategy is that while we are able to minister very specifically and missionally to the various people groups of the neighborhood, we can also draw them to what we share together as a church. Some of this happens in the natural overlap of ministries, such as young urban professionals serving at one of our meals, but in other times we are far more intentional about it. It is a testimony to the power of the gospel when individuals from our various people groups gather together at our Sunday afternoon service. It is a snapshot of heaven to see a young professional in his business casual clothes worshiping side by side with a guy wearing half-dollar-size stretch earrings. Beyond that, it is extremely helpful in developing a well-rounded, biblically based, urban theology to have such diverse perspectives on the gospel as people from divergent worldviews are discipled.

A MISSIONARY TRAINING FIELD

God has blessed C3 over the years with a seemingly endless stream of college students, mission teams, and summer and semester missionaries from both our denomination and a variety of other organizations. While every church, in the perpetual flux of ministry, experiences the reality of people exiting the proverbial "back door," Keller points out that this reality is intensified for those in an urban setting.[11] We have found that in actuality C3 does not even have a "front door" but rather more of a "revolving door." God blesses us with help for a time and it is our role to train them in missionary methodology to postmoderns while they are here. This often happens through the teachable moments that arise during the intense challenges and opportunities this field poses to those who serve here. This intersection of biblical exegesis with harsh reality makes C3 a wonderful training laboratory for those entering the ministry.

My supervisor and mentor Keith Draper, Executive Director of the Chicago Metropolitan Baptist Association (SBC), always says that ministry experience in an urban setting should be calculated in dog years. That is why medical programs have people serve in urban centers for their internships. They experience so many more strange realities in a far shorter time. For us, the temporary help that missionaries give us is a blessing, but is far outweighed by the impact we are allowed to have on Jesus' Kingdom mission by training these missionaries.

I have personally learned along the way just how invaluable this hands-on reality training really is. Having had the honor of cutting my ministry teeth on this kind of mission field is a blessing I am not thankful for often enough. It is not everywhere that you learn to preach with the possibility of a drunken warlock interrupting your application points with a bizarre tirade. Nor does everyone have the experience of watching a mentally disturbed discipleship contact run down the street and leap into an alley. We are one of the few churches in America that has had the honor of baptizing people out of Wicca, and one that knows the pain of seeing some of those who have come so far slip back into their previous life. Weekly we experience adventures that many people in other ministry settings would not even believe if we described them in detail.

Discipling Others

Far more enjoyable than my own training has been the privilege I have had to disciple others through their artistic experiences here. I was honored to disciple one young man from the hard-core culture for more than a year. He and his wife are now working toward becoming missionaries to Eastern Europe. Another individual was a resident artist for us and is now a Wycliffe missionary. He designed a great water-fountain display for the front of our church that offers bottled water to people making their way to one of the neighborhood festivals. We also hosted a book-signing for one of our members and took a trip in a large van to Colorado to record a CD of original music for our praise band. One of our past team leaders is now ministering in Texas, and another is a worship pastor in California. We are very thankful that God continues to give us the opportunity to showcase the creativity of our members, and often to launch them toward their future ministry endeavors.

God continues to send additional missionaries to be part of our church. One longtime couple is taking steps to prepare for missions in Western Europe. I remember when the husband was just learning to deal with the idiosyncrasies of ministering to the Goth culture and I had to help him process a confrontation with one of our "people of peace" (Luke 10:6). Another witnessed one of the street kids physically beating one of her seeker friends on our corner. The assailant is now in jail, and still being ministered to by another member who serves in ministry to the people of the street.

Internships

Numerous college student interns have already left us for other mission fields, like one who is serving children in Mexico. She was a missionary kid and said that she learned what it meant to "be the church" during her college years with us. Others are still serving our community, preparing for when they will go overseas. One has just become a cell group leader and is planning to use his training in a future ministry of Bible translation in the two-thirds world. We even have a suburban school that buses students in on Monday nights to be the hands and feet of Jesus ministering in our Food and Friends community meal. They once had to clean up the urine of a drunken guest who confused our clothing closet with the restroom.

Mission Teams

Mission teams from a variety of churches and organizations have served in our church. The particular challenge is to train people in the realities of urban ministry when we only have a week to work with them. Many groups have had an incredible impact drawing in guests and serving the community through surveys, flyer distributions, and acts of service. We even have an older couple who comes from Iowa twice a year to serve as my secretary and maintenance crew. We also once had a college mission team that made the local news for sacrificing their spring break in coming to work with us.

Not all groups are so helpful. Sometimes they come with their own agendas and hang-ups. We had one group from a Midwestern state that arrived at our church in the middle of one of our Goth nights. They were experiencing controversy in their own church over worship style, and could not get past our method of outreach to the community. They displayed a poor attitude over the entire week of their stay in Chicago. The leader even mimicked the behavior of the gay community while walking on Halsted Street. Our graduate student intern, who was guiding this group, had her more-than-capable hands full in keeping them from damaging our relationship with the neighborhood.

Longer-term summer or semester missionaries are usually a deep blessing to the church and community, and particularly open to the training we provide. They come intentionally on mission, and God has taught us through each of them as well. The very experience of living in close quarters in our facility in our neighborhood is a life-changing experience for many of them.

One summer missionary experienced firsthand the challenges of ministering in the Goth culture. She was in a ministry conversation with one of the guests when a mentally unstable individual verbally assaulted that person, and then called the police on herself. I had to follow up that encounter with the State's attorney to drop the charges. Another summer missionary had to help smooth over relational tensions when one of the street kids began shouting Spanish obscenities at someone who was passing by. As it turned out, this person was the roommate of someone who attends our speech club. We had to carefully navigate a way to continue to minister to both parties.

A recent semester missionary had to kick out a transvestite prostitute for inappropriate advances on another male guest during one of our events. Another wrestled with how to minister to a mentally disturbed and spiritually oppressed guest who was offering false prophetic statements to other guests. One youth pastor from the South is planning to spend his sabbatical month with us after having led a number of trips to our neighborhood. As one of our semester missionaries reflected: "I have a kind of reverse culture shock when I go back home. Here [at C3] it is clear why I am a believer in Christ and need Him so deeply."

Finally, C3 is getting involved in starting daughter churches and networking with other denominational churches that are reaching out to the next generation in the city. Our experiences are proving helpful to these other missions. Because of the brokenness of our surroundings, Chicagoland Community Church is a wonderful place to learn the beautiful lessons of God's love. Although there is great darkness in our community, we have found that the Lord Jesus shines all the brighter in stark relief.

CONCLUSION: STILL LEARNING

Many questions remain as we forge ahead to meet the dynamic challenges of our community. One challenge we are wrestling with is how to best minister to those who visit our worship service first rather than coming in through an outreach event and being drawn from there into a cell group. How do we avoid segregating our visitors into cells that were created as an outreach opportunity to a particular people group? How do we accomplish multiple purposes with such a limited number of potential leaders? We are still learning, even as our visiting mission teams are learning. We often find that we learn together as they bring fresh eyes to the field.

We have been shown a few things with absolute certainty in our ministry in Lakeview, and these seem to be transferable ministry principles that can be applied to any mission field:

1. The more challenging a ministry environment, the more necessary a missional focus. Intentional outreach is urgent in such a rapidly transforming and transient neighborhood.

2. The more difficult the discipleship challenges, the more vital is relational ministry. In settings where the majority of people have a great distance to cover in order to reflect the values of the Kingdom, life change is going to be difficult and building trust is absolutely necessary.

3. The most important thing is simply trying to follow Jesus by the power of the Holy Spirit, to the glory of God the Father, in whatever ministry environment He has placed you. As one of my church planting friends says, "Jesus is far more concerned about our obedience than He is about our success."

4. Finally, ministry challenges can be the perfect training ground for new ministers and missionaries. A person learns how to serve best in situations that face actual resistance where one must learn to sincerely trust God.

We pray that someday God will allow our church to branch out and multiply in other center city neighborhoods of Chicago as well, but for now we are simply very thankful He has gifted us with such a wonderful primary neighborhood in which to relearn what real ministry and real discipleship are all about.

Back in our church facility, on the other side of the sanctuary, is another multimedia poster made by the same team of summer missionaries. It quotes another verse from the same psalm: "He will have no fear of bad news; his heart is steadfast, trusting in the Lord" (Psalm 112:7). As a church, C3 has faced more than its share of bad news, ridiculous situations, and impossible challenges. Nearly everything that can go wrong for a church plant has gone wrong for C3. In the midst of that, however, God has shown Himself to be faithful. He has taught us that while bad news may still come, there really is no need to be afraid. He is worthy of our trust even in challenging situations, and He can use those situations to teach us and others more about His Kingdom and the wonders of who He is.

REFLECTION QUESTIONS

1. What are some passages of Scripture through which God has deeply impacted your perspective on your own ministry? What might God be trying to teach you through the unique ministry environment in which He has placed you?

2. How would it transform the way that you ministered to others if you focused more on the relational aspects of ministry and less on the organizational ones?

3. Who are some people in your life who are potentially leaders for the next generation? What are you doing proactively to give them the ministry experiences they need to be great missionaries?

Native to Chicago's Far South Side, **TOM KUBIAK** has a
burden to see Christ's true Church engaged in the ministry of
reconciliation throughout the city—vertically and horizontally.
He rejoices in God for his lovely wife, Joanna, and their
children, David, Leah, and Sarah. They relocated to the
city-center South Loop in 1999. Tom is the founding pastor
and preaching elder of this integrated, non-denominational,
neighborhood ministry.

CHAPTER 17

CHURCH IN THE CITY CENTER:
Diversity and Constant Change
Tom Kubiak

Introduction: Up Close and Personal

I n the epicenter of a world-class city such as Chicago, we find the types of businesses, enterprises, and attractions that drive this city of "broad shoulders" from its core: Chicago Board of Trade, Chicago Stock Exchange, Sears Tower, numerous universities, Grant Park, Field Museum, Shedd Aquarium, Soldier Field, and McCormick Place, to name just a few. These institutions are located within the South Loop neighborhood. With the influx of hundreds of thousands of workers on weekdays, tourists from around the world, and metro-area fun-seekers on weekends coming for a variety of festivals, it is tempting to make two false assumptions: that any attempt to engage in gospel ministry must be large scale and that there will naturally be a personal disconnect for Christ-followers at churches within the city center.

When we examine the life and ministry of our Lord Jesus Christ as He walked in our world two thousand years ago, it is striking to observe how Jesus made such a profound difference in people's lives in the most up close and personal ways (John 1:14, 35–51; 2:1–12; 3:1–21; 4:1–30). Dr. Ray Bakke describes both a theological and practical paradigm shift for gospel outreach upon evaluating the 1970s crusade type of evangelism as well as the strategy in losing the Vietnam War.[1] In both cases, people were attempting to accomplish their task from a distance—far away from the "real audience."

Jesus spent lots of time with a small group of people. This led me to an understanding that to reach the city, one had to focus on narrowcasting versus broadcasting. This was a huge shift in my thinking. In Any City, USA, folks read the same newspaper and watch the same TV stations; they are reached by broadcast, from the typesetter to the telecaster. I began to see that in the city we needed to focus on a narrowcasting medium. The bigger the city, the narrower the focus; the more personal and relational evangelism must be. This is the reverse of the way folks think, which is big city, big meetings, and big strategies. But the opposite is true: the bigger the city, the smaller the focus. By putting all our emphasis on broadcasting, we lose cities at the cost of millions of dollars, under the delusion that we are reaching a large group of people.[2]

Based on Jesus' model of simply sharing all of life together in relationship with the people around Him as well as this paradigm shift recognized by Bakke, South Loop Community Church (SLCC) has established this type of niche in the city center. We are driven to engage our local context and culture in personal, meaningful ways. We concur with Dr. Howard Hendricks that "you can influence people from a distance, but you impact them up close."[3]

STATISTICS AND TRENDS IN CITY-CENTER CONTEXT

Not Your Stereotypical "Inner City"

Most Christ-followers assume that city-center, and inner-city, ministry takes place strictly among urban blight, the economically poor, and the homeless. Since the mid-1980s, Chicago has been at the forefront of American cities strategically bringing in residential development to create a new hybrid community within the city center. In 2005, the *Chicago Sun-Times* carried a feature series on "The New Downtown,"[4] highlighting the expansion of its boundaries and the strong inflow of new residents. The first article in this series, "Our Extreme Makeover," described how a once-struggling downtown discovered new vibrancy.

The heart of Chicago pounds stronger than ever. You can hear it over the daily thrumming of Chicago life, amid the tourists scavenging North Michigan Avenue, through the 24-hour cycle of the Loop, to the new neighborhoods [read, South Loop] carved from freight yards and warehouses on the Near South Side. . . . The regenerated downtown has had the biggest impact on business on State Street—Chicago's new college town. A collection of schools in the South Loop brings thousands of students onto State Street, where stores now cater to them.[5]

In another article, "The New Downtown by Day," the newspaper summarized the city center now as "a blur of workers, shoppers, tourists—and even people who live there."[6] You can count my family, as well as more than half of our congregation, among those who reside in the South Loop neighborhood—where we can get up close and personal with those we are attempting to reach with the gospel of Jesus Christ. *Chicago* magazine described our community as "the hottest neighborhood in the country,"[7] while we locals often call it "Craneville" (referring to the large number of cranes used to construct high-rise buildings).

Our latest survey research revealed the following statistics on this city-center community:

> *The lifestyle diversity in the area is somewhat high with 16 of the 50 U.S. lifestyle segments represented. The top individual segment is "Affluent Educated Urbanites" representing 24.1% of all households. The racial/ ethnic diversity is extremely high. Among individual groups, Anglos represent 46% of the population and all other racial/ethnic groups make up a substantial 54% which is well above the national average of 33%. The largest of these groups, African-Americans, accounts for 33.1% of the total population. Hispanics/Latinos are projected to be the fastest growing group increasing by 43.9% between 2006 and 2011. The area [South Loop proper] can be described as "extremely non-traditional" due to the below average presence of married persons and two-parent families. The overall education level in the area is very high . . . with college graduates accounting for 56.0% of those over 25 in the area. Concerns which are likely to exceed the national average include: Affordable Housing, Racial/Ethnic Prejudice, Finding Companionship, Neighborhood Gangs, Social Injustice, and Neighborhood Crime and Safety.[8]*

Can Opposites Attract?

One of the intriguing factors of the greater city-center and South Loop community, which also drew me to plant SLCC here, is the disparity between local neighborhoods and even sub-neighborhoods within our primary one. In 2002, the *Chicago Sun-Times* did a fascinating job of revealing how diverse our city-center community is:

> *The Near South Side is an area where two Chicago extremes exist side by side. It's among the poorest areas of the city for African-Americans, a place where half the black households made less than $14,173 in 1999 and where one in three people lived below the poverty line. It's also the wealthiest white area in the city, a new analysis of recently released data shows. The*

median income in white households there was $88,489 in 1999. About a
quarter of the Near South Side's residents are white.[9]

Our "Percept" survey based on 2006 data also showed that household income levels exceeded national averages in both the top segment ($150,000 and
up) and the low segment (under $15,000).[10] In a separate survey quadrant using
data from the immediate southern periphery of the South Loop, the research
showed:

> *Struggling Urban Diversity representing 41.0% of all households. The*
> *next lifestyle groups in ranking were Rising Multi-Ethnic Urbanites and*
> *Struggling Black Households. African-Americans account for 61.3% of the*
> *population, with Anglos representing 8.8% of it. Based upon the number*
> *of years completed and college enrollment, the overall education level [for*
> *struggling minorities] in the area is somewhat low. Household income was*
> *outside the range of national norms—particularly in the bottom segment*
> *(under $15,000).*[11]

The greater South Loop neighborhood includes hardly any single-family,
detached housing structures. Most residential development is multi-family, low-
rise, mid-rise, and high-rise facilities. A mixture of high-end residences co-exists
with Chicago Housing Authority (CHA) low-income and mixed-income projects. There are senior-citizen buildings as well as single-residency occupancy units
(SROs—usually accommodating fixed-income and/or disabled residents) in the
community. Most construction and housing development is vertical, with space
in the city center at a premium. Parking space is becoming increasingly difficult
to find.

Describing such density and disparity of the city-center population, particularly in the greater South Loop community, reminds me of a conversation
I had at the Moody Bible Institute (MBI) Annual Pastors' Conference in May
of 1999 (while I was transitioning downtown to start SLCC). Over lunch in the
Student Dining Room, several of us pastors were getting acquainted and sharing
our ministry contexts. Upon hearing of my new ministry call to plant a church in
the city center, one pastor posed this unsurprising question: "Who are you going
to target?"

I replied, "Everyone in our local neighborhood." I could tell by the smirk
on this pastor's face that he thought this forty-year-old church planter must have
"just fallen off the back of the pickup truck."

My acquaintance explained, "Well, it's natural for 'like to attract like' in kind."

Then, in one of those blessed, Holy Spirit–inspired—as well as sanctification-testing—moments, the Lord led me to respond, "You're right, it is 'natural' for 'like to attract like' but, last I checked, the transforming gospel of Christ is the 'supernatural' power to draw all people to God and His Church." Although I held myself in check, I confess that I was ready to pontificate on basic scriptural teaching, such as making disciples of all the ethnic groups (Matt. 28:18–20), sharing the Good News of Jesus with every creature (Mark 16:15), Peter's vision from God to help him accept the Gentiles (Acts 10:9–33), the integrated church at Antioch (Acts 13:1), evidence of real faith where there is impartiality (James 2:1–9), and what the glory of heaven will look like when we all meet the Lamb of God (Rev. 5:9; 7:9).

As SLCC lives and serves the Lord in the city center with such disparity, we claim the reconciling power of Christ's gospel to attract a diversity of people to Himself.

Don't forget that you Gentiles used to be outsiders. You were called "uncircumcised heathens" by the Jews, who were proud of their circumcision, even though it affected only their bodies and not their hearts. In those days you were living apart from Christ. . . . Once you were far away from God, but now you have been brought near to him through the blood of Christ. For Christ himself has brought peace to us. He united Jews and Gentiles into one people when, in his own body on the cross, he broke down the wall of hostility that separated us. He did this by ending the system of law with its commandments and regulations. He made peace between Jews and Gentiles by creating in himself one new people from the two groups. Together as one body, Christ reconciled both groups to God by means of his death on the cross, and our hostility toward each other was put to death. He brought this Good News of peace to you Gentiles who were far away from him, and peace to the Jews who were near. Now all of us can come to the Father through the same Holy Spirit because of what Christ has done for us. (Ephesians 2:11–18 NLT)

Our church is convinced that we are being used of God to be "salt and light" (Matt. 5:13–16), through engaging in personal ministry in the city center. Our niche is to impact non-Christians up close!

PROFILE OF SOUTH LOOP COMMUNITY CHURCH MINISTRY

Born-Again Identity

By God's grace and sufficiency, I was privileged to start SLCC in October 2000. Native to Chicago, with my early years in Roseland on the city's Far South

Side, I have always been eager to see the church immersed in multi-ethnic, cross-economic, multi-generational, and holistic Gospel ministry. SLCC is continuing to blossom into this biblically rooted pattern. Our city-center ministry is nondenominational, elder-led, intentionally integrated, and committed to the fusion of scriptural orthodoxy and cultural relevance. Knowing the vital importance of being driven by God-honoring truths and principles in the city center's pluralistic culture, we constantly remind ourselves of who the Lord has called us to be:[12]

South Loop Community Church exists to be used of God in helping people become fully functioning followers of Christ.

These are the pillars of SLCC in twenty-first-century Chicago:

- We value the expository preaching and teaching of God's Word without apology. (Acts 2:42; 20:24–27; 2 Tim. 4:1–5; Hebrews 4:12)

- We value the power of prayer to accomplish what only God can do. (Jer. 33:3; John 15:5; Acts 2:42–43; James 5:16)

- We value sincere, God-focused praise and worship. (Psalm 95:1–7; John 4:23–24; 12:32; Acts 2:46–47; Rom. 11:33–36)

- We value thorough, holistic disciple-making. (Matt. 9:36–38; 28:18–20; Acts 2:47; 4:19–20, 33; Rom. 1:16; 2 Cor. 5:14–20)

- We value the love, truth, and sharing found in biblical community. (Acts 2:42, 44–46; 4:31–32; Rom. 12:3–5; 1 Cor. 12:5–7; Phil. 2:1–8)

Our ministry is attempting to create its own cultural identity that reflects the cross-cultural dynamics of the city center without compromising biblical integrity in doctrine and mission. For example, we combine expository preaching of God's Word—even forty to fifty minutes' worth—with contemporary styles of worship and music. Our church refuses to compare itself and its ministries to other gospel-based churches; but, rather, it respects what other healthy congregations are doing for Christ in the city. We allow God, the Giver of the spiritual gifts, to shape and mold our own congregation's capacities. Knowing the diverse representation of attendees, our services seek to be more reflective of the nuances each people group brings: regular seasons of spontaneous prayer, high-tech media, expressive praise and worship, even extended worship service time (typically one-and-a-half to two hours in length). The community of Christ-followers thrives on authenticity, accountability, and personal engagement with life and ministry.

With religious pluralism so prevalent in the city center, we find it crucial to equip God's people effectively in embracing an accurate Gospel and articulating it with such purity in our communities. In the spirit of grace, SLCC seeks to proclaim the Good News of Jesus Christ in words and deeds that demonstrate the transformational difference the Gospel makes in lives as well as neighborhoods (1 Thess. 1:4–10). It is critical for any city-center church, and any ministry for that matter, to have a firm grasp of soteriology (Matt. 7:13–14).

Family Snapshot

For most of SLCC's history, more than 50 percent of the Sunday service attendees have been able to walk to our meeting place (Sherwood Conservatory of Music) on a nice-weather day. This statistic reveals our deep commitment to minister effectively to local residents and our heart for this community. The ethnic makeup of our congregation is 45 percent white, 28 percent African-American, 16 percent Pan-Asian, 8 percent Haitian, and 3 percent Latino. At this point, the praise band and worship team—numbering on average a dozen persons—consists of five African-Americans, five Pan-Asians, one Haitian, and one white person.

We are still a work in progress, as it relates to being more than colorful—but truly an integrated community of believers in Christ. We stress the "75 percent" philosophy that Pastor James Forbes articulated:

> *A truly diverse congregation where anybody enjoys more than seventy-five percent of what's going on is not thoroughly integrated. So that if you're going to be an integrated church you have to be prepared to think, "Hey, this is great, I enjoyed at least seventy-five percent of it," because twenty-five percent you should grant for somebody's precious liturgical expression that is probably odious to you; otherwise it's not integrating. So an integrating church is characterized by the need to be content with less than total satisfaction with everything. You have to factor in a willingness to absorb some things that are not dear to you but may be precious to some of those coming in.*[13]

Of course, this principle is based on the apostle Paul's words: "Don't be selfish; don't try to impress others. Be humble, thinking of others as better than yourselves. Don't look out only for your own interests, but take an interest in others, too" (Phil. 2:3–4 NLT). People in the congregation, as well as outside the church, can take greater notice of the Gospel when this type of ministry is up close and personal.

Incarnational "24/7" Ministry

A goal of Chicago Mayor Richard M. Daley has been to create a vibrant downtown that basically functions around the clock, both commercially and residentially. In similar fashion, SLCC is committed to valuing people over programs—which manifests itself in assimilating into the local city-center context so as to experience the ebb and flow of life in the heart of Chicago. In other words, when the unchurched and non-Christian residents observe how we church members interact with all aspects of community activity, they begin to see how the gospel functions in their world—and the difference Jesus Christ can make! Rather than elaborate on specific programming, I will simply share with you a few examples of the opportunities that arise as a result of incarnational ministry.

In short, as a pastoral colleague puts it, "Jesus didn't commute!"[14] John 1:14 reads, "So the Word became human and made his home among us. He was full of unfailing love and faithfulness. And we have seen his glory, the glory of the Father's one and only Son" (NLT).

RECOMMENDATIONS AND TRANSFERABLE PRINCIPLES

Where the Heart Is

Despite the complexities, frenetic pace, disparities, and multifaceted costs of the city center, the Lord impressed on me the necessity and value of living within my church-planting ministry context. Relocating my family of five in 1999 to the South Loop has proven to be extraordinarily opportunistic. "Home is where the heart is!" Just as the Christian Community Development Association (CCDA)[15] promotes this type of strategy, living in the neighborhood clearly makes us stakeholders in the community. A sense of rootedness also lends itself to longevity of ministry. In networking so closely with existing social structures, my family has been afforded platforms from which to testify to Christ (schools, athletics, neighborhood boards).

Sure, there are practical benefits of residing in our own ministry environment such as no congested traffic commute and saving the corresponding time and fuel consumption, let alone losing the emotional and mental exhaustion associated with it. In our neighborhood, research shows that 35 percent of households have no vehicles and 50 percent have just one vehicle. Thirty-one percent of households use public transportation to get to work, with 24 percent walking to work on a regular basis.[16] However, the most significant value of incarnational ministry is to completely immerse ourselves in the matters of life, relationships, business, and work that our entire community faces daily. This sort of identification is an enormous asset for effective gospel ministry.

Intensity Calls for Simplicity

One fascinating challenge for most city-center dwellers is to streamline their lifestyle. Due to the density of population and limited storage space, we have a refreshing need for simplicity as well as creativity and ingenuity. In other words, these limitations and the intensity of critical life issues in the city's center force us to focus on what matters most to God! In this type of urban environment, there is not the time—nor the capacity—to get distracted with most of the typical materialistic concerns that bombard the church today.

This is one of many reasons that it is not wise for outsiders to superimpose their ministry paradigms into the urban center. Every ministry context is unique, and requires prayerful deliberation in reference to the best gospel-advancing goals for the community. SLCC prioritizes simplicity, even as it relates to ministry involvement. Rather than weigh Christ-followers down with an inordinate number of programs, emphasis is placed most on incarnating the gospel of Christ through the natural network of contacts and opportunities in the neighborhood. The stakes and threats in the heart of the city are so high that the church must keep the main thing the main thing, and not allow itself to get distracted with peripheral issues. We welcome a sense of simplicity and attempt to do a few things well for the glory of God.

"Being" the Church Outside the Walls

A built-in benefit for SLCC in its early years has been the fact that we lease space for Sunday worship services at Sherwood Conservatory of Music and offices in the neighborhood, just a few blocks from Sears Tower. While we are presently in the process of acquiring our first church-owned local facility, we have appreciated the mind-set of being the church—people—on a mission throughout our local neighborhood.

Since my family lives in the South Loop neighborhood and all three of my children have attended the local, selective enrollment high school, I have been afforded a number of avenues through which to volunteer—and represent Jesus Christ in the process. Back in 2000, another parent and I started the Sports Booster Club at Jones College Prep High School (JCP).[17] I have served as the president of the booster club the last seven years. This volunteer role has allowed me to work with, and witness the gospel to, other parents in the school. In the process, we have sought to create a more vibrant school spirit for an educational institution that is located downtown (on State Street) and that has had limited athletic facilities for several years.

Serving on JCP's Local School Council for five years—and counting—has given me the privilege of having more direct influence in the education of my children as well as that of other students. Chicago's Local School Councils are quite unusual and powerful: they have the authority to hire, or fire, principals, and they approve the school's budget and school improvement plan. As a Christ-follower, I desire to represent Him as well as campaign for better education in typically underserved areas of the city center. This reflects the holistic nature of the gospel. If there are avenues through which God's people can move and serve in order to bring justice and righteousness, then I believe we should use them.

"Keeping It Real"

We find plenty of gross injustice within our cities, and we ought to be the front-runners in carrying out a holistic, Good News ministry to the disenfranchised in our neighborhoods. SLCC aims to assist and empower the needy in ways that do not diminish their dignity, but enhance it. This is a challenging area of ministry, and we are still growing in it. Yet by God's grace we've created an incarnational climate in which the poor and needy are welcomed alongside urban professionals. Everyone has something to contribute to the body of Christ and His Kingdom work—whether time, spiritual gifts, encouragement, insight, or some degree of their God-given resources.

Our church has been able to assist formerly homeless individuals get back on their feet—finding housing, employment, and connectedness to the local community of Christ-followers. We have not had a 100 percent success rate, but several in our fellowship have been rescued, redeemed, and reconciled through the power of Christ and the love of His church. We have had formerly homeless persons playing music in our praise band, leading prayer sessions, teaching small groups, spearheading community outreaches, as well as counseling those currently in a state of addiction or despair.

Finding affordable housing for folks in the heart of the city is a social justice component for Christ-followers. Here is another holistic aspect of gospel ministry that tests the sincerity of an integrated church's compassion, mercy, and righteousness. We are presently considering the level of our congregation's involvement with advocacy—in the civil and legal arena—and the possible creation of a church-sponsored facility that provides lower-income folks quality housing in our area. The most effective learning and vision-casting comes when we engage our diversity of people up close and personal. In the city center, we find people from every social strata.

As our high school has witnessed a demographic shift in recent years, both racially and socioeconomically, a pioneering effort has been launched to not only maintain diversity but also promote social justice. When my son, my oldest child, started high school (2000), Jones College Prep had 90 to 95 percent low-income students (free or reduced lunch). By the time my two daughters matriculated at the school (2003-present), the number of low-income students dropped to 55 percent.

When we live in the heart of the city, we more clearly see the inequities that exist. Our school leaders discovered that many students throughout Chicago not only attend low-performing elementary schools in poverty-stricken communities, but also that these students are not even aware of the opportunities to seek higher-performing education. Quite often, these students are ignorant of the high school application process and they lack the family or community support to pursue better education. Our Targeted Recruitment and Support Program identifies a few neighborhoods with the combination of low-performing schools, high degree of poverty, and a large population of minorities. We then go out to educate these communities about our high school, the application and admission process, and the support structures we have in place for them (both in their community as well as in our school). Chicago Public Schools views our program as a prototype that may very well be replicated in other select high schools in the city.

It is a challenge to be confronted with injustice, but it's also a blessing to be the holy change-agent for equitable advancement. This represents a tremendous example of having a "heart for the community." People need to see what Jesus looks like when He advocates for the disenfranchised in our cities today.

WHOSE KINGDOM ARE WE BUILDING, ANYWAY?

Since moving into the South Loop in 1999, I started seeking another pastoral friendship for encouragement, friendship, and prayer support. The Lord led me and Tim Douma, founding pastor of Loop Christian Ministries in the greater South Loop, to get connected in Christian fellowship. We began meeting monthly to share what is happening in our lives, families, and ministries and then to pray together. From that point, we decided to invite other city-center church planters and pastors, eventually forming a loose-knit group of evangelicals who have a heart for the city. Now, anywhere from three to thirteen church leaders gather on a monthly basis to mutually strengthen each other and hold each other up in prayer. We know that of all that the disciples asked Jesus to teach them, it was the plea, "Lord, teach us to pray" (Luke 11:1), that is found in Scripture. I cannot tell you how refreshing it is to network with these other city servants and to realize that God is at work elsewhere in our city!

Even when I rehearse the mighty, miraculous work of God in birthing SLCC in 2000, I cannot forget how the Lord led the historic Moody Church to support our church plant—despite the fact that they hardly knew us. When Pastor

Erwin Lutzer and the elders of their church recognized the hand of God in establishing this new work in the South Loop, they "adopted" us without making us "jump through a bunch of hoops" or mandating that we become members of their church. Their spirit of cooperation was an awesome testimony to Kingdom-building beyond our own local enterprises. Their gesture certainly influenced me toward not being selfish with ministry endeavors.

With a huge spike in teen violence over the past school year in Chicago, a team of pastors—primarily from the South and West Sides—have banded together to form "Pastors on the Move to Save Our Children." This collaborative effort is not about merely marching down the streets of our city with a bullhorn after a homicide. Rather, our pastoral group works at hosting neighborhood events that draw young people, and their parents, to a park or community center through offering free food and listening. Attendees must complete an information form before receiving their free food: name, address, phone numbers, school, concerns, prayer requests, and other needs (such as housing, employment, or spiritual).

After the big outdoor event, data are compiled for the closest local churches to follow up on these people—offering spiritual assistance, mentoring, and the resources that various city service departments of Chicago can provide. This outreach is not about individual pastors, church names, or reputation-building, but it's about being the Church—with a capital "C"—in word and deed to our city and its hurting people. What a huge factor in keeping us Kingdom-focused (Matt. 25:45)!

The city center is a highly transient area: from the destitute and homeless who move around the city to the high mobility of urban professionals. Pastor Charles Lyons of Armitage Baptist Church is known for declaring, "In the city, it's like preaching to a parade!"[18] Our relatively young ministry has lost large numbers of people to the suburbs and to job transfers out of state. In the process, we've learned "how to say good-bye" in a way that glorifies God. We are faced with the choice of either resenting the turnover or celebrating the time we have been able to invest in people spiritually and then blessing them on their way. Our church has chosen the latter and rejoices in the Lord's broader Kingdom work that expands in concentric circles from the city center. We honor, applaud, pray for, and send these people forward in transition.

CONCLUSION: DESTINATION, VACATION, OR RESIDENT LOCATION?

Countless people see the heart of the city as merely a work destination or pleasure-filled vacation. I hope and pray for more laborers for the harvest (Matt. 9:38) that are up to the challenge of incarnational ministry as city-center residents.

SLCC is definitely in process, but we remain committed to gospel outreach and transformational living that is up close and personal. Our vision is for managed growth, with a priority on planting daughter congregations throughout this needy city. May the gospel of Jesus Christ reverberate throughout the city—starting from its core—in word and deed!

REFLECTION QUESTIONS

1. Consider getting involved in a local neighborhood church ministry. If this will involve moving your home or church, what are the steps you need to take to accomplish it?

2. Evaluate your capacity to be satisfied, in your church, with less than total satisfaction. Meditate on Philippians 2:1–5; 4:10–13, then clarify the non-essential, cultural issues that you need to release and appreciate in your fellow worshippers.

3. Study the following Scriptures as they relate to personal ministry engagement with others: Matthew 9:9–13; Mark 1:14–20; 3:13–19; John 1:35–46; 2 Timothy 2:1–7. Now, identify specific individuals whom you can disciple and mentor as well as those who can build spiritually into you. Pray over these potential relationships and then discuss the possibilities with these people.

4. Prove your acceptance and appreciation of God working outside your "box." Schedule prayer time with other pastors or leaders; network with other churches toward a common goal for your city; practice saying "good-bye" to faithful folks who move away from your ministry.

Recommended Reading List

Bakke, Ray, and John Sharpe. *Street Signs: A New Direction in Urban Ministry.* Birmingham: New Hope, 2006.

Conn, Harvie M., ed. *Planting and Growing Urban Churches.* Grand Rapids, Mich.: Baker, 1997 (especially the chapter on "Networking" by Robert C. Linthicum, beginning on p. 164).

DeYoung, Curtiss Paul, Michael O. Emerson, George Yancey, and Karen Chai Kim. *United by Faith: The Multiracial Congregation as an Answer to the Problem of Race.* New York: Oxford, 2003.

Edington, Howard, with Lyle Schaller. *Downtown Church: The Heart of the City.* Nashville: Abingdon, 1996.

Emerson, Michael, with Rodney M. Woo. *People of the Dream: Multiracial Congregations in the United States.* Princeton, N.J.: Princeton Univ. Press, 2006.

Greenway, Roger S. *Together Again: Kinship of Word and Deed.* Monrovia: MARC, 1998.

Schaller, Lyle E. *Center City Churches: The New Urban Frontier.* Nashville: Abingdon, 1993.

White, Randy. *Journey to the Center of the City: Making a Difference in an Urban Neighborhood.* Downers Grove, Ill.: InterVarsity, 1996.

Part Three

MINISTERING TO
SUBURBAN NEEDS

GLEN KEHREIN, along with his wife, Lonni, and family, have lived on Chicago's West Side since the early 1970s when they founded Circle Urban Ministries (www.circleurban.org). Glen and Lonni's journey has taught them principles of racial reconciliation, urban ministry, and redemption. Other writings of Glen's can be found in *Restoring Communities at Risk*, *A Heart for the City*, and *Breaking Down Walls*.

Introduction to Ministering to Suburban Needs

Glen Kehrein

THE CHURCH: HOMOGENOUS UNITS BECOMING THE DIVERSE BODY OF CHRIST

Three years after World War II concluded, several major events changed the course of history. In 1948, the State of Israel became a realized dream, drawing hundreds of thousands of Jews, many having just recently been liberated from the Nazi POW camps.

Across the Atlantic on July 26 of that same year, President Harry S. Truman signed Executive Orders 9980 and 9981. The former order was intended to eliminate racial discrimination in federal employment, and the latter desegregated the United States military. It was the beginning of America living up to its own long-deferred declaration of its values that had been nearly two hundred years in gestation.

With slightly less notability, 1948 also was the year of my birth. The postwar baby boom produced a generation that became witnesses to and creators of more societal change, more rapidly, than ever before in United States history. The world "boomers" were born into seems ancient and quaint compared to the one they will eventually depart.

I have been a participant observer of this dynamic my whole life. Through my high school years, life was isolated in a small town where the only people of color were migrant "Texicans" shipped up to help the Jolly Green Giant put his corn and peas into cans. Within twenty-four hours of the last ear of corn getting husked they were out of town.

It was not until I migrated to Chicago for college that I interacted with

African-Americans. Rooted in a life experience of racial homogeneity, I had little understanding of the massive social changes happening around me and echoing through the nation and world. (For a fuller description see my chapter in this section.) America was changing. That the young country would change was inevitable given its conflicting values. "Liberty for all" and the preservation of "white privilege" had been on a collision course since the beginning. The only question was, Would the mid-twentieth century produce another civil clash akin to the one in the previous century?

AN URBAN FAULT LINE

In the mid-1960s Chicago was not the place to sustain oblivious bliss. It was located upon a major fault line of the shifting tectonic social plates. When I moved to the urban campus of Moody Bible Institute in the summer of 1966, the city was riveted by another recent migrant. Dr. Martin Luther King Jr., fresh from the long-fought civil rights victories of the South, was taking his quest north. If I was even aware of the national and local news being made just a few miles away, it hardly affected my life. While located in the heart of the city and just blocks from the infamous African-American Cabrini-Green housing project, Moody's campus was a white island that reinforced much of the religious and cultural isolation of my rearing.

Although Chicago was one of the major theaters upon which the drama of social change was playing in the 1960s, it was certainly not the only one. Change was sweeping the country. While citizen clashes in cities like Chicago, Detroit, Birmingham, and Selma were captured by the media, real societal changes were being negotiated in Washington, D.C.'s corridors of power. National legislation extended democracy to everyone through civil rights, voting, and open housing laws. Restrictive immigration laws,[1] rooted just as securely as was slavery by our founding fathers,[2] were finally liberalized by Congress in 1965,[3] ensuring that the "huddled masses yearning to breathe free" would now include non-Europeans and non-whites.

The resistant status quo citizens (whose forefathers had been those huddled masses from Europe) had, themselves, drunk richly from the land of milk and honey due primarily to legislative advantages put into effect in the foundational years of the new country. But the myth they had spun, and indeed believed, was that the sole reason for their success was that they and their forefathers had worked harder, saved more, and earned every bit of their place of privilege in the land of opportunity. And, as such, they did not welcome others—especially others they perceived as so different from and inferior to themselves.

The tides of change cannot be held back for long. By the same token, however, legalizing entry to the playing field is not the same as leveling it. Change can be a slow, nearly imperceptible process where you awaken one day to see a new landscape. Time has had an impact on America and who is an American. In the forty years since the social legislation of the 1960s, many changes have brought significant leveling. While it is possible to find communities as racially isolated as the one I was reared in, they are fewer and fewer. My chapter gives a detailed account of the historical developments of the racial and cultural diversity evolving this country into a mosaic of the people groups of the world. Demographers tell us that by the middle of this century the combined total of minorities will surpass the Anglo aggregate.[4] Diversity is an unmistakable reality today and will only increase in its prominence.

Perhaps, like me, you have noticed this reality. Throughout our children's school years, with the generosity of friends our family traveled out of Chicago to a little getaway spot on a lake several hours northeast of the city in Michigan. The nearby small town reminded me of my "white bread" youth with no minorities in sight. Black friends we took with us—children and adults—received stares from the locals as if they had emerged from a flying saucer. But twenty-five years later all that has changed. Black folks now reside there, and their numbers visibly increase each time we visit. Our current getaway spot in the woods is several hours west of Chicago outside a small town about the size of the one I grew up in. However, Mexican restaurants are springing up on Main Street and bilingual servers are now needed at McDonald's. Not fifteen minutes away is De Pue, Illinois, with a mostly Hispanic population.

Christians have spread throughout the globe with an evangelistic zeal to reach the 10/40 Window, but the record at home is much more subdued and segregated. While today more church leaders are looking at it critically, the Homogeneous Unit Principle, promoted by Donald McGavran and C. Peter Wagner,[5] became doctrinaire, core church-growth strategy of the 1980s and 1990s. Megachurches promoted numerical church growth as the measure of success by embracing the values of reaching out to "our kind." In this way the baby-boomer generation embraced a sanctified rationale that resulted in churches almost as segregated as those of previous generations.

RACIALLY CHANGING CHURCHES

However, a new wind is blowing, and the chapters in this section reflect a new embracing of diversity and racial reconciliation in the church. Pastors Dan Gute and Winfred Neely share their church stories in the racially changing southern suburbs of Chicago. To the far west of the city another dynamic of a multicultural community presents other challenges. These churches are not cookie-cutter models to be franchised everywhere. Rather they represent real-life efforts carried out by Christ-followers attempting to break down social barriers.

Additional hope should be gleaned from the fact that such efforts are springing up in communities everywhere. Fifteen years ago, biblical racial reconciliation was a foreign concept to most. When Raleigh Washington and I wrote *Breaking Down Walls* it was the first time Moody Press had published a book on the concept. Other evangelical publishers were no different. But a slow, building tide embracing biblical reconciliation and diversity began to emerge around that time. While the movement has not exploded into a tsunami, neither has it retreated. Young emerging church leaders are raising up churches with reconciliation as core theological values.

Racial awareness is extending into mainstream evangelicalism as well. The Willow Creek Association (WCA), formulated upon the successful principles and practices of the megachurch Willow Creek Community Church (Barrington, IL), is demonstrating a remarkable embrace of diversity and biblical social justice. The highpoint of WCA's year is its annual leadership conference, which is broadcast via satellite across the globe and viewed by millions. The intentional cultural/racial inclusiveness, starkly absent several years ago, cannot be missed by the most casual or even disinterested attendee. WCA now boasts a membership of around 20,000 churches, many of whom "catch a cold, if Willow sneezes." The long-term impact of this awakening should not be underestimated, especially when combined with the missions effort, P.E.A.C.E, of Rick Warren and Saddleback Church in California.[6]

Movement is breaking out institutionally as well. Minnesota was known for the PBS comedy radio show *The Prairie Home Companion* and "Sven and Ollie" jokes. Historically the Twin Cities area understood racial reconciliation to be when Swedes and Norwegians could drink coffee from the same pot. Today minorities are migrating to the area and several Christian organizations are reflecting this change. Bethel University, located in the Minneapolis suburb of Arden Hills, has created a college major in racial reconciliation. Another institution of Scandinavian heritage, the Evangelical Free Church of America, changed its mission statement to read, "We exist to glorify God by multiplying churches among all people".[7] Buttressing the statement is a major "biblical diversity" initiative under the direction of the denominational president's office. Such intentionality is showing results. The largest number of new church plants of the EFCA is now in minority communities—a stark contrast to just a few years ago. That this once "whitest of white" conservative group is embracing diversity is of no small note.

Something is afoot.

Chapters in this section, indeed this entire book, are not meant to be an expert's guide. Each author would tell you he or she is building the car while traveling down the road. There are no experts, only fellow explorers. Our guide is the Holy Spirit; our map, the Scriptures. Our steps are faltering and tentative. But we are moving. We welcome the reader to this path and the contribution you are making and will make to this high calling.

GLEN KEHREIN, along with his wife, Lonni, and family, have lived on Chicago's West Side since the early 1970s when they founded Circle Urban Ministries (www.circleurban.org). Glen and Lonni's journey has taught them principles of racial reconciliation, urban ministry, and redemption. Other writings of Glen's can be found in *Restoring Communities at Risk*, *A Heart for the City*, and *Breaking Down Walls*.

CHAPTER 18

THE TIMES THEY ARE A-CHANGING:

The Suburbanization of Poverty

Glen Kehrein

The line it is drawn
The curse it is cast
The slow one now
Will later be fast
As the present now
Will later be past
The order is
Rapidly fadin'.
And the first one now
Will later be last
For the times they are a-changin'.
—*Bob Dylan, 1963*

Introduction: Way Down South in the Land of Cotton

Change was brewing in the placid midpoint of the twentieth century. It is always brewing, often overlooked or unanticipated. In the postwar era many Americans drew security from the booming economy and the gathering superpower status of their country. This thin veneer, captured by *Leave It to Beaver*, an iconic American television situational comedy depicting an idealized American family, was about to show its first cracks in 1955.

Few took notice on a December afternoon in 1955 when a recent seminary graduate and newly appointed pastor accepted a position with an obscure grass-roots group called the Mississippi Improvement Association. Yet the Montgomery, Alabama, bus boycott drew energy from the arrest of a diminutive, yet courageous, Negro seamstress who failed to yield her bus seat. From this humble beginning the Civil Rights Movement, festering since the deconstruction of Reconstruction, was to finally force America to live up to its creed of liberty for all.

Another massive change involving the same people group of disenfranchised Americans was also firmly afoot. After centuries of conscripted labor, African-Americans were no longer a necessary labor force in the Southern agrarian economy. The mechanical cotton picker could do the work of fifty field hands, rendering the sharecropper all but obsolete by the end of the Second World War. Millions looked anew to the industrial jobs created in the North, beginning what was to be called "The Great Migration." Nicholas Lemann explains,

> *Black Americans moved from the South to the North; five million of them moved after 1940, during the time of the mechanization of cotton farming. In 1970, when the migration ended, black America was only half Southern, and less than a quarter rural; "urban" had become a euphemism for "black." The black migration was one of the largest and most rapid mass internal movements of people in history—perhaps the greatest not caused by immediate threat of execution or starvation.[1]*

One would be hard pressed to overstate the social significance of this demographic shift, yet few Northern leaders seemed to understand until the realities were upon them. Rare and unheeded warnings and questions came from David Cohn in 1948:

> *The coming problem of agricultural displacement in the Delta and the whole South is of huge proportions and must concern the entire nation. . . . Five million people will be removed from the land within the next few years. They must go somewhere. But where? They must do something. But what? They must be housed. But where is the housing? . . . How will they be industrially absorbed?*
>
> *. . . There are other issues involved here of an even greater gravity. If tens of thousands of Southern Negroes descend upon communities totally unprepared for them psychologically and industrially, what will the effect be upon race relations in the United States? Will the Negro problem be transferred from the South to other parts of the nation who have hitherto been concerned with it only as carping critics of the South? Will the victims of farm mechanizations become the victims of race conflict?*

There is an enormous tragedy in the making unless the United States acts, and acts promptly, upon a problem that affects millions of people and the whole social structure of the nation.[2]

The "where?" of course, became Northern industrialized cities and, indeed, racial conflict followed. Charles Silberman, writing in 1963, observed, "White Northerners have been able to persuade themselves that racism is a peculiarly Southern phenomenon in part, at least, because their contacts with Negroes have been infrequent and casual."[3] Racial conflict north of the Mason-Dixon Line should not have come as a surprise. Even French social observer Alexis de Tocqueville, while enthralled with the young democracy more than 150 years ago, found slavery and racism contradictory to the ideals of the young country.

I see that in a certain portion of the territory of the United States at the present day the legal barrier which separated the two races is galling away, but not that which exists in the manners of the country; slavery recedes, but the prejudice to which it has given birth is immovable. Whoever has inhabited the United States must have perceived that in those parts of the Union in which the Negroes are no longer slaves they have in no wise drawn nearer to the whites. On the contrary, the prejudice of race appears to be stronger in the states that have abolished slavery than in those where it still exists; and nowhere is it so intolerant as in those states where servitude has never been known.[4]

WHITE BY INTENT AND PURPOSE

Previously, urban slum existence in the United States had been a temporary socioeconomical state of the immigrant poor. Chicago socialite Jane Addams found purpose in life in providing "uplift" to the "huddled masses yearning to breathe free" through the settlement house movement begun at her now famous Hull House. In a generation or two, an uneducated, illiterate immigrant family transitioned from generations of historic poverty in the old country into the burgeoning middle class in the young land of opportunity.

Drawn together by family, culture, language, and tradition, Euro-ethnic groups consolidated into neighborhoods. By the early twentieth century, every major Northern city had become a miniature Europe, complete with Little Italy, Germantown, Little Warsaw, Greek Town, and the like. That these communities were of European descent, and not Korea Town, Little Japan, or Little Mexico, was not a happenstance. The "whiteness" or Euro-American-ness had been the plan since the country's founding, institutionalized through the power of immigration and naturalization as expressed by the "Father of the constitution," James Madison:

> *When we are considering the advantages that may result from an easy mode of naturalization, we ought also to consider the cautions necessary to guard against abuse. It is no doubt very desirable that we should hold out as many inducements as possible for the worthy part of mankind to come and settle amongst us, and throw their fortunes into a common lot with ours. But why is this desirable? Not merely to swell the catalogue of people. No, sir, it is to increase the wealth and strength of the community; and those who acquire the rights of citizenship, without adding to the strength or wealth of the community are not the people we are in want of.[5]*

The young country had expansive goals with vast lands that needed settlement. However, the settlers were to remain a strictly controlled white majority with the entitlement of U.S. citizenship limited to whites and codified by legislation to establish the uniform naturalization rule. Madison's concerns were heeded when citizenship was withheld from anyone who was not white in the 1790 Naturalization Act:

> *That any alien, being a free white person, who shall have resided within the limits and under the jurisdiction of the United States for the term of two years, may be admitted to become a citizen thereof, on application to any common law court of record, in any one of the States wherein he shall have resided for the term of one year at least . . .[6]*

In the 150 years that followed the Naturalization Act, the United States spread from sea to shining sea and European immigrants poured into the country to drink from the intoxicating brew of capitalism. More than 600,000 people responded to newspaperman Horace Greeley's call to go West to take advantage of the Homestead Act's offer of 160 acres of free land. To qualify for the giveaway all one needed was to be the head of a family, at least twenty-one years of age, a citizen or expecting to become one, and not have taken arms against the Union. Lacking citizenship, non-whites "need not apply." Like the failed hope of "Forty Acres and a Mule," distribution of capital was denied to non-whites. Signed into law by President Lincoln in 1862, eventually 1.6 million families were granted 270 million acres (10 percent of all of the land in the United States).

Growth and Conflict at the Hub of Little Europe

Expansionism brought growth to all of the industrial cities, but none more dramatically than Chicago, which was ideally located to serve as the young nation's transportation and manufacturing hub.

> Chicago was also, many people thought, the most typically American of the nation's big cities, a scene of boiling economic activity and technological ingenuity, American industrialism's supreme urban creation. In an unreservedly commercial country, it was, visiting novelist Frank Norris described of late-nineteenth-century Chicago: "All around, on every side in every direction, the vast machinery of Commonwealth clashed and thundered from dawn to dark and from dark till dawn. . . . Here, of all her cities, throbbed the true life—the true power and spirit of America." Chicago was "the only great city in the world to which all its citizens have come for the one common, avowed object of making money."[7]

Capital investment spurred development in every direction, even across Lake Michigan. Chicago was a city with jobs where hard work could produce stock in the American dream. After digging the Illinois and Michigan canals, the Irish settled southwest of downtown in Bridgeport, the Germans (Chicago's largest ethnic group) settled along Milwaukee Avenue to the northwest, and Little Italy was carved out of the Near West Side. The creation of the "Chicago bungalow" and "two flats" sprang up in every direction. When public transportation, notably the famous "el" (elevated) train expanded, like spokes of a wheel, outward from "The Loop," more and more immigrants, and then their successive generations, filled in the open spaces.

Tight, ethnically based communities grew and thrived with the times. Successive generations created more Chicago neighborhoods out of the prairie sod, growing increasingly ethnically mixed. The exception to this was the black residents. Chicago's very first resident, a fur trader, Jean Baptiste Pointe du Sable, was of African and French descent (circa 1780). However, blacks numbered only about 30,000 of a total population of 1.7 million at the turn of the twentieth century. The end of World War I brought a wave of African-American job seekers that doubled that population. The Great Depression, however, slowed the growth to a trickle through the 1930s.

If an article had even appeared in the *Chicago Tribune* on October 2, 1944, about an event four miles south of Clarksdale, Mississippi, it is doubtful that even one Chicago West Sider or South Sider would have bothered a glance. Yet the events of that day on the Hopson plantation were to change—some would say displace—life for nearly every one of them. The hullabaloo was over the first public demonstration of a working, production-ready model of the mechanical cotton picker. For millions of Southern blacks the machine was to break the bond

301

of working the soil that had existed for generations. Within a few short years a wave of African-Americans headed to Chicago and eventually into those Irish, German, Italian, Polish, and Ukrainian neighborhoods.

One thing made their journey to the "promised land" more perilous than any other immigrant group before them—their race. No other single group engendered the corporate guile as did the children of the immigrants from Africa. Sure enough, each European group experienced vile prejudices from the ones previously established. The most notably extreme treatment was visited upon the Irish. The deep-seated feelings were rooted back home:

> *Eighteenth-century Ireland presents a classic case of racial oppression. Catholics there were known as native Irish, Celts, or Gaels (as well as "Papists" and other equally derogatory names), rather than a nation. The Penal Laws imposed upon them a caste status out of which no Catholic, no matter how wealthy, could escape. The racial and class hierarchy was enforced by the Dissenters, who were mostly Presbyterian farmers, mechanics, and small tradesmen, descendants of soldiers settled by Cromwell and Scots settled later in Ulster.[8]*

While Irish "white" skin afforded them immigrant and naturalization status as defined by the act of 1790, old prejudices were not about to die away, especially in a country run by the WASP establishment. In the early years Irish were frequently referred to as a "nigger turned inside out";[9] the Negroes, for their part, were sometimes called "smoked Irish."[10] According to a popular quip of the day a Negro said, "My master is a great tyrant. He treats me as bad as if I was a common Irishman."[11] Irish were portrayed with ape-like features in political cartoons, and help-wanted ads routinely included the subtext, "Irish need not apply."

Yet in a generation or two, "the unwashed" assimilated into the mainstream "melting pot."[12] In Chicago the Irish eventually took over city hall and the public establishment and operated the famous Regular Democratic Party (i.e., "The Chicago Machine"), now on its second rendition under Richard M. Daley, son of its modern founder. Nationally, the Irish reached prominence when Joseph Kennedy, former banker, whiskey runner during Prohibition, and ambassador to England, accomplished the impossible by getting his son, an Irish Catholic, elected President of the United States. The Irish had become white.

When JFK was still the junior senator from Massachusetts, it was obvious that despite what was happening in "the Beaver's neighborhood," "the times, they were a-changing." Passage on the Illinois Central Railroad was accessible and cheap. In only a day's trip the whole world changed for black rural Southerners who had never seen snow or lived outside the reach of Jim Crow. Chicago, indeed, must have seemed to be a promised land. But, like the biblical land with which many black religious persons drew affinity, this promised land was occupied. There were no longer swamps to drain or prairies to tame; the pie had been cut, and re-cut and parceled and subdivided. Homes were built, neighborhoods created, churches established, lives being lived out. While the Irish might have previously assimilated, these Americans, despite their heritage in America of five, six, or seven generations, hit a stone wall of resistance to integration of any form.

Resistance to blacks moving into white communities preceded a wholesale exodus, often referred to as "white flight," and resulted in the transformation of most major cities. Until the 1940s black Chicagoans were largely confined to the "Black Belt," a narrow strip of land on the South Side and the Near West Side that had been an immigrant entry slum. But that was about to change. In the next twenty years nearly one million blacks made Chicago their home. At first, the only housing to be had was in the old, deteriorated slums long worn out by generations of immigrants. But even the old slums did not have nearly the capacity required. The *Chicago Defender* wrote, "In the past we have had occasion to protest holdup rents for ramshackle hovels. Today, however, there are no broken down hovels to be had at any price."[13]

The Birth of Suburbs

Returning war veterans added to the housing pressure; soon the market responded with new construction and the birth of modern suburbia. In the first fifteen years after the end of World War II, 688,222 new homes were built in the Chicago metropolitan area, located either in the suburbs or the farthest reaches of the city.[14]

The other building boom taking place was over at the Chicago Housing Authority, part of a federal initiative to clean slum housing and build thousands of units meant to offer short-term housing. However, soon "the projects" became part of the corporate city strategy to contain the burgeoning black population. Construction continued at a rapid pace through the 1950s and into the 1960s. Decisions about site locations for public housing clearly revealed a plan to segregate poor blacks entirely. Massive projects such as the Robert Taylor Homes on the South Side became vertical ghettos stretching for blocks and blocks, creating the largest public housing project in the world. Eventually the CHA tenant roster ballooned to 142,000, larger than all Illinois cities except two. Yet that total was not even 20 percent of the black census.

Ethnic hostilities born in the old countries and nurtured in the new gave way to a type of melting-pot solidarity of racial territorialism. There was a unified effort to contain the black inhabitants within the expanding South and West

Side ghettos. Amanda Seligman, professor of history and urban studies at the University of Wisconsin-Milwaukee and author of *Block by Block: Neighborhoods and Public Policy on Chicago's West Side,* said that during the 1950s and 1960s many whites tried to discourage black newcomers by gathering in mobs at black homes and organizing white solidarity movements. "Finally, when none of those strategies worked, they removed themselves from the neighborhoods," Seligman said of the white West Siders.[15]

While it was obvious that blacks needed to live somewhere, nobody wanted them to live next door. As though created through some grand scheme—but in reality merely reflecting common racial values—every aspect of the social structure conspired to resist the expanding black community.

> *The African-American in-migrants clustered into ghettos. Some cities maintained the segregation by imposing zoning requirements on the size and quality of dwellings or by forcing blacks to get permission to move in from the whites in the area. Where legal impediments did not exist, whites founded improvement associations and protective leagues that drew up race-restrictive covenants and made gentlemen's agreements. Government leaders and the courts countenanced the obstructions in the name of peace, order, and private property rights.*
>
> *When covenants and agreements failed to maintain racial separation, whites used violence to keep blacks out. No northern city seemed able to escape racial tension. In New York City, numerous conflicts occurred over housing in suburban sections. Chicago saw the most extensive violence, including one of the most destructive race riots in the nation's history.[16]*

While growth of the black population could not be stopped, some measure of control was accomplished. Real-estate brokers, who stood to gain significant commissions, steered black buyers and renters to the fringes of the black communities. White panic could be ignited when one black family crossed the invisible barrier into "our neighborhood." Soon homes went on the market and white flight was on. This story was repeated hundreds of thousands of times across the West and South Sides of Chicago as well as all Northern cities.

Nothing Remains the Same

Perhaps I was, and yet may remain, completely naive to consider the church as a positive force for racial progress. Is it foolish to believe that the teachings of Jesus might be relevant to one of the most recalcitrant of human struggles? Most Americans have no memory of the Great Migration and think of Northern African-American ghettos as demographically stagnant. Suburban whites often think of minorities as living "in there" somewhere, deep in the recesses of the inner city.

Yet "nothing is more dynamic than change." If Yogi Berra didn't say that, he could have.

The push and pull of human movement has been a constant reality in this country and particularly in our urban centers. Past legal constraints designed to limit the opportunities have been lifted. A succession of Fair Housing Laws and Presidential Executive Orders beginning in the 1960s reduced active segregation by offering minorities some measure of recourse against housing discrimination. Blacks and Hispanics began to experience housing choices denied to previous generations. Economic and social advancement meant that more and more minorities could now follow the same path as other Americans. Middle-class minorities began to migrate out of the cities, leaving larger and larger concentrations of what sociologists began to call the permanent underclass.

Old patterns of white flight seem to persist even when property values are not threatened. When African-Americans expanded into Chicago's southern middle-class suburbs, race was still the deciding motivator of white flight.

Like many of its south suburban neighbors, Country Club Hills became home to hundreds of new minority residents during the 1980s. But unlike Riverdale, Country Club Hills saw little increase in its poor, dispelling the notion that where there are blacks and Latinos, there is poverty.

In 1980, Country Club Hills was 11.9 percent African-American. By 1990, it was 57 percent black. Meanwhile, whites have left in droves. The white population dropped from 11,980, or 85.7 percent of the population in 1980, to 5,881, or 38.1 percent in 1990.[17]

URBAN DEVELOPMENT

The highest concentration of the underclass was in large public housing projects. But those communities are disappearing and displacing most of their residents. The U.S. Department of Housing and Urban Development (HUD), under heavy criticism for warehousing people in socially irresponsible housing conditions, declared large-scale low-income housing projects to be abject failures and encouraged local housing authorities to tear down housing projects. By the end of 2009, all fifty-three of Chicago's public housing high-rises will be gone, uprooting forty thousand people.[18] "Mixed housing," a blend of subsidized and market-rate housing, became the Federal housing strategy. However, far fewer units were constructed for low-income residents than were displaced. New Orleans, pre-Katrina, serves up an example of the national trend.

> *In 2002 in New Orleans, after the St. Thomas project was demolished, only 9 percent of the units in the redevelopment were affordable to the people who used to live there, even though the community was originally promised that half the new units would be affordable, according to a report by Brod Bagert, Jr., the son of a prominent New Orleans lawyer and politician who wrote his master's thesis for the London School of Economics on the issue.[19]*

> *Over the past few years Congress has eliminated several important rights held by public housing residents. For instance, there used to be a law that for every public housing unit demolished, another unit had to be built. This was known as the one-for-one replacement housing requirement and was repealed by the 1995 Rescission Act. On the Section 8 side, tenants were traditionally entitled to renew their leases so long as they complied with them. Now, however, Section 8 landlords may evict tenants without cause at the end of their lease terms. Some protections remain, but in many areas Congress is ceding policy-making authority to local PHAs.[20]*

The reduction of public housing units pushed the poor to find housing elsewhere. However, with affordable units at a premium and almost none being created in the cities, a predictable out-migration of minorities is the result. Where are they going? Everywhere—from the cities of moderate size, to older suburban communities and even into small towns where older, smaller housing is moderately affordable.

Other market forces are fueling this out-migration as well. Gentrification (the return of people of means to the city) took root in the 1970s with the emergence of a new breed of city dwellers—the yuppies (young urban professionals), many of whom were also DINKs (double income, no kids). First seen as an aberration, gentrification has become a movement that grew in the '80s and took off in the '90s. Today nearly every major city is experiencing redevelopment of inner-city communities.

Chicago, always proud of its vibrant downtown, did not rest upon its laurels; rather it fueled the movement by making its "Loop" (downtown) more inviting. Chicago's park system had always been a point of pride, but today the restored Navy Pier and Millennium Park bring millions of visitors. City inducements have spawned hundreds of new eateries, shops, and even museums and theaters that make downtown Chicago one of the most attractive cities for urban residents.

Not only are new combination office/residential towers being built within the Loop, residential development is booming in every direction outward. Old industrial warehouses turn into loft apartments, and long neglected "brownstones" and "Victorians" are reclaimed. Formerly seedy parts of Chicago are becoming "yuppiedom," and in the process turning once tax delinquent property back to the tax rolls at many times the previous value. A returning tax base could not be better news for city hall, as Mayor Richard M. Daley signaled in 1993 when he himself moved from his childhood home in the Irish bastion of Bridgeport to the new Central Station development on the Near South Side. With Central Station, developers have transformed the once-vacant railroad land near the city's center into a middle- and upper-middle-class gated community of homes.

Much of this new development ventures into low-income communities where properties can be purchased cheaply, rehabbed into modern residences, and "flipped" for a handsome profit. No longer is the development contained to the fringes of the Loop. A trip west on Madison Avenue, a street devastated by riots following Dr. Martin Luther King Jr.'s murder, reveals brand-new $350,000 condos being constructed five miles from the Loop. Displaced rental residents and low-income owners who cannot afford property tax increases are joining the pursuit of affordable housing outside the city.

IMPACT OF CURRENT IMMIGRATION TRENDS

Just as few cities considered the net impact of the technological advances in the cotton industry, few gave much thought to Immigration and Nationality Act amendments of 1965. America's citizenry, engineered by immigration quotas since its founding, was 89 percent Euro-American and 10 percent African-American in 1965. Nineteen sixty-five changed that course dramatically.

The largest demographic shift has, obviously, been Hispanic. Large gateway cities continue to attract immigrant numbers into their inner cities as they have for generations, but the city is no longer the only port of entry.

> *To begin with, the great Latino gateways—Los Angeles, New York, Miami, and Chicago—will continue to house massive concentrations of Hispanics. Yet even so, the growth rates that slowed in these vast metros in the 1990s are not likely to pick up and may slow even further. Of course, this in no way means the Latino population will necessarily stabilize in those cities. Rather, the great mainstays may be seeing a continued influx of new arrivals and a simultaneous outflow of Latinos leaving in search of better jobs, housing, and quality of life in other destinations.*
> *Meanwhile, the move to the suburban fringes will surely continue as*

growth slows in already crowded central cities. Family composition and gender data as well as other indicators suggest that suburbs, particularly those on the periphery of these great gateways, are themselves becoming ports of entry where immigrants settle without ever having stopped in the old urban barrios. Then, too, Latino families in search of the classic American suburban dream are also moving to the outskirts where housing is cheaper. Accordingly, more and more Latinos will be flocking to the suburbs in the coming decades.[21]

Just as in the city, suburban communities consistently experience white flight and significant demographic shifting. Immediately to the west of Chicago's boundary sits suburban Cicero, established by Czechs, Poles, and Italians who vehemently and even violently prevented black infiltration for decades and even attracted the attention of Dr. Martin Luther King Jr. when he was crusading for open housing laws. In a negotiated settlement brought on by civil rights lawsuits, the town of Cicero accepted a Fair Housing Resolution. The Hispanic community, however, was the group ready to take advantage of the opportunity. Classic white flight followed. According to U.S. Census figures, the Mexican-origin population exploded from 9 percent in 1980 to 37 percent in 1990 and 77 percent in 2000. Without a doubt the next census will reveal whites to be in single digits.

Hispanics (and other immigrant groups) are no longer following the standard path of previous generations. The city is no longer seen as the only port of entry and immigrants are as likely to relocate to a small town or suburb as to a large city center. Many of us are caught unaware today. A long-time resident walks into the local Wal-Mart and is shocked by the racial diversity. Most white people react with visceral discomfort and begin to question their future. "Can I be comfortable here anymore?" or "Is this still my neighborhood?" While overt racism has certainly been reduced, this discomfort is the same basis that has always fueled white flight.

CONCLUSION: DOES CHRIST MAKE A DIFFERENCE?

While the previous description has been quite clinical, I have experienced racial change up front and personally. While I was beginning to study the dynamics I have described, God called my wife and me to move into the racially changing Austin community on Chicago's West Side in 1973. White exodus was in full bloom with 75 percent of the homes for sale. It seemed to us that the "salt and light" impact of the body of Christ had been missing from the equation. What position did Christians take when they attended the meetings of the local "improvement committee" and heard the vile racial attacks? How did "worldly" talk about property values square with "spiritual" talk of loving your neighbor? Did it make any difference whatsoever that Christians lived in those communities? Was their perspective any different from that of their neighbors? Were they hearing sermons that would bring Christ's perspective?

In short, the resounding answer to these questions is no. Not one of the twenty-seven evangelical churches survived the racial change. Some relocated (to fields "white unto harvest" one might cynically inquire?); others just closed. None adapted.

Are the 1960s and 1970s ancient history, or might the church and its parishioners learn from our past?

Anecdotal information provides contradictory evidence. One church in my denomination recently moved for the fourth time—twice in Chicago, then to a south Chicago suburb, and finally to Indiana! Yet another church—a megachurch locating in an inner-ring, ethnically changing suburb of Minneapolis—has done the opposite. The highly respected senior pastor has made it his mission (and led the church to adopt the same) to understand how to become a relevant faith community welcoming and serving the newly arriving neighbors.

Another sign of hope is the opportunity these changes bring to break down barriers of race, class, and geography. Will ethnically changing suburban communities cause churches to see dealing with minorities as a local issue and no longer just "in there"? Will their needs cause the urban and suburban ministries to partner for the purpose of sharing resources, knowledge, and mission strategy?

Another sign of hope is that emerging postmodern church leaders, while some of their theology has been questioned, have a clear upside advantage in this arena. They are much less shackled by overt historic racism. Multiculturalism, racial reconciliation, and diversity are finding expression in the creation of "New Wineskin" churches and networks of churches encouraging the body of Christ to reflect the world we are to reach.

But this chapter of the church amidst demographic change is just now being written. You and I have the great opportunity to contribute to it by learning from the realities and mistakes of the past.

REFLECTION QUESTIONS

1. Have you studied the history of your city or town and community? How is history unfolding today?

2. What is happening around you demographically? Is the ethnic makeup changing in your community or city? With whom could you engage to become better informed?

3. Does your church reflect the ethnic/racial makeup of your city or town? If not, why do you think that is so?

4. Is your congregation talking about the changes happening in your city or town? Is it preparing for change? What is the likely future?

WINFRED NEELY is Professor of Pastoral Studies at the
Moody Bible Institute, and Church Planting Pastor of Living
Hope Community Church in South Holland, Illinois. He holds
the Doctor of Ministry degree from Trinity Evangelical Divinity
School, Deerfield, Illinois, and degrees from Wheaton College
Graduate School and Trinity International University.

CHAPTER 19

SEIZING THE MOMENT:

Churches in Racially Changing Communities

Winfred Neely

Introduction: Growing Up in Chicago

I grew up on the South Side of Chicago. My family lived in the Ida B. Wells housing project and I went to Doolittle Elementary School, across the street. We lived in Ida B. Wells until the middle of my sixth-grade year, when every middle-class and working-class African-American family moved out of the projects to greener social and cultural pastures on the South Side of the city. My proud and industrious parents purchased a three-flat building. The year was 1965.

My new community was largely white. My new sixth-grade teacher at Cook Elementary School was white, and most of the students in my class were white. I made friends with white children. My next-door neighbors were white, and I remember leaning across the fence, having warm and pleasant conversations with them, but I had no idea that under the calm surface of neighborly civility strong undercurrents of racial fears raged. Within the space of about two-and-a-half years the Auburn Gresham neighborhood was virtually all black.

In the middle of my freshman year at Calumet High School, Daddy came down with kidney disease, and was no longer able to work or maintain the building. Since he worked for the railroad, he had a good insurance policy with health benefits. Daddy also managed money extremely well. So my parents sold the building and purchased a home further east on the South Side of Chicago. Our new address was in the idyllic community of Calumet Heights. Calumet Heights was quiet. African-American doctors, lawyers, teachers, judges, and other professional and working-class people lived in the community. During the summer children and teenagers hung out at Stony Island Park. The upscale Pill Hill was about five blocks away. The year was 1969 and Calumet Heights was about 60 percent African-American. In the space of about two years that community was virtually all black.

I lived through racial transition in two communities growing up in Chicago. At the time I did not give much thought to the implications of racial change in a neighborhood, and the role of the church in such communities did not even register as a blip on the radar screen of my mind. In my teenage mind, the church was the most irrelevant factor in the equation of racial change in a neighborhood. Indeed, the church was a part of the problem and often the first institution to leave the changing community!

As an adult I did not think I would be swimming again in the choppy waters of racial transition in a community, but that is precisely where I am today. I am an ordained minister of the Christian and Missionary Alliance. The Midwest District of the C&MA had an Alliance church in South Holland, Illinois. The struggling church was gasping for breath. The district leadership decided to close the church and plant another church in the village. My wife and I are the church planting couple. In August 2002, Stephne and I moved to South Holland to plant Living Hope Community Church. Much of what is communicated in this chapter has been gleaned during my last five years of church planting work in South Holland, and refined during my doctoral work at Trinity Evangelical Divinity School.

DÉJÀ VU: ANOTHER WAKE-UP CALL

The pastor's words stunned me: "Every Reformed church in South Holland is in crisis."[1] The crisis is not doctrinal or theological per se. All of the Reformed churches in the village are orthodox and sound in teaching for the most part. The crisis in these churches is rooted and growing in the sociological soil of racial transition. Middle-class and upper-middle-class African-Americans are moving into the village, and white people are moving out.[2] Many members of some of the historic churches have moved away from the vicinity of their church buildings. On Sunday morning there is a strange dynamic going on. Numerous white people, who no longer live in the village, drive into it to attend worship services at their respective church buildings.[3] But this has resulted in the internal, structural weakening of the historic churches in the area. A good number of the members of these churches moved to other communities and joined churches that are more racially and culturally congenial. These factors, combined with the historic churches' inability to biblically and creatively engage the emerging community,

314

has resulted in a sociological crisis in the Reformed churches and other predominantly white churches in the area.

The crisis is doubly sad in view of South Holland's history. South Holland is one of the southern suburbs of Chicago. The Dutch settled and incorporated South Holland in 1846. In the village, they built Reformed churches and schools and lived out the implications of the gospel of Christ in business and social life. The Underground Railroad passed through South Holland. South Holland was in essence a Dutch Reformed Christian community, and even today the Reformed legacy is felt in the village: the sale of alcohol is prohibited in South Holland and most businesses are closed on Sunday in honor of the Lord's Day. But 162 years after its founding, South Holland is in the process of racial transition. Today the residents are 75 percent African-American and their presence is continually on the rise. At the time of writing, we are witnessing the consequences of a sociological crisis in the Reformed and historic churches in South Holland.

I live in South Holland, and I love the people and the place, and I cherish our Reformed legacy. South Holland is a wonderful town, but the Reformed and historic churches' inability or lack of will to deal creatively and biblically with racial transition is troubling.

Walter Ziegenhals was the head and founder of the Churches in Transition Project in Chicago, born in the heat of the massive racial changes that took place in Chicago during the 1960s and 1970s. The purpose of the Project was to assure the presence of viable United Churches of Christ in African-American and Latino communities in Chicago.[4] Ziegenhals understands the range of problems associated with ministry practice in a racially transitioning community.

> *A congregation in a community facing or undergoing racial transition is confronted with a complex of problems. Normally, these include such factors as aging and declining membership; a diminishing financial base; insufficient or inadequate leadership; racial fears (as well as ethnic, cultural, and class fears); movement of the membership away from the church building; inability to understand the interrelation between the community's fate and the church's future; estrangement from new neighbors . . . and difficulty in defining the mission of the church beyond meeting the needs of the present membership.[5]*

If local churches in transitioning neighborhoods and towns like South Holland are going to impact their communities, they must move from maintenance mode to mission mode and relate the Great Commission to the emerging community. There must be a shift from the first gear of racial, cultural, and class fears[6] to the fifth gear of creative, missional engagement. Sociological shifts in transitioning communities require radical adjustments and fresh contextualized thinking in the way local churches in these neighborhoods do ministry, express worship, and strategize to win the lost.

THE BIBLICAL PERSPECTIVE

When a church adapts its strategy and methods to its current cultural environment, that church is acting in a biblical manner. Paul adapted his preaching and his evangelistic strategies to connect with the culture that he was trying to reach. For example, in Acts 13, Paul's preaching context was a synagogue. Before he was asked to speak, portions of Scripture from the Law and the Prophets were read. In all likelihood, Paul drew the contents of his sermon from these texts.[7] His listeners, Jews and Godfearers, were familiar with the Old Testament. Paul therefore made his case for the Messiahship of the Lord Jesus by using historical narration of facts from the Old Testament that reached their fulfillment and climax in Christ.

In Acts 17, Paul preached in essence the same message, but his approach was different. Here his context was the Areopagus, and his listeners were pagan polytheists who like to think and discuss new ideas. He built a bridge from where they were to the gospel. The people of Athens were not familiar with the Old Testament, nor did they consider it to be a final authority in the matters of religion and philosophy. Therefore, in this message, Paul quoted pagan poets whose insights were consistent with biblical revelation in order to communicate to the Athenians the good news about Christ. Paul's overriding concern was not to do anything that would hinder the gospel. Of course, in the church Paul would open up the Scriptures and expound and preach God's Word regardless of who his listeners were, but in his evangelistic efforts he was willing to use different approaches, depending on the culture and the context. He summed up his evangelistic approach by saying, "I have become all things to all men so that by all possible means I might save some. I do all this for the sake of the gospel, that I may share in its blessings" (1 Cor. 9:22–23).

Paul exhorted the young churches to follow his example in this regard. He says:

> *So whether you eat or drink or whatever you do, do it all for the glory of God. Do not cause anyone to stumble, whether Jews, Greeks or the church of God—even as I try to please everybody in every way. For I am not seeking my own good but the good of the many, so that they may be saved. Follow my example, as I follow the example of Christ. (1 Cor. 10:31–11:1)*

When a local church refuses to adapt to its current environment in order to win the lost to Christ, when a local body of believers refuses to become all things to all people in order to share in the blessings of the gospel in its ministry context, she is being disobedient to Christ or is uninformed about her role in that community. Millard Erickson eloquently writes:

> *The church must be versatile and flexible in adjusting its methods and procedures to the changing situation of the world in which it finds itself. It must go where needy persons are to be found, even if that means geographical or cultural change. It must not cling to all of its old ways. As the world to which it is trying to minister changes, the church will adapts its ministry accordingly, but without altering its direction.[8]*

In doing this the church is actually modeling itself after the Lord Jesus. Erickson comes to the same conclusion:

> *As the church adapts, it will be emulating its Lord, who did not hesitate to come to earth to redeem humanity. In doing so, he took on the conditions of the human race (Phil. 2:5–8). In similar fashion the body of Christ will preserve the basic message with which it has been entrusted, and continue to fulfill the major functions of its task, but will make all legitimate changes which are necessary in order to carry out its Lord's purposes. . . . If the church has a sense of mission like that of its Lord . . . it will find ways to reach people wherever they are.[9]*

FAILURE TO RISE TO THE OCCASION

Churches, however, struggle with adapting to their environment in transitioning communities. Jones and Wilson have no illusions about the difficulty involved in this adjustment. They note, "As a residential area of a city changes, a church located therein will have to change its programs if it is going to minister effectively to a heterogeneous constituency."[10]

Given the difficulty involved, and the small chances of success, it ought not be surprising that some churches in changing communities never make the sociological adjustments, and consequently die. For example, several churches in South Holland have disbanded and sold their properties—these churches have died. Jones and Wilson comment on the death of some churches:

> *There are some churches that cannot possibly continue to exist. They slipped past the point of no return before they realized or accepted the gravity of their situation, or after considering all alternatives they realized that*

317

sociological changes and a weakened internal church structure precluded the continuing ministry of the congregation. . . . Some churches will die because they did not plan, and other churches will plan the dissolution of the congregation and turn their assets over to the denomination to be used to establish new congregations. . . . They will thank God for the privilege of serving together in the days gone by and will go forward in faith and hope that out of the ashes on the old church will rise the foundations for another church in another place.[11]

Dying with dignity and raising foundations in another place for a new congregation is one solution for a church in a transitional community. Other solutions are: (1) die a lingering and often painful death; (2) choose to die suddenly; (3) choose to merge with another congregation; or (4) sell the property and relocate to another neighborhood or nearby state that is more congenial in culture, race, or class. All of the above solutions, with the exception of the fourth one, lead to death in one way or another.

What is disturbing about the above solutions is how deeply rooted they are in the perspective of those who are leaving the community. Charles Chaney insightfully observes:

Most of the published rhetoric and philosophy on transitional communities and churches is focused on the people who are leaving, not on those who are arriving. Communities are described according to the classical sociological categories. They move from new development stage to the post-transitional stage. The life cycle of institutions is applied to churches and collated with the stages of community development. The whole picture is one of decline and deterioration and decay, moving inevitably toward death. This is all true from the point of view of the long-term resident. But from the perspective of the new residents, the community is one of hope, not despair. They are moving to better homes, leaving less desirable conditions.[12]

Despair for those who are moving out and hope for those who are moving in. The emerging community is hopeful. Churches in transitioning communities, and those who are planting churches in those communities, must look at the sociological situation mainly from the perspective of the emerging community. In this connection, Allen and Bullard offered a keen perspective about the core issue:

The post-transitional stage . . . can be the newly developing stage of a community in disguise. The cycle of the community stages begins again, and new patterns of relating . . . are established. . . . This is the real opportunity for the church in the changing community, i.e., the ability to perceive the new community which is emerging and to build the future band upon it.[13]

THE GREAT OPPORTUNITY

In light of Allen and Bullard's insight and in view of what has been discussed so far in this chapter, I propose the following: Instead of being a cause of despair, the transitioning community presents the church with an opportunity—an opportunity to renew and restructure existing churches or plant churches that can relate meaningfully to the sociological context and concerns of the emerging community.

The transitioning community presents the church with the opportunity to renew and restructure existing churches in view of missional engagement. Churches in transitioning communities need renewal. Cultural and class waters run deep in the soul of national American life. In order to overcome the entrenched hindrances of class, culture, and race in a transitioning community, the existing churches will need to experience renewal. Renewal is the work of the Spirit in restoring His people in an extraordinary way to normal Christianity, resulting in personal and collective reformation through the Word of God.

John Stott is helpful in further clarifying the scope of renewal:

> *Protestants use a different vocabulary to describe the continuously needed restoring and refreshing in the church. Our two favorite words are "reform," indicating the kind of reformation of faith and life according to Scripture which took place in the sixteenth century, and "revival," denoting an altogether supernatural visitation of a church or community by God, bringing conviction, repentance, confession, the conversion of sinners and the recovery of backsliders. "Reformation" usually stresses the power of the Word of God, and "revival" the power of the Spirit of God, in his work of restoring the church. Perhaps we should keep the word "renewal" to describe a movement which combines revival by God's Spirit with reformation by his Word. Since the Word is the Spirit's sword, there is bound to be something lopsided about contemplating either without the other.*[14]

Churches in transitioning communities are faced with their desperate need for renewal. Prayer and fasting, repentance, seeking the face of God, giving our wills to Christ, and obedience to the Bible are some of the steps that local churches earnestly pursuing Christ must take in order to experience renewal and have the consequent spiritual power necessary to effectively engage the emerging community.

These churches need to restructure themselves for missional engagement. It is easy to underestimate the power of church structures to promote or hinder the gospel of Christ. Yet it is obvious from history that structures play a huge role in the life of churches. For example, after the sixteenth-century Protestant Reformation, the Catholic Church planted churches across the globe. In fact, "The Roman Catholic Church, between 1500 and 1700, won more converts in the pagan world than it lost to Protestants in Europe."[15] Why were they so successful? One reason is the way that they were structured. At this time the Catholic Church had religious orders or missional structures that functioned as mission agencies for the papacy:

> As papal mission agencies . . . the various Religious Orders engaged ever more energetically in missions, and vied with one another in spreading the gospel. In the first place, the older missionary orders renewed their activities—the Franciscans and Dominicans, and also the Augustinians and Carmelites after their internal reform.[16]

Yet the Protestants who had truly recovered the gospel would not engage in world missions for another two hundred years! Of course, they misunderstood their responsibility to carry out the Great Commission, but there was also another problem. The Protestant churches of the Reformation had viable congregational structures, but they did not have missional structures. It was not until the nineteenth century, when Protestants had structured themselves for mission, that the power and vitality of Protestantism was released, resulting in the advance of Christ's Kingdom across the planet.

Ralph Winter's insights are helpful here:

> Organizationally speaking, however, the vehicle that allowed the Protestant movement to become vital was the structural development of the sodality,[17] which harvested the vital "voluntarism" latent in Protestantism, and surfaced in new mission agencies of all kinds, both at home and overseas.[18]

In short, instead of focusing only on their congregational life, renewed churches in transitioning communities must develop missionary structures that facilitate their missional engagement with the emerging community. They must organize church life in a way that helps instead of hinders mission involvement in the community. In a real sense, they have to take for granted that they are an ecclesiological and a missionary community, and that their community is a mission field, and act accordingly.

Stuart Murray notes, "Missionary communities do not structure themselves for maintenance . . . but to engage in mission. Their form is determined by the message they are wanting to incarnate, and by the context in which they are engaging in mission."[19] A renewed church, or a local congregation of people in the quest of promoting renewal, must understand their context. Making a diagnosis of the context and the issues in the community, the local church is then in a position to structure itself to engage in mission.

THE NEED FOR CHURCH PLANTING

The transitioning community presents the Church with the opportunity to plant churches that can relate the gospel of Christ meaningfully to the sociological context and concerns of the emerging community. Given the fact that many churches will not experience renewal, tap into Christ's power, and make the structural adjustments necessary to engage in mission in transitioning communities, one way to seize the opportunity is to plant churches that can creatively engage the emerging community. It would be foolish for church leaders, church planters, and other concerned parties to bury their heads in the sands of a maintenance mind-set, while the winds of sociological change are blowing all around us. No, we must seize the moment for Christ and His Kingdom! Planting a new kind of church is one way to advance the cause of Christ in a transitioning community. Stuart Murray goes right to the heart of the matter.

> *Church planting is not about just establishing more churches. . . .*
> *Allowing this to become the preoccupation of the church planters or*
> *denominational strategists would be a serious mistake. Church planting*
> *is an opportunity for theological reflection and renewal, for asking radical*
> *questions about the nature of the church and its task in contemporary*
> *society, and for the developing of new kinds of churches. New churches are*
> *needed, not only to bring the Christian community closer to where people*
> *are geographically, but closer to where they are culturally, sociologically, and*
> *spiritually.[20]*

Who takes the lead in this matter of church planting in transitioning communities? Leadership may come from denominational leaders who have a heart for the community in question. If one of their churches is in the changing community, instead of selling the property, they can close the old church and use its building to plant a new church that is able to affirm long-time residents and also reach out to new people who are moving into the community. That solves the problem of finding a building. The big issue is finding the church planter. The church planter and the community must fit. Denominational leaders should look for a church planter who is able to relate to the people of the emerging community. Ideally, church planting should be a team effort.

Churches in another community may desire to birth a church in the area. Perhaps some of their people live in the community or nearby, and desire to plant a church in the area. The mother church will provide the church planting team, a core group of people, and financial support for several years. Also, based on a thorough diagnosis of the community, 501(c)(3) ministry arms may be developed in order to reach out and minister to the needs of the whole person. The mission is to redeem the neighborhood as a whole, and not just a narrow spiritual slice of community life. Perhaps relationships can be built with people in some of the historic churches and with believers who desire to stay in the community. Some of their churches are dying and some of their churches are relocating, but some of the members may decide that they are going to be a part of a church where they live, desiring to make a Kingdom difference in their community. People like this should be welcomed in the new church in the transitioning community. While the new church planting team is organizing itself to reach the emerging community, it must welcome all people in the community.

There are many ways to plant a church. It is good for church planters and those involved in the church planting effort to remember the words of Peter Wagner: "Each church planting endeavor carries its own set of circumstances that will help determine which method is best."[21]

Keep in mind that church planting is not a short-term effort. The church planter should commit to being a part of the effort for at least ten years. Steve Sjogren and Rob Lewin give the following counsel to church planters:

> Here's what we recommend: Put away all thoughts regarding leaving for ten years. Put it in your palm pilot for ten years from this month: reevaluate my commitment to this city. That's what I (Steve) did. Then years later I saw that note and laughed. I was spending so much time serving the people of the city that all I could do was chuckle at the ridiculousness of leaving. Why ten years instead of three? Ten years might as well be forever.[22]

In at-risk transitioning communities, a minimum commitment of fifteen years is the norm. Longevity is key in successful church-planting efforts.

CONCLUSION: CHURCH PLANTING IS EXHAUSTING WORK!

Planting a church is one of the most physically and spiritually exhausting things that a person can do. You will feel exhausted mentally and physically, and there will be times when the temptation to quit will be almost unbearable! Do not quit. Make a commitment to the people and place. Persevere. There is no microwave approach to maturity in Christ. It takes time to build a church and establish credibility in a community. A commitment to stay will give you a long-term perspective on the ministry. Over time you will have the benefit of longevity in one place.

A word needs to be said about the attempt to plant regional churches in transitioning communities. Some churches are not willing to make the missional adjustments required to win the lost, so they attempt to become a regional church. A regional church draws its membership from a wide area, but does not focus on the community. This is a poor substitute for carrying out the Great Commission.

There are sociological reasons for planting churches. When existing churches in changing communities are not able or not willing to make the required cultural and sociological adjustment to win the emerging community to Christ, then it is time for new kinds of churches to be planted, churches that relate to where people are culturally and socially.

Although there is no formula for renewing or planting new churches in transitioning communities, the principles are clear: (1) We are responsible to carry out the Great Commission where we live (Matt. 28:19–20); (2) God calls us to become all things to all people in order to win them to Christ (1 Cor. 9:19–23); (3) longevity adds stability and long-range perspective to ministry efforts; (4) divine power and enablement is necessary for missional impact in the community (Acts 1:8; 4:33; 6:8); (5) success is measured in the number of lives transformed by the gospel (Acts 2:41; 4:4; 6:7; 9:31, 42; 10:44–48; 11:19–26); (6) success is counted in redeemed people used of God to transform the places where they live (Isa. 49:8; 58:12; 61:1–4; Zech. 8:5); and (7) prayer is the most powerful means of grace and Kingdom advancement at the disposal of every follower of Christ (Acts 2:42; 4:24–31; 6:4, 12:5; Eph. 6:18–20; Col. 4:2–4; James 5:16–18)!

It is my hope and expectation that the twenty-first century will see more prayerful, creative, and thoughtful engagement of the church of Christ in racially changing communities.

REFLECTION QUESTIONS

1. Historically, Protestant churches have not done well in racially changing communities. Why do you think this is true?

2. What would the Lord Jesus want from a local church that finds herself in the midst of a cultural and racial transition in a suburban community like South Holland? Be specific and concrete.

3. What is it about church planting that makes it such hard work? Why is longevity in church planting ministry important?

4. What are the practical implications of 1 Corinthians 9:19–23 for the ministry of your church in your racially changing community?

Recommended Reading List

Barna, George. *The Power of Vision*. Ventura, Calif.: Regal, 1992.

———. *Turning Vision into Action*. Ventura, Calif.: Regal, 1996.

Coleman, Robert E. *The Master Plan of Evangelism*. Grand Rapids. Mich.: Revell, 1963.

Francis, Hozell C. *Church Planting in the African-American Context*. Grand Rapids: Zondervan, 1999.

Gordon, Wayne with Randall Frame. *Real Hope in Chicago*. Grand Rapids: Zondervan, 1995.

Murray, Stuart. *Church Planting: Laying Foundations*. Stottsdale, Pa.: Herald Press, 2001.

Neely, Winfred O. *Church Planting in a Racially Changing Community*. Deerfield, Ill.: Published Doctor of Ministry Project, 2005.

Rainer, Thom. *Effective Evangelistic Churches*. Nashville: Broadman and Holman, 1996.

———. *High Expectations*. Nashville: Broadman and Holman, 1999.

Robinson, Martin, and Dwight Smith. *Invading Secular Space*. Grand Rapids: Monarch Books, 2003.

Sjogren, Steve, and Rob Lewin. *Community of Kindness: A Refreshing New Approach to Planting and Growing a Church*. Ventura: Regal, 2003.

Stetzer, Edward. *Planting New Churches in a Postmodern Age*. Nashville: Broadman and Holman, 2003.

Towns, Elmer, C. Peter Wagner, and Thom S. Rainer. *The Everychurch Guide to Growth*. Nashville: Broadman and Holman, 1998.

Wagner, C. Peter. *Church Planting for a Greater Harvest*. Ventura: Regal, 1984.

Winter, Ralph. *The Two Structures of God's Redemptive Mission*. South Pasadena: William Carey Library, 1974.

ALVIN BIBBS has a Master of Arts Degree in Christian leadership development from Fuller Theological Seminary. He is the Executive Director of Multi-Cultural Church Relations for the Willow Creek Association in South Barrington, Illinois. He is assisting the WCA in developing a more ethnically diverse movement in order to serve prevailing churches around the country. His role has special emphases geared toward the values of radical compassion, racial reconciliation, social justice, and leadership development for the sake of the Church.

CHAPTER 20

MOBILIZING THE SUBURBAN CHURCH:

Moving Toward a Lifestyle of Compassion

Alvin C. Bibbs Sr.

Introduction: Setting the Stage

n 1996, God placed a unique call upon my life to *Head west, young man.* For some leaders, heading west might mean traveling to beautiful sunny Southern California. However, for me it meant traveling about forty-five minutes northwest—outside of the city limits of Chicago. So much for the palm trees, sandy beaches, and hanging out with a few Hollywood stars.

The assignment that God placed in front of me was challenging, exciting, and frightening. However, I sensed that God was truly up to something special that I could not ignore or simply dismiss. That something special was accepting an invitation to join the staff of Willow Creek Community Church in South Barrington, Illinois. Willow, after many years of intense evangelistic ministry, felt it was time to aggressively step outside of its *culture* and *comfort zone* to build relationships with families that were facing tremendous social inequalities.

The majority of these groups were living below the poverty level within the United States and other parts of the world. At this point in Willow's history there was not a clear path or full-blown strategy in place to reach beyond the comforts of the highly resourced northwest suburbs of Chicago. So, with the support of an incredible team of staff members and a handful of unpaid staff volunteers, we aggressively moved forward to build a mobilization infrastructure that could stand the test of time.

The purpose of this chapter is to share some very important principles to support you and your team members in mobilizing a suburban church for cross-cultural compassion and social justice ministry. God's Kingdom is expanded as His people steward their time, spiritual gifts, and material resources into His service.

Too often we have placed labels on the poor or even the marginalized in our society. Historically, it has been an "us" and "them" dialogue versus a "them" and "all of us" dialogue.

WHY MOBILIZE VOLUNTEERS?

The first thing that needs to happen before a church attempts to mobilize volunteers is to be clear on the mission. Tell the church why it is important. I discovered the power of mission early on in my tenure at Willow. One of our mission statements that God laid upon our hearts was "To extend as servants into under-resourced communities so that local churches and ministries can be empowered to transform lives for Christ."

It did not take long for this mission statement to find a home within the core fabric of the Willow Creek Community Church culture. It was fascinating to watch regular attenders and members get really excited about the focus and intentionality of this mission statement. They sensed a major shift in how the church senior leadership viewed life outside the walls of Willow.

Perhaps you are wondering, *So, what is at the heart of this mission statement, and what makes it so powerful?* The answer to that question would be the notion to "extend." It is very clear within the Scriptures (the Great Commission, Matt. 28:18–20) that we are to go and make disciples of all people. In addition, in Isaiah 58:6–9, we are asked rhetorically whether God's call is

> *to loose the chains of injustice and untie the cords of the yoke, to set the oppressed free and break every yoke? Is it not to share your food with the hungry and to provide the poor wanderer with shelter—when you see the naked to clothe him, and not to turn away from your own flesh and blood? Then your light will break forth like the dawn, and your healing will quickly appear; then your righteousness will go before you, and the glory of the Lord will be your rear guard. Then you will call, and the Lord will answer; you will cry for help, and he will say: Here am I.*

Throughout Scripture, God calls His followers to move toward and relieve the suffering of the hurting, those with few resources, and the least of these (Matt. 25:40). We clearly learn of God's passion for the oppressed in Isaiah 58. Furthermore, God is promising to heal and be ever so present to those individuals and communities of people who obey this call to extend compassion.

That is why the notion of extension is a nonnegotiable from a Christian perspective. We need to assist members from a local church to understand that it is not just about a leader up front telling them how and why they should extend God's love to the hurting in society. It is the Word of God reminding them of their Christian responsibilities when it comes to compassion and social disparities in the land.

Principles

Here are the main themes for close attention when mobilizing a suburban church into holistic acts of compassion. The most important message of all is to obey God. Therefore:

1. God calls us to do good. (Gal. 6:2)

2. God expects His followers to consistently serve the hurting and poor. (Matt. 25:40)

3. God reveals His transforming power as we serve the hurting and poor. (2 Cor. 4:7; 13:4)

4. Volunteers experience God's presence as they develop relationships with the hurting and poor. (2 Cor. 12:9)

5. God promises to protect and provide for those who serve the hurting and the poor. (Isa. 58:6–8)

6. God deliberately designed each one of us uniquely for His Kingdom purposes. (Eph. 2:10; Isa. 43:21)

Here's a story of one volunteer who obeyed God's call upon his life to serve at a homeless shelter on our church campus in partnership with PADS (Public Action to Deliver Shelter):

> *A staff member asked me to serve as a volunteer leader. At first, I didn't see myself capable or desirous of leading this ministry. It didn't take long for God to show how He was going to help and guide me in this role. That was all the confirmation I needed.*
>
> *God changed my life as I helped people going through difficult times. For probably the first time in my life, I have really felt that I am serving where God wants me.*
>
> *Hearing about and watching the way God changes the lives of our guests and volunteers makes me feel so passionate about this ministry.*

> *I am fortunate to have a job that allows me flexibility. I usually can meet with volunteers or staff at their convenience and come into our site any hour it is open.*

What a tremendous gift to watch God transform one life right before our eyes—here is a leader who did not catch the vision at first, but out of obedience received a greater gift in blessing others.

Remember that in order to successfully mobilize a suburban church into holistic acts of compassion, an integrated platform must link *people, process,* and potential ministry *partners.*

People

The people who are serving on behalf of your organization deserve to know as much as possible about the various groups they will eventually be serving. Keeping the volunteers in the dark limits effective serving experiences. Take the extra time to highlight some of the key players involved in the serving experience. This could happen in a number of different ways. For example, put together a short video vignette of a community leader from the neighborhood where the volunteers will serve. Or, invite another pastor to speak at one of your church services or churchwide ministry functions where a cross section of your members might be present. Help your volunteers envision the people they will be serving before the actual event takes place.

Process

Second is *process*. A colleague who managed the internal volunteer operations at Willow and I spent hours traveling together, discussing how the internal and external systems around our church worked in order to navigate effective serving experiences within and beyond our church walls. We exchanged notes along the way and discovered the similarities in our ministries to serve volunteers within the organization.

We came to realize that if a local church did not have a solid on-ramp for potential volunteers to serve, the likelihood of them serving probably was not that great. We owe it to the volunteers to know how our processes and systems work, and to communicate that well. Every church must have in place a sound, comprehensive system to eliminate confusion and frustrations for volunteers before and after any serving experience.

Partners

Third would be the identification and selection process of ministry *partners.*

Collaborating with like-minded leaders and organizations is not as easy as you might think. Unfortunately, for many generations churches across North America have stumbled in a mighty way in this area. For that reason, I would strongly recommend that every leader take as much time as necessary in identifying and selecting partners for your church to invest in long term. In identifying potential partners, the first assignment for you is to revisit your desired mission and vision for your church.

The reality is quite simple: there is a lot of need in the world, but unfortunately your church cannot eradicate it all. The worst thing your church can do is to try to do too much and leave the entire church and its leaders wounded. When that happens, those to whom it has promised ministry are also left with broken promises and unmet needs, and less trust for the church. To avoid that happening, put together a plan of action that aligns with your mission and vision. That will make life a whole lot easier for everyone involved, especially those who will be eventually representing your church out in the field. In selecting potential partners, assess their overall ability to absorb volunteers effectively and ensure that their mission objectives and values align with the ones that you have in place for your church.

Of course, we can't overlook all of the administrative needs, liabilities, and logistics affiliated with serving and partnership. For that reason, pray that God would send the best leader with the ideal gift mix to lead and navigate these very important functions on behalf of your church.

WHAT ARE YOU MOBILIZING THEM TO DO?

Frequently, within suburban church settings, we confuse church members with mixed messages related to *blessing* and *serving* the poor. We often communicate from our pulpits that we are fully devoted to the needs of the poor, and then as a follow-up we give a different message from the pulpit. It goes something like this: "We have discovered in recent weeks that our church is not positioned financially to reach beyond our church walls to establish relationships with under-resourced communities as originally planned. We are going to need additional time to figure out the best organizational strategy before we can move forward effectively."

That message has damaged far too many hearts of those sitting in the pews on Sunday morning. The tragedy of the preceding statement is that often the suburban church mind-set has only been focused on financial resources versus the spiritual transformation of its members through points of engagement with poor families, communities, and leaders.

By no means am I suggesting that the financial assistance is not important, because it is. However, what about the heart, soul, and spiritual awakening and transformation that occurs within the life of the volunteer? Managing church-wide expectations is a huge part of the process. Here are a few important questions that every suburban church should ask internally before venturing out beyond the church walls:

1. What is the *ultimate goal* that your church has in mind when it comes to mobilizing volunteers?

2. Is this mission to serve the poor embedded in your *church's strategic plan*?

3. Do you have a *system* in place to mobilize volunteers into under-resourced neighborhoods?

4. Have you *equipped or trained* your members to the point that they are prepared for this type of venture?

5. Are you at a place organizationally to hire full- or even part-time *employees* to facilitate this cross-cultural ministry?

6. What *percentage of your congregation* do you truly expect to be involved?

7. Is this an *intergenerational* serving ministry?

8. Have you studied the *legal liabilities* affiliated with a ministry to serve the poor?

9. How will your church members respond to the social justice conversations they will encounter out in the field? Are you ready for that as a church?

10. Has this vision been covered in prayer?

These are just a few examples of what a suburban church should be wrestling with before serving the poor. That is why it is critical that suburban churches go through a process of educating, equipping, exposing, engaging, and then enlisting massive numbers of volunteers to serve in marginalized communities on behalf of their local church.

Educating

Educating your church members happens every weekend from the pulpit. The value of serving, and the church being mobilized into society and the world, is a biblical mandate that every church should embrace. This does not need to happen every weekend; however, an intentional effort must be visible in order for the value to stick! Get creative in your sermon series and embed the value through dramas and other forms of art.

Equipping

Other training venues throughout the year can look at equipping your people—including your adult ministries, student ministries, small groups, and new members' class. The teaching platforms are endless within any church setting if positioned effectively.

Exposing

Exposing church staff and key influencers from your congregation to ministries and communities where potential investment will be made is one of the best tactical strategies senior leadership from a suburban church can make. This, of course, takes all of the guesswork away from future conversations that could hinder progress in mobilization plans. Exposed, well-informed leaders can make God-honoring decisions about the organizations or the people with whom they will eventually cultivate partnerships.

Engaging

Engaging ethnic leaders in their ministry environment sends a huge message of just how serious your church and leadership team is about pursuing a mutually edifying relationship with them.

These are great moments to do life together and grow in relationship and understanding about a given community. Eventually what begins to transpire is a comfort level by suburban leaders in trusting the direction and wisdom of the ethnic leader.

This is not as simple as it sounds. Suburban leaders are accustomed to being the ones in control and making all of the decisions. Now, in some regards, the roles have reversed. Relational connections are one of the most important endeavors for any church that is prayerfully considering serving beyond its walls in a sustainable way.

Duane Elmer quotes the late Paul Hiebert on the significance of interpersonal relationships: "No task is more important in the first years of ministry in a new culture than building of trusting relationships with the people."

ENLISTING VOLUNTEERS

Enlisting volunteers is only as difficult as you make it. Some suburban churches are still not sure of the best processes and systems to have in place when putting the call out for servants. In some cases, not only is the system and structure broken, but leaders are not really sure how things will work once the volunteers arrive at their serving destination. This is absolutely unacceptable because it could place the volunteers in some very uncomfortable situations. We must have done our research.

The opportunities for volunteers are unlimited and will pay huge Kingdom dividends. The final section will bring to light a few expected outcomes from their serving investment.

GIVING IT ALL BACK TO GOD

In the end, all service is given to God. Truly our ultimate goal is to give glory and honor to God through our acts of compassion. In the process, four expected outcomes occur: first, the outcome for the Kingdom of God; second, for your church; third, for those who receive; and fourth, for the volunteer.

God's Kingdom is expanded as people steward their time, spiritual gifts, and material resources toward initiatives to ease the suffering of people who have tremendous needs. Through that process God is pleased by our collective efforts and looks down on us with joy and satisfaction knowing that we care.

For the bride of Christ, the Church, things are not business as usual any longer. The compassion gauge within your church culture continues to move aggressively to the right. Regular attenders and members within your church cannot wait for the next serving initiative. There is a level of fulfillment that was not present in previous years. Through this process, more churchwide ministries become active in serving the poor and hurting than ever before in the history of your church. The intergenerational connections are fluid without the previous barriers. Children and junior high school students are engaged on a very high level serving alongside their peers. As this process unfolds, give God the praise He so deserves.

For those who receive, service brings joy and thanksgiving that the ministries and people connected with them feel with them. For years they have despaired in underdeveloped communities. Then God, in all of His wisdom and power, gave a vision to a pastor, and through that pastor inspired a congregation to get off the pews and move toward the lonely and suffering to make a difference for Him. That is the power of God at work. By the Holy Spirit's power working through sinful people, lives and communities are transformed.

Volunteers continue to serve and move ever closer to a lifestyle of compassion that says, "Serving the poor in my backyard, down the street, in the city, or even a few thousand miles away from home is a priority in my life." They say to themselves, "If God so loved the world that He sent His only Son into the world to die for us, then it should be a nonnegotiable for us to at least leave this world in better shape than the way we found it."

CONCLUSION: TRANSFORMED BY COMPASSION

When volunteers make a positive difference in the lives of people served, most often the people who serve are the most transformed by their compassion experiences. The exposure to a new culture, a new environment, and new people and places draws people out of their own experiences and paradigms. Volunteers often leave ministry experiences having a new perspective and a changed idea of what it means to minister. More often than not, churches and volunteers are the students, and the poor, or those in need, are the teachers and guides.

REFLECTION QUESTIONS

1. Are you and/or your church/ministry aware of marginalized people in your city or town? Who are they, and what are their needs?

2. Are other churches and ministries in your area reaching out to the marginalized? What are they doing? How can you help?

3. Are you personally ministering to the marginalized? Can you do more?

TONY DANHELKA is an ordained minister and a co-founder of Riverwoods Christian Center in St. Charles, Illinois. He and his wife, Donna, moved to the Fox River Valley in 1976 to begin and develop the mission of Riverwoods. They have one son, Anthony David, known to many as TJ. Tony's heart is to partner with local Fox River Valley churches to come together across cultural and denominational lines in unity to better address efforts of strategic prayer, caring through community development, and sharing the Good News of Jesus Christ.

CHAPTER 21

URBAN ISSUES IN SUBURBAN TOWNS?
Poverty Among Luxury
Tony Danhelka

Introduction: The Luxurious Fox River Valley

A simple thirty-five-mile drive directly west from the heart of Chicago's lakefront is a collar community known to locals as the Fox River Valley. It is a series of large and small towns nestled in along the banks of the Fox River, which flows southward from the northern Illinois border toward the Illinois River. The area has been targeted for luxury housing, recreation, shopping, biking, boating, fishing, and resorts of many kinds for nearly 150 years.

Two of the largest cities in Illinois sit as twins of the western flank of Chicagoland. Elgin, to the north, with a city limits population of just over 100,000 people,[1] and Aurora, with about 175,000 people,[2] to the south. The railroads came from Chicago to these two cities in the 1800s. Before long these small resort villages grew into industrial giants with many of the same issues as their dominating sister city of Chicago.

The Elgin Watch Company popularized Elgin throughout the world.

Elgin was founded in 1864, right as the civil war was coming to an end. The first watch Elgin made, an 18 sized B W Raymond railroad grade watch, was finished in 1867 and over the next 100 years, they went on to produce about 60 million watches. Elgin produced their first wristwatch around 1910, leading most other American watch companies by many years. Elgin was originally called the "National Watch Company." The name never really stuck and in 1874, they changed their name to the "Elgin National Watch Company" because most of the watch trade and public were calling them "watches from Elgin." They kept that name until the late 1960s when they stopped producing watches and changed their name to the "Elgin National Industries."[3]

Aurora became known as the "City of Lights" in the late 1800s due to its being one of the first cities with electric streetlights throughout.

Joseph McCarty, a pioneer from New York State, came west seeking a new home. Reaching the Fox Valley, he built the first campfire in April of 1834 on the island, which is now the site of downtown Aurora. He thought that the Fox River location was an ideal place for a new community and told his brother, Samuel. It was not long before Samuel arrived, family was sent for, and a permanent settlement was taking roots. The settlement was named McCarty Mills for the brothers' grist mill and sawmill. In 1837, when a Post Office was established, the village became Aurora, goddess of the dawn. Later, when the City was the first in the United States to use electric lights for publicly lighting the entire City, it achieved the nickname of "City of Lights."[4]

Many people view the luxurious Fox River Valley as the "Golden Corridor." You can take an expressway thirty-five miles out of Chicago and get off at any of the Elgin exits and travel south, parallel to the banks of the Fox River, and see luxury homes, shopping centers, bike paths, beautiful quaint villages with seasonal festivals that draw hundreds of thousands of tourists, and your pick of seemingly every imaginable restaurant.

Yet a more careful drive through the Fox River Valley reveals more than fifteen economically stressed housing communities and residential areas, most of which are tucked away in hidden corners. In these communities live more than 40,000 people,[5] which include 16,500 children living below the federal standards of poverty.[6] Many ministries focus on poverty in the megacities like Chicago. God burdened our hearts with the needy in the adjoining Fox River Valley.

THE CHALLENGE BEGINS

In 1965, a youth minister called me into his office. I was two years out of high school and a relatively new convert to Christianity. The Bible had become very important in my life. I had discovered hundreds of passages of Scripture that demonstrated God's bent for the poor and needy.[7] We were discussing what has become my life verse, 2 Chronicles 7:14. A pretty young lady (who later became my wife) came in to discuss something with the pastor. She was introduced to me as the president of the youth group. She turned to me and asked if I would be willing to join a group of college students who volunteered on Sundays during the summer helping to run a children's church at the Wayside Cross Rescue Mission in Aurora. She said that most of the children came from areas of poverty around Aurora.

I laughed in my mind, *Poverty in the Fox Valley? There couldn't be! This I have to see!* See I did. God touched my heart with a passion for these hidden youth and families of the Fox River Valley.

Over the next seven years I owned a business, was drafted into the army, and then began college. God used these experiences to continually burn into my heart the children I had met in Aurora. These youth became more than poverty-area statistics to me. Devontae, Pedro, Terrone, Annabel, LaMar, Antonio, Dante, and Destiny were real-life youth with often hidden potential.

During high school I was branded a "remedial student." All of my classes were with other remedial students. I was caught up in heavy alcohol abuse and hated school. Neighbors prayed and loved me into the Kingdom of God. Upon graduation, I was involved in an alcohol-related car accident in which I almost lost my life. I woke up in the hospital and prayed, "God, if You are out there like my neighbors say You are, I welcome You to forgive my many sins and I accept Jesus, Your Son, as my Savior."

The neighbors took me to their church, the Western Springs Baptist Church, the only church that Billy Graham ever pastored. Then I was drafted into the army and trained for Vietnam in Tiger Land boot camp in Fort Polk, Louisiana. Upon completion of the training, I received orders to report to Fort Sill in Oklahoma for "advanced nuclear weapons training."

I remember the commander at Fort Sill welcoming us. He told us we were hand-selected and if we got good grades in the training we would be stationed in Georgia or Europe. If not, we would be sent to Vietnam for our tour of duty. For the first time in my life I was motivated to learn. A few months later, after much study, I graduated from the training with excellent grades and was sent to a base in Germany. I thought to myself, *How many children in the Fox Valley poverty areas have been scripted as "remedial" and believed it as I did for so many years?* What if they had a caring community of Christian believers to build significant relationships with them, introduce them to an alternative life in Christ, and motivate them to learn? How many could break out of the cycle of poverty and be given a chance at developing their potential?

Mentor John Perkins

God blessed me with mentors along the way. He gave me people of great integrity who taught me and modeled for me how to love Jesus. Men like John Bauer, my first boss; Arthur Melvin, a dynamic businessman; Vic Cottrell, a college professor; and Bill Leslie, an inner-city pastor.

In the early 1970s, my wife and I took multiple trips down to Mendenhall, Mississippi. We wanted to learn firsthand about Dr. John Perkins and the Voice of Calvary ministries. We shadowed Dr. Perkins in and out of meetings for days, learning the ways he implemented what became known as "the 3 R's": Relocation, Reconciliation, and Redistribution. This was four years before his first book was released in 1976, *Let Justice Roll Down*. The Fox Valley housing communities seemed much different from rural Southern communities segregated into deplorable conditions. However, many of the issues were the same—low self-esteem, minimal education, prejudice, undeveloped job skills, and hopelessness.

Earning the Right to Be Heard

The Fox River Valley housing communities were ignored by most churches and sadly thought of by many believers as a necessary collection place for the "lazy and unlucky." Most people did not know they existed.

A question loomed for us: How do we earn the right to be heard among the youth and families living in these housing communities? We were not welcome to live there. A waiting list of thousands wanted to get into these projects from other larger cities, primarily Chicago. As we tagged along with John Perkins, we noticed that he would go out to a Christian camp from time to time. Not far from Mendenhall, in Pearl, Mississippi, was Camp Pioneer. It was directed at the time by one of the founders, Maurice Bingham.

We watched Dr. Perkins share the gospel of hope in Christ with the youth at the camp. We witnessed how he was earning the right to be heard in this Christian camp environment. We were very aware at the time of a Christian camp in the heart of the Fox River Valley that was interested in reorganization.

John Perkins came to us in 1975 and drove up and down the Fox Valley with my wife and me. We showed him the camp and talked about the desires of the two ownership groups to discuss launching a new ministry. Dr. Perkins was among the people who encouraged us to step out in faith and see where God would take us with this adventure.

Christian Camping

Most of 1975 was spent discussing the details about launching a new Fox River Valley ministry with the leaders from two Christian organizations that owned the property, Champ Boutwell from the Midwest Advent Christian Camp Meeting Association[8] and Paul Johannaber from the Wayside Cross Rescue Mission.[9] Together the two organizations owned eighty-five acres of forested land with eight hundred yards of frontage on the Fox River and twenty-seven buildings that were built in the 1930s. We talked about becoming a new Christian camping ministry with a heart for the youth and families in the impoverished areas around Aurora and Elgin.

Launching Riverwoods

My wife and I moved onto the camp property in August 1976. By March 1977 we worked through the details of beginning a new ministry. We officially launched Riverwoods Christian Center (www.RiverwoodsChristianCenter.org) on March 16, 1977, by signing the completed incorporation papers.

The early years were spent converting the old buildings into usable year-round facilities and identifying fifteen housing and residential areas in the Fox River Valley where the poorest of the poor lived. God blessed us by quickly sending us three one-year "interns," who raised their own support, and there was an already established part-time maintenance man on the property. An old, well-seasoned bus was donated to help us pick up the campers that first summer.

The managers and caseworkers in charge of the housing communities in the Fox River Valley welcomed us with open arms. It greatly helped that we were born out of the Wayside Cross Rescue Mission, which was well established as a caregiver to the needy. We recruited twenty-five teenagers and college students that first summer to become the counselors and staff. We agreed that all the campers would come from the most needy areas of Aurora and Elgin and that they would not pay anything to come to camp.

We provided the campers a week of canoeing, boating, nature walks, sports, games, great meals, and chapel times.

MEGACITY ISSUES IN SUBURBAN TOWNS

It did not take long for us to discover that these youth and their families were dealing with major issues of life at far too young an age. We met Aaron, Wilma, Bernard, Rose, Anthony, and so many more teens and parents facing issues like gangs, drugs, alcohol abuse, kids having kids, quick-tempered anger, many fatherless homes, and a lack of desire to attend school. A week of camp was good. It provided healthy meals, a new safe and clean environment in a camp setting, getting to know exciting counselors who had a living faith in Jesus Christ, and lots of fun activities. We built relationships and earned the right to be heard. By the end of the week campers were much more willing to listen to presentations of the gospel and encouragement to make lifestyle changes. Yet, we knew we had to do more than provide a week at camp for the youth.

We began to get to know the church pastors and congregations that were close to each of the communities we served. Many of them were small and under-resourced themselves. We knew we had to recruit and mobilize a caring Christian force of volunteers to work with our campers year-round. At first we set up "kids' clubs" in the nearby churches and schools with gyms. It became at least a weekly meeting place to continue speaking into the lives of the campers. They loved the night of games, Bible stories, treats, and getting to know the regular volunteers.

Informal Annual Needs Assessment Survey

The one-year interns and the maintenance man all became full-time staff in the first couple of years. John Perkins encouraged our young staff to do a basic survey each year of the "felt needs" of the residents in each of the areas we served. We went door-to-door asking a few questions:

1. What are your basic needs that are not being met?

2. Who are the people or groups in your community that are trying to help you meet these basic needs?

3. Do you attend any local church?

4. What are specific ways I could pray for your family and community?

The response was consistent. The greatest felt need of 80 percent of the parents or guardians was, "Help keep our children busy with productive activities and out of the gangs!" They were often unaware of anyone who wanted to help them with any of their needs. Most organizations expected them to go to their buildings and offices in the downtown areas of Aurora or Elgin. Transportation was a major problem for some, and language barriers for others.

Far too many of the parents would laugh at us and say things like, "So you want to help? We remember others who have come by to offer help, but after a few attempts they disappeared, and you will too."

The Birth of Advocacy

By the early 1980s, we realized we needed to go from a "camp with a heart for the youth in economically stressed areas" to a "camp that goes home with the campers!" We started praying for full-time, Christian social-worker-type youth ministers who would live in or near the areas we served. One of our original interns, Jessie Gottschall, became our first advocate. We decided that an advocate would work full-time year-round in one of our fifteen communities. A new advocate is often introduced to our children and families through our now extensive summer camp operation. Then the advocates network with churches around the community they serve. As they complete the door-to-door needs assessment, they start mobilizing a caring force to address felt needs.

In time the advocates realized they needed to place major emphases on the teen years. We could often motivate the younger children to attend our meetings, memorize Bible verses, attend church, pray, improve school grades, and better cooperate with their parents. However, when they hit their teen years and hormones started flowing through their bodies, far too many of them got caught up in the gangs, drugs, drive-by shootings, and early pregnancy. We pulled back on some of the community-wide and parental activities we were doing and focused time and energy on better supporting our teens.

Aaron first came to Riverwoods summer camp as a ten-year-old. He was a cooperative and enjoyable child. He wanted to learn and have fun. Three years later his attitude and behavior took a major change for the worse. He became angry, disruptive, and sharp with his words. His mom loved Jesus. They had moved from a neighborhood in Aurora to a housing community now called Jericho Circle. The gangs recruited Aaron, and he quickly became one of the enforcers. We had a relationship with Aaron, but he had become a tough guy. At the end of the school year a couple of our staff met with Aaron's mom and worked out a deal. With his mom's permission, our staff went to a gang meeting, picked up Aaron, and drove him out to Riverwoods for all eight weeks of the summer.

We watched his heart soften and he renewed his commitment to Christ near the end of the summer. He went home in late August and the gang rejected him without harm, claiming, "He got religion!" Aaron went on to graduate from high school, adopt his sister's child, marry, raise a family, become a deacon in his church, volunteer weekly with street teens, and become a Riverwoods board member. He was the first teen to go through an eight-week teen resident camp program with us. His adopted daughter, now in her teens, has recently enjoyed the highly developed "College Bound" eight-week program. The positive cycle continues.

The "College Bound" activities and resident training sessions in the summer have impacted the lives of many high school youth. We also developed a computer lab at our headquarters camp and brought in minority business people to teach these classes. Our advocates work specifically with parents and guardians on improving parenting skills before and during their youths' teen years as well.

COMMUNITY MINISTRY WITH A CHRISTIAN CAMP

As the number of advocates grew throughout the Aurora and Elgin communities, we came to the conclusion that Riverwoods was actually a community ministry that was uniquely headquartered in a dynamic Christian camp only thirty minutes away from any area we served. It was a significant paradigm shift for us, that camp could be a ministry base for more than camp. Through the years the camp facility demanded much attention in resources and upkeep. However, the heart of what we were doing was in the community.

It has been a hard adjustment for our donors and volunteers to make with us. It is easy to capture the profound impact a Christian camp can make on a young life. It is much harder for many people to capture the effectiveness and activities of an advocate working in the homes and schools of the youth and families we serve. The families we serve caught on very quickly, however. They love it when their very own Riverwoods advocate is part of their daily lives. Well, most of the time they love it! Tough love is a challenge for us all along the way.

PRAYER, CARE, AND SHARE: UNIFYING THE CHURCH

We have our great success stories, like Aaron, but also profound failures in working with our families. In 1995, Riverwoods began to experience a fresh wind of renewal spiritually. It started as a time of burnout and distress for some of us. In time, the Lord met us in our need and brought a fresh zeal to call our staff, donors, volunteers, and the communities to a renewed heart for prayer. As one of the founders of Riverwoods, I was led by that "still small voice" of Jesus to step out in greater acts of faith and obedience to invite the churches our advocates worked with to unite for prayer. We traveled to other communities in the United States and beyond and witnessed a similar move of the Holy Spirit calling local churches to unite under the headship of Christ to care for the hurting and share the eternal message of Good News in Jesus Christ. In fact, in Argentina we saw the spiritual atmosphere of a city the size of Aurora or Elgin that developed a much greater hunger for more of Jesus, and lived it out in caring for the needy and sharing their renewed faith in Christ.

My wife and I flew to San Nicholas, Argentina, in 1997. We were invited by the Harvest Evangelism team[10] to join 110 foreigners who flew in from ten countries for three weeks of training on city transformation. We spent mornings in training about how to unite pastors, strategically prayer walk a city, break into creative evangelism teams, and empower the needy. We went out into the community for witness and caring encounters during the afternoons. The first week saw little response. About one week into our meetings the majority of Protestant pastors from local congregations joined our morning training. Our leader, Ed Silvoso, invited them to repent of being divided by their secondary differences and forgive each other for not uniting in prayer, caring for the hurting, and sharing the gospel.

The Holy Spirit moved deeply in their hearts. The pastors asked for forgiveness one after another. They cried together, hugged each other, and expressed their need to unite. That afternoon we went to the same parks, street corners, and needy neighborhoods. But what a change from the community! People were suddenly open, positive, friendly, and very responsive to the gospel message and expressions of love. It was the most obvious transformation of the spiritual climate over a city that we had ever witnessed. We returned to the Fox River Valley with a renewed commitment to the strategic relationship between the earnest prayers of focused intercessors, unified repentance of church leadership, and the work of the Holy Spirit.

Welcoming and Sustaining the Holy Spirit

The Riverwoods board of directors took a bold step and approved the hiring of an executive director to take over the day-to-day activities. This freed me up to invest half of my time working with pastors and Christian businesspeople. The paramount question became, "How do we better welcome and sustain a greater move of the Holy Spirit over the Fox River Valley housing communities and region?" Our experiences in Argentina taught us that a major part of the answer was tied to an appropriate unifying of the local church in promoting unified prayer, caring for people's needs, and sharing the gospel. We read books on revival, fasting, intercession, and hearing the voice of God. When the churches unite to hear God's voice, there often is an explosion of the power of God.

The Joys of Fund-raising

Finances have been a big challenge through the years. The vision always seems greater than the apparent resources. What are the best ways of believing God for the people and financial resources to fund a ministry that serves the children and families living in economically stressed communities? During the founding years we prayerfully developed five ways of raising the necessary funds: We sent out direct mail appeals to our growing mailing list. We created events to cultivate donors, like an annual phonathon, summer concerts, a banquet with table hosts who invited new friends, and a spring golf outing. There were also foundation requests, and church and service club presentations that cast the vision of Riverwoods and helped with greater visibility. But greater than all of these are the *one-on-one visits* in prospects' homes or businesses.

About five years into the Riverwoods adventure, the board recruited a fund-raising consultant to come and evaluate our ability to raise $250,000 for a new building. After talking to our board of directors and staff individually, he said that we were not in a position to raise the money because all of the board members had different views of what was the primary mission of Riverwoods. Some saw it as a camp, some saw it as a community ministry, and some saw it as a retreat center. He challenged us to create a one-sentence mission statement that everyone agreed to and memorized. Then he challenged the board members (most of whom were not personal financial supporters of Riverwoods) to become major donors and recruit others to join them.

The consultant encouraged me to begin visiting ten to twenty families a month in their homes. He trained me to set up appointments with the husband and wife at their kitchen tables to tell the unique Riverwoods story, share the financial needs, and ask if they could help with a monthly gift over the next three years. It was amazing how many families were willing to meet with us. We now have a growing family of donors in each of the fifty states. Our excellent management team has a twenty-year plan and is able to annually set and hold to three-year and one-year goals and budgets.

TWELVE TRANSFERABLE PRINCIPLES

Many principles can be gleaned to better deal with the issues of poverty in the suburbs. Here are twelve that inspired me along the way:

1. God clearly reveals in the Bible His bent toward helping the poor.

2. Youth who grow up in economically stressed communities that are scripted as remedial non-achievers can be properly motivated to develop their God-given potential.

3. Identifying and developing positive mentors as role models is strategic to every human being's future success.

4. Many suburbs have hidden economically stressed housing communities and residential areas with all the "big city" issues of poverty, gangs, and drugs.

5. God is still calling believers to earn the right to be heard among people living in economically stressed areas by building intentional relationships and breaking away to safe environments like Christian camps.

6. A week in a Christian camping environment can often have major life-

changing transformation, both now and for eternity.

7. Community caregivers need to be diligent in recruiting and mobilizing a Christian caring force of volunteers.

8. A simple needs assessment survey is easy to administer and meets residents at their point of need.

9. Much additional focus and attention needs to be given to the turbulent teen years for lasting change.

10. The relationships established by an intentional long-term advocate is very important.

11. Unifying local pastors, ministry leaders, and businesspeople through repentance of differences and challenging them to come together for prayer, caring for the needy, and sharing the gospel welcomes and sustains a greater visitation of the Holy Spirit on a region and neighborhood.

12. Fund-raising is all about developing a unified compelling mission statement, developing relationships, and asking for the donation.

CONCLUSION: WORTH IT ALL

Riverwoods is alive and well addressing the needs of children, youth, and families from housing communities up and down the Fox River Valley. But far more than new construction at the headquarters camp, dynamic board leadership, a growing professional staff, and donors that are sacrificially committed to our mission are the lives of the people in the communities that have been affected along the way.

My ninety-two-year-old parents recently died of natural causes three months apart. The same Latino mortician, Rebecca, came to the home both times. The second time she came I had just arrived from Riverwoods wearing my Riverwoods shirt. As she walked into the home she noticed my shirt and asked, "Oh, do you know something about Riverwoods?" I confirmed that I was one of the founders thirty-plus years ago. She smiled and said that she was a Riverwoods camper from 1979, 1980, and 1981. She said that she lived in the Fox View Housing Project in Carpentersville at the time, which is one of the fifteen housing communities that we have served since 1977. She was able to quote the names of her counselors and others who influenced her life. There she stood, a successful career woman who overcame great odds. She said that Riverwoods was the one shining light in her childhood.

Yes, it has been exciting to watch hundreds of youth grow up in the weekly Riverwoods contacts. Some of them have disappeared and then resurfaced like Rebecca. Others have kept close contact with us. Either way we love to know that there are youth who are now in adulthood and are living positive lives compared to the generations on welfare before them.

REFLECTION QUESTIONS

1. Why are mentors important? Who are three people that God has used to positively influence your life?

2. Why are suburban welfare and section eight housing communities ignored by most churches and seen as regrettably necessary by many believers? Are you familiar with any low-income housing community within five miles of your home?

3. Did you ever attend a Christian residential summer camp during your childhood? What lasting memories do you have from camping? Why is Christian camping a unique way to earn the right to be heard with youth and families from economically stressed areas?

4. How can you best mobilize a "Christian caring force" in your neighborhood to welcome and sustain a greater move of the Holy Spirit to change the spiritual climate in the neighborhood you serve?

Recommended Reading List

Bright, Bill. *The Coming Revival.* Orlando: New Life Publications, 1995.

Griffin, Bob. *Firestorms of Revival.* Lake Mary, Fla.: Creation House, 2006.

Grubb, Norman. *Rees Howells: Intercessor.* Ft. Washington, Pa.: Christian Literature Crusade, 1952.

Hawthorne, Steve, and Graham Kendrick. *Prayer-Walking.* Lake Mary, Fla.: Charisma House, 1993.

Perkins, John. *Let Justice Roll Down.* Ventura, Calif.: Regal Books, 1976.

———. *Restoring At-Risk Communities.* Grand Rapids, Mich.: Baker, 1995.

Pier, Mac, and Katie Sweeting. *The Power of a City at Prayer.* Downers Grove, Ill.: InterVarsity, 2002.

Sheets, Dutch. *Intercessory Prayer.* Ventura, Calif.: Regal, 1996.

Silvoso, Ed. *Prayer Evangelism.* Ventura, Calif.: Regal, 2000.

Virkler, Mark, and Patti Virkler. *Dialogue with God.* Gainesville, Fla.: Bridge-Logos,
Revised 2005.

MARTY SCHOENLEBER was the founding pastor of New Song Evangelical Free Church in Bolingbrook, Illinois. He received his B.A. in ancient history from the University of Maryland and the M.Div. from the International School of Theology in San Bernardino, California. Currently he serves as the Church Planting Missionary Consultant for the Great Lakes District of the Evangelical Free Church.

CHAPTER 22

BECOMING A MULTI-ETHNIC SUBURBAN CHURCH:
Intentional International Diversity

Marty Schoenleber

Introduction: Ministering to Suburban Needs

O. J. Simpson had just been found not guilty of the murder of his estranged wife, Nicole. The nation quickly divided. The majority of the white population could not believe the verdict. Why had the jury not found the evidence of guilt compelling? But around the country, the majority of black Americans celebrated and rejoiced at the verdict.

I remember one surreal moment. The television newscast showed two African-American students in front of a crowd of white students on an elite college campus in the Chicago area. The students were looking through a storefront window where the newscast of the verdict was just hitting the screen. Surrounded by a crowd of white students, the two black students heard the verdict and the eruption of disbelief behind them, and then a knowing, but very simple, smile of a secret shared passed between them. What was that look? Were they in some way pleased with the decision? No, that's the wrong word. Satisfaction, that was it. They were satisfied with the verdict.

A few days later, I was speaking with one of the African-American members of our multi-ethnic congregation. New Song Church is situated in Bolingbrook, Illinois, a town of seventy thousand. The church is composed of people who were born in twenty-three different countries. That alone makes us unique. It makes us diverse ethnically, culturally, and economically. It also means that every week is a new adventure in learning what it means to be a follower of Christ in twenty-first-century America.

"Geri," I said, "tell me what's going on in the divide over the O. J. Simpson verdict. Why is black America satisfied with the judgment? Tell me what you think is going on."

My black-skinned sister sat down, took a deep breath, and began to educate me. "Honestly, most blacks that I know, think that O. J. was guilty. I don't believe anyone is celebrating that a murderer is going free. What's being celebrated is that finally, one of us had enough money to show that the system is not color-blind. If you have enough money to buy the right lawyer, you can buy the verdict you want. It was just good to see a black person prove the system doesn't work."

MY JOURNEY

I was a teenager in the idealistic and embryonic dawning of public discourse on racial issues that was the 1960s. I grew up in an all-white and mostly Catholic suburb of Philadelphia. Nuns and priests and good Catholic laymen crossed my vision at school, but there were no black or Asian or Hispanic faces in the weekly activity of my life. "We" were German and Italian and Irish and Polish, with a smattering of Jewish ethnicity in the area, but we were all "white." The only contact I had with black people was through the television, unless you count the minstrel show that the local Catholic church put on with a bunch of white people painted up in blackface.

When I moved on to Archbishop Wood High School in 1969, my own awareness of color had begun to awaken. The nuns and other teachers of my grammar school exposed us to some of the civil rights literature of the period. One nun helped us to see the positive side of President Johnson's "war against poverty" and the struggle for justice in the civil rights movement. During those years, and later in college, books like *Talley's Corner* began to alert me to the privilege that was accorded me simply because my skin was white.[1] They also began to make me more aware of the kinds of institutional racism that lay below the surface of everyday life.

Still, I suppose the first place I interacted with non-white students was on the athletic fields. Playing football and running track brought me in contact with others my age from schools that had a more diverse student body. This contact was superficial and distant. However, all of these things plus Dr. Martin Luther King's rhetoric, the music of the band Chicago, and a religion teacher's influence at Archbishop Wood High School helped to fan into a flame the desire to live in a world where people "would be judged not by the color of their skin, but by the content of their character."[2]

College was a new experience. I ran track with teammates from all types of backgrounds. My classrooms were filled with other ethnicities, accents, and even the opposite sex (except for two classes, Archbishop Wood was not coed). For the first time, my teachers had different hues. Through the ministry of Campus Crusade for Christ, I came to know the Lord personally and also developed my first real friendship with someone who was non-white.

Stan was the best friend I had in college and also one of the smartest. He had a twin brother at Howard, another brother at Tuskegee, and a fourth at still another mostly black college. I remember his disappointment when he learned that the one girl in our mostly white fellowship whose skin was dark, a beauty whose parents were from India, listed herself as Caucasian for the United States census. When Stan learned what to me was an insignificant piece of information, his sense of aloneness was almost palpable. There truly was no one "like him" in our entire movement. The experience served to heighten my awareness of "difference."

All of this history probably sounds trite and inconsequential to a person of color, but it was significant in forming the multi-ethnic and multicultural vision that has been played out in New Song Church. Eventually, I went on staff with the ministry of Campus Crusade and was assigned to the International School of Theology. It was a chance to continue the kind of modest ministry to faculty that I had begun at the University of Maryland. I was not a peer academically, but I was able to relate with faculty and administration on a professional level.

During my time at the seminary, I was exposed to the provocative and expanding literature of the church growth movement. One new idea was the so-called Homogeneous Unit Principle, or HUP. The principle was first formulated by Donald McGavran, the founding dean of the Fuller Theological Seminary missions department. Simply stated, HUP, according to McGavran, is that "people like to become Christians without crossing racial, linguistic or class barriers."[3] Acting on this idea, church growth advocates encouraged the development of strategies that would evangelize groups without requiring people to leave the comfort of their traditional associations of race, language, and class. The net result of these new strategies, in case after case, seemed to be the growth of churches—larger churches, more conversions, bigger buildings, more programs, bigger budgets, and a larger profile in the community.

What made me suspicious was that the Homogeneous Unit Principle did not seem to fit with what I read in the book of Acts. Furthermore, it did not look like the scenes describing the saints before the throne of God in Revelation, and it seemed to throw away a powerful picture of the gospel in action—namely, its ability to speak to the human heart across barriers of race, language, and caste. It failed to capitalize on the opportunity for the Church to say that something supernatural was possible because of the gospel of Jesus Christ—bringing together people from radically different backgrounds under the Lordship of a sovereign, sacrificing, and risen Savior.

Is not a church that demonstrates to the world a picture of diversity and unity, love and community with one another across these types of barriers a powerful testimony to the supremacy of Christ? Someday, God's people will all be together for eternity, and there is no indication in Scripture of ethnic enclaves in heaven. Did not God create the ethnic and cultural diversity that we have? I know that in every culture there are things that are simply evil, but many things in different cultures are just different. Not wrong, different.

On the one-tenth of a mile trip to the end of my street, I will pass a Muslim neighbor from Pakistan, a Korean neighbor, a first-generation Polish neighbor, four African-American neighbors, two mixed-race couples, one Hispanic family, and five white families. When the kids show up at the end of our little cul-de-sac to play kickball, it looks like a United Nations grammar school playground. The reality today is that the twenty-first-century suburb in many metropolitan areas is *more* diverse than some of the communities within our major cities. With these thoughts and realities in mind, I began to ask other questions concerning how to "do church" in the contemporary suburban landscape.

RETHINKING THE SUBURBAN CHURCH

How can a church in the traditionally white suburban expanses of America begin to affirm the value of diversity in its congregation and better reflect the changing demography of its community? If a church displayed the power of the gospel to overcome racial, social, linguistic, and economic barriers, would its evangelistic efforts find listening ears? Is not a multi-ethnic ministry, with all of its attendant complexities and problems, a potent display of the "manifold grace of God" (1 Peter 4:10 KJV)? Wouldn't such a display shake the foundations of those who deny the gospel? Isn't that partly what happened in the first century (Acts 17; Gal. 3:24–29)?

Out of those questions a decidedly non-homogeneous unit principle ministry philosophy began to emerge for a new church in the town of Bolingbrook, Illinois. Thirty-five minutes from downtown Chicago, within forty minutes of both regional airports, Bolingbrook is a town without a downtown. A slowdown in the economy in the 1970s caused this bedroom community to take a nosedive economically. Houses were boarded up, home prices went down, and the reputation of the town was trashed. But then things began to turn. An aggressive and savvy mayor took the reins and pursued the dual track of making Bolingbrook both business and family friendly. By the late 1980s it was becoming one of the hottest real estate markets in Chicagoland, and one of the most culturally diverse.

In 1988, I drove through Bolingbrook on the way to the adjoining town of Naperville. As I passed through Bolingbrook, the thought hit me, *This is the kind of town that needs a church like I have been thinking about. It has the ethnic diversity, and the social and economic mix for a church that would work to bring people together around the gospel.*

I was naive. But God seemed to be moving my heart toward the most challenging experiment of my life. In the summer of 1990 my wife and two children moved from Southern California to Illinois. Over the next year we prayed, planned, got to know our neighbors, served in the community, had another child, and began to understand the rhythms of our new mission field.

We arrived just ahead of what was going to become a significant influx of Hispanics, mostly from Mexico, and right alongside a large collection of peoples from Muslim-dominated countries. A sizeable number of families (now more than five hundred) came from the Philippines. From Asia, China, Japan, and Korea, populations were all growing in number. Then there were the "invisible ethnics"—first-generation Europeans who brought a different culture and set of values but melted in to the white landscape. In addition, Haitians blended in with refugees from Ghana, Nigeria, Ethiopia, and Sierra Leone. All these and more were finding their way to Bolingbrook and creating the test tube for the approach to ministry we would take. One night twenty-two émigrés from Sierra Leone and Ghana showed up at our English as a Second Language classes. We quickly found that the ministry of proclamation had to be supplemented by significant ministry to the whole person.

CORE VALUES FOR MULTI-ETHNIC MINISTRY

What were the foundational pillars upon which we stood?

1. The gospel, not marketing, is the power of God unto salvation (Rom. 1:16).

2. No matter what their color or culture, people are the same in their basic human need for grace, forgiveness, purpose, and hope (Jer. 17:9; Rom. 3:23).

3. Every community with ethnic diversity needs at least one church that seeks to declare and model to its nonbelieving neighbors that we are one in Christ at the foot of the cross (Rev. 7:9–12).

4. The rich need the poor more than the poor need the rich (Luke 6:20–23).

5. Revivals begin in have-not communities more often than in have communities (1 Cor. 1:26).

6. A church that showed the world great diversity coupled with great love for one another would bring great glory to God and great joy to the world (John 13:35). We wanted to become that church.

We began to move forward with our plans to become a multi-ethnic, multi-cultural church. Part of what drove our vision was the concept that "every culture and ethnicity, every socio-economic and even political group sees both more and less of God and His will because of the spectacles with which they approach the Scripture and life."[4] That principle causes us to value different perspectives as well as to have a healthy suspicion about our own and others' interpretation both of Scripture and culture. It causes us to cultivate a Berean-like heart (Acts 17:10–15), not only with regard to the Scripture but also as it pertains to ethnicity and culture.

That vision has kept us on the East Side of town with the "poor" and the greatest ethnic diversity in our community. It has yielded a food pantry ministry that last year funneled twenty-two to twenty-five tons of food to the needy of our community and a nine-hundred-square-foot clothing pantry that helps to keep children warm and parents appropriately dressed for job interviews. Additionally, an eighteen-hundred-square-foot modern health clinic has seen more than two thousand patients since we opened it four years ago. It is staffed completely by volunteers from more than a dozen different churches. We attempt to care for the whole person and the whole community.

In 2004, we added an office for the county social service agency housing counselor. The county pays the salary; we provide the office. In fall 2008 a dental care office was added to the clinic to complement the general practice, optometry, physical therapy, and chiropractic care that is already offered. In addition, our staff, elders, and trained lay counselors offer biblical counseling to our community. We are able to provide direct and personal help without a bureaucratic referral process that might rob the person we are trying to help of dignity.

Becoming Intentional in Reaching a Variety of Cultures

This learning experience is sometimes filled with failure. It is also filled with surprising joys and discoveries. But it starts with intentionality, taking risks, and humility.

Dr. Ken Horiuchi is a Japanese pastor and church planter who makes frequent trips to America and our church. We have developed a partnership over the years to cooperate on evangelistic projects here, in Japan, and in the Philippines. One year we sent the chaplain of the Chicago Bulls and his wife along with our youth pastor to do basketball clinics in Japan as an evangelistic outreach. Another year, we sent Michael Jordan's mother and sister to Japan to do a book signing tour. Michael's sister, Roslyn, a dynamic believer in Christ and a current Moody Graduate School student, would introduce her mother. Mrs. Jordan would speak, and then her daughter would return, sing a song, and present the gospel. On this side of the partnership, we have been involved in training Japanese interns to plant churches in Japan, housing Japanese exchange students, and many other evangelistic projects.

Numerous times I asked Dr. Horiuchi if he wanted me to pick him up or take him to the airport for one of his overseas flights. Finally, after turning me down for about two years, my Japanese friend pulled me aside and told me, "In Japan, if you ask the question, it means you don't want to do it. In my culture, you would say something like, 'I will come and pick you up.'"

This godly servant of Christ had tolerated me essentially insulting him for two years before he told me of my cultural ignorance. Another time, I was making small talk with an elderly Filipino man. "That's a nice-looking jacket, Ed," I said about a bronze suede half coat that my friend was wearing. The next day, the jacket was gift wrapped in a box and sitting on my office desk. I did not realize how powerful the words of an American authority figure (in this case, his pastor) were in the ears of a man whose country had been liberated by United States armed forces in World War II.

Early in the church's life we began to notice a disturbing trend. Few African-Americans were coming to meetings outside of Sunday morning worship. They had little participation in business meetings, training sessions, or even social events. As we analyzed and questioned our members, we began to understand a number of contributing factors. One, in our area, many black families have dinner much later than many of our white families. Planning a meeting at 7 P.M. was almost a guarantee to eliminate our African-American families. Two, many blacks have had the uncomfortable experience of having white Christians disregard or discount their input in planning and strategy sessions. When you experience that enough, you begin to think, *If I'm not going to be listened to, why go?*

What Lessons Did We Learn?

These experiences and many others have convinced us that the only way to become a truly multi-ethnic church is to be intentional in everything you do. It starts with a desire to reflect the diversity of God's creation in the peoples of the earth. Heaven is going to be multi-ethnic. In fact, with the global movement of the majority of believers to the Southern hemisphere, heaven is going to be far more colorful than many white Christians are prepared for.[5] The multi-ethnic church must be willing to take risks that move it out of comfortable and familiar patterns of ministry. The homogeneous unit principle is a reality that needs to be recognized. People do, no matter what their color or culture, like their comfort zones.

Unless a church works to overcome people's natural (and I would add, fallen) desire to segregate into tribal units, it will never be successful in bridging the gap between peoples. But there is a huge payoff to learning together and learning from one another. We learn to value and appreciate our differences and we reflect the love of Christ both to the rest of the body of Christ in our area and to the unbelieving community as well. We also experience new depths of meaning in the gospel itself.

One year I planned a weekend retreat for those in our worship ministry. We traveled to a town in the Western suburbs of Chicago to get away from the busyness of ministry. Among the team was the leader of our drama ministry, an African-American woman, who had never been on a retreat of this nature. On Saturday afternoon, in a team building exercise, I sent everyone out into the community on a scavenger hunt. Mary (not her real name) spoke of her reservations about the planned adventure. "I am uncomfortable out here. I don't see a lot of black people in this community, and I wonder how they are going to respond to me."

Her white sister in Christ, seeing Mary's anxiety, spoke words of comfort and courage, "Mary, I'll be with you and I will lay my life down for you." That was enough to put a glow of acceptance on Mary's face and create an unbreakable bond of friendship. It also showed both of them their oneness in Christ at a deeper level than either had known or guessed at before that moment.

Relationships and opportunities like that experienced by Mary and her white sister-in-Christ can only happen when we are purposeful and take risks. When we segregate ourselves into comfortable ethnic enclaves, we never get close enough to one another to hear the hurts and pains and fears that keep us apart. You cannot love those whom you will not spend time with.

In a multi-ethnic congregation, you are always in danger of stepping on someone's cultural toes. That is no reason to avoid the process, but rather an opportunity to learn how to express our oneness in Christ in a way that says to the world, "Something supernatural is going on here." This otherworldly quality of our lives is supposed to be one of the defining (and attractive) characteristics and tangible proofs that we are in Christ. We have moved from darkness to light when the quality of our love is not only in word but in deed (John 13:35; Eph. 5:8; 1 Thess. 5:4–5; James 1:19–27). This is what the apostle Paul is driving at in his letter to the Corinthians when he tells them they are acting like "mere men" (1 Cor. 3:1–4). Pursuing multi-ethnic ministry gives occasion to lean into the Spirit for the grace to love one another despite the cultural differences we may encounter.

I want our community to watch our people step out of their cars in the parking lot on Sunday morning and see a black family meet up with a white family, an African-garbed family meet up with a Hispanic family, an Indian couple meet up with a mixed-race couple, an Asian and a white person greet, and a group of college-age or high school-age students of various ethnicities meet and greet and embrace one another in obvious love and care. I want the community at large to marvel at how different we look and how much we love one another. I want people to be stunned at the way our church family cares for special-needs children and adults and come to the unmistakable conclusion that "God is with this people." I want the reputation of New Song to be that we break the pattern of Sunday morning being the most segregated time of the week in American culture. I want people to see that we give more than lip service to what is carved in stone outside the front the door of the church—"Starting Churches that Honor God by Developing People Who Live Passionately for and Like Christ." That requires a bold trust in the sovereignty of God and the power of the gospel to transform lives.

How Is Multi-ethnic Ministry Nourished?

The commitment and encouragement to risk needs to be continually nourished by new experiences and new challenges to the congregation. At New Song, I regularly recommend books, quote non-white role models, plan pulpit exchanges, and offer other inter-ethnic cooperation and experiences for our people. We have hosted and served two black churches during building and land purchases and had pulpit swaps with African-American pastors for one to four weeks at a time. In addition, we have intentionally invited guest speakers of color, including some who needed to be translated. We have swapped worship teams with other churches and been intentional to both recognize and cultivate non-white leadership. All of these experiences help the congregation to embrace the larger vision of multi-ethnic ministry. And yet we have a long, long way to go. Even as I write these words I am aware that some of the intentionality that I just wrote about needs refurbishing. A church that wants to be effective in its multi-ethnic vision can never stop praying and working at the process.

Do Your Illustrations Give a Multi-ethnic Flavor?

Selection of illustration material is important too. If I roll out an illustration that grabs from the black cultural experience to make a point, it serves its function, but may sail over the head of most white people in the congregation. But my black members' ears perk up at the mention of a Colin Powell, Phillis Wheatley,

Frederick Douglass, George Washington Carver, Jesse Jackson, Oprah Winfrey, Clarence Thomas, Rosa Parks, Dr. Martin Luther King, Condoleezza Rice, or Andrew Young. I suspect that often one of the things that passes through my black members' minds about me is, "That white boy doesn't understand our situation, but he's trying." Trying to be respectful is important and valued. When the speaker is able to speak about the contemporary situation in Sierra Leone, or the atmosphere surrounding the Jena Six, or the plight of immigrants from Mexico, or the situation of union workers being squeezed by foreign labor, it provides an atmosphere that people of color find hospitable and safe.

White pastors need to use black cultural heroes for illustrations in messages. Black pastors need to do the same with other cultures, as do Hispanics and any other group that is seeking to be truly multi-ethnic and inclusive in its approaches. When a person of one culture makes an effort to value and affirm another culture, it is noticed and it is appreciated. Churches that have ESL classes (English as a Second Language) may need to begin to rethink ministry if they really want to reach Spanish-speaking peoples. I am not saying that we should stop offering ESL. But perhaps it would be more effective to start SSL classes (Spanish as a Second Language) for the non-Spanish speakers that we currently have, in addition to ESL. All immigrants to any country should learn the language of that country whether or not they are seeking to become citizens of that nation. But that is a different issue. We need to think about adaptation to reach those who are on our doorsteps rather than waiting for them to develop the language skills to hear the gospel from our lips.

PRACTICAL CONVERSATION STARTERS

Here are a few questions for beginning to get to know someone with a different background.

1. "What's your favorite pie?" Your ethnic brother answers and then you say, "My wife and I would love to have you over for some _____ pie. Does Friday night work?"

2. "Tell me your story. How did you and your family arrive in the neighborhood?"

3. "How is worship in America different from your home country?"

4. "What do you like most about your American experience?" "What do you miss most from your own culture?"

Promoting a Multi-ethnic Leadership

White churches are notorious for making their plans and then inviting participation of blacks in the agenda that whites have already established. Churches need to work hard at creating opportunities to include other ethnicities in their decision-making and ministry-shaping plans. Look for people of color (or in the black church, people of less pigment) whom God might be raising up to leadership in your midst. Since it is impossible to over-communicate anything in a church, senior leadership must keep telling the congregation of your intent to become multicolored in your worship and fellowship.

Every person in the non-dominant culture of your church probably needs to be pursued if he is going to feel accepted as a full participant in the ministry. The dominant culture, be it black, white, Asian, or Hispanic, must pursue the culture it desires to include. People must be rushed as though they were freshmen desired by a fraternity or sorority. The minority culture is always asking the question, "Will I be accepted by this group?" The first step to answering that question satisfactorily in others' minds is to pursue them aggressively and listen to them honestly.

The Importance of Books

"Readers are leaders and leaders are readers," is one of Saddleback Community Church pastor Rick Warren's favorite slogans. Becoming truly missional requires new thoughts and perspectives. Fortunately numerous new perspective-expanding books suggest new wineskins for ministry. It would be hard to understate the value of these resources in seeking to develop a missional mind-set toward multi-ethnic ministry. The books I have found particularly insightful are included in a recommended reading list at the end of this chapter.

The list may be a little intimidating, so where should the novice begin? Struggling to learn how to do what God had called me to do, I ran into a book edited by Michael Emerson and Christian Smith called *Divided by Faith*. It was enthralling, frustrating, exciting, inspiring, thought provoking, and infuriating all at once. It shows how white churches, particularly suburban ones, have often unintentionally made the racial divide in churches worse. It shows the barriers that must be breached and how easy it is to stumble even with the best intentions.

Frustrated but not ready to give up, I found the address of Dr. Emerson and sent him an e-mail to ask if I could set up a phone appointment to discuss the contents of the book. A date was set and the phone call made. I told him that his book was all of those things I noted in the previous paragraph. I also told him that I was not ready to quit on the multi-ethnic experiment. I just needed some pointers on which way to go with all of the information with which I had been challenged in his book. Professor Emerson was understanding but frank. He said that he empathized with my struggle. He said that he and his co-author knew that the book would be discouraging to some, but that their purpose was to uncover the difficulties and barriers to multi-ethnic ministry so that solid patterns of ministry could develop. He promised that in a second book, he and his co-authors hoped to make a case for how multi-ethnic ministry was biblical and worthy of pursuing, despite all the difficulties. That book has now been published under the title *United by Faith*.

Whenever people ask, "How can I learn to do multi-ethnic ministry?" I tell them to start by reading these two books. Reading them is an education in its own right. You will also find yourself on your knees, which is the right place to begin a multi-ethnic ministry. Know that it will be difficult. Read as a learner. Read as a man or woman going into a foreign country. These resources are invaluable tour guides for multi-ethnic ministry, and every minute invested in them will be paid back a hundredfold.

The Mission Field at Our Door

The nations have come to us. Ethnic diversity in our communities is a reality. As we step out the front door of our homes or apartments, from a cultural and ethnic perspective the world is at our doorsteps. Ministry here is not like ministry in a monocultural nation like Japan. (The total number of non-Japanese in the entire island nation does not represent more than 6/10 of 1 percent of the population.)

According to the 2000 census, Bolingbrook is 62 percent white, 18 percent black, 13 percent Hispanic, 6 percent Asian, and 2 percent other. Since then, all the "minority" numbers have gone up with the largest increase in the Asian and Hispanic numbers. Within those five broad categories is astounding diversity. For example, in our church, we have Ghanians, Nigerians, Sierra Leonese, and African-Americans. Each of these might look "black" to the eye. But all of these are distinct people groups with different cultures and languages and ways of interpreting the world. In our church, under the category of Asian would be Chinese, Japanese, Korean, Filipino, and Cambodian as well as Taiwanese, Korean-American, and Chinese-American. Unfortunately, New Song Church is the exception in such diversity. Diversity is everywhere in American culture except in the local church. Thankfully, though still a minority, there are growing number of notable exceptions.[6]

CONCLUSION: WALK ACROSS THE STREET

The new urbanized environment of the suburbs depersonalizes humanity, trivializes one's sense of significance, and calls into question one's most basic beliefs. As a result of the confluence of multiple ethnicities, languages, beliefs, and cultures, the individual feels small and isolated. This is the environment of today's suburb. Today's pastoral leadership needs to work through the existing networks of relationships to reach these diverse populations.

Proper training and vision are imperative. How are our monoculture churches prepared to reach and train the masses of ethnic peoples in our backyards? Do we have any real vision of how to love and incorporate them into our churches? This is not only a "white suburban church" issue. Traditionally, black churches are also significantly behind the curve when it comes to reaching out to other peoples. Together, black and white churches, which are the majority of the churches in America, need to form an alliance to reach the multitudes that God is placing around us.

We can no longer afford to tolerate disharmony in our expression of our gospel witness. Nor can we remain parochially bound to the "tribe" of our background or skin color. Red, yellow, black, white, and brown people need us to take the gospel to them and provide opportunities for them in the fellowship and the leadership of our church families. They have gifts given to them by the Holy Spirit (1 Cor. 14; Eph. 4:7–8). God has placed them in the house or apartment next door (Acts 17:26). Our job is to walk across the street and welcome them into our homes, our lives, and our churches.

REFLECTION QUESTIONS

1. Discuss: "There is no influence without contact." How does this relate to multi-ethnic ministry?

2. Acts 17:26 says that God has established the boundaries and times of the peoples of the earth. What does this mean as it relates to the neighbors on your block?

3. Second Corinthians 5:17–21 says that we are ambassadors of reconciliation to the people around us. Ambassadors often work in situations where nations are estranged for some reason. Who are the people in your community who are estranged both from God and from your church?

4. In what practical ways can you help your neighbors to find reconciliation with God?

Recommended Reading List

Bakke, Ray, and Jim Hart. *The Urban Christian: Effective Ministry in Today's Urban World.* Downers Grove, Ill.: InterVarsity, 1987.

Branch, Taylor. *Parting the Waters: America in the King Years 1954–1963.* New York: Touchstone, 1988.

Emerson, Michael O., Curtiss Paul DeYoung, George Yancey, and Karen Chai Kim, eds. *United by Faith: The Multiracial Congregation as an Answer to the Problem of Race.* New York: Oxford, 2003.

Emerson, Michael O., and Christian Smith, eds. *Divided by Faith: Evangelical Religion and the Problem of Race in America.* New York: Oxford, 2000.

Gilbreath, Edward. *Reconciliation Blues: A Black Evangelical's Inside View of White Christianity.* Downers Grove, Ill.: InterVarsity, 2006.

Gordon, Wayne, with Randall Frame, *Real Hope in Chicago.* Grand Rapids, Mich.: Zondervan, 1995.

Harris, Paula, and Doug Schaupp. *Being White: Finding Our Place in a Multiethnic World.* Downers Grove, Ill.: InterVarsity, 2004.

Kozol, Jonathan. *Savage Inequalities: Children in America's Schools.* New York: Crown Publishers, 1991.

McFeely, William S. *Frederick Douglass.* New York: Norton, 1991.

McLean, Gordon. *Cities of Lonesome Fear.* Chicago: Moody, 1991.

Perkins, John. *Let Justice Roll Down.* Ventura, Calif.: Regal, 1976.

Perry, Dwight. *Breaking Down Barriers: A Black Evangelical Explains the Black Church.* Grand Rapids, Mich.: Baker, 1998.

Reed, Gregory J. *Economic Empowerment Through the Church: A Blueprint for Community Development.* Grand Rapids, Mich.: Zondervan, 1993.

Shuler, Clarence. *Winning the Race to Unity: Is Racial Reconciliation Really Working?* Chicago: Moody, 1998.

Younger, George D. *The Church and Urban Power Structure.* Louisville, Ky.: Westminster Press, 1963.

DANIEL GUTE grew up in Guatemala, Central America, the son of missionaries. He is a graduate of the Moody Bible Institute, Wheaton College, and Trinity Evangelical Divinity School. He has served on the pastoral staff of Lorimer Baptist Church in Dolton, Illinois, since 1983. He and his wife, Diann, have three children, Sarah, Derek, and Melinda.

CHAPTER 23

THE GREAT COMMUNITY:
A Pathway from Diversity to Unity
Daniel J. Gute

Introduction: An Uphill Climb

"I t will never work. You'll lose half of your people and two-thirds of your funding," was the counsel from the national church office. Then again, the year before we had been told that if something did not turn around, at the current rate of decline we would be dead in five years. It left us with a "what have we got to lose" kind of attitude. But I am getting ahead of the story.

Similar circumstances have presented themselves over and over again for suburban churches near urban centers, and so it was for Lorimer Baptist Church of Dolton, Illinois, a suburb bordering Chicago's southern city limit. The community around the church changes, while the congregation does not. So what is a church to do?

Transitional ministries, those that have changed from one ethnicity to another, whether by sale of the property or by more gradual attrition of one ethnicity with the arrival of another, are a dime a dozen in most urban areas. It has been our desire and our commitment not to simply transition but to remain an intentionally multi-ethnic congregation. Whether or not our dream will remain reality, or for how long, is yet to be seen, but this is the story of our journey.

While fairly rare on the South Side and in the south suburban region of Chicago when we began in 1990, multi-ethnic congregations have become more common today. Many churches have done a better job of it than we have, yet people have been gracious to say, "You can be a model for others!" Perhaps. My observation, however, has been that far too often we tend to make models out of what God did in one place and one time—He may work with you differently.

But I do believe there are principles that have been discovered, that when applied, while producing a different look, can achieve the same overall results. We can see a multi-ethnic as well as multi-generational and socioeconomically diverse congregation, committed to reconciliation, building bridges across the chasms of culture and class that so frequently (and tragically) divide us. We call this "the Great Community," the overflow of the Great Commandment (Matt. 22:37–40) and Great Commission (Matt. 28:18–20) in a changing neighborhood.

Our hope is to at least encourage churches in diverse communities to consider an alternative to segregated Sunday morning gatherings and separated body life throughout the week. When we are separate, we fail to be what Jesus prayed for in John 17:20–23—that we be unified, not by culture or class, but by the cause for which He came, "that the world may know that you sent me and have loved them as you loved me."

THE PATTERN—LORIMER'S FIRST 100 YEARS

Founded as a mission Sunday school by the Immanuel Baptist Church of Chicago (pastored at the time by Dr. George C. Lorimer, for whom the church was subsequently named) and then congregationalized in 1890, Lorimer Baptist Church began as the Langley Avenue Baptist Church between 71st and 72nd Streets on what was then Chicago's Far South Side, outside of the city limits.

It was renamed Bethel Baptist Church and then in 1909 again renamed Lorimer Memorial Baptist Church. In 1922 a new building was dedicated on the corner of 73rd and St. Lawrence Avenue. In 1947 the congregation moved to a new building at 85th and St. Lawrence. Then in 1958 it moved yet again to its present location in Dolton, Illinois. Each of these moves was being spurred along by an encroaching minority population, following the pattern now known as "white flight."

I joined the staff as Lorimer's youth pastor in 1983. The church was well-established, white European, conservative, and traditional in worship and ministry style. One of my first conversations with a leading family was about the changing community and the inevitable need for Lorimer to move again.

In 1988–89 the church underwent a significant evaluation with the help of an outside consultant. The community was changing racially and there was significant unrest within the congregation, but no consensus on what to do. Then came some rapid departures over discontentment with internal factors, and the ongoing longevity of the church came to be seriously questioned as we approached our centennial year. In January 1990, the senior pastor resigned. We celebrated our centennial in April under a cloud of ambivalence, and then in the summer of that year, under the direction of an interim pastor, the church wrestled with issues of identity and its future.

TIME FOR CHANGE

The interim pastor introduced the entire leadership team to C. Peter Wagner's book *Your Church Can Be Healthy*,[1] which describes in medical motif the diseases that churches acquire. One of those chapters was titled *"Ethnikitis,"* describing a church of one ethnicity in the community of another. With an overwhelming consensus that this could have been a case study of Lorimer Church, seven options were suggested for future direction. These included closing the church or moving the church, as had been the pattern, or merging with another ministry.

One of the options was to choose to stay in the Dolton community, hire a white senior pastor because the congregation was almost all white, and hire an African-American associate to intentionally become a multi-ethnic church that would reflect the community and surrounding region. While my frustration and disillusionment at this point had me actively looking for another ministry, that option sounded right to me: biblical, missional, and practical, even if improbable. I began to champion the church's selection of that option.

Throughout that summer the elders and the congregation met to discuss the options. About the middle of August, while I was on a personal retreat preparing for fall ministry, the phone rang. It was the interim pastor calling and suggesting that if I believed that Lorimer should become multi-ethnic, then perhaps I should consider leading them in the process. I did not want to hear that. I did not want to stay. But as my wife and I talked about the possibility, it became increasingly clear to me that God had raised me up and brought me here "for such a time as this."

I had grown up on the mission field and been exposed to three cultures simultaneously—the American culture of our home and mission school, the national Hispanic culture, and the Mayan culture among whom my parents ministered. I had majored in missions at Moody Bible Institute, preparing to go back to the mission field, and had my undergraduate degree in cultural anthropology from Wheaton College. Since graduating from Moody, I had been involved in youth ministry in Chicago's south suburban region, half of that time in multi-ethnic Chicago Heights where our youth ministry had been both racially and socio-economically diverse.

As discussions continued we shared with the elders and congregation our conclusion, that if the church would choose to stay in Dolton and seek to become a multi-ethnic ministry, I would be willing to candidate to be their pastor. On

August 26 the church voted to stay. It extended a call to me on September 16 and I began in that position October 9, 1990.

Nobody on the outside thought it would work . . . and on the inside we were not too sure either. In our limited circle of awareness, we did not know of another single church that had done what we were attempting to do—to take an established white church and have it become and stay a multi-ethnic ministry. But we did believe it was right, that it was God's calling on our lives and consistent with His Word and His purpose for the Church.

It was then that we heard those words from our association's national office, "You'll lose half of your people and two-thirds of your funding." Admittedly, a sense of desperation helped the risk-taking part of this. After all, almost anything is better than death. Some of us in leadership argued, "If we're going to die anyway, why not go out being biblical and attempting to look like the church that Jesus called us to be!"

God was gracious to not let the negative predictions come true. Only three families left immediately after the decision was made. And while the exodus was steady from that point on for several years, God was always bringing more people in the front door than were going out the back door. While the majority of those who were joining the church were African-American, we welcomed many members who were white and Hispanic as well.

Pastor Michael Walton joined the staff in November 1990. He and his family more than doubled the existing black population in the congregation. My pitch to Michael, as we talked about the possibility of our pastoral partnership, was to "come be a missionary to 'white folks' and help us figure this out." It is only appropriate to acknowledge the significance of the contribution that Michael and his wife and children had in helping our dream become reality, and at times with significant personal cost to them. Michael served Lorimer as associate pastor for eight years before moving on to another ministry.

The Eight Principles

While we were unaware of other churches that had done what we were attempting to do, I did know Reverend Raleigh Washington, the founding pastor of Rock of Our Salvation Evangelical Free Church in Chicago's West Side Austin community. He and I had been in seminary together. Rock Church was an intentionally multi-ethnic ministry, but it had started that way. Dr. Washington was not sure about the application of the principles to a well-established ministry, but he and his ministry partner, Dr. Glen Kehrein, were gracious to have breakfast with Michael and me a number of times to offer their perspective on our process. When their book *Breaking Down Walls*[2] was published in 1993, it became a road map for us on our journey. Over the years we have consistently taught and sought to practice the eight principles of reconciliation that are outlined in the last half of that book. We have preached them, taught them in Sunday school classes and small groups, introduced them in membership orientation, presented them in seminar formats, written about them in newsletters, and referenced them in almost every discussion about race relations.

Here is a summary of those principles in the words of Raleigh and Glen, with their definitions and the biblical references from which they are derived:

1. Commitment to Relationship—Ruth 1:16

Racial reconciliation is built upon the foundation of committed relationships.

2. Intentionality—Ephesians 2:14–15

Intentionality is the purposeful, positive, and planned activity that facilitates reconciliation.

3. Sincerity—John 15:15

Sincerity is the willingness to be vulnerable, including self-disclosure of feelings, attitudes, differences, and perceptions, with the goal of resolution and building trust.

4. Sensitivity—Ephesians 4:15–16

Sensitivity is the intentional acquisition of knowledge in order to relate empathetically to a person of a different race and culture.

5. Interdependence—2 Corinthians 8:12–14

Interdependence recognizes our differences but realizes that we each offer something that the other person needs, resulting in equality in the relationship.

6. Sacrifice—Philippians 2:3–4

Sacrifice is the willingness to relinquish an established status or position to genuinely adopt a lesser position in order to facilitate cross-cultural relationships.

7. Empowerment—2 Corinthians 8:9

Empowerment is the use of repentance and forgiveness to create complete freedom in a cross-cultural relationship and to enable the other person to function with wholeness.

8. Call—2 Corinthians 5:17–21

We are all called to be involved in the ministry of reconciliation, but some are gifted with a special call to be racial reconcilers.[3]

These principles gave us guidelines with which to work through our relationships within the changing church family, but it did not come naturally nor did it come easily. When cultures collided we found that we needed more than a set of principles; we needed a path to follow, a place to engage relationally. Over the years we came to recognize a process that has helped people understand where they are and where they go next as we answer the question, "What do we do with the differences between us?"

"What Do We Do with the Differences?"

We expect the people of Lorimer to maintain a commitment to reconciliation on multiple fronts: most visibly cultural and ethnic, inevitably generational, and most recently socioeconomic. In each of these arenas of life we experience differences, challenging differences, and the answer to the questions about our difference serve as a map of the path from diversity to unity in the body of Christ, the Church.

Over the years that the south suburban region of Chicago has been experiencing racial transition, it has most frequently been marked with tension, but sometimes with wonderful harmony. In communities that have embraced the changing demographics, there have been significant strides in both the political and business arenas. The educational institutions have not fared as well, because many families opt for private education or move out of the area. But dead last on the list have been the churches, in their openness to embracing and experiencing diversity. For some churches, white, black, and Hispanic, their identity is so tightly interwoven with their ethnic and cultural traditions that considering multi-ethnicity challenges the very core of their identity. Culture and ethnicity, whether by design or default, have taken precedence over Christ's intercession for our unity (John 17:20–23).

Lorimer Church has sought to be intentional about not just reflecting the diversity around us, but being reconciled where segregation maintains its greatest stronghold, in the fellowship of believers in Jesus. It seems only reasonable that in a community in which blacks, whites, and Hispanics live and work and go to school and play and shop side by side, that there also ought to be places where we share the benefits of worshiping together. This enables us to experience what Paul wrote in Ephesians 4:4–6, "one body and one Spirit . . . one hope . . . one Lord, one faith, one baptism; one God and Father of all." It is our unity over our diversity that gives testimony to the power of the gospel, not the perpetuation of some cultural expression of our Christian experience.

Admittedly, racial reconciliation is not the first priority of the Church. Its mission is to make disciples. But in John 17, Jesus clearly prayed for our unity in Him (and not just within mono-ethnic churches). This unity, before a watching world, speaks volumes about the power of that good news—the fact that it can really make a difference in lives and communities. While in other arenas, business, civic, commercial, and educational, we can get along publicly, often there is never more than a surface cordiality. It is in the context of sharing life in Christ— "doing church together"—that we come to accept and affirm and appreciate one another. The timeless truth is that God made us beautifully diverse so that we can experience a mutually beneficial dependence.

THE FIVE A'S

So how do we come to not only recognize our differences but grow to genuinely benefit from those differences in our shared relationship in Christ? I want to suggest five steps (the Five A's) that need to be experienced in succession as we climb the path up the mountain of reconciliation, whether it be generational, racial, or socioeconomic.

Acknowledge the Differences

The first step is to acknowledge the differences.

In the excellent book *One Blood: The Biblical Answer to Racism*,[4] the authors present the truth that there is really only one race of people . . . the human race. All of us can trace our parentage back to Adam and Eve, who were made in the image of God (Gen. 1:26–27) and into whom He breathed life (Gen. 2:7).

Genetically the things that we commonly use to draw distinctions are a mere fraction of what it means to be a human being. Nevertheless we recognize early in life that however insignificant they are genetically, these differences between us are real. Within the oneness of our humanity God has created an awesome array of diversity. We are designer people . . . every one of us . . . down to the number of hairs on our heads, our fingerprints, and even the DNA by which we can be identified. Certainly we should celebrate as we read in Psalm 139:14 that we are "fearfully and wonderfully made." We need to be able to say to and with one another, "You're not like me and I'm not like you," remembering that we are God-designed. Before His throne in Revelation 7:9, in a context of worship, we see a multitude of people too large to count "from every nation, tribe, people and language." God is honored by the diversity and by those differences.

Most of us enjoy seeing a bright bouquet of flowers; we appreciate the diversity that contributes to its beauty. We would never ignore those differences out of fear of hurting one of the flowers' feelings, would we? Of course, that is a ridiculous thought! But we do that all the time in our relationship with people who are not like us. We dishonor God's creative work and one another when we ignore (or even worse, deny) the differences. You often hear people say, with regard to race relations, "Oh, I don't see color." I believe this devalues who God has made another person to be. Color blindness is a distinct disadvantage to the person who suffers from it. God did not make us different to have the differences ignored, but to give us an opportunity to be others-focused and always learning.

Reconciliation, then, begins with acknowledging the differences. But we cannot stay on that level and experience all that God has for us. The next step is to accept the differences.

Accept the Differences

In Romans 15:7 we are commanded, "Accept one another, then, just as Christ accepted you, in order to bring praise to God."

While our goal in the body of Christ is unity, it does not mean "uniformity"— we do not all have to be alike to worship together. God wants us to be conformed to the image of Christ, to display Christlikeness, but it does not mean that we are all the same.

God has given us different personality types and interests, different physical appearances (including skin color and tones), different natural talents and spiritual gifts, different intellectual capacities and proficiencies, different cultures and family heritages, and in each of them God would have us hear Him say, "Accept one another."

Quite naturally we want other people to be like us. Anthropologists call that innate tendency "ethnocentrism," the belief that my culture, my way of doing things, is the best. It looks at everything through my own cultural lenses. When people are more proud of and committed to their ethnic heritage than to their identity in Christ, racial reconciliation becomes a huge challenge.

Accepting one another means coming to grips with the reality that there are other legitimate expressions of life, including our life in Christ. It means saying to one another, "You don't need to be like me . . . and I don't need to be like you." What would be the day-to-day practical outworking of really accepting one another instead of just tolerating each other? I think we would find ourselves moving on to the third step, where we affirm the differences.

Affirm the Differences

After God's creative work with all of its variety, including plants and animals and finally human beings, His assessment was that it was "very good" (Gen. 1:31). He liked what He saw. I believe He still does, and He wants us to affirm it too.

In 1 Corinthians 12, Paul is writing about the church, using the analogy of the body consisting of many parts. Beyond merely accepting this fact, we are to affirm those other parts, validating their existence, their importance, their place, their contribution. Verses 17–20 remind us, "If the whole body were an eye, where would the sense of hearing be? If the whole body were an ear, where would the sense of smell be? But in fact God has arranged the parts in the body, every one of them, just as he wanted them to be. If they were all one part, where would the body be? As it is, there are many parts, but one body."

To "affirm" is to recognize the value of another, including the differences. It is being able to say to one another, "I like you—especially in the ways that are different from me." An expression of joy instead of an attitude of jealousy pervades the body in celebration of the differences.

Once we recognize the value of another person, it ought to be easy to move to the fourth step, to appreciate the differences.

Appreciate the Differences

The thought continues in 1 Corinthians 12:21–26:

> *The eye cannot say to the hand, "I don't need you!" And the head cannot say to the feet, "I don't need you!" On the contrary, those parts of the body that seem to be weaker are indispensable, and the parts that we think are less honorable we treat with special honor. And the parts that are unpresentable are treated with special modesty, while our presentable parts need no special treatment. But God has combined the members of the body and has given greater honor to the parts that lacked it, so that there should be no division in the body, but that its parts should have equal concern for each other. If one part suffers, every part suffers with it; if one part is honored, every part rejoices with it.*

This is written in regard to our spiritual gifts within the church, but it is equally applicable to our personalities, natural abilities, and even our ethnicities. As we acknowledge the differences among us and accept and affirm the differences in each other's lives, we will benefit from and be enriched by those differences. At this stage we can genuinely say to someone different from ourselves, "I need you . . . and you need me."

That appreciation leads then to a fifth and final step, where we appropriate the differences.

Appropriate the Differences

To appropriate is "to make use of," to add to our experience something that we learn from another. Recipes that reflect others' ethnic heritage and have become part of our family tradition is an example of appropriation. Our lives are enriched by experiencing and embracing elements from another culture. You can know that pleases our heavenly Father. He must smile and say, "Look, they're sharing!"

Paul wrote to the Philippians, "Whatever you have learned or received or heard from me, or seen in me—put it into practice" (4:9). As we appropriate the differences, we say to one another, "Show me, teach me, help me." The goal is not to minimize the differences between us but to *intentionalize* the relationships through which our understanding of those differences moves from being an *irritant* to being *interesting* to being *important* to being *indispensable*.

SOME LESSONS LEARNED

As I have opportunity to tell Lorimer's story, one question is pretty common: "What is the most surprising lesson you've learned?"

My answer remains, "How much alike we are—how much we have in common."

Then comes a flood of questions—"But isn't worship hard?"

"Yes, but it tends to be for every church."

"Isn't fellowship difficult?"

"Yes, but it's a common challenge for every church."

What we have to pay extra attention to because of our multi-ethnicity are things every church ought to be paying attention to, because simply put, life is all about relationships.

When we began in 1990, we had three African-American and two Hispanic adult members, and only 3 percent of the congregation lived in the village of Dolton. Today we are approximately 70 percent African-American, 25 percent Caucasian, 5 percent Hispanic, and almost 30 percent of our congregation comes from Dolton. We have come to believe that the local church should be a reflection of God's family, guided by the Word of God, instead of the conventional wisdom of the world in which we live, the "birds of a feather flock together" mind-set. We believe that our unity in diversity should reflect the heart of God, the true body of Christ, and the work of the Spirit, which Jesus declared would be a great means for evangelism (John 17:20–23).

Lorimer Church does look and sound a little different from when we began the process in 1990, and together we have learned some things along the way.

1. If you are going to pursue multi-ethnic ministry, reflecting the Kingdom of God in the local congregation, you must lead from conviction and not conventional wisdom. There are critics in abundance within every ethnic group, but it is our conviction that the principle of homogeneity (meaning "of the same or similar kind"), while good sociology and pragmatic missiology, is faulty ecclesiology—it fails to grow the Church after the pattern of diversity and inclusion that Jesus designed for it. Dr. Rod Cooper describes the principle well in his chapter "People Just Like Me" that appears in the book *Building Unity in the Church of the New Millennium*. He writes,

> *This principle states, "People like to become Christians without crossing racial, linguistic, or class barriers." Even though advocates of this perspective would argue it has biblical merits, this writer is hard pressed to find such a basis. It would seem that regarding ethnically homogenous churches, this philosophy is based more on a sociological principle than a biblical one. The driving ideas behind this type of philosophy are couched in the need for effective evangelism and the maintaining of the group's "cultural" identity. Although this seems quite noble, even biblical, it perpetuates a "separate but equal" mentality within the church, which can subtly maintain racist and separatist attitudes toward the [racially different and] socioeconomically deprived in the name of bringing people to Christ.*[5]

2. The Kingdom of God takes precedence over culture, and being Christlike over any ethnic loyalty. It is not wrong to appreciate who God made you to be with the background that He has given you, but that cultural heritage becomes a hindrance when it is allowed to separate you from others who don't share in it.

3. People are people. We have similar needs, concerns, dreams, and problems; and we all have a story worth telling. Fear of the unknown is the number one reason people avoid others who are different than they are, but hearing their stories creates a familiarity.

4. Sin is sin—and it does the same things to people, all people, regardless of your ethnicity.

5. Every cultural group has wide variety within it, and no single person can accurately or appropriately speak for an entire ethnic group. There is no more a "black perspective or opinion" on an issue than there is a white or Hispanic opinion.

6. Black and Hispanic churches fight and split over issues like music just like white churches do. Worship wars and relational challenges know no ethnic boundaries.

7. Life and ministry will be characterized by commitment, not convenience, and must rise from conviction rather than the priority of preference. For example, people generally evaluate worship with statements like, "I really liked that!" or maybe more often, "I really *didn't* like that!" Our preferences can no longer be the criteria for evaluation. The question must be "Did God like it?" and the commitment must be "to accept one another" (Rom. 15:7) and "to serve one another" (Gal. 5:13).

8. We must be willing to let people leave. Each of the options presented to our congregation during our transition into this process had this tag line attached: *We encourage everyone to stay, but we will also give you permission to leave.* People-pleasing and racial reconciliation are not a good mix. Calling people to wholeness and holiness must take precedence over serving people's history and happiness.

9. Staffing is key to your credibility. A lot of churches have minorities attending, sometimes in significant numbers, but the leadership remains entirely of the majority culture. While this may reflect integration, it does not represent reconciliation. There must be visibly diverse and intentionally shared leadership. These would include every area of church life: pastoral staff or elders (at the time of this writing Lorimer does not have a Hispanic pastor on staff, but we have had one, and we are working toward that again), the worship team, and platform participants. This also involves those who oversee ministry programs and the ministry teams with which they work. Small group leadership and hopefully the small groups themselves should reflect the diversity of the congregation.

10. There needs to be opportunity created for safe, honest conversation about racial issues. Usually these conversations are just informational. Rarely are they confrontational. Still the commitment by all must be to "speak the truth in love" to one another (Eph. 4:15).

11. The Eight Principles of Reconciliation need to be championed regularly. Actually, they apply to any relationship (marriage, neighborhood, workplace, and classroom) and in any church. Any church that seeks to understand and live by these principles will be healthier, but in a multi-ethnic congregation you do not have the option to ignore them.

12. It's necessary to keep the agenda of racial reconciliation on the front burner. It never goes away. There are always newcomers entering the congregation who need help in understanding how you came to be as you are and how they can contribute to the process.

CONCLUSION: KINGDOM DREAMS

Beyond the principles is a process that will lead you up these steps where you will experience the benefits of being part of an intentionally multi-ethnic congregation. It is what Jesus had in mind for us as His body. He is the basis for our unity and is so much bigger than any of the differences that would separate us.

Our dream, should the Lord allow, is to ring the south suburban region of Chicago with churches that will live out Christ's message of reconciliation, bridging the gaps that historically have separated us and diminished our witness to a watching world.

While Lorimer Church has experienced God's blessing in our multi-ethnicity, building a bridge across the culture gap, we now begin to address another gap that divides Christ's Church, the class gap, the socioeconomic differences. May God grant us His grace as we continue to learn and apply His principles and processes to build a bridge over this chasm too.

REFLECTION QUESTIONS

1. Describe an experience you had in a multi-ethnic church or worship service. What stood out to you as beneficial that was outside your normal worship experience?

2. On the pathway up the steps of acknowledgement, acceptance, affirmation, appreciation, and appropriation, where are you and what evidences do you point to of that step in your experience?

3. According to John 17:20–23, what is the purpose and power of our unity despite our diversity?

4. From the list of lessons learned, which resonated with you as something that you also have observed, and which one was the biggest surprise?

Recommended Reading List

Evans, Tony. *Let's Get to Know Each Other: What White Christians and Black Christians Need to Know About Each Other*. Nashville: Nelson, 1995.

Gilbreath, Edward. *Reconciliation Blues: A Black Evangelical's Inside View of White Christianity*. Downers Grove, Ill.: InterVarsity, 2006.

Ham, Ken, Carl Wieland, and Don Batten. *One Blood: The Biblical Answer to Racism*. Green Forest, Ark.: Master Books, Inc., 1999.

Peart, Norman Anthony. *Separate No More: Understanding and Developing Racial Reconciliation in Your Church*. Grand Rapids, Mich.: Baker, 2000.

Perkins, Spencer, and Chris Rice. *More Than Equals: Racial Healing for the Sake of the gospel*. Downers Grove, Ill.: InterVarsity, 1993.

Shuler, Clarence. *Winning the Race to Unity: Is Racial Reconciliation Really Working?* Chicago: Moody, 1998.

Part Four

PARACHURCH
MINISTRIES

CLIVE CRAIGEN has spent nearly twenty years of his life in urban ministry, both working with youth and in church planting. He received his B.A. from Grace College and his M.A. in inner city studies education from Northeastern Illinois University. He is also a graduate of the DeVos Urban Leadership Initiative (Chicago 2000). He currently serves as Assistant Professor of Urban Ministry at Moody Bible Institute, co-shepherds a house church in Chicago, and works as a student mobilizer for Go2 Church Planting Ministries.

Introduction to Parachurch Ministries

Clive Craigen

URBAN MINISTRY: IT'S MORE THAN YOU THINK!

lmost twenty years ago my wife and I moved into the Humboldt Park neighborhood to begin working with Inner City Impact. Our journey into a life of urban ministry began four years earlier while we were still in college. We traveled three weekends a semester to the inner city of Indianapolis to work with the youth at a rescue mission. That tentative first step continues to this day. We started out working with children and youth. These young people were growing up in a rough neighborhood. Violence, drugs, gangs, inadequate education, and many more issues were played out in the lives, families, and neighborhood in which we lived, worked, and worshipped.

When we started working in Chicago almost two decades ago, inner city ministry meant one of two things, working with the homeless or working with children and youth who were at risk. Other things were happening, but urban ministry was about the poor. And while urban ministry still means that, it has come to encompass so much more.

The urban context and particularly Chicago have been profoundly changed by a number of trends. Gentrification and the resulting relocation of people with resources back into the city have created pockets of suburbia upon the landscape of urban America. People have brought with them their lifestyles, their comforts, their conveniences, and even their churches. This relocation of wealth and influence has caused a radical realignment in the city and suburbs. Property values and taxes rise, taking the cost of living beyond the means of a typical urban family.

Furthermore, this relocation and "renewal" has contributed to the suburbanization of the poor. In their quest for affordable housing and available jobs, a growing number of the urban poor have relocated to the suburbs. Chicago is not alone in experiencing this phenomenon. It is occurring across the urban landscape of North America.

Furthermore, Chicago has also experienced a growing influx of immigrants and refugees from Africa, Asia, and South America. Alongside its historic Polish, Italian, Irish, African-American, and Puerto Rican ethnic enclaves are people living from all over the globe. There are Indian, Pakistani, Arab, Vietnamese, Korean, Mexican, Haitian, and African communities. People from everywhere are now calling Chicago home. Chicago has become a snapshot of the world.

The internationalization of the city, the gentrification of its neighborhoods, and the suburbanization of the urban poor have left an undeniable footprint upon the city and upon urban ministry. Because Chicago and other cities continue to have tough neighborhoods characterized by poverty and violence, there will always be a place for traditional urban ministry. It also continues to have historic neighborhoods in which the majority of the residents share the same ethnic heritage. The city looks like a checkerboard with government-subsidized housing buttressed against million-dollar condo developments. Working-class ethnic neighborhoods find themselves in close proximity to the wealthy.

The shifting reality on the streets cries out about the complexity of urban ministry. It involves working with both the very young and the very old, and all those in between. It includes those who have just arrived from other countries and those who are on their third generation of public aid. It involves those who only speak English and those who speak no English. It encompasses the homeless, the working poor, the middle class, and the wealthy. Everything from literacy to food distribution, from housing to medical care, from job training to English language instruction is required. From traditional venues to unconventional ones, ministry takes place day in and day out, week in and week out all year long. We see traditional programs in athletics and recreation and ventures in economic entrepreneurship and the arts. Urban ministry involves all of the above and more. This context and its complexity require all the skill, innovation, and creativity that can be mustered.

My reflections upon this section of the book and on the multitude of ministries working across the city of Chicago leads me to thank God for the many organizations and ministries: large and small, those with historical roots and those that are newcomers to the city, and ministries run by professionals and those led by volunteers. This committed company of mostly unknown, unheralded, and unsung heroes will rarely make the news, but they continue to serve

God and the city.

Most have paid a price for their faithful service. They have experienced financial troubles, physical problems, marriage difficulties, and a host of other trials. They have the scars and limps that come from doing life and ministry in urban America.

God will not allow them to give up. And they really do believe in the power of the gospel to transform lives, families, and neighborhoods. They continue pouring out their lives as a drink offering for the glory of God. They are not perfect, and they would not always agree with each other, but they keep faithfully serving.

This section has highlighted a few ministries in Chicago, but it is really a shout out to all the ministries and people, the big and the small, the veterans and the newcomers who faithfully go about the work of making disciples.

CHAPTER 24

LOVING THE SEXUALLY BROKEN:
The World of Male Prostitution (Emmaus Ministries)

John Green

Introduction: The View from the Wall

The pale yellow glow of the streetlight flickers. Cars cruise slowly by, and young men stroll the sidewalks around me. The darkness, physical and spiritual, seems to press down on all.

I am holding up a wall. My back presses against the coarse brick. My right leg is bent upward, my foot flat against the wall. I am a silent sentry on Hubbard Street in Chicago. It is a good wall to lean against.

From my sentry post I can see about a dozen guys "hustling" and about two dozen "johns" cruising in their cars. This area of Chicago has been known for male prostitution ("hustling") for about five decades. The men who prostitute themselves here (hustlers) sell their services to many types of customers (johns): visitors staying in the nearby hotels, perhaps conventioneers in town for a week, or men who work in the nearby "Loop" and lie to their families that they are "staying late at work."

One john eyes me up and down as he slowly passes by. I laugh. He is not going to get a "date" out of me. Some of the johns I recognize from the years I have been down here. Some turn their heads when they see me, their guilt getting the best of them.

They make me angry, these predators. The hustlers I work with at Emmaus Ministries chose to do this to put food in their mouths or support a family, although some do it more to support a drug habit now. But for most of them prostitution began as a way to survive. But these johns seem like predators. Many are older white males from the 'burbs (suburbs). Some are driving cars that are worth about five years' salary for me. Some have baby seats in the back, giving silent testimony to the wife and family who are oblivious to Daddy's midnight jaunts.

It is not a nice world that I see from my wall.

Across the street from my post, Tim is making a fool of himself yelling and laughing. He is one of those guys who is always up, always smiling, even when trying to sell himself. He screams "hello" as he sees me and jaywalks over. I tell him to be careful, he might get arrested for that. We laugh.

I move off the wall and shake his hand. With the smooth movements of a practiced hustler, he pivots so he can keep an eye on the passing cars. He is talking to me but his eyes constantly look to the street behind me, watching the passing predators for any sign of interest. A john pulls up and Tim stops in midsentence. "Be back in a few" he whispers, and without another word gets in the car.

ACT 1, SCENE 2

Around the corner comes Randy. Five rehab tries and still counting, he still is a major coke (cocaine) fiend. But youth and a strong heart might see him through it. He is surprised that I do not give him one of my usual lectures. I am all lectured out, I say. I tell him that I pray the next time I see him it is not on a slab at the morgue. He walks away in silence.

Tim is back in twenty minutes.

He shows me the two twenty-dollar bills and says it is worth it. "Gotta go man," he says, slapping me a handshake. He heads down to McDonald's, as he does after every "date," to wash his mouth out. "It's worth it." Yeah, right.

Anthony comes around the corner with a new guy named Mike. Mike eyes me suspiciously. Anthony assures him that I am not a cop and goes on to tell him about the camping trip I took him and three other hustlers on last year. Mike introduces himself and takes one of my cards. I explain our ministry a little to him. He has only been hustling for two weeks, and his eyes light up when I tell him that there is a place he can go and get some help to get off the streets. While we talk, Tim joins us and takes Anthony aside and down the street to talk privately.

"I don't want to do this anymore," Mike says to me quietly, making sure Anthony cannot hear him. "Can you really help me?" he asks with a hint of desperation. I tell him I will do my best and encourage him again to come by the ministry tomorrow. Anthony and Tim, meanwhile, are walking back toward us. They are trying to decide whether or not to go with a john down to 84th Street on the South Side of Chicago. The "date" is new and neither of them knows him, but he is willing to pay five hundred dollars.

The john has been trying to pick someone up all night. The guys are leery of new people. Jeffrey Dahmer and John Wayne Gacy[1] were both "new people" when they cruised this block. That is one of the real dangers these guys face. Nobody cares about them, which makes them easy targets for killers and crazies. Anthony needs the cash, so he gets in the car on its next lap around the corner. I say a silent prayer.

While all that was going on, Mike has been talking to me about his growing up in the church. We talk about God, Jesus, sin, forgiveness. Mike is a bit of a theologian. His mom, he says, told him that God wants us to be happy. I disagree with him.

God does not promise us that we will be happy, I say, but He does promise us joy. I explain to Mike how a Christian who is persecuted is not going to be happy, but he can be joyful even in the midst of such pain and struggle. Mike smiles and says he understands. He says he has to get back to business and shakes my hand. Be joyful, I say.

It has been three hours and my sentry time is done. I leave my wall and begin to walk toward my car to head uptown to another strip. Johns cruise and hustlers stroll around me. But the darkness does not seem so overwhelming; the Light has shone.

Jesus gave us a clear command: "Go into all the world and preach the gospel to all creation" (Mark 16:15). When most of us in the Church hear that, we think immediately of "mission territory," faraway places where valiant people of faith have gone for centuries to share the good news. But going "into all whole world" includes the dark places in our midst. Since 1990 Emmaus Ministries has been dedicated to "making Jesus known on the streets." We are an evangelical ministry of Roman Catholic and Protestant Christians reaching out to men involved in prostitution.

MALE PROSTITUTION—AN OVERVIEW

Male prostitution is not a recent phenomenon, although it is not discussed as commonly as female prostitution. Male prostitutes are first mentioned during biblical times as temple prostitutes. Prostitution of men has always been as prevalent as female prostitution and has often involved children and adolescents.[2]

According to the literature, there are four basic types of male prostitutes. The first are street hustlers. Street hustlers are considered the lowest class of prostitutes because they are survival-oriented and cannot anticipate the future. Street hustlers are likely to self-identify as heterosexual or bisexual and often have an extensive history of physical or sexual abuse.

Bar hustling is another form of prostitution. These men are more concentrated in exclusively gay neighborhoods. Bar hustlers often have a history of sexual abuse and are more likely to identify themselves as homosexual. Some men put themselves through college or graduate school through bar hustling. Two other forms of prostitution are call/professional men and "kept boys." These men generally work for specific clients and are considered higher class than street and bar hustlers. Emmaus Ministries works among street and bar hustlers.

Internet prostitution, a new form of hustling, has gained popularity over the past five years. Male escort websites and agencies allow men to advertise with pictures, text, and contact information for a small fee. Another way men are able to use the Internet to set up "tricks" is through message boards or chat rooms. Emmaus Ministries is currently looking into different ways we could reach out to this community.

COMMON CHARACTERISTICS

Although there is no "typical" hustler, several characteristics are common. Most men in prostitution are young and from low- to middle-income families. A significant number have been physically or sexually abused. They are generally high school dropouts, unskilled, and unemployed. Men in prostitution often have other criminal involvement and abuse alcohol and/or drugs. Many of these men come to the streets as runaways or throwaways and are dependent on social services for food, clothing, and housing.[3]

Most hustlers begin their involvement in prostitution as a means for quick cash. They may be supporting families, trying to make it from one meal to the next, or looking for love from a significant male. After several weeks of hustling, most young men become addicted to drugs or alcohol. They put themselves in a high-risk lifestyle for contracting a variety of sexually transmitted diseases, including AIDS. These men are also vulnerable to the random violence indigenous to the streets.

The extensive use of cocaine in lower-class neighborhoods has qualitatively changed street-level prostitution. "No one we talked with who had a firsthand knowledge of prostitution as it existed before the ascendancy of cocaine in the 1980s believed otherwise.... Several respondents, both female and male, attested that prostitutes during pre-cocaine days were more likely to set aside money for living expenses, nice clothes, and personal hygiene, whereas now almost all of a habitual cocaine user's money is spent on the drug."[4]

Young men who resort to prostitution encounter other great risks. Whether from the violence of street life, disease, or substance abuse, most of these hustlers will die as young men if they stay on the streets. This has taken Emmaus ministers into various bars and clubs of the gay community. Street ministers come in contact with a variety of people groups, including men and women in prostitution, substance abusers, homeless teenagers, adult men and women on the street, and the women and men of the gay, lesbian, and transvestite bars.

THE COLD, HARD FACTS

The Hustler

- In 1970, 20.7 percent of prostitution arrests in the United States were males. By 1998, the number had risen to 42 percent.[5]

- Nationwide arrests for male prostitution rose 16 percent in the years between 1989 and 1998. Arrests for female prostitution dropped 13.3 percent during the same period.[6]

- Eighty-two percent of male prostitutes come from families where the father was absent, alcoholic, or abusive.[7]

- The majority of men arrested for hustling in Chicago during 2004 were between the ages of twenty-five and forty-four. It is estimated that men enter prostitution between the ages of eleven and twenty-five.[8]

- Out of the 1,374 men arrested in Chicago for prostitution in 2004, 207 were white and 535 were black.[9]

- Male prostitutes in the United States often have economic motivations for their work due to the structural, material conditions that force men to sell sex. "[They] usually have low levels of formal education and their work choices are limited to unskilled labor, which pays them much less than the 'easy money' provided by sex work."[10]

- Most prostitutes have histories of childhood abuse, including sexual abuse, as well as more recent accounts of homelessness, alcoholism, and drug misuse. Many suffer from post-traumatic stress disorder (PTSD) caused by the nature of their work.[11]

- In a sample of 224 male street prostitutes, 17.9 percent identified themselves as homosexual, 46.4 percent as heterosexual, and 35.7 percent as bisexual. Fifty percent of those identified as homosexual tested HIV positive, as did 18.5 percent of the heterosexuals, and 36.5 percent of the bisexuals; 62.5 percent of the self-identified homosexuals were hepatitis positive, as were 45.8 percent of the self-identified heterosexuals, and 70.2 percent of the self-identified bisexuals.[12]

- In the same study, 53 percent of the male prostitutes reported a history of injection drug use, 76 percent a history of cocaine use, and 61 percent a history of crack use.[13]

- Child sexual abuse victims are the most likely to be arrested as adults for prostitution.[14]

- Male prostitutes usually have had significantly earlier sexual experiences, an older first sexual partner, a male as a first sexual partner, consumed more cocaine, were more depressed, and were more likely to have contracted a sexually transmitted disease compared with others of a similar socioeconomic status.[15]

The Customer

- Most of the hustlers' customers consider themselves to be heterosexual or bisexual.[16]

- Customers engage in high-risk sexual behavior with the hustlers. In the majority of cases, a condom is not used. This increases the risk of transmission of HIV and other sexually transmitted diseases to the customer and his other partner(s).

OUR PHILOSOPHY OF MINISTRY

Emmaus Ministries is a Christian outreach to men involved in sexual exploitation on the streets of Chicago. Through nightly outreach teams, a daytime drop-in center, and a residential home, Emmaus staff and volunteers assist men out of prostitution and toward faith in Jesus Christ. Emmaus Ministries seeks to make Jesus known in Chicago's "night community." This includes a wide variety of people groups—men and women in prostitution, substance abusers, homeless teens and adults, and patrons of gay, lesbian, and transvestite bars. Emmaus is primarily concerned with young adult male prostitutes.

Relationship as the Basis for Ministry

As Jesus walked with the disciples on the road to Emmaus, so we too walk with young men on the street. We attentively listen to their stories, share with them from the Scriptures, and build community with them as Jesus did in the breaking of the bread. Where we can, we lead them to Jesus, and we provide assistance and support during transition away from street life.

Our clients are often those most wounded on the streets. Men involved in sexual exploitation often attempt to use services in the homeless community. However, because of their lifestyle, they are often rejected and abused by the mainstream homeless culture. These young men are truly the ostracized among the overlooked.

We unite the body of Christ in ministry to them. We are dedicated to bringing Protestants and Catholics together in a Christ-centered, grassroots ministry of evangelism and service. "As Evangelicals and Catholics, we pray that our unity in the love of Christ will become ever more evident as a sign to the world of God's reconciling power."[17]

COMPONENTS OF OUR MINISTRY

Outreach

Emmaus reaches out to adult young men in prostitution through a three-phase development plan. The first phase of Emmaus ministry is street outreach. Emmaus outreach ministers go out on the streets in male/female pairs to do outreach from 10:00 P.M. to 2:00 A.M. most nights of the week. Wearing identifiable shirts and name badges, they walk the streets and go into the bars and dance clubs where hustlers gather. Emmaus teams visit these places regularly, establishing a Christian presence and developing long-term friendships with the patrons. Through these friendships, outreach ministers connect men with existing resources for food, housing, or medical attention. Most of all, they extend to these young men the loving touch and words of Christ Jesus.

Ministry Center

The second phase of ministry is located in the North Side neighborhood of Uptown, the Emmaus ministry center—a place of hospitality, prayer, and discipleship that welcomes the men referred by Emmaus outreach ministers or fellow hustlers. During the day, men come to the ministry center and are provided with clothing, meals, showers, laundry facilities, counseling, discipleship, Bible studies, referrals to social service agencies, job-search assistance, GED preparation, and contact with local churches. The men are given daily chores and they set goals for themselves pertaining to jobs, education, lifestyle, and their relationship with God.

Periodic outings and times to get away from the city help the men have a break from street life and a chance to reflect on and make decisions about the direction of their lives.

Emmaus House

The third phase of ministry is a residential home. The Emmaus House mission is to provide transitional housing in a supportive and encouraging environment for the men of Emmaus Ministries while they make progressive steps away from street life and toward healthy, interdependent living. Each morning, residents gather for devotions and prayer before leaving the house to pursue their goals, such as attending school, a job-training program, recovery or counseling meetings, or beginning work at a job. In the evening, residents and staff share dinner together and participate in nightly classes such as Bible studies, recovery meetings, and discussions relevant to the issues in their lives. The night ends with each person telling about his day and then praying as a community.

While in the Emmaus House, each resident meets one-on-one at least once a week with a House staff member called a navigator. The navigator and resident work to develop the resident's goals and schedule each week, as well as provide a safe place for each resident to share his concerns, joys, and thoughts and explore and/or grow in his faith in Jesus Christ.

Ministries of Education

Emmaus is committed to a ministry of education: helping to sensitize, teach, and train the body of Christ for ministry in the night community. The educational ministries director oversees all ministries of education. Educational activities include volunteer opportunities, Kaio community memberships, immersion nights, speaking, and music engagements.

The Kaio Community

Kaio is a Greek verb meaning "to set on fire." You will find it in Luke 24:32 as the two disciples who walked the Emmaus road with Jesus describe their hearts "burning" within them. The Kaio community at Emmaus Ministries offers people the opportunity to spend a year serving, learning, and being open to God's guidance. In return, we cover each person's room, board, medical expenses, public transportation, and a weekly twenty-dollar stipend.

Stories from the Streets

"Stories from the Streets" is a flexible program that can be tailored to fit various formats. The full program consists of approximately one hour of stories communicated through music and dramatic monologue. Rooted in our guys' own words, these stories are moving and engaging, are sometimes amusing, and always offer an opportunity to understand these men who are truly the "ostracized among the overlooked."

GOD'S GRACE AT WORK IN THE MOST BROKEN . . .

As I walked into the room, the boy lying in the hospital bed before me did not stir. In the bed next to him, through a thin curtain, I heard an Asian couple talking in a language I could not understand. *All My Children* blared from their television set hanging like a vulture on the wall.

Looking down at Mike I saw a tough street kid in a child's body. Our staff met Mike at Illinois Masonic Hospital, where he had a bullet lodged behind his left ear from a street-related shooting. At the time he was eighteen years of age. Our outreach volunteers had known him for a few years, but he had always eluded them.

Most teen boys are fighting acne, battling their sisters over the bathroom, and playing sports. Not everyone experiences these everyday adolescent happenings, however. After being tossed from relative to relative, Mike followed in his mother's footsteps and began a life of street prostitution, drug abuse, and perpetual homelessness at the tender age of fourteen.

In the ensuing years, after that initial hospital visit, we walked with Mike through prison terms, stays in the hospital, and mighty battles to leave the streets. The bullet behind his ear has moved into his brain, causing regular seizures and a stroke several years ago. It is now too dangerous to be removed.

Mike is a success today. With our encouragement he has persevered through all of the suffering and brokenness. He is no longer a client of Emmaus, but part of our extended family. He now lives in southern Illinois and calls us once or twice a month to check in. For a few years he has been clean of drugs and has held down a job at a warehouse. Several years ago, in a moment of grace in prayer with some of our volunteers, Mike gave his heart to God and has been growing in his faith ever since. His mother became a Christian some time ago, and is now off the streets and married. Mike has a growing relationship with her and other relatives including his grandmother.

Building Relationships with Men in Prostitution

Emmaus Ministries is one of the few ministries that exist to reach men involved in prostitution. Our outreach ministers build relationships through being a predictable presence on the streets and spending time on the men's "turf" before we ask them to come to us. Showing a willingness to learn and to listen to the men communicates that we value them as people and desire to have relationships with them.

What do you need to know to involve yourself in such a ministry and build such relationships? Although it may be difficult to initiate a conversation with someone who appears so different from yourself, treat him as you would any other person and do a lot more listening than talking.

Be aware of your body language and make sure you are communicating your interest in the person through your facial expressions and gestures. Be sure that your words and your body language are consistent. It is understandable that you may feel uncomfortable, but consider this as part of the learning experience and remember that your world may be as foreign to them as theirs is to you.

When approaching a man to converse, do not approach him from the back, as this may seem threatening. Stay with your partner and watch out for each other as you seek to make contact with the men. Stay in areas that are visible and do not get in a car with anyone.

A good way to make contact with a man is to offer to buy him a meal or a cup of coffee. This gives you a chance to converse face-to-face while also meeting a physical need. You may be asked for money, but it is more helpful to share a meal with him. It gives you an opportunity to get to know him. Oftentimes simply being available by sitting, standing, or waiting on a strategic corner and allowing men to approach you is astonishingly productive; attraction versus promotion is the rule.

If you spend time in a bar, sit in one place so that you are available for conversation or interact with others through playing pool or darts. Be aware of pornography that may be going on and sit with your back to the television screens. You may want to order a drink or two while in the bar; our outreach ministers cannot order alcohol. It is customary to put a five- or ten-dollar bill on the counter and let the bartender tell you the price and give you your change. Leave a one-dollar tip, or two dollars if you are there for several hours. If you have an opportunity, converse with bartenders and others who work in the bars, being mindful that they are at work. This is another way to build relationships and have a presence in the bar.

Sharing the Gospel

The gospel can be communicated on outreach through several different means. Part of sharing the gospel is just a presence on the streets where people are lost; it is like being with the prodigal son in the distant country. Another way of sharing the gospel is through serving men: meeting their need for food or conversation, or referring them to services that will bring them closer to the fullness of life that God intends for them. Finally, sharing the gospel involves verbally communicating who Jesus is, His love for everyone on the street, how our sin separates us from God, and how everyone can know and experience the love of God through a relationship with Jesus.

Outreach ministers need to know their testimony and be able to communicate it in a way that is clear and understandable by anyone. Be aware of the Christian terms we use that people outside of the Church do not know or understand. Also, think about the meaning behind the terms you use and whether or not you are communicating what you think you are communicating. It may be helpful to have a few verses memorized that you can share with men you meet on the street.

CONCLUSION: EMMAUS IN LIFE AND DEATH

For all of the manifestations of the Lord and His power in our men's lives, our staff and volunteers are brought down to the valley by the tragedies. There have been many of them throughout the years. Street prostitution is not a safe occupation. Between violent tricks, the random violence of the streets, serial killers, drug overdoses, exposure to the elements, and illness such as HIV/AIDS, men do not often make it to age forty. But in the midst of tragedy, we also see the work of God and experience the joy of new life.

Anthony was living out the final hours of his life, his body ravaged by hepatitis and AIDS. One of our staff members had been ministering to Anthony, both in and out of the hospital, working with our ministry director to help get his medical care and other affairs in order, and even throwing a special birthday party for him. Our staff had also been taking Anthony to church on Sundays and to a healing service on Wednesday nights. Members of the congregation made him feel welcome and gathered around him in prayer. But despite our best efforts, we felt that his heart was hardening to the gospel as the fear of death set in.

An infection ultimately claimed Anthony's life. He was taken to the hospital on Friday morning, and the doctors predicted he would not make it through the weekend. Family members, consisting of an aunt and a handful of cousins, were called to his bedside. (Anthony's mother passed away when he was a young teen, and he did not know his father. His older brother, who had guided him through much of his life, was now in jail.)

Friday evening, with Anthony drifting in and out of consciousness, we asked him whether or not he wanted to accept Christ. He indicated that he did, and that he also wanted to be baptized. In the ICU of Weiss hospital in Uptown, with tubes running in and out of him and electronic monitors humming and chirping, an intimate baptismal ceremony was held around Anthony's bedside in the presence of family and a couple of our Emmaus guys. Later that evening, he slipped into a coma. He passed away the following day.

In the ensuing days, we were able to help his few remaining family members cover the cost of a simple burial, and we remembered his life and processed his death with our guys. We wrote the obituary and planned the memorial service and reception, as a witness of Christ's love to Anthony's family. We stood with our men as they chose to reconnect with their families and make commitments (or recommitments) to Christ, and we were once again reminded of why we are serving at this ministry.

The pioneer missionary C. T. Studd said, "Some wish to live within the sound of church and chapel bells. I want to run a rescue shop within a yard of hell."[18] We stand with these young men (and an increasing number of teen boys) at the impasse between spiritual and physical life and death.

REFLECTION QUESTIONS

1. Did you know anything about male prostitution before reading this chapter? What might be some of the reasons society does not talk about this issue?

2. What does C. T. Studd's quote mean to you? What does it look like to "run a rescue shop within a yard of hell" in today's culture and society?

3. Are you open to doing ministry with the sexually broken? What would it take? How could you or your church get involved in such a ministry?

Recommended Reading List

Bakke, Ray. *A Theology as Big as the City*. Downers Grove, Ill.: InterVarsity, 1997.

Hayes, John B. *Sub-merge*. Ventura, Calif.: Regal, 2006.

Hilfiker, David. *Not All of Us Are Saints*. New York: Farrar, Straus and Giroux, 2004.

Jewell, Dawn Herzog. *Escaping the Devil's Bedroom: Sex Trafficking, Global Prostitution, and the gospel's Transforming Power*. Oxford, United Kingdom: Monarch Books, 2008.

Loconte, Joe. *Seducing the Samaritan: How Government Contracts Are Reshaping Social Services*. Boston: Pioneer Institute for Public Policy Research, 1997.

Payne, Ruby K. *A Framework for Understanding Poverty*. Highlands, Tex.: aha! Process, Inc., 1996.

MARY KIM is a graduate of Moody Graduate School with a Master of Arts in Biblical Studies. She was born in Seoul, Korea, but moved to Los Angeles in 1980 with her Salvation Army parents and two brothers to open the Korean ministry of the Salvation Army in the United States. Mary has served on two summer mission teams to the Republic of Georgia. She is currently a student at The Salvation Army College for Officer Training in Chicago's Lakeview neighborhood.

MAJOR DAVID HARVEY has always been passionate about program and community development. Before becoming a Salvation Army officer, he was a Community Center Director and Youth Director in Dearborn, Michigan. As a Salvation Army officer, he has served as a pastor in Oak Creek and Green Bay, Wisconsin; Divisional Youth Leader in Indianapolis, Indiana; Territorial Youth Secretary in South America; Curriculum Director at The Salvation Army College for Officer Training; and presently is the administrator for the Chicago Kroc Center.

As a Salvation Army Officer, **MAJOR DARLENE HARVEY** has served as a pastor in Oak Creek and Green Bay, Wisconsin; Divisional Youth Leader in Indianapolis, Indiana; in community development and projects in South America; as Family Care Director at The Salvation Army College for Officer Training; and presently is working on the Kroc Center project. The Harveys have two sons.

CHAPTER 25

HEART TO GOD AND HAND TO MAN:

The Salvation Army in Chicago

Mary Kim and Dave and Darlene Harvey

Introduction: Chicago's Far South Side

"Our students face homelessness, gangs, little job opportunity when they get out, pregnancy, home violence, and little healthy social structure. How can we educate these children until these needs are met?"
(Principal, Far South Side high school)

"Our young people and young adults need doors opened for them to opportunity, or they cannot change and have no reason to change."
(Pastor, West Pullman church)

"My kids don't have anything to do down here. There are no structured or safe activities in the area. It is too dangerous to let them go outside. I would rather they be in my house playing games or watching TV then getting hurt in the neighborhood. We need somewhere that I can send my grandchildren and know they are safe and being mentored until I can pick them up."
(Grandparent, Roseland community)

One of the current challenges in Chicago is the Far South Side. Recent years of development planning and reconstruction are changing Chicago through the gentrification of the center city.[1] What used to be federal high rise and row houses is now vacant land or new townhouse developments.[2] What used to be skid row, the area of homelessness, prostitution, and addiction, is now full of million-dollar condos that are bringing Chicago's elite back to the city.[3] But where have the poor gone? Where are the new social challenges of those poor to be found? Chicago's Far South Side.

THE ARMY'S BEGINNINGS

The history of the Salvation Army has always been in an urban setting. William and Catherine Booth, the co-founders, had hearts for the city. The Salvation Army began in the East Side of London, in 1865, when William was seeking God to redefine his ministry as a new Methodist Connection pastor. He had just departed from his denominational ties as he felt that his church was apathetic to the poor and marginalized. Booth's premise was that Christians needed to go to the people on the streets. William Booth said of his calling:

> When I saw those masses of poor people, so many of them evidently without God or hope in the world, and found that they so readily and eagerly listened to me, following from Open-Air Meeting to tent, and accepting, in many instances, my invitation to kneel at the Savior's feet there and then, my whole heart went out to them. I walked back to our West End home and said to my wife . . . "O Kate, I have found my destiny! These are the people for whose salvation I have been longing all these years. As I passed by the doors of the flaming gin-palaces tonight I seemed to hear a voice sounding in my ears 'where can you go and find such heathen as these, and where is there so great a need for your labors?' And there and then in my soul I offered myself and you and the children up to this great work. Those people shall be our people, and they shall have our God for their God."[4]

The Salvation Army began as a street ministry on the East Side of London, England, called the "Christian Mission." From its humble beginnings, it has spread to 113 countries, preaching the gospel in 175 languages. Its mission statement says, "The Salvation Army, an international movement, is an evangelical part of the universal Christian Church. Its message is based on the Bible. Its ministry is motivated by the love of God. Its mission is to preach the gospel of Jesus Christ and to meet human needs in His name without discrimination."[5]

At the Salvation Army International Congress in 2000, General John Gowans stressed that the mission of the Salvation Army continues to be "to save souls, grow saints and serve suffering humanity."[6] The motto that has been used through the years to describe its work is "Heart to God and Hand to Man."[7]

Evangelism

The primary focus for William Booth's ministry was the salvation of souls.

In his book *Come Join Our Army,* R. G. Moyles explains some of the innovative means used by William Booth and the early Salvationists to attract those who would not otherwise attend church. His strategy was to go to the people on the streets and use unusual measures to attract them, such as the circus, color, drama, and music. They used advertisements like people-sized sandwich boards for their marches to announce speakers like "Cheap Jack" and "Hallelujah Pigeon-Flyer," speaking on topics like "Great Charges on the Devil" and "Salvation Hurricanes." One time Bramwell Booth, son of the founder, actually preached a sermon from a coffin after he had been carried around town for a funeral processional.[8]

Another unique aspect of the Salvation Army was its inclusion of women in ministry. Under the Victorian society when women could not vote, attend college, hold professional positions, or own property, women found a meaningful role as clergy, or called officers, as well as volunteers, evangelists, and missionaries within the Army. "Stories describing the impact of female preachers were common during the formative era of the Salvation Army. Often young women—who made up almost half of William Booth's early officers—led the pioneering ventures of the Army."[9]

The Salvation Army provided women liberation, excitement, and adventure. This was made possible because of the foundation that had been laid by Catherine Booth, the co-founder. Much of the Salvation Army's theology can be attributed to her as she was well educated and, at heart, a theologian. While her husband was at work ministering to the down and out on the East Side of London, she was busy with preaching campaigns to the more affluent on the West Side of London. In many ways it was her ministry that financially supported the Booths' mission. Many women were instrumental in starting new works for the Salvation Army, including the unofficial opening in the United States by Eliza Shirley and the official opening by George Railton and the seven "Hallelujah Lassies" (another term for charismatic women). William Booth was known to say, "My best men are women."[10]

Challenge of Social Ills and Sin

From its beginnings, the Salvation Army has been proactive in addressing the social ills and sins in society. Although its primary focus was the salvation of souls and evangelism, the Salvation Army established the motto "Soup, Soap, and Salvation," meaning a person needed to be met where he was and his physical needs had to be addressed before the gospel could be presented to him. The social problems of this time also included alcoholism, domestic violence, child labor, child neglect, prostitution, poverty, lack of shelter, and hunger. By 1870, the Salvation Army had established soup kitchens and counseling centers to address these needs. However, food was offered to people at a low cost instead of free. This was meant to maintain the recipient's dignity.[11]

William Booth was so moved by the social conditions of the poor in England that he wrote a controversial book in 1890 about the plight of the poor, *In Darkest England and the Way Out*. In it he outlined a program to help the poor and needy, something he termed "The Cab Horse Charter," claiming that in England, cab horses were better cared for than millions of the poorest people: "When a horse is down he is helped up, and while he lives he has food, shelter and work."[12] He outlined programs that provided assistance for individuals to be helped up, and to receive food, shelter, and opportunities for work. He placed the programs under three distinct umbrellas:

- A City Colony to provide shelters for the homeless, rescue homes for "wayward" girls, slum brigades, industrial homes, a safety match factory, and other short-term social services.

- A Farm Colony where men rescued from the City Colony could be retrained and rehabilitated.

- Colonies Overseas (in Canada, Australia, or South Africa) where those rehabilitated might make new lives for themselves.[13]

The public embraced this scheme enthusiastically. Within the first eight months, more than 200,000 copies of *Darkest England* were sold and nearly 100,000 pounds were donated to support the endeavor. The City Colony was deemed to be one of the best-organized, most successful privately sponsored social-reclamation ventures in the history of British social welfare.[14]

The Salvation Army was active in helping girls who were trapped in prostitution by providing shelter, sharing the gospel, helping them find a new way of life, or returning them to their parents' home. It also became increasingly clear that underage girls were deceived and trapped into this lifestyle. The age of consent was only thirteen and British Parliament had been waffling on a bill to raise it to sixteen. The Salvation Army helped move this bill by involving Mr. W. T. Stead, an editor of the *Pall Mall Gazette*, in writing articles that exposed the evils of prostitution. Mr. Stead was also involved with the Salvation Army in staging a "sting operation," which confirmed that an underage girl could be purchased for illegal purposes. The Salvation Army led the public reform by enlisting 330,000 signatures for a petition that was presented to Parliament. The legal age of consent was raised to sixteen. A thanksgiving meeting was held in Exeter Hall and thousands of Salvationists and other English citizens throughout England rejoiced over what many perceived as a grand moral victory. The Army prepared to set up homes to care for young girls who would be out on the streets as a result of the ruling.[15]

Another area of social reform involved making working conditions better for those who were involved in manufacturing matches. Because of poor working conditions in match factories, many workers contracted the disease called "phossy jaw." This disease ate away the roof of the mouth and the inside of the nose. William Booth opened a new match box factory to make "safety matches." Employees did not have to worry about contracting this serious illness. This also made a statement to society that the working class had the right to work in conditions that did not produce serious illness. It demonstrated the necessity of Christians getting involved in social justice.[16]

The Army in Chicago

The Army began its ministry in Chicago in February 1885, with Captain William Evans, his wife, and their assistant, Captain Edward Gay, on a street corner with a drum and concertina at Bush Temple, Chicago Avenue and Clark Street. Chicago became a great center of Salvationist activity in the country. Within the first year, Commissioner Frank Smith claimed that one thousand people had been saved in Army meetings. Chicago #8 Corps held thirty-nine outdoor meetings every week.[17] From "Salvage Brigades" in 1892, where old clothes and discards were collected and repaired, and the 1925 introduction of family shelters to get people off the streets, to the 1976 introduction of holistic alcoholic treatment for men and women, the Salvation Army has been working to help families find Christ through social outreach.[18]

Tom Seay Corps and Service Center: A Modern-Day "City Colony" in Chicago

The "City Colony" model of providing shelter for the homeless continues in every city where the Salvation Army exists. In Chicago, in the North Side community of Uptown, the premier Salvation Army ministry to homeless men, women, and their families is the Salvation Army Tom Seay Corps and Service Center. Tom Seay Corps came into existence in 1973 as a dream of famed Chicago philanthropist Tom Seay. The program initially served a growing population of homeless teens with a crisis housing unit on the upper floor, which became a men's overnight warming shelter in the 1980s and was closed in May 2007. The Corps has changed names and ministries three times, but never its focus and mission to save souls. That Tom Seay is located in Uptown is no accident, as the largest population of the homeless in any zip code continues to be Chicago's Uptown neighborhood.[19]

Tom Seay serves homeless and marginalized men and women in SRO's (sleeping room only) housing units that do not allow cooking. Tom Seay serves breakfast and lunch 365 days a year. In addition to nightly shelter and daily meals, Tom Seay offers pre-GED classes, laundry, addiction groups, mailroom services, AIDS testing, a weekly free medical clinic, computer lab, food pantry, clothing room, and showering facilities. Daily devotions are held in the morning and three worship services on Sunday. Tom Seay Corps is staffed by a team of thirty-two employees, eight of whom are bi-vocational pastors, in addition to the three Salvation Army officers.

Major John Price, Corps Officer of Tom Seay, puts it all into Kingdom perspective:

> *The battle for us has been and still continues to be to "keep the main thing the main thing." The question for us becomes: Where can we go to serve the people who need our help the most? Right now, it's Uptown. The neighborhood may change in twenty years, but the need will not. We are making a difference in our corner of the world, one life at a time. Providing dignity, hope, and encouragement with a hand up, not a hand down, is part of our service to others in Christ's name.*

Harbor Light Center: A Modern-Day "Farm Colony" in Chicago

The Chicago Harbor Light Center, on the Near West Side, is a "Farm Colony" of sorts where addicted people are retrained and rehabilitated. It has been serving homeless alcoholic men in Chicago since 1888. The Harbor Light Center opened an outpatient psychiatric clinic and a medical clinic on skid row in 1959, where they provided counseling and outpatient medical services by professionals in the fields of psychology, medicine, and sociology. The outpatient clinic continually incorporated new developments in the field of addiction and its treatment, and stayed relevant to the needs of its clients. After 1976, new programs were initiated: a residential treatment and halfway house, which were funded by the State Department of Alcoholism, and programs redesigned to treat alcoholics and drug addicts together.

Clients have typically gone through residential treatment programs or are still capable of stopping use of drugs/alcohol on their own for a period of time that is long enough for them to get involved in outpatient treatment and self-help groups such as AA and NA to prevent relapses and strengthen recovery. During the recovery process, clients live in the Center community or in structured living environments such as group homes.

The majority of clients at the time of their admission into the Harbor Light are homeless (about 80 percent), unemployed (about 90 percent), have no income (about 77 percent), and typically bring multiple problems such as legal-status issues, unemployment, physical conditions/illness, mental illness, and re-lationship/family problems. Besides the funded programs such as the residential treatment and halfway house, the Harbor Light has auxiliary services such as job referrals, adult education, computer training, job readiness training, and oppor-tunities to get involved with the spiritual activities of the Center, which augment and enhance the treatment and recovery process of the individual client.

Early leaders of the Salvation Army social ministries learned that it was vision and a love for God that could change a man's future. Envoy Walter McClintock was an architect who had lost his career due to alcoholism. He had been con-verted through the Salvation Army's ministry and was called to lead the Harbor Light Center where he saw men sobered and changed each day. His wife, Eunice, was a nurse who was able to do her part in serving the health needs of the men as they worked through the program. These individuals, like so many others, help demonstrate to us that it is not always the education of a person, but his heart for ministry, that can change the world for Christ. Two great truths that should encourage your ministry are: (1) If God moves your heart to make a difference, He will see you through even though you may not feel the most qualified, and (2) Some of your best ministry leaders may come from the fruits of your current ministry programs.

La Villita Corps: a Modern-Day "Colony Overseas" in Chicago

The Salvation Army La Villita Corps (or in Spanish, *Ejército de Salvación)* is an example of a "Colony Overseas." In the early 1980s, a long-time soldier (member) of the Army moved from Chile to Chicago. When he arrived, he saw a need to reach the growing immigrant population from Mexico that was living in the South Side 26th Street area known as La Villita, translated as "Little Village." Like many other communities in Chicago during the early part of the twenti-eth century, this section of Chicago was European—mostly German and Polish. During the last part of the century, it became Mexican.

The Mexican culture is very Catholic, so to "change religion," as they said, felt like they were going against their cultural heritage, their nationality, and their families. Loyalty is very important in the Mexican culture. However, the spiritual needs of these new immigrants, the holistic ministry that the Salvation Army was positioned to offer, and the care and love of the pioneer members of La Villita Corps began a work that after these many years has seen several officers and two locations. The La Villita Corps has grown to a community of around 160 people who worship together and share life. In addition to religious services throughout the week, La Villita Corps has an after-school program, English as a Second Lan-guage classes, a food pantry, and emergency assistance.

When asked about some current challenges that La Villita Corps is facing when it comes to holistic urban ministry, La Villita Administrator Carlos Moran replied:

> *The biggest challenge is the "illegal status" in terms of immigration for most of the population. The fear of being deported, divided families, and not being able to reunite because of legal issues are real fears in the community. A big problem is the idea that somehow immigrants are using tax dollars for services, when in reality they are hard workers, who pay taxes in every sale and service they buy, who receive little or no protection, and who contribute to the economy as good consumers.*

At La Villita Corps and elsewhere, Moran concludes, "When people come as immigrants, they are looking for a change. They are willing to develop new loyalties, and to have something to remember their mother country. We try to provide an environment of grace and understanding, a place where they feel they belong."

STOP-IT: A Modern-Day "Social Reform" Issue in Chicago

The Salvation Army continues to be involved in issues of social reform and justice. One such area of involvement has been the issue of human trafficking, a modern-day form of slavery. According to the Department of Health and Human Services, victims of human trafficking are subjected to force, fraud, or coercion for the purpose of sexual exploitation or forced labor. Victims are young children, teenagers, men, and women. After drug dealing, human trafficking is tied with the illegal arms industry as the second largest criminal industry in the world today, and it is the fastest growing.[20]

In October 2006, the Salvation Army received a three year grant from the Department of Health and Human Services and STOP-IT began. STOP-IT, Salvation Army's Trafficking Outreach Program and Intervention Techniques, has three objectives:

1. Outreach to victims of trafficking, providing support, and planning to assist in safe exit from trafficking.

2. Train community service providers regarding trafficking.

3. Raise public awareness on trafficking indicators.

STOP-IT, and other Salvation Army programs and services for social reform, justice, and welfare, flow out of the Army's mission to save souls, grow saints, and serve suffering humanity in the name and love of Jesus Christ. "The New

Covenant brought hope through Jesus Christ to fulfill the commands of the Old Covenant for living out justice and mercy," states Maribeth Velazquez Swanson, LCSW, Program Administrator for STOP-IT. She continues:

> *So, with our faith in Jesus and our Spirit-led organization, the Salvation Army is battling to eradicate the insidious plague of human trafficking, through prevention, training professionals and the faith community, and partnering with other organizations to raise awareness that human trafficking doesn't just happen "over there," but right here in the greater Chicago Metropolitan region. How we do this doesn't matter as much as why we do this. Our core belief that all people are created in the image of God is foundational to all of our efforts. When we have the privilege to directly support the rescue and restoration of a victim, we serve not only through our professional knowledge and experience of working with traumatized individuals, but with the understanding of God's character and our commitment to reflect His character to the weak and broken. "Thou, O Lord, art a God full of compassion, and gracious, long-suffering, and plenteous in mercy and truth" (Psalm 86:15 KJV).*

Many social conditions that were challenges in the early days of the Salvation Army continue to be opportunities for Christian organizations and churches to give their hearts to God and hands to man. The great needs in Chicago include poverty, low graduation rates in the most challenged schools, unemployment, underemployment, no health insurance coverage, child care issues, teen parenting, sexually transmitted diseases, drug and alcohol abuse, and homelessness. The Salvation Army continues to address these needs in a relevant and holistic manner, using the best of what we have to offer in the name and love of Jesus Christ.

The Ray and Joan Kroc Corps Community Center Project

Thirty communities across the country have been chosen to receive a gift from the Joan Kroc Estate to use the arts and sports to introduce disciplines in the lives of children that will guide them in future decisions and careers.

In Chicago, we have been approved for such a center and are finalizing plans for implementation for this center to be on Chicago's Far South Side. This center will be located in West Pullman, and will serve a three-mile radius of other Chicago communities such as Roseland, Morgan Park, Beverly, Pullman, and the southern suburbs of Harvey, Dolton, Riverdale, and Calumet Park. All of these communities have been in the newspapers regularly with problems of gangs and violence as well as corruption. To many, these areas are "the forgotten southside."[21]

COMMUNITY DEMOGRAPHIC MATRIX FOR WEST PULLMAN COMMUNITIES							
COMMUNITY	POP	RACIAL DEMOGRAPHICS				% OF INDIVID BELOW Age 18	MEDIAN INCOME	% OF INDIVID BELOW POVERTY
		WHITE	BLACK	HISPANIC	OTHER			
Beverly	21,992	63%	32%	3%	3%	30%	$66,823	4%
Morgan Park	25,226	30%	67%	2%	1%	30%	$53,133	12%
Pullman	8,921	8%	81%	9%	1%	32%	$30,966	22%
Riverdale	15,055	11%	86%	3%	0%	50%	$13,178	56%
Roseland	52,723	1%	98%	1%	0%	32%	$32,237	18%
Washington Hts	29,843	1%	98%	1%	1%	28%	$43,201	12%
West Pullman	36,649	1%	94%	5%	1%	36%	$39,601	22%
Suburbs								
Calumet Park	8,516	12%	83%	5%	0%	32%	$45,357	12%
Blue Island	23,463	54%	24%	22%	0%	33%	$36,520	13%
Harvey	30,000	10%	81%	9%	0%	39%	$31,958	22%
TOTALS	**252,388**	**19%**	**74%**	**6%**	**1%**	**34%**	**$39,297**	**19%**

Source: U.S. Census Bureau, Census 2000
Source: Metro Chicago Information Center

Chicago's Far South Side neighborhoods are undergoing a challenging reality. While creating a plan for steady revitalization, with the goal of becoming safe, affordable communities for working families, they have seen a growth in families moving to this area from Chicago's inner-city federal housing projects that have been knocked down. Within a three-mile radius of the proposed site of our future ministry center at 119th and Loomis, there are 255,000 people, more than a third of whom are under eighteen. These neighborhoods have the city's highest prevalence of high school dropouts; more than 30 percent of students do not complete school, and 36,477 adults do not have their high school diploma, which represents 21.1 percent of the adult population. This is 10.3 percent below the national average.[22]

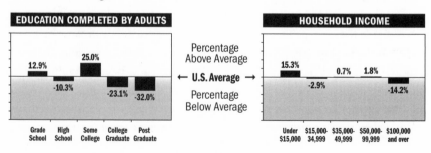

412

Nine of the twelve Chicago neighborhoods with greater than 25 percent of residents living in poverty are located in the greater service area. These include Englewood, West Pullman, Pullman, Riverdale, Roseland, Calumet Park, Harvey, Dolton, and Morgan Park. The Salvation Army has recently conducted two studies in these areas. A 1999 study by MCIC found that the top two unmet human service needs in Chicago are for gang alternatives and youth/teen centers. In July 2006, MCIC did a more specific study for the Far South Side of Chicago and found that needs such as affordable housing, child care, and job training, while important, are in fact less urgently needed than the type of community center currently envisioned. The real needs in the community include:

- *Recreational programs* that target youth and young adults, offering a variety of sports (soccer, golf, swimming) and all-season programming, especially after school.

- *Education and family components* such as tutoring and mentoring within and across age groups, reading groups, and special workshops to address family life skills, including financial planning and budgeting, stress management, and parenting classes for single parents.

- *Social services* that link community members to existing organizations and services and foster relationships between adults and youth, families, and seniors.

- *Health education and screenings,* and nutrition and mental health workshops for adults and seniors.

- *Arts and cultural programs* to increase exposure to performing arts like dance, poetry, music, and drama, especially for youth and families.[23]

Every church in America would do well to have a community needs assessment done for its area. What it has shown the Salvation Army is that the Ray and Joan Kroc Corps Community Center is a great way to move in to a community with few hopes and dreams on the horizon. It is what Mayor Richard M. Daley of Chicago intuitively understood was the key when he said, "While government could never rebuild souls, it is organizations like this that help rebuild the souls and lives of those most in need. And we must continue to support their efforts."[24]

The Salvation Army has this unique opportunity to fit the dream of Joan Kroc into its holistic mission. Her dream was to open centers of Olympic-level training in sports as well as professional training and performance opportunities in the arts for young people in urban, high risk areas.

Mrs. Kroc grew up in Minneapolis in a low-income family. People who believed in her gave her two gifts she treasured. One was a pair of skates and lessons that she used to win a Junior Skating Competition in that city. A sponsor also paid for piano lessons, which later landed her a musician's job in a restaurant where she met Ray Kroc, the founder of McDonald's.[25]

The belief in the potential of people is what will carry on Joan Kroc's legacy in these new centers throughout the country. The Salvation Army will use state-of-the-art sports training facilities to teach underprivileged kids and their families sports disciplines that will equip them for life's challenges and bring scholarship opportunities to kids, especially boys, who now only have a 3 percent chance of graduating from college.[26]

A Kroc Center will also use the arts to open doors for young people to see a discipline with fine arts and music that may guide their futures. To find the root of the problems facing our young people is the key to opening the door to their futures.

TRANSFERABLE PRINCIPLES FOR URBAN MINISTRY

While there is no such thing as the perfect church, we all need to evaluate our ministries and communities. We need to make sure that our mission of reaching the world for Christ is not conflicting with the way we treat people outside of our churches. People are hungry for the love of God, as expressed through a gospel that meets their physical needs and points them to independence from governmental support while finding freedom in Christ. Here are some examples of a new community perspective that will help any church in its pursuit to extend its heart to God and hand to man.

Help Others Without Judging

If we are honest, we often want to turn our heads when we see a man or woman sitting on the street with cup in hand, or people who come to our church door with the smell of booze on their breath. We know that the need we see is only the tip of the iceberg of problems they are facing. But what our struggling communities need today are people who will listen, people who will not judge them and be open to hear their stories and point them to a church or other support systems that will help meet the multifaceted needs they might be facing.

Discover the Greater Need

We must enter each ministry opportunity with a fresh set of eyes that will help us see beyond the immediate to what could be. Christ has given His life for these people and offered hope, peace, and restoration. We (the Harveys) were working with a school in the Milwaukee area where teen pregnancy was on the rise. The school was expelling young mothers from school because they were missing class days to take care of their babies. The school would not acknowledge their need, and the community did not know where to start to tackle this issue.

We were located across the street from the school and decided to start a daycare for infants of adolescents. In this way, the young moms could know their kids were safe, they could attend school, and they could even come to the Corps during lunch to be with their babies. The visible need was pregnant teens. The greater need was for girls to know they were loved and could still make it in life if they moved forward to accept their responsibility and find God's plan for their lives.

Every Person Deserves a Chance Without Discrimination

The Church today needs to evaluate the reality of discrimination in our communities, both without and within the Church. We find in many of our drug and alcoholic treatment programs that it can take a man three to seven times in and out of the program before he can break his addiction. One of the hallmarks of the Salvation Army is that it takes the cases and people that no other organizations will help. We have been called "the net at the bottom of social need." When you fall through the cracks, the Salvation Army will find a way to get you on your feet. Suburban churches and Christians, who have been blessed with resources and influence, need to increase their support for families in their communities and in the surrounding cities. They must not discriminate against those in need but help them get on their feet by using their influence to get them jobs in areas that would normally turn their backs, help get them clothed, and assist them to care for their families and support their churches.

See the Possibilities, not Just the Person Before You

When we see those in such deep need, we need to remember, "But for the grace of God, there go I." We have been blessed by God to have education and a ministry heart to change the world. Someone believed in us and helped keep us on the path of God. We need to have that same support for others who cross our path. Not to treat them as numbers, but to pray to God that He would reveal one person, or one family, that He wants us to focus on, even if it is outside of our comfort zone.

I remember visiting a home of one of my scouts to give him an award he had missed the Sunday before in church. When I entered the home, the father was sitting in a chair, watching television with a beer in his hand. He kept the back of his chair to me because, as he later revealed, he was scared to death to have a pastor in his house. God placed that man and family on my heart, and through continued visits and family tragedies, they eventually came to the Lord. Today, they are officers in our movement. I often thank God that He did not allow me to write them off as another derelict family who hates God and wants nothing to do with the church. All of us needed a chance to experience a friend who pointed us to salvation.

It Takes Many Doors to Find the One God Has Equipped You to Open

Churches have different strengths and passions. We need to accept our uniqueness and reach out to people with needs that our strengths can help. If we cannot help them, at least we should listen and point them to people, churches, or organizations whose skills and resources match those needs. Evangelism groups have told us that it takes three to seven touches before someone accepts the gospel. It may also take several social assistance touches for a family to realize its true need and find a door to God and independence.

Work Together for the Greater Good

We do not need to win this world to Christ alone. The Salvation Army, for example, is comprised of more external volunteers, churches, and collaborative organizations than internal support. In your community you can organize or join local church or social service networks that can make a better impact by coordinating ministries. Or, your church could work with your local Salvation Army or social service organizations to volunteer and take a family in need to the place where God has created them to be.

CONCLUSION: DOING THE MOST GOOD IN THE 'HOOD

The recent national slogan for the Salvation Army is "Doing the Most Good"—taking the resources of dollars and volunteers that God sends our way and using them to reach the maximum number of people in need with the maximum outcome possible. For Chicago, we say, "Doing the Most Good in the 'Hood," targeting Chicago's most challenging communities with new centers and initiatives that will transform individuals, families, and communities. May God challenge us to get out of our churches and work to change lives, one family or individual at a time. May He grant us the humility to work together in doing the greater good in this work in His name.

REFLECTION QUESTIONS

1. William Booth received his vision for ministry when walking through the East Side of London. Where have you walked that you have seen God's vision for your ministry? What impression has God placed on your heart? Can you say, as he did, "Those people shall be our people and they shall have our God for their God"?

2. What might God be calling you to do in your community to bring about change that will not only help people, but bring them dignity and respect through involvement and work?

3. What churches or Salvation Army centers are you collaborating with in ministry to your city? Are you the "lone ranger," or are there others you can unite with to bring about a larger impact in your greater community?

Recommended Reading List

Brook, Stephen. *God's Army: The Story of the Salvation Army.* Philadelphia: Trans-Atlantic Publications, 1999.

Hattersley, Roy. *Blood & Fire: William and Catherine Booth and Their Salvation Army.* New York: Doubleday, 2000.

Ludwig, Charles. *Mother of an Army.* Minneapolis: Bethany House, 1987.

McKinley, Edward H. *Marching to Glory: The History of the Salvation Army in the United States of America.* Atlanta: Salvation Army Supplies, 1986.

Troutt, Margaret. *The General Was a Lady: The Story of Evangeline Booth.* Nashville: A. J. Hollman Co., 1980.

Yaxley, Trevor. *William & Catherine: The Life and Legacy of the Booths, Founders of the Salvation Army.* Minneapolis: Bethany House, 2003.

DAVID ANDERSON is a psychologist and Executive Director of Lydia Home Association. He received his B.A. in community health at Northern Illinois University and his Psy.D. from the Chicago School of Professional Psychology. He has been married for twenty-five years to Karen and has two birth children (Nathan and Audrey), one adoptive child (Connor), and one foster son (Nick) who has two children of his own.

CHAPTER 26

UNLEASHING THE FAMILY:
Safe Families for Vulnerable Children (Lydia Home)

David Anderson

Introduction: Safe Families for Children

During the final week of 2007, Chicago was shocked by the actions of a young mother who quietly exited a train with her three-year-old daughter, leaving her two sons, ages six and four, behind. Fellow passengers frantically attempted to get the mother's attention, but she walked away, abandoning her young boys.[1]

Similar scenarios of parents being unable or unwilling to care for their children occur with greater frequency than many of us are aware. State child-welfare emergency hotlines throughout the nation reportedly receive more than five million calls each year of suspected child abuse or neglect. Of those calls, about one million meet the State's criteria for abuse, thus activating services.[2] What happens to the remaining four million families? Someone who knows them or knows of them was concerned enough to make a report to authorities, yet their situation remains unchanged. And what of the additional countless families that are in crisis but are not identified? Safe Families for Children is a program that allows God's people to give meaningful, life-changing support to families in crisis.

CURRENT SAFETY NET

The current public system in place to care for and protect children is called the child welfare system, or Department of Children and Family Services (DCFS), Department of Human Services (DHS), etc. This system is given the mandate to remove abused or neglected children from their parents' custody, at which time the children become "wards of the State." This system of care is controversial and, at times, fraught with errors. Yet there are few good alternatives.

Developed by most states in the 1940s and 1950s, this concept of the government protecting children from their parents is only two or three generations old. Prior to this, the Church and other faith-driven organizations were at the forefront of caring for vulnerable children. The Christian Church was active in providing a safe haven for children who were abandoned or neglected by their parents. In fact, throughout history, the church and other religious organizations were the safety net for discarded and vulnerable children. Church history is filled with accounts of believers rescuing "exposed" infants in ancient Rome, taking in orphans, caring for the sick and the elderly, and sheltering pilgrims. Many orphanages, hospitals, and asylums were first developed by Christians putting their faith into practice.[3]

However, with the development of state-run systems of care within the last fifty to sixty years, the Church has relinquished its role. As the government has stepped up, the Church stepped back, to the point of becoming irrelevant to the real and significant needs of hurting families. A handful of Christian families brave the foster care system. However, the Church is no longer a visible presence in helping the very groups we are commanded to help—the orphans and widows.

A THEOLOGY OF ORPHANS AND WIDOWS

Throughout Scripture, there are numerous references to widows and children. Few would argue with the assertion that children are the most vulnerable "people group" in our society, requiring special attention and protection. In fact, James associates the care of orphans and widows with one's purity of faith. He writes, "Religion that God our Father accepts as pure and faultless is this: to look after orphans and widows in their distress and to keep oneself from being polluted by the world" (James 1:27). In Lamentations 2:19, Jeremiah cries, "Arise, cry out in the night, as the watches of the night begin; pour out your heart like water in the presence of the Lord. Lift up your hands to him for the lives of your children, who faint from hunger at the head of every street." Asaph the songwriter pleads, "Defend the cause of the weak and fatherless; maintain the rights of the poor and oppressed. Rescue the weak and needy; deliver them from the hand of the wicked" (Ps. 82:3–4).

David further describes God's concern for orphans and widows, "Father to the fatherless, defender of widows—this is God, whose dwelling is holy. God places the lonely in families; he sets the prisoners free and gives them joy" (Ps. 68:

5–6 NLT). Isaiah adds, "Learn to do right! Seek justice, encourage the oppressed. Defend the cause of the fatherless, plead the case of the widow" (Isa. 1:17). God clearly states that they need protection: "Do not take advantage of a widow or an orphan. If you do and they cry out to me, I will certainly hear their cry. My anger will be aroused, and I will kill you with the sword; your wives will become widows and your children fatherless" (Exodus 22:22–24).

Jesus valued children. His words are direct, "Let the little children come to me, and do not hinder them, for the kingdom of heaven belongs to such as these" (Matt. 19:14). He also warned those who would mistreat them, "But if anyone causes one of these little ones who believe in me to sin, it would be better for him to have a large millstone hung around his neck and to be drowned in the depths of the sea" (Matt. 18:6).

THE EARLY CHURCH'S CARE

When the early church was fully alive in engaging the culture and significantly impacting the "least of these," the practice of offering care to strangers (hospitality) became a distinguishing characteristic.[4] These Christians became known for their acts of kindness and service. Babies who were deformed or of the wrong sex were discarded on the waste heaps outside the city. The Christians would gather the unwanted babies and raise them as if they were their own. The Christian writer Tertullian (A.D. 200) wrote, "It is our care of the helpless, our practice of lovingkindness that brands us in the eyes of many of our opponents."[5]

As in ancient times, children today continue to be hurt by societal ills that have filtered down to the family. Christians are concerned and disturbed by reports like the two boys abandoned on the train, but often do not know how to make a difference. That is where the ministry of Safe Families for Children comes in. Safe Families is a movement of hundreds of Christian families who have opened their homes to care for children whose parents are struggling. By demonstrating biblical hospitality, Safe Families returns the church to the forefront of caring for "orphans and widows."

LONELY BUT NOT ALONE

Kim came to the United States from China to begin her post-graduate studies at the University of Iowa. After two years, when her father became ill and was no longer able to send money for her educational costs, Kim made the painful decision to drop out of school. She moved to Chicago and began working as a cashier.

Shy and feeling very lonely, Kim became involved with the first boyfriend she ever had and became pregnant. Her boyfriend pressured her to end the pregnancy, and Kim broke up with him. Eight and a half months pregnant, she was experiencing much shame regarding her behavior and anxiety over how she could ever build a secure life for herself and her child. She had no one to turn to. She went to an adoption agency to give up her child, but the agency referred her to Safe Families because of her ambivalence.

When Kim came to Safe Families for help, the staff explained that she could place her newborn with Safe Family volunteers while she earned the money needed to get an apartment and to get better established. Kim wept with relief. Not long after this meeting Kim delivered a beautiful baby boy, who went to stay with Safe Families volunteers. Kim named the baby after the Safe Family father, and she requested that they become his godparents. The family had a great opportunity to share their faith in word and deed, and their relationship with Kim continued long after the baby was returned to her care. They have become her extended family.

Safe Families for Children

Kim and others like her would only be able to access the help of the State child welfare agency by being an abusive or a neglectful parent. This is not a criticism of these State agencies; investigating and intervening in abusive situations is their mandate. But we must not assume that State welfare agencies can solve the problem of countless children unprotected in unsafe homes where there is crisis or serious stress. With the changing economy, many more families are experiencing financial crisis, unemployment, and homelessness. Others are dealing with family violence, parental drug and/or alcohol abuse, illness, or incarceration. According to the Children's Defense Fund, children living in families with incomes less than fifteen thousand dollars are twenty-two times more likely to be abused (physically or sexually) or neglected (insufficient food, clothing, housing, or supervision) than children living in families with incomes of thirty thousand dollars or more.[6] Children with parents who abuse drugs or alcohol are four times more likely to be abused than those who do not. The number of poor children under age eighteen was 12.8 million (17.4 percent), or one child in six. The number of poor children under age five was 4.2 million (20.7 percent), or one child in five.[7]

During crises, many parents are not capable of providing a safe and caring environment and are at increased risk for abusing or neglecting their children. Historically the extended family often stepped in to support parents by taking care of children for short periods of time, and neighbors came alongside families in crisis. However, many urban families are socially isolated and their extended family is not available. The children in a family traumatized by crisis become especially at risk for neglect or abuse as their parents struggle to cope with crushing circumstances and emotions.

Safe Families for Children (SFFC) is a network of hundreds of host families in metro Chicago who are passionate about helping and caring for at-risk children and their parents. Designed to extend and strengthen the community safety net for at-risk families, Safe Families is a positive alternative to the State child welfare system. The voluntary and non-coercive nature of Safe Families is a hallmark of the program. Free from punitive interactions and coerciveness, parents in crisis are able to place their children (newborns through parenting teens) in safe homes, still maintaining custody of their children. The objectives of Safe Families are to (1) deflect children from the State child welfare system, (2) prevent child abuse and neglect, and (3) provide a family in crisis with the necessary support while demonstrating the love and compassion of Jesus Christ. Many parents struggle in their roles because of limited informal social supports and unavailable extended family support. Many Safe Families have become the extended family that the struggling parent never had. Additionally, by temporarily freeing parents from the responsibility of caring for their child, SFFC provides parents with time to address personal issues without fear of losing custody of their child or children.

Besides meeting the needs of families in crisis, Safe Families serves as a bridge in several ways. Resource-rich families who desire to share their blessings are connected with resource-limited families. Suburban families who typically are isolated from the struggles of those trapped in poverty are connected with urban families struggling daily to make ends meet. Finally, the ministry connects the public sector (State agencies) and the Church as the welfare system increasingly has seen Safe Families as a resource for families who are at risk but do not fall within their abuse/neglect criteria.

From Depression to Life Change

Bridges were built when Donna handed her two children over to Safe Families volunteers Mike and Katy Wright. Suffering from depression and feeling overwhelmed, Donna had been habitually tucking her daughters, Alexandria, age four, and Taylor, age two, into bed and leaving the apartment to do drugs and attempt to escape her problems. She had no family to help. At one point, she called DCFS to hand over her children, but the State referred her to Safe Families.

"I was depressed, and things had gotten to the point that I almost didn't care about anything," Donna recalled. "But I did want to get better, so I agreed to have my kids placed with the Wrights. I started meeting with a counselor to work through issues related to my own abuse I'd experienced as a kid. I didn't realize until then how stressed out and angry I had become."

Donna, who lived in Chicago, began visiting her children at the Wrights' suburban home and eventually began spending weekends with the family, which included Mike and Katy's four children, ages ten to fifteen. Today she recognizes God's hand in providing her with a friend/mentor like Katy at that critical point in her life.

"Katy wouldn't give up on me and wouldn't let me give up on myself," she stated. "She challenged me to think differently about life and my kids and God. Katy was exactly what I needed in order to change."

During the four months that Alexandria and Taylor were living with the Wrights, Donna received Christ as her Savior and became involved in a supportive church home where she was baptized by the Wrights. She is now regularly attending a home group Bible study, meeting weekly with a mentor, and ministering to the youth in her church. She has also become a devoted mother, spending hours helping her children with their schoolwork and reaching out to other overwhelmed mothers.

"Safe Families made it possible for me to get the help I needed without losing my kids to the State, and I'll always be thankful for that," Donna said. "I think about how bad off I was before I met the Wrights, and I know God has really blessed me."

BIBLICAL HOSPITALITY

The Wrights, along with other Safe Families, epitomize the biblical command for all Christians to live lives characterized by hospitality. We are witnessing an extraordinary movement of care as families join this wave of biblical hospitality by using their homes for Kingdom purposes. In so doing, the Church returns to the forefront of caring for children, as it had been throughout history.

The hospitality of the Bible is dangerous, demanding, and deliberate. It is radical, far different from the lifestyle with which we may be accustomed. While the Safe Families program provides as many safeguards as reasonably possible, opening our doors to strangers can be risky. Our own children can be exposed to undesirable language and behaviors. The needs of children newly separated from their parents and feeling stressed will demand more of our time and energy. Our children will need to sacrifice and exercise patience as they share their possessions and their parents with those to whom we are ministering. However, the blessings run deep when we practice biblical hospitality and demonstrate to the world that the Christian family, in obedience to Christ, can be a powerful source of change in our society.

Overwhelmed

Pam experienced the power of biblical hospitality after coming to us in a desperate state. She had eight children, ages six months to sixteen years old, and was raising them alone, without any support from their fathers. Barely making it by any standard, the last straw came when Pam lost her job, was evicted, and became homeless. She and her children lived in a van for a period of time and then moved in with "friends," who reported her to child welfare officials. An investigation was underway, and Pam began to see that losing her children was a very real possibility.

We heard about Pam's situation from a friend of the ministry, who asked if we would be willing to care for the children through our Safe Families program. Within days, five of our volunteer families took in Pam's eight children, initially planning on care lasting about three months. As our staff got to know Pam, though, we realized she would need more time. So we asked our volunteers if they could keep her children for a year. All said yes.

Among those volunteers were Peter and Cindy Baldwin and their four children, who cared for Trinity, Pam's six-month-old daughter.

"We are totally committed to this baby, and to seeing Pam's family be reunited someday," Cindy said during Trinity's stay with them. "Our reason for doing it is simple —God wants us to help people in need. After all, these are His children too."

Pam found a food service position at a suburban school and secured housing. All of her children were able to go home in far less time than anticipated. Pam's fear of losing them to the State system was assuaged because of Christian families practicing hospitality.

Hospitality Defined

But what exactly is hospitality? We often think of inviting friends and family to our home for food and socializing as hospitality; however, that may be more accurately defined as entertaining. Entertaining is enjoyable and often strengthens relationships, but it is not to be confused with biblical hospitality. Likewise, we refer to hotel and restaurant establishments as part of the "hospitality industry." Unfortunately, that is often the extent to which many of us understand and live out hospitality. The practice of hospitality, apart from the hospitality industry, is nearly extinct in our society.

Somewhere along the way we have changed and watered down the original meaning of this concept. The Greek word for hospitality is *philoxenia*, which means "love of strangers." We do not often put the words *love* and *stranger* in the same sentence. Fear of strangers is a much more common thought than love of strangers.

However, biblical hospitality is powerful and instrumental in reaching our world with the gospel of Christ. In our postmodern age, hospitality is an essential practice that needs to accompany our verbal proclamation of faith in order to restore our credibility to a society that sees us as being anti-gay, overly political, hypocritical, insincere, sheltered, and judgmental.

The practice of Christian hospitality was most vibrant during the first five centuries of the church. It provided credibility (word and deed) and distinguished the Church from its surrounding environment. The teachings of the New Testament command all of God's people to be hospitable, and the early Church believed it and lived it out. This involved loving and welcoming strangers into their homes. Hospitality was not seen as a special gift that only a few possessed, but rather as a command for all Christians. Hospitality was one of the foundational ministries of the early Church. Christians were to regard hospitality to strangers as a fundamental expression of the gospel.

The New Testament makes frequent mention of hospitality. Peter, with insight into the difficulty of living a life of hospitality, encourages us to "offer hospitality to one another without grumbling" (1 Peter 4:9). Hebrews also alludes to the fact that the practice of hospitality can be mysterious and have its rewards. "Do not forget to entertain strangers, for by so doing some people have entertained angels" (Heb. 13:2). Paul instructs Christians to "practice hospitality" (Rom. 12:13), because hospitality does not come naturally and it often goes against our nature. Not only were all Christians encouraged to live lives of hospitality, but leaders were especially instructed to be hospitable. In fact, hospitality is a characteristic that was to be used to identify those who should be considered for leadership. "Now the overseer must be above reproach, the husband of but one wife, temperate, self-controlled, respectable, hospitable, able to teach" (1 Tim. 3:2).

Choices, Consequences, and Compassion

Nadia came to the United States from Slovakia as part of a church choir performing in a Slovakian church in Chicago. To her friends' surprise, she married a man shortly after meeting him. After the birth of their first child, Nadia's husband became physically abusive to her and left her for another woman. With three months to go until the birth of her second child, Nadia came to Safe Families seeking assistance. In broken English, she struggled to convey her anxieties about separating from her children and allowing them to be cared for by "strangers."

Nadia was anxious about the future of her young family.

A few months later, Nadia's son, Jona, was born, and she agreed to place him and his one-year-old sister, Jobelia, in the home of Safe Families caregivers. By living out biblical hospitality, the Safe Family had a unique opportunity to demonstrate Christ's love to a mother who was overwhelmed and homeless. Nadia was able to get her life back on track and have her children returned to her care.

BARRIERS TO HOSPITALITY

When people consider the challenge of opening their homes to others, a number of concerns arise. These concerns can lead to barriers that hinder people from practicing the discipline of hospitality.

Castle Mentality

Much of our income is invested into our homes. Because we invest so much, we may develop a perspective that our homes are our castles, something of significant value. That perspective can easily shift to our homes and their contents becoming our idols. I once spoke at a fairly wealthy church, and a couple came up afterward indicating an interest in opening their home to a child but wanted a guarantee that their possessions would not be harmed. When told that I could not make such a promise, they walked away discouraged. I could not help but think of the rich young ruler who walked away from Jesus because of his possessions (Mark 10:17–25). This is probably the biggest challenge for our wealthy North American church. The practice of hospitality is an alternative to a life focused on consumption and materialism. God lends us our homes and possessions to use for Kingdom purposes, not just for our own comfort and entertainment. Hospitality ensures that we maintain a right relationship with our possessions.

Fortress Mentality

With so many problems and negative influences in our world, it is natural to desire a "safe place" to which we can withdraw. Often our homes become this "safe place" with figuratively high walls and deep moats. The desire for safety and protection is not wrong. However, it can have a detrimental effect as we are lulled into thinking our safety comes from our fortress rather than trusting in Christ for His protection. This fortress mentality also keeps others out who desperately need to be exposed to the extraordinary love of Christ as expressed in relationships within a family. When was the last time a neighbor, a stranger, or an acquaintance crossed the threshold of your front door?

Haven Mentality

Our homes have become our sanctuaries for refueling and restoration. Certainly this is important. However, hospitality and restoration are not necessarily mutually exclusive. The Lord often uses a variety of people and places to restore us, even our guests. Reliance on our home for restoration may detract us from other ways to be restored, such as fully using all we are and have for His purpose. "As the deer pants for streams of water, so my soul pants for you, O God" (Ps. 42:1). Additionally, the joy of seeing God at work in someone's life is a tremendously rejuvenating experience that we may inadvertently exclude ourselves from when we fail to open our doors to others.

Time

Time is the most often reported reason that people give for being unable to open their homes. Families are quite busy running to school meetings, soccer games, church activities, etc. Many Christian families would like to find the time to mentor or tutor a child, visit a homeless shelter, or reach out to their neighbors. A ministry like Safe Families provides very busy families opportunities to serve because we bring the needs to them and the children are integrated into their routines.

ROLE OF THE FAMILY IN MINISTRY

This type of integration into the family not only has a healing effect on the at-risk children, it also allows the host family to participate together in life-changing ministry. There are few opportunities today for an entire family to minister together. Church programs and ministries are usually divided by age and sometimes gender. This is helpful in meeting the specific needs of various groups. However, when possible, ministering together as a family promotes unity and allows our children real experience in living out their faith. The Christian family is one of the most powerful sources of change in our society. Our homes are a powerful change agent. Rather than sheltering our families, we need to unleash them for ministry. It is easy for us to see our families as fragile, requiring us to handle them with care by defending and protecting rather than unleashing.

Few sports teams ever win games by focusing solely on defensive strategies. If the Church is going to make a significant impact in our society, we have to use our homes and change our strategies from being predominantly defensive to an offensive game plan. Our families are not as fragile as we think.

Healthy churches understand the importance of both reaching out and caring for their own (discipleship). If one or the other is out of line or nonexistent, problems often occur. Might this also be the same for our families? Healthy families must care for their own (raise their children) but also reach out to others as a family. By not recognizing the need to reach out, the Church is less effective and our families miss out on a unique blessing—and some suffer the consequences of a lack of purpose.

The section on hospitality in the book of Hebrews (13:2) seems to imply that there may be a surprise ("some people have entertained angels") for hosts as they live out hospitality. Many of our Safe Families attest to the fact that they received more of a blessing than they gave. It makes sense. When a family is given a life-changing purpose that requires the involvement of every member, new life and energy is breathed into the family. Some have said that their family now has a purpose beyond just raising the next generation. "Blessed are the merciful, for they will be shown mercy" (Matt. 5:7).

Unloved

The Kimball family experienced this joy of ministry as they provided one young mother with something she had never experienced: unconditional love. Samantha's baby, Africa, had been born prematurely a month earlier and was about to be released from the hospital. The last thing this mother wanted to do was to take her home where her mother and brother were smoking crack cocaine and dealing drugs. In desperation, Samantha went to a local adoption agency. The adoption counselor, seeing Samantha's commitment to Africa and desire to raise her, sent Samantha to us.

We matched Samantha with Safe Families volunteers Chad and Holly Kimball, who live on the South Side of Chicago with their two preschool daughters. They picked up Africa at the hospital and cared for her while Samantha continued looking for housing and employment.

During that time, Samantha spent many afternoons with Africa and the Kimballs. Holly recalled, "Samantha said to me, 'I didn't know there were people in the world like you. I've never experienced love from anyone like this before.' I told her that we were willing to sacrifice for her because Jesus sacrificed His life for us. She listened closely while I shared the gospel with her, and I could tell she was touched."

A solution to Samantha's problem came just five days later, when she found housing and enrolled in a work/study program at a local trade school. "I fell in love with Africa, and it was hard to say good-bye," said Holly. "It was such a blessing to be part of God's plan to keep this little family together."

A Personal Note

My wife and I committed our home to the Lord's use early in our marriage. During the past twenty-four years, we have had the privilege of having a variety of people, including adults, children, teens, an elderly parent, and a disabled relative live with us. We have never regretted sharing our home with any guest. Last year, through the Safe Families Program, we took in a two-year-old boy whose mother was working to free herself from her drug addiction and other behaviors that supported it. Her son had behavior problems and numerous disabilities. He could not talk, did not follow instructions, and was aggressive. In fact, the Safe Families program considered not accepting him and sending him to the State because of his behavioral problems and the numerous diagnoses he had. However, when my son and daughter learned that a child was going to have to become a ward of the State because there were no other options for him, they convinced my wife and me to take him in. We had thought our nest was full because we had my mother-in-law (who was ill) and my nephew (who was in a wheelchair).

We decided to trust the Lord with this challenge and we took him in. We prayed daily as a family that this child would learn to communicate. He did, and subsequently his behavior improved. In a fairly short period of time, his improvement was so remarkable that there was little evidence of the numerous disabilities he was diagnosed with. We also ministered to his mother, who was surprised that such love would be shown by strangers to her and her son. On one visit, she asked why we were doing this for her, because she knew we were not getting paid. What an opportunity to testify to the hospitality we have all been shown by God as we moved from being enemies to being His cherished children. However, the time with her was shorter than we anticipated as she was abused by her boyfriend and found dead in a hotel room. Although our children are now adolescents, we adjusted our lifestyle and adopted this adorable little boy that the Lord placed in our care.

CONCLUSION: LIFE-CHANGING HOSPITALITY

Is it possible to create a safety net in our communities so children have a place to go while their parents struggle with their own life challenges? Yes, it is possible. However, it only happens when we unleash our families and help them overcome the barriers to biblical hospitality. Commissioning and supporting families to open their homes and minister to children and their parents has made a significant statement to the watching world longing to see authentic generosity.

Is the hospitality of the Bible more than just having people over to our homes for coffee and cake or participating on the hospitality committee of our church?

Is hospitality only for a select few, or should it be an expectation for all Christians? Hospitality is a powerful and effective discipline that can change our world.

Safe Families has hundreds of families opening their homes. It is the largest volunteer movement providing homes for children in the United States. While the program originated in Chicago, Illinois, other State governments are taking steps to support a Safe Families movement in their own state.

REFLECTION QUESTIONS

1. We have all heard news reports of children being abused and neglected. Many of us are in danger of becoming calloused to these situations where our hearts are no longer stirred. Are you still moved by these injustices? If not, what do you need to do to soften your heart?

2. Do you know anyone who seems to have mastered the discipline of hospitality? If so, what is it about their lives that put them in this category? What barriers do you struggle with when thinking about opening up your home?

3. A premise of this chapter is that the Christian home/family is an untapped yet powerful source of change in our society. Do you agree? What is it about the Christian family that gives it this potential?

4. Just like the church, a healthy family needs to effectively care for its own and reach out to others. How can your church implement these principles?

Recommended Reading List

Bakke, Ray. *A Theology as Big as the City*. Downers Grove, Ill.: InterVarsity, 1997.

Lupton, Robert D. *Compassion, Justice and the Christian Life*. Ventura, Calif.: Regal, 2007.

McDonald, Patrick. *Reaching Children in Need*. Eastbourne, England: Kingsway Publications, 2000.

Pohl, Christine D. *Making Room: Recovering Hospitality as a Christian Tradition*. Grand Rapids, Mich.: Eerdmans, 1999.

DAVID AND BETH KANELOS have served as Young Life Area Directors since 1985, reaching out to a multi-culturally diverse population of urban teenagers on Chicago's North Side. In 2004, they received the Young Life "Senior Staff Award of Excellence" in honor of their years of commitment to one community. David received his B.A. from Western Michigan University, and did graduate work in counseling at DePaul University and in theology at Fuller Seminary. Beth has a B.F.A. from the University of Illinois. David and Beth raised their son and daughter in Chicago.

CHAPTER 27

IN SEARCH OF LOST SHEEP:
How Young Life Reaches North Side Teenagers
Dave and Beth Kanelos

Introduction: A Teenage Mission Field

"**S**uppose one of you has a hundred sheep and loses one of them. Does he not leave the ninety-nine in the open country and go after the lost sheep until he finds it? And when he finds it, he joyfully puts it on his shoulders and goes home. Then he calls his friends and neighbors together and says, 'Rejoice with me; I have found my lost sheep.'" (Luke 15:3–6)

More than thirty thousand students attend the twenty-some public and private schools on the North Side of Chicago. To many of these students, life seems filled with endless possibilities, numerous forks in the road, many choices, and much to experience. With the strong influence of media, peer pressure, and a lack of parental involvement or positive role models, young people are left looking for direction in a society where right and wrong have become a blur. Though in desperate need of direction and guidance, many young people rarely step into a church. They are hurt, insecure, broken, neglected, self-centered, skeptical, rebellious, sexually active, media sponges, abandoned, abused, seeking independence, wandering around aimlessly, looking for love and acceptance. They are like the lost sheep.

Matthew says of Jesus, "When he saw the crowds, he had compassion on them, because they were harassed and helpless, like sheep without a shepherd" (Matt. 9:36).

The mission of Young Life is to actively seek and guide lost teenagers and bring them to a personal relationship with Jesus Christ. Young Life's founder, Jim Rayburn, said, "Our young people today are waiting for somebody to care about them enough to take the time and trouble to pour out compassion on them, to prove their friendship, to bridge this tragic and terrible gap that exists in our culture between teenagers and adults—to emulate the example of Jesus Christ."[1]

YOUNG LIFE: A BRIEF OVERVIEW AND HISTORY

Young Life has been reaching adolescents since 1940 and is now involved in the lives of more than one million teenagers in the United States and around the world.[2]

In 1938, Jim Rayburn, a young Presbyterian youth minister and seminary student in Gainesville, Texas, was challenged by his pastor to work exclusively with unchurched kids.[3] Rayburn's own words testify to the struggle going on in his heart: "He [the pastor] was pushing on me all the time. He didn't care if I did any work around the church. He just wanted to see those kids reached for Christ. He said, 'Don't monkey around with the people who come to church. I'll take care of them. You go on down to that high school.'"[4] Rayburn began to learn about the complex subculture of high school kids and their cliques. After experimenting with various approaches to meet teenagers, he found he was most effective in reaching the popular kids, student leaders in the school, who began to invite their friends. He was often criticized for this method, but was getting positive results in that many kids were listening to the message of Jesus Christ.[5] In 1940, Rayburn started a weekly youth club meeting in the homes of the various students in the early evening. There was singing, a skit or two, and a basic message about Jesus Christ.

This simple idea has led to an international ministry that has expanded to reaching junior and senior high schools students in suburban, urban, and rural settings, as well as those with disabilities (Young Life Capernaum Project) and teenage moms (Young Lives). "Young Life now has more than 4,500 ministries in 50 states and 52 countries."[6]

By 1972, Young Life had begun ministries in approximately 25 multi-ethnic and urban areas. Today, Young Life is in more than 175 urban communities meeting the unique needs of inner-city, racially underrepresented, and poor young people.[7]

Young Life Expands to Urban Communities

During its first twenty years, Young Life's ministry was mostly focused on suburban high school students. In the 1960s, some Young Life staff and the national

Board of Directors began to realize the need to minister to urban communities.

In the 1960s, George Sheffer, one of the leaders of this urban movement, came to Chicago to start Young Life with the help of students from Wheaton College in Wheaton, Illinois. About four years later, as the student volunteers prepared to move on, Wally Urban, a Young Life staff member from Minneapolis, moved to the South Side of Chicago. Soon, Wally was asked to follow up with the kids from Marshall High School on the West Side. Reflecting on his time in the city, Wally said, "It didn't seem much different than hanging out with suburban kids. You just hang out where kids are, spend time with them shooting baskets or running around."[8]

In 1966, Young Life urban continued to develop as Sheffer hired Jim Chesney to work on the West Side of the city.[9] One of the many challenges facing this fledgling ministry was race. Sheffer, Chesney, Verley Sangster, and Wally Urban were white men called and committed to reaching kids in an African-American community. Through the power of the Holy Spirit these men produced lasting results. Because of their dedication to the gospel and their social action, they were able to transcend their many differences and find unity in the body of Christ.

Sheffer notes:

> *On the West Side, where Jim Chesney and I combined a proclamation of the gospel with our social action, kid after kid moved on into college or other training. We threatened, coaxed, promised—did everything we could think of to help them get through high school. There were twenty who graduated from college out of that early West Side group—some of them beautiful Christians, serving their own people in a number of significant ways.*[10]

A Call to the City

In 1985, after serving as volunteer Young Life leaders for six years in Oak Park, a western suburb of Chicago, God called us (two Caucasians who grew up in middle-class suburbs) to work on the Young Life staff with a culturally diverse population of teenagers from more than twenty different ethnic groups on the North Side of Chicago. Previously, we had worked in secular settings. I (Dave) had worked in insurance and social work, counseling runaway kids and troubled families. My wife, Beth, was an art teacher in a district that emphasized multi-cultural diversity. This new adventure with the Lord was taking us out of our comfort zone, on a mission to reach city kids with God's love, using the same quality relational ministry we had seen in Young Life in the suburbs. When we moved, our son, Jacob, was three years old and Beth was pregnant with our daughter, Jessie. We had concerns about living in the city: our family's safety, quality education, raising funds to support the ministry, and finding community in such a diverse place.

YOUNG LIFE FOCUSES ON THE C'S

Christ Centered

Young Life's founder, Jim Rayburn, was passionate about Christ, which becomes obvious in the focus of the mission: "Young Life is Jesus Christ and don't you ever forget it. That's not just what we are about, that is all we are about."[11] When Jesus walked the earth, He upset the status quo by loving sinners and hanging out with them, by restoring their dignity no matter who they were or what they had done. It is because of Christ's transformative love that Young Life staff and volunteers love God and are committed to share their lives and His love with kids, through an incarnational or relational approach. "We loved you so much that we were delighted to share with you not only the gospel of God but our lives as well, because you had become so dear to us" (1 Thess. 2:8).

The work that Young Life leaders do is aptly described by Rebecca Pippert, who writes, "We are not to shout the gospel from a safe and respectable distance and remain detached. We must open our lives enough to let people see that we too laugh and hurt and cry."[12] Young Life leaders spend time with kids and develop friendships, while living lives that reflect Jesus. Kids are more likely to listen to a message about Jesus Christ from someone they know and respect.

Young Life deploys a network of paid staff and volunteer leaders who co-labor in the seed planting and harvest. Leaders make a commitment to volunteer a minimum of one year so that they can develop deeper relationships with kids. Most leaders stay longer, as they invest in the lives of kids, exemplifying Christ, and offering them hope and guidance.

Volunteer leader Larry, a home appraiser, invested a lot of his time in Roger, a junior at Senn High School on the North Side. Roger dropped out of high school, but Larry took an interest in helping him prepare for his GED. Fifteen years later, Roger became a volunteer Young Life leader and began investing time into Edgard, a high school junior. Committed volunteers like Larry and Roger are a large reason why Young Life works. Each leader exemplifies the sincere love of Jesus through sacrifice and action, which has made an impact on many generations.

Contact Work

Extensive research supports the harsh reality that the overwhelming majority of youth will not voluntarily walk into a church. "Church is boring," is a statement we recently heard from Raymond,* a high school junior. To young people church is foreign, alienating, scary, boring, or simply something they do not see a need for. To the younger, nonbelieving generation, Christians are perceived primarily in a negative light: 87 percent of sixteen- to twenty-nine-year-olds consider Christians judgmental, 85 percent label us hypocrites, 78 percent view us as old-fashioned, and 75 percent consider us to be overly political. Modern Christianity is most commonly described by non-Christian young people (91 percent) and young churchgoers (80 percent) as anti-homosexual.[13] Unfortunately, according to Barna's research, Christians are not known by their love but rather by what they dislike.

Rayburn understood that the bridge between the younger generation and the church has collapsed. He realized that each year, fewer and fewer kids were making it to the pews. "We can't wait for teenagers to come to us. We've got to go to them wherever they are—soda fountains, basketball games, street corners, everywhere. We've got to learn to talk with them, to think about things they think about."[14]

This sense of urgency, of seeking out the lost rather than waiting around for them, is the basis for Young Life's incarnational ministry. Because God urgently pursues us, we urgently pursue kids. Young Life staff and leaders hang out when kids are coming out of school, monitor a lunchroom, sponsor a club or tutor at a school, coach a team, attend sporting events, create a drop-in center where teens come after school, volunteer at a park, sponsor band shows for local teen bands, and hang out at local fast food places. Through this contact work, leaders are able to model Christ's love as they develop relationships with young people. Like Jesus, we must not be afraid to get dirty, be vulnerable, and ultimately, get hurt. "We as adults must roll up our sleeves and go to adolescents, listen to them, and unconditionally care for them."[15]

Young Life ministry requires leaders to literally get dirty. As leaders develop friendships with kids, they invite them to Young Life events, which can and do include anything from shaving cream fights, garbage can milkshakes, turkey bowling, trips to Six Flags, all-night bus tours that include bowling and laser tag, Karaoke, weekend and weeklong camps, concerts, movies, and more. The purpose of these events is to draw kids into a safe environment where they can hang out with friends and have lots of laughs and fun. Jim Rayburn called this "earning the right to be heard," or loving kids first, rebuilding that bridge of trust and friendship and only after rebuilding that bridge, using words to evangelize.[16] We attempt to reach kids who so desperately need Christ, kids "[who] are without hope, peace, forgiveness, direction, identity, purpose, understanding as to who they are, where they come from or, most of all, where they are going."[17]

Windy Gap

In spring 1972, during my (Beth's) sophomore year at Palatine High School (in Palatine, Illinois, a Chicago suburb), one of my cheerleader friends, Luann, was talking about something called Young Life Club and invited me to a shaving cream fight to take place after the Club on Tuesday night. It sounded like fun, so I went and had a great time. I do not remember a thing about the Club meeting, but the shaving cream fight was crazy. During the following weeks, I continued to attend Young Life Clubs and heard about a camp trip in the summer to Windy Gap, a Young Life camp in North Carolina. I signed up to go, even though none of my close friends were going. As soon as the bus hit the road, the leaders got up and began meeting all the kids. It was a kind of contagious, friendly enthusiasm that helped me feel accepted and loved.

That week at Windy Gap was phenomenal. I remember the crazy games, swimming, horseback riding, and mini-biking. But most of all, I remember the twenty-minute quiet time on the fifth night of camp when everyone went off by themselves to think about and talk to God. As I reflected on my life, I thought about how I had always gone to church with my parents, was confirmed in the church, went to youth group, sang in the choir, played in the bell choir, and said the "Now I lay me down to sleep" prayer every night, but, how, even after an entire life spent in the church, something was missing. I did not have a personal faith in God. At Young Life camp, I heard about Jesus' love, acceptance, and forgiveness like I had never heard before. During those twenty minutes, sitting on the edge of the lake staring at the stars, I found what was missing: a deep, meaningful, personal relationship with Christ.

After camp, I regularly attended Campaigners, a weekly Bible study that met on Sunday afternoons at the home of Cliff Anderson, the Young Life Director in Palatine. There we had basic lessons about how to study the Bible and pray, and how to deal with teenage life issues such as temptation and peer pressure. The Young Life leaders were there to support me, walk beside me, and teach me how to live the Christian life.

During the summer of 2007, we took our Young Life group from Chicago to Windy Gap, and I had the opportunity to sit at the same spot staring at the stars, reflecting on thirty-five years of knowing Christ, thanks to the seeds planted in me through Young Life during my high school years.

Just as we "earn the right to be heard" with kids, we earn the right to be heard in schools and in the community. We have been active at Lane Tech High School in Chicago since 1989. Lane Tech is a North Side school with 4,200 students, representing more than thirty different nationalities. Through volunteering and serving at the school, we earned the respect and trust of the administration and security guards. We developed an after-school YL Club on Mondays, which is a fun-filled hour of mixers and games. Leaders can meet kids, hang out with them, and invite them to Club meetings, events, and trips. Young Life Club is one of one hundred clubs and sports that students can get involved in at Lane.

Club

For many high school kids, their adventure with Young Life begins at "Club." A suburban Young Life Club traditionally meets in the home of one of the students, where all the furniture is cleared out of one room and kids sit on the floor. Typically, in the city, a youth center, park field house, or a church basement is used for Club.

The first time Daniel* came to Club, which met in a youth center on a local college campus, he pushed the campus emergency alarm and was immediately caught by a security guard who threatened to have him arrested. He apologized and said he did not know what the button was for. He ran down the block and I (Dave) found him in a bus stop crying. As we talked, he told me that he could barely read and that he hated himself because he was stupid and always getting into trouble. I convinced him to come back inside to the Club meeting and promised that no one would make fun of him. I later found out that he was in a special school, and when he was accused of wrongdoing, he would either fight or run away from the situation. Weekly, as he came to Club and acted out, I would take him to the office with two leaders, and calmly and respectfully ask him for his side of the story. Regardless of whether we punished him or not, we made him understand that we liked him, wanted him in Young Life, and that our rules existed not to put him down, but to make sure that nothing could happen in Club that would keep everyone from having a good time.

Through all his problems and our disciplining him, his behavior has improved as he has experienced tough love in a reasonable and compassionate structure.

We begin Club by singing a few upbeat pop songs that kids can relate to, being careful to choose songs that are neutral or positive in content. Teens also love some of the oldies, such as "Lean on Me" or "Stand by Me." The last two songs in Club are slower and more contemplative, so that kids can begin to consider the Christian content of the lyrics. Songs such as "He Knows My Name," "Prince of Peace," and "Light the Fire" have become favorites with our kids, even those who are unchurched.

At the end of Club, one of the leaders will share a short message using terms that non-churched kids can understand; in other words, no "Christian lingo." The Club message is basic so that the one furthest away from God might understand. In order to catch the attention of the teens, the leader will share a funny story about growing up, a news article, or a clip from a current television show or movie. The leader will read a passage from the Bible, clearly communicating the greatest story ever told, of Jesus and His love. The entire message is usually only ten minutes or less. Throughout the semester, the messages build on each other as the gospel unfolds. We keep things short and high energy because, as Jim Rayburn said, "It is a sin to bore a kid with the gospel."[18]

One example of how God worked through our Club ministry involves four high school boys, three Palestinian and one Egyptian, all Muslim. These boys were invited to Young Life Club by girls they knew at school. They liked it and got permission from their parents to attend Club weekly. They joined our basketball team and were all starters. With two strong platforms for relationships, they soon became good friends of the Young Life leaders.

One night, after using his Bible in a Club talk, Dave put his Bible on the carpeted floor. Afterward, one of the guys came up and in all respect said, "Why do you put the Bible on the floor? A Muslim would never put the Koran on the floor."

Before Club another week, one of the guys stopped us (Dave and Beth) to thank us for sending him a birthday card. He said, "This was the first birthday card I've ever got in the mail." I (Dave) was wondering what these young Muslim guys thought about the gospel message that they were hearing weekly at Club. As I drove them home, they always took the backseat of the van, so that they would be the last ones to be dropped off. I overheard a discussion they were having. One guy asked the others what they thought about Jesus: Is He the Son of God or a prophet? Can a person find God without having to work for it? Then the question came up, How would their families react to them if they became Christians?

I did not have time to respond to what I heard that night because I had to drop them off. Over their remaining time in Young Life, I began to ask them questions about the messages. They were curious and we talked a lot about the differences between Islam and Christianity. As far as I know, none of them made commitments to Christ, but I had the satisfaction that they would know how to find or pursue Him when God led them to do so. Young Life leaders hang with teenagers regardless of their decision to follow Christ or not. They respect them and continue to be their friends.

Camp

Camp trips take kids out of the city, away from their usual surroundings, responsibilities, family stress, peer pressure, and into the quiet solitude and beauty of God's creation. In order for kids to afford these trips, we offer a variety of fundraisers such as pancake breakfasts, candy sales, work days, walk-a-thons, yard sales, and car washes. Kids work side by side with the leaders and begin to develop relationships while they earn their way to camp.

Young Life's summer camps are beautiful resorts made for teenagers and filled with a fun, relaxed environment, exceptional entertainment, adventurous activities, great accommodations, and lots of good food. Rayburn believed that the key to running a successful camp was quality and excellence. "We talk about the King of Kings; let's act like he's the one in charge! We're gonna get the classiest camps in the country."[19] "It was the best week of my life!" is a comment heard from most kids who attend camp.

Young Life has found it important to remove the distractions of everyday life in order to set up a platform where kids can really hear, see, and experience God at camp. Therefore, we have them check in all their electronic equipment when they arrive: the cell phones, iPods, video games, computers, etc. They moan about it at first, thinking they cannot live without their music or text messaging, but eventually they all adjust, often without even realizing it. On day five of a seven-day camp, the whole camp gets a twenty-minute quiet time to consider the message of Jesus dying for our sins and God's message of love for them. Many decisions for Christ are made on this night, and the transformation begins. Removing the distractions allows kids to more fully engage in relationships, reflect on their lives, and listen to what God is saying through their interaction with their leaders and through the camp speaker.

Through discussions in cabin time, relationships between kids and leaders grow deeper in an atmosphere of love and acceptance. Leaders have the chance to clarify the message and answer questions that are raised on spiritual and life issues in a place where confidentiality is maintained. At a winter weekend camp during cabin time, Flako told the cabin that he and two other guys who came to Christ in Young Life were trying to stay out of a gang around their high school. He had known the gang recruiter since they were kids in the neighborhood, and the more he refused them, the more threatening they got. I (Dave) counseled him to tell his parents and call the police, but he said this would lead to reprisals. He said that if he and his friends had to fight to stay out of the gang, they would. We prayed in the cabin that God would give them a way out without anyone getting hurt. I kept up with the situation, and in the spring, they told me things were getting worse. I wanted to call their parents, but they refused to let me. In May, Flako told me that when he was pulling out of the school parking lot, the gang recruiter smashed the rear window of his car with a tire iron. He said that he prayed to the

Lord and did not fight back, but sped into the other lane and got away as fast as he could. The transformation of Flako's life began through camp and cabin times and gave him the self-control to not be vengeful.

Camp is both a relationship come to fruition and a new beginning. Throughout the year, leaders are working with kids, praying for them and hanging out with them, with the hope that they will go to camp. For Young Life leaders, getting kids to camp is the result of earning the right to be heard and of developing relationships. For kids, getting to camp is the chance for them to hear the gospel in a place with few distractions. It is a chance for them to see tangible examples of heaven on earth; it is a broken yet hopeful glimpse of the restoration. Whether it is a weekend or weeklong camp, it is a memorable shared experience that brings kids closer to their leaders and most important to their Creator. It gives them the courage and strength to persevere and face whatever challenges await them at home and reminds them that they do not have to face their problems alone.

Campaigners

As a follow-up to camp, we encourage the teenagers to come to Campaigners, a study that helps them explore the Bible and talk more in depth about how it applies to their lives. We talk about the foundations of Christianity as well as life issues from a biblical perspective. The goal is to help students obey the Great Commandment: to love God and to love our neighbors, families, friends, peers, those of various backgrounds and cultures, and the less fortunate, as we love ourselves (Luke 10:27).

Community Service Projects

Service projects challenge kids to give back to the community while helping them earn the forty hours of community service required by the Chicago Public Schools for graduation. If a minimum of ten hours are not completed at the end of each year, the student will be demoted. We recruit students to help with canned food drives, Kiwanis Peanut Day, neighborhood clean-up projects, serving in a soup kitchen, Christmas caroling in nursing homes, serving at a camp, working with Habitat for Humanity, and more. It is a valuable time for leaders to bond with young people, as they work together toward a common goal of serving the community. Taking poor kids to serve poor people has a powerful impact on the lives of all involved.

One of the most valuable service projects has been helping with Hurricane Katrina relief projects in D'Iberville, Mississippi. Shortly after Katrina hit the gulf coast in August 2005, we began a pocket-change collection at Young Life Club to send to this small town that had been devastated by Katrina. We have taken five work trips over spring and winter breaks, traveling by bus with more than thirty kids and leaders to work on projects coordinated by the D'Iberville Volunteer Foundation. In preparation for each trip, we do a four-week orientation and Bible study. Through this experience, Chicago high school kids and leaders learned about service, goodwill, leadership, and team work, and gained a greater appreciation for the world outside of their own lives.

Indelibly imbedded in our minds and hearts are the images of collapsed houses and schools, piles of debris, shredded plastic bags hanging in trees, and mailboxes or cement steps on a property where a house once stood. We will never forget the people's thankfulness to be alive, faith, perseverance, and hope in the midst of the chaos. The most powerful moment on our final trip to Mississippi was seeing Tommy, a tough city kid who was expelled from school for fighting, look the directors of the D'Iberville Foundation in the eye and say, "You and the people of D'Iberville have helped me love God by serving people."

Community Relations

Christ understood the importance of relationships. He knew that in order to gain respect, credibility, and support for ministry, we would need to live in a way that engages our neighbors. In Matthew 5:16 Jesus exhorts us, "Let your light shine before men, that they may see your good deeds and praise your Father in heaven." It is because of this exhortation that Young Life takes such an active role in its surrounding community. We participate in projects with our local alderman, such as community clean-up days. It is important to have open communication with our community relations officer in our police district, and frequent discussions on gang developments and legal issues related to teenagers. Through these relationships, this broader participation in our neighborhoods, we create unity in our fragmented communities.

We work in a community with no walls, where kids live all over the city and attend more than twenty different high schools. They do not necessarily go to school in their own neighborhood, but travel by public transportation to attend a better school in a safer neighborhood. Even though much of the North Side of Chicago is being gentrified and property values are soaring, the high schools in our area are still filled with underprivileged and underrepresented kids. We reach out to a multi-cultural, diverse population of youth where English is often their second language at home. Their nationalities include Polish, Ukrainian, Romanian, Assyrian, Mexican, Cuban, Puerto Rican, Ecuadorian, Colombian, Peruvian, Guatemalan, Filipino, Pakistani, Indian, African-American, Bosnian, Vietnamese, Cambodian, Chinese, Japanese, and more.

As members of our local Kiwanis Club, we serve as advisors to the Key Club at Lane Tech High School, a service club of eighty members run by high school students. This endorsement from Kiwanis opened doors for us to be inside the school, spending time developing relationships with teenagers and administrators as we work on service projects together. After serving the school and earning its respect for a number of years, the school gave us I.D. badges and we are welcome there anytime.

Committee and Church

Our Committee members, representing a variety of local churches and professions, keep us accountable by meeting monthly to review our activities and expenses, offer prayer support, and help us plan fundraisers to support the ministry. It is difficult raising money in the city because we are dealing with poor kids whose families have few resources. We often have to meet the physical needs of kids by providing them with food and transportation. We are always trying to attract new donors because of the transitional nature of the city.

As believers in Christ, we understand the importance of being involved with a cohesive body of believers, which is why we maintain close ties to the Church, getting to know local pastors and youth pastors, although Young Life is non-denominational. Not only does the Church offer us and our fellow leaders physical, spiritual, and emotional support, it offers the same to our kids. By developing long-term relationships with kids, we hope and pray that they will develop a long-term relationship with Christ. Young Life's goal is to reach kids for Christ and either lead them into a new church home or direct them back to their family church where they can continue to follow Christ and be nurtured in their faith for a lifetime.[20]

Changed Lives

Looking back on twenty-three years, we are thankful for how God has guided and provided for our ministry to thousands of kids. He enabled us to buy a home in the city and rear our two children, both of whom are now college graduates. We are confident that the reason we have served this long is because of God's grace. Persevering through the bumps and potholes continues to make us more dependent on Him as we try to figure out how to reach adolescents for Christ. The reward is seeing God's miraculous work in the lives of those kids we meet along the path. As Matthew 13:3–8 suggests, we may not always see the results, but though we may not see or understand, we must still obey and trust:

> *Then he told them many things in parables, saying: "A farmer went out to sow his seed. As he was scattering the seed, some fell along the path, and*

the birds came and ate it up. Some fell on rocky places, where it did not have much soil. It sprang up quickly, because the soil was shallow. But when the sun came up, the plants were scorched, and they withered because they had no root. Other seed fell among thorns, which grew up and choked the plants. Still other seed fell on good soil, where it produced a crop—a hundred, sixty or thirty times what was sown. "

Diana's* story is one of a seed that developed and grew but was later choked out by the thorns. We met Diana her freshman year, when she came to the Young Life Garbage Can Milkshake, the big kickoff for the Club year at Lane. Diana was an insecure, quiet, heavyset Goth girl from a dysfunctional, alcoholic family. She joined two after-school Clubs: Young Life and the "Room for All Club" (a club that welcomes students who are gay and straight) at the high school, as she was seeking a place to belong. She participated in all the Young Life Clubs and trips and accepted Christ at camp the summer after her freshman year. She started growing in her faith, began reading the Bible she received at camp, and came to Bible studies after the trip. The summer after her junior year, she worked for a month on work crew at the Young Life camp in Michigan. She felt loved and supported and grew in her faith.

Even though she was growing in her faith, she continued to attend the Room for All Club, often asking us where God stood on the issue of homosexuality. We discussed what the Bible says about this issue, encouraging her to continue her friendships but to be careful. Diana graduated and went to a small college in Wisconsin, where she had a roommate who brought her back into the homosexual lifestyle. When she came back to visit Club the next year, she said, "I can't be a Christian anymore." After investing so much time in Diana, we were sad and disappointed in her choices but pray that she will come back to the Lord one day soon.

Edgard was a lost kid who would never have sought out the church on his own, but was found by Young Life leaders who loved him for who he was and directed him toward Christ.

Edgard started coming to Young Life when he was fourteen. He was born in Chicago, but was sent to live in the Philippines with his dad when he was two years old. His father was a drunk and often abused him. He was often dressed in rags and ran through the streets all day without shoes. At the age of six, Edgard returned to the States where he attended Catholic church and Sunday school, learned important passages, and got confirmed. Edgard eventually stopped going to church, and in high school he began to struggle with anger and pressure from his mother to work and maintain good grades.

When he was fourteen he heard about Young Life from his older brother. After participating in Club and going to camps, Edgard turned "halfway to God," but still struggled with fighting, tagging, graffiti, and vandalism. He started hanging out with the wrong crowd and began smoking weed regularly and listening to music on his iPod to relax and escape. He had a saying, "I feel so high, I'm in heaven," but he knew he still had problems. His grades were low; he did not graduate on time and had to go to summer school. It was then that he began to question what he was going to do with his life. During the summer of 2007, Edgard began going to church with one of his Young Life leaders, where he was both challenged and encouraged.

One night in June, Edgard rode his bike over to our house in the pouring rain. After we gave him some dinner and dry clothes he told us about what he was learning at church and his relationship with God. While we talked, we suggested that Edgard volunteer to work at a Young Life camp. At the camp, Edgard got a chance to develop his relationship with God and serve others in a Christian community. The following fall, Edgard enrolled in the Marines, where he was awarded for outstanding character and performance in training and was meritoriously promoted. Edgard says:

> *Throughout the challenges of boot camp, I was able to overcome all of its obstacles. In times when I felt weak, the bond I had with God lifted up my spirit and made me not give up. I know that all through my life, something was pulling me up, someone was reaching for me. I realize now that it was God who had a strong hold on me. Young Life guided me during my lost teenage years, to positive people and to a deeper relationship with God. Young Life was perfect for me. It turned my life in a positive direction where I am most happy. It helped me find who I am and who God is.*

CONCLUSION: THE CHALLENGE

How can we reach the lost sheep, the lost kids in our communities who do not go to church? Accept the fact that for most non-Christian kids, church is not attractive, but the person of Christ is curiously attractive. Go to where kids are, develop relationships with them, earn their trust, find out what they need and want from life, earn the right to be heard by sharing your life with them, and then share the gospel. Whether or not kids find a personal relationship with Christ, continue to love and care for them over the long haul. Seeds have been planted, so pray that God will cause the growth. A good youth outreach is not built solely on programming or a meeting place, but is built on relationships created around love, respect, and hospitality.

REFLECTION QUESTIONS

1. How can you or your church work together with Young Life to reach teens in your city?

2. What is your church's attitude toward nonbelieving teens in your community? Would non-Christian teenagers feel comfortable coming into your church? Why or why not?

3. Who are the lost teenagers in your city? Where do they hang out? What are their needs?

4. What are you doing to reach out to them with the love of Christ?

* Indicates name change throughout the chapter.

DONNITA TRAVIS is Executive Director and Founder of By the Hand Club. After serving as a volunteer with children in Cabrini-Green for five years, Donnita stepped down as president of an advertising agency in 2001 to establish By the Hand. Located in the Cabrini-Green, Altgeld-Murray, Austin, and Englewood neighborhoods, By the Hand is dedicated to helping more than six hundred children have new and abundant life. Donnita was in advertising for eighteen years, received her M.B.A. from Northwestern Kellogg School of Management in 1995, and was named to Today's Chicago Woman "100 Women Making a Difference" in 1998.

SARAH JAMES received her B.A. at the University of Indianapolis in Elementary Education. Sarah came to Chicago to get her Master's degree in urban ministry at the Moody Graduate School. She is the Director of By the Hand Club for Kids, an after-school program in Chicago that serves over 600 children in under-resourced neighborhoods. Sarah has recently been given guardianship of two brothers from Cabrini-Green, Keewaun (fourteen) and Trayvon (ten).

CHAPTER 28

USING PRINCIPLES OF EXCELLENCE TO CHANGE YOUNG LIVES:

By the Hand Club for Kids

Donnita Travis and Sarah James

Introduction: A New Model for After-School Ministry

God has birthed a ministry in the city of Chicago that is changing hundreds of young lives. It is an after-school program that is using principles of excellence to radically transform the lowest performing children from overcrowded and underfunded Chicago public schools in the city's most under-resourced neighborhoods.

"YES, WE WANT HIM!"

"I always liked to go out in the playground and look for trouble. I loved trouble. In fact, trouble was like my hobby. Then one day, I heard gunshots and I woke up and saw my mother's head bloody and knew my papa did it."

Keewaun was six years old when he witnessed his mother's tragic death. Two years later the assistant principal of his school recommended him to be a part of By the Hand Club for Kids (formerly Kids' Club). We will never forget the first day we visited his classroom. His teacher, Miss Avrom, told us, "Keewaun doesn't know his ABCs, and until someone helps him with eyeglasses, we can't even test him to see what he needs." She went on to say, "He could use some help with hygiene and clothes." Miss Avrom took a deep breath and said, "I don't know if you even want him."

We smiled and reassured her, "Yes, we want him!"

By the Hand Club was founded for the Keewauns of the world. Started in

Cabrini-Green in 2001, By the Hand is located strategically throughout some of Chicago's most impoverished neighborhoods, where overcrowded and underfunded schools abound. It is a Christ-centered after-school program with an emphasis on academics and a commitment to loving the whole child—mind, body, and soul.

BY THE HAND CLUB NEIGHBORHOODS—SPRING 2008[1]			
	CABRINI-GREEN	ALTGELD-MURRAY	AUSTIN
Black	98%	99%	95%
Under 18 Years Old	48%	48%	34%
In College Male	0%	1%	2%
In College Female	2%	2%	3%
Female Headed Households	86%	75%	62%
Per Capita Income	$5,525	$7,662	$11,969
Schools in Academic Warning	75%	66%	61%

For a child to attend By the Hand Club, he has to be recommended by his school principal as a child in critical need of intervention. We literally and figuratively take kids by the hand (thus our name) and walk alongside them from the time they enter our program until they are walking independently with the Lord. We tutor them to academic excellence. We mentor them with the love of Christ, and we care for them as our own.

Every child who comes to By the Hand Club is struggling academically, which often signals more serious issues such as behavior problems or a chaotic home life.

A NATIONAL EVIL

In May 2006, while attending an Urban Youth Workers Institute Conference at Azusa Pacific University in Azusa, California, Dr. John Perkins, founder of the Christian Community Development Association (CCDA), gathered together a small group of individuals he considered the emerging leaders in CCDA. He challenged them by saying, "I am not responsible for your generation. I attacked the issues of my day. We dealt with racism and homelessness and housing and the breakdown of the family. Now you have to stand up and deal with the problems of your generation."

As Christians, we are to reflect the character of God to a hurting world. Undoubtedly, one of the biggest of our day is the poor education of today's urban youth.

While there is a range of statistics and considerable debate regarding what constitutes a "dropout," according to the Manhattan Institute for Policy Research, the national dropout rate for African-American students is 44 percent.[2]

This is not only a threat to our nation, it is a present-day evil. Satan is using poor education to destroy today's inner-city youth. Seventy percent of prison inmates cannot read above a fourth grade level.[3] Further, some states determine how many prison cells to build based on fourth-grade failure rates.[4]

Why would Satan want our youth to remain uneducated? For starters, they will not be able to fully study the Word of God. Second Timothy 2:15 says, "Do your best to present yourself to God as one approved, a workman who does not need to be ashamed and who correctly handles the word of truth."

Further, it is difficult for our children to transcend the barriers of race discrimination, class, or background to achieve their God-given potential without a good education.

CHICAGO WORKS!

The tagline for the city of Chicago is "Chicago Works!" But, when it comes to education, Chicago, like many other big cities, does not work. In Chicago, 61 percent, or nearly two-thirds, of African-American males drop out of high school. This is compared to 42 percent of white males.[5] In 2005–2006, 12,871 students dropped out of Chicago Public Schools. At an estimated social services cost to taxpayers of $127,000 for every high school dropout, this will cost taxpayers $163 billion.[6]

Although it is easy to blame Chicago Public Schools, we must realize that government does not hold the answers. At best, the public education system can only bring about improvement, not transformation, in the lives of our children.

CHANGING FROM THE INSIDE OUT

Six weeks after his coming to By the Hand, we took Keewaun to his first eyeglass appointment. The optometrist did not use the traditional "E" to test his vision because Keewaun could not recognize the alphabet. He had to use pictures and numbers to test his vision. We found out Keewaun is very nearsighted. He picked out a pair of red-framed glasses because he was on the Big Red Team at By the Hand. When Keewaun slipped his new eyeglasses on his face, he smiled and said, "Wow, this is what everybody looks like!"

Also, we were able to take Keewaun shopping at Target for new winter clothes, a coat, and shoes. Keewaun enjoyed riding in the cart as we went up and down the isles. Of course, we had to make an unexpected stop at the toy aisle to pick out a football! Everything we bought seemed to be red, Keewaun's new favorite color. He fell asleep on the way home from his big adventure.

Learning and Growing

Soon we saw Keewaun's attitude toward school improving. He started bringing his homework to By the Hand. One day, Keewaun was sitting at homework time with his Team Leader, Ms. Sarah, who was helping him with his spelling words. After printing one of his words, Keewaun looked up and said, "What is a roller coaster?" Ms. Sarah tried to explain, but the look on his face said he still did not really understand. A month later, By the Hand took all the kids to Six Flags Great America. Ms. Sarah took Keewaun and some of the other kids on their first roller-coaster ride. Afterward, Keewaun said with a big smile on his face, "Now I know what a roller coaster is!"

Three times a week, Ms. Sarah met Keewaun at his apartment building to take him to school. This helped to reduce his tardiness and absenteeism. She sat with him during the school hours to give him some one-on-one attention. It was during that opportunity that Ms. Sarah felt Keewaun's pain as he was teased by other kids for his clothes, shoes, or for being put in special education classes.

During the summer months, a volunteer named Ms. Tigist helped Keewaun complete a reading curriculum. That summer Keewaun's confidence in his academics began to grow. He started picking up books to read on his own.

One evening, when Ms. Sarah took kids home from By the Hand, the boys started asking how you get Jesus in your heart. After Ms. Sarah explained, Keewaun said, "I think I should wait until I am older to pray. I am too little." Ms. Sarah reminded the boys that if Jesus is knocking on your heart now, then this is the time to invite Him to be Lord and Savior of your life. Keewaun thought for a minute and said, "OK, then I want to pray right now."

Keewaun began to understand the voice of the Holy Spirit early on. One evening he decided to approach his uncle and ask him if he could try some weed. Many boys his age were trying it. As he started walking toward his uncle, he saw a book lying on the table that By the Hand had given to his family. He sounded out the letters B-I-B-L-E . . . Bible. Even though he still could not read very well, Keewaun said, "I looked at the Bible, flipped through the pages, and knew I shouldn't try the weed."

Keewaun Making an Impact: This Generation and the Next

At the end of a week at summer camp, Keewaun asked Ms. Sarah if she would take him to church. Keewaun not only started going to church but his little brother, Trayvon, came with him. Then Keewaun brought his cousins, Reshaun,

Travis, Devonshay, and Dee and his friend Benjamin. All the boys began learning about God at church and Sunday school.

One Sunday morning, when Ms. Sarah went to pick up all the boys for church, their grandmother told her about an older cousin getting shot on the playground the night before. Ms. Sarah began to think about how she was going to counsel the boys. Before she spoke a word, Reshaun said, "Ms. Sarah, guess what happened last night? Keewaun read us the story of Jesus' death and resurrection! We all listened to him as he read the Bible to us."

Keewaun added, "I felt like going down to the playground last night but something told me not to go down there. So, I got the Bible and read to everyone." Apparently, at the same time Keewaun was reading the Bible, their cousin was getting shot.

On a cold February night, after their great-grandmother's funeral, Ms. Sarah went over to see all the boys and their family. The boys came down to the van and told Ms. Sarah about the funeral. Ms. Sarah used this as an opportunity and asked them, "If you were to die today, where would you go?"

One cousin yelled out, "Heaven."

Ms. Sarah answered, "How do you know?"

Another cousin said, "I go to church."

Keewaun looked at Ms. Sarah and shook his head no. He then spoke up and told the boys how you ask Jesus to forgive your sins and ask Him to be in your heart. Ms. Sarah asked the boys if they wanted to pray. Reshaun, Devonshay, and Dee all prayed to receive Christ that night in the van. Immediately, after the boys prayed, Reshaun yelled as loud as he could, "Ms. Sarah, Jesus just pulled the sin right out of my heart."

It is hard to imagine where Keewaun would be without By the Hand Club. Recently, Keewaun asked his senior pastor, Dr. Erwin Lutzer at the Moody Church, where God was when his dad shot and killed his mother. Pastor Lutzer said, "Right there with you, Keewaun. God knew this would happen and that is why He put Ms. Sarah and the other leaders from By the Hand in your life."

On the flipside, thanks be to God, it is not hard to imagine what Keewaun's life will be like now. He explained it best when he said, "Ms. Sarah, when I grow up I am going to have me a house, a wife, a car, and a motorcycle. And then I'm gonna get me some kids. And take them places like you take us. And I'm going to teach them about God."

DO NOT USE A FIRE HOSE TO WATER A HOUSE PLANT

From day one, By the Hand felt God's call to serve children who needed help the most—children scoring in the lowest academic ranges in the poorest performing schools in the most under-resourced neighborhoods. In other words, children who did not stand a chance without "critical," or what By the Hand calls "divine," intervention.

In order to make sure that the kids who need it the most are served first, By the Hand only accepts children who are referred by their school principal as making a 2.0 or below grade point average in reading and math on their report cards and scoring at the 25th percentile or below in reading and math on their Illinois Standardized Achievement Tests (ISAT).

Once the children are enrolled in By the Hand, our vision is to help them have an abundant and eternal life. The way we go about doing this is by caring for the whole child—mind, body, and soul. This holistic approach, just like we saw with Keewaun, is key because the children referred to By the Hand Club often come with considerable and sometimes incapacitating needs—mind, body, and soul. How can children improve in school when their stressor chemicals are so high that it affects their learning and memory, or their eyesight is so poor that they cannot see? Or how can they have hope for today, much less for the future, without Christ in their life?

In order to care for our children holistically, By the Hand Club hires full-time staff who oversee the after-school programming three days a week and spend the other two days of the school week doing home and school visits. This approach is resource intensive, but necessary, based on the extensive needs of our children.

We recently had the opportunity to compare notes with another Christian after-school program in Chicago. Like us, they are based in an under-resourced neighborhood, but they primarily serve working families whose children attend a charter school. The primary need of these children is after-school care while their parents are at work, and the ministry model is more "service-based" than "needs-based." As a result, this program operates five days a week to serve its working parents, is open fewer hours a day, and offers a more supplemental homework, enrichment, and spiritual curriculum. This is absolutely the right approach given their vision, mission, and needs of their children and families. In fact, implementing a more resource-intensive approach would be like using a fire hose to water a houseplant. It would not be very good for the plant and would waste a lot of water.

WHY BUSINESS PRINCIPLES CAN WORK IN MINISTRY

Businesses principles can work in ministry. In ministry, the number one principle of excellence is to begin with a God-given vision and mission. By the Hand Club's vision and mission is to take children in critical need by the hand

and help them have abundant and eternal life—mind, body, and soul. While the vision and mission are forward looking, they guide and inform our work for today. The moment we lose sight of our vision and mission, we begin to drift and become ineffective.

Next we have very concrete and measurable goals. It seems that in ministry there is a tendency to downplay results either because we know we must rely on God for the results or because results in ministry are difficult to measure. After all, we do not exist to make a profit. We exist to change lives and glorify God. Yes, it is true that we rely on God for the results, but who is to say that God will not use principles of excellence to produce greater results? For example, we have noticed at By the Hand Club that when we measure and report results in ministry areas they seem to improve. In the business world this is known as the Hawthorne Effect, based on a series of experiments on factory workers carried out between 1924 and 1932, which showed improvement caused by observing worker performance.

So, at By the Hand we measure and report on every aspect of the ministry that we want to improve: attendance, retention, grades, behavior, test scores, home visits, school visits, classroom management, etc. This lets us know how we are doing in each of these areas so that we can adjust for improvement along the way, and it lets us know when something isn't working so that we can stop doing it and try something else.

Yes, it can be difficult in ministry to quantify whether or not lives are being changed, but that should not stop us from trying. Compared to business, stakes in ministry are higher, and the money is not ours. Therefore, we should work even harder to quantify results.

Consider the parable of the talents (Matt. 25:14–30). The master entrusted his three servants with his property. Two were productive and their master told them, "Well done, good and faithful servant! You have been faithful with a few things; I will put you in charge of many things" (vv. 21, 23). The other one was unproductive and the master called him "you wicked, lazy servant" (v. 26), taking his talent and giving it to the one with ten. God expects us to be faithful and productive, especially in matters relating to the kingdom of heaven.

These are some of the principles of excellence that By the Hand has used to help improve our efforts over the years. By the Hand was started as a ministry of the Moody Church serving sixteen children who lived in the Cabrini-Green housing project. Today, By the Hand is a separate 501(c)(3) charitable organization and serves five hundred children in three of Chicago's poorest communities. While all of the children were recommended by their school principals as needing critical academic intervention, they finished the 2006–2007 school year with remarkable, or should we say "miraculous," results:

BY THE HAND CLUB PRINCIPLES OF EXCELLENCE	
VISION (What)	To take children in critical need by the hand and help them have abundant and eternal life.
MISSION (How)	An after-school program that cares for the whole child— mind, body, and soul.

GOALS (Measurable Outcomes)	
MIND	Test above the 25th percentile on ISAT tests
	Pass all classes (preferably A's, B's, and C's)
	Behave positively at school, home, community, and By the Hand Club
BODY	Attend school and By the Hand Club regularly
	Have medical coverage
	Receive consistent eye, hearing, dental, and physical care
	Eat a healthy and nutritious diet
SOUL	Know Jesus as Lord and Savior
	Know how to share their faith
	Attend Sunday school and church
	Have a strong discipline of prayer and Bible study

BY THE HAND CLUB RESULTS — 2006-2007 SCHOOL YEAR	
MIND	84 percent of our children passed all of their classes (a 12 percent increase from 1st quarter)
	47 percent made all A's, B's, and C's (a 27 percent increase from 1st quarter)
	Average GPA was 2.53 (a 7 percent increase from 1st quarter)
	Average ISAT reading score was close to the nation's average at the 42nd percentile (a 71 percent improvement from the 24th percentile in 2005–2006)
BODY	100 percent were offered a hot, nutritious meal each day at By the Hand
	100 percent were up-to-date on physicals and immunizations
	100 percent received eye exams and eyeglasses as needed
SOUL	100 percent completed Kids' Evangelism Explosion
	67 percent of our children are Christians
	41 percent made a profession of faith this year
	31 percent are in church

VALUES (How We Behave)	METRICS (How We Measure)
1. Holiness	Monthly Home Visits > 80% Homes
2. Excellence	Monthly School Visits > 80% Classrooms
3. Learning	Children w/Failing Grades 0%
4. Passion	Children w/All ABC's > 75%
5. Unity	Children w/ISAT's above the 25th percentile > 80%
6. Servant Leadership	Children Completing Kids' Evangelism Explosion 100%
	Children Attending Church 100%

CHANGING YOUNG LIVES, ONE LIFE AT A TIME

While Keewaun's story seems exceptionally daunting, it is not that unusual. Take Natasha, for example. She often recalls, "I used to get into lots of fights. I loved to fight. Most of the time I started them!"

When Natasha first joined By the Hand Club, she had straight D's and F's on her report card and regularly got suspended at school for, you guessed it, fighting. She was a very angry young girl, but she had every reason to be. Her dad was in jail and her mother was using drugs—once even selling Natasha's gym shoes for a few dollars to get high. Natasha was living with her grandmother. No one knew until Natasha confided in her leader at By the Hand Club that a neighborhood man had molested her repeatedly while she was growing up. Everywhere she turned there was rejection, pain, and isolation. No wonder she got into a lot of fights!

But after joining By the Hand Club, Natasha began to receive the love and attention that she was desperately craving. She was one of those kids who always came around even when the Club was not meeting. Natasha would come by and ask if she could help with anything. She could be found cleaning out closets, getting name tags ready for the next week, or unpacking toys for the Club Store. Natasha now had a circle of loving, caring adults around her, allowing her to see what it looks like to walk with Christ daily. It was through this consistent contact and mentoring with the staff and volunteers that Natasha began to grow.

Even so, Natasha really struggled with her anger toward her mother. You could sense her pain as she would write in her journal at By the Hand, "My problem is that my mom won't come see me, call me or talk to me. I hate that, but I still love her. I am going to still be the same loving person I am."

One afternoon, Natasha came to By the Hand Club angry because a girl had called her mother a name at school. Natasha said, "I'm going to fight her tomorrow." But her leader, Ms. Sheila, showed Natasha Hebrews 13:5, "God has said,

'Never will I leave you; never will I forsake you.'" She recalls this as a turning point in her life. "I memorized that verse that week. I learned that God will never leave me or forsake me no matter what kind of trouble, hurt, or pain I may be in. Every time I wanted to get angry and fight someone, I remembered these words. It helped me to know that somebody really cares. It taught me that God will always be there for me, even if other people aren't." Natasha has not been in a fight since.

One day in chapel, Natasha heard for the first time how she could be the light of the world (Matt. 5:14). She wanted to be that light in a dark world and gave her life to the Lord. She said, "Now I can help my mom get clean off drugs by telling her who God is."

Ms. Sheila took a group of girls to get their eye exams. Natasha learned that, like Keewaun, she was extremely nearsighted. When she got new eyeglasses, her grades began to improve in school.

When her grandmother could not get off work to take her to the clinic, By the Hand took her for her school physical and immunizations. Otherwise, Natasha would have missed several days of school before these were updated. Probably the biggest breakthrough for Natasha came one night after girls' Bible study at By the Hand. A guest speaker had shared with the girls about how God had helped her overcome a past of sexual abuse. That night Natasha confided in Ms. Sheila that she too was a victim of sexual abuse. We were able to get Natasha the professional Christian counseling needed to begin the process of restoration and healing. At the time of this writing, she has been in counseling for three years and, thanks be to God, is making great progress.

A lot of fighting goes on in Natasha's home. Ms. Bethany from By the Hand Club remembers one night in particular, "Natasha called us right after getting home from By the Hand because people in her family were fighting and threatening her." At 10:30 P.M., Bethany and a volunteer picked up Natasha and the three of them drove around for an hour. Finally, they returned to Natasha's building where her grandfather was waiting for her outside. He assured Natasha that everything was calm again and she could come back home. Natasha went back upstairs.

Natasha had a way to escape her home life that night. Ms. Bethany said, "We really didn't know what to do or where to go. But we did know that Natasha needed us to just be there with her. So we were there."

WHAT IS THE BOTTOM LINE?

Have a Clear Vision, Mission, and Well-Defined Goals

In order to have a clear vision and mission, you will need to pray and ask God for His guidance and direction. This not only forces you to seek God's calling for your ministry, but once you have it, will help you stay focused and committed over the long haul.

At By the Hand Club, we have a strong sense that God has called us to help children who live in high risk urban neighborhoods to have abundant and eternal life by loving the whole child. So, it does not matter how tough things get, this is our calling and it is a matter of obedience. We would not dream of quitting until God says so.

Also, when people want us to do something ministry related, but not directly fitting our vision and mission, this clear sense of calling keeps us from drifting off course. In other words, our clear vision and mission helps prevent us from doing the "good" that would get in the way of doing God's "best."

Goals are simply specific and measurable things we want to accomplish based on our vision and mission. Since By the Hand Club is ministering holistically to children, we define what we want our children to achieve in very specific and measurable terms—mind, body, and soul.

Measure It and It Will Improve

At By the Hand we measure and report on everything imaginable, often celebrating results in staff meetings or posting them on office bulletin boards.

Do Not Overspiritualize Matters in Your Ministry

In ministry, we sometimes are tempted to relegate matters to just the spiritual realm, making us so heavenly minded that we are of no earthly good. Two areas come to mind related to our discussion:

- The gospel is not just sharing the good news of eternal life with a dying world, it is also sharing the love of Jesus with a hurting world. Just like Jesus told His twelve when He sent them out in Matthew 10:8, we are to "heal the sick, raise the dead, cleanse those who have leprosy, drive out demons. Freely you have received, freely give." Moreover, when we do this for others, we are doing this to Christ Himself, as Matthew 25:40 explains, "The King will reply, 'I tell you the truth, whatever you did for one of the least of these brothers of mine, you did for me.'" Finally, as Dr. John Fuder, professor at the Moody Bible Institute, points out, there are more than three thousand references in the Bible to caring for the disenfranchised, the poor, the orphaned, the stranger, the widow, and the other marginalized in our world.[7] How can we love people enough to care about their eternal well-being and not love them enough to care for their well-being today?

- Just because God is ultimately responsible for the results does not mean that we have an excuse to neglect our duty. Ministry happens when God's intervention combines with our personal responsibility. We are His hands, His feet, and His love to a hurting and dying world. His plans will prevail, but the question is will it be through us or someone else? We do not want to miss out on being a part of what He is doing.

Rely on God, Not Clever Techniques

No matter how ingenious our methods, if they are not God-ordained they will fail to accomplish His work. Besides, even the most advanced human techniques are nothing in comparison to God's omnipotence. Just think about how limited we are in every way while God is completely unlimited. We cannot change a heart, much less save a soul. We like to work hard at By the Hand because God deserves it, not because He depends on it. We plan and work as if the results depended on us, but never forget we depend completely on God.

CONCLUSION: WHAT ARE YOUR PRINCIPLES OF EXCELLENCE?

Today, Keewaun is reading books and winning spelling bees. That is not all he wants to win; he wants to be a preacher one of these days and win souls like Dr. Erwin Lutzer. Natasha makes A's and B's on her report card and is one of the top students in her class at a private high school. She is in church every Sunday and still praying and trusting that God will use her witness to save her mom.

If we had not used the principles of excellence outlined here, we are convinced that we would have failed God and failed these precious children.

The most important thing is for each organization to find its God-given approach to ministry. While we can certainly learn from each other, we will fail if we try to carbon copy what works for another ministry in our own. We each need to find what will work best for us based on what God is calling us to do, our vision and mission, whom we are serving, and how best to meet their needs. In other words, we each need to create our own principles of excellence, or better yet, catch His principles of excellence, for changing young lives.

REFLECTION QUESTIONS

1. How does Satan use lack of education to destroy youth today?

2. What can Christians do that government cannot do to address the problems of our age?

3. What are some pitfalls ministries must guard against when taking a results-oriented approach?

4. If you are a ministry leader, how can you use principles of excellence to improve your overall ministry effectiveness?

BRAD STANLEY is the founder of Youth With A Mission Chicago and has been its Director for the last seventeen years. Based in the Rogers Park neighborhood, Brad has helped to develop and facilitate evangelism, discipleship, and practical helps ministry among the city's diverse ethnic and subculture communities. Brad and his family have worked with Youth With A Mission for the past twenty-two years and have served in more than twenty nations.

CHAPTER 29

AGGRESSIVE EVANGELISM:
Taking the Gospel to the Streets (YWAM)

Brad Stanley

Introduction: A Surprising Discovery

The street drama had just finished. As the team quickly moved out into the small crowd of onlookers, I grabbed one of our interpreters, from a local Vietnamese church, and approached a woman who looked to be in her sixties. We greeted her, asking her questions about her family and where she lived, and began to talk to her about the drama. After describing to her the gospel message, I asked her if she had ever considered the message that Jesus brought to the world. I will never forget her response. "Who is this Jesus? I have never heard of him. Does he live here?"

The shocking reality is that this conversation did not take place in Vietnam, but on the corner of Kenmore and Argyle in Chicago. Furthermore, this lady had lived in that neighborhood for forty years. In four decades, living in a major city in North America, she had never heard of the person of Jesus Christ. Her culture, language, and relational networks had isolated her from the influence of the church.

The cultural and social diversity of the modern city has made it increasingly easier to live and function in isolation from the traditional reach of the Church. The dynamic of relationships within today's cities is no longer based on geographical proximity but on the basis of function or cultural affinity. The average urban dweller has more of an acquaintance with those from his cultural or occupational marketplace than with those who live in walking distance from his residence.

THE NEED FOR AGGRESSIVE EVANGELISM

Much like the story of this woman from the "Little Vietnam" community of Chicago, many who live in the city may never truly hear the gospel unless someone is sent to them. Aubrey Malphurs sums it up well in his book *Planting Growing Churches*. He says, "The evangelical church will not survive unless it aggressively pursues unchurched lost people outside its 'four walls.' It must adopt an 'invasion' or 'penetration' mentality. The days have long passed when the church could sit back and wait for lost people to come to it."[1] *Webster's New World Dictionary* defines aggressive as "boldly hostile; quarrelsome."[2] Productive and fruitful evangelism can never be hostile or quarrelsome in its approach toward people. However, like Malphurs' suggestion for an "invasion or penetration mentality," I would suggest that the Church has advanced historically to the degree it was willing to be hostile in Satan's territory and quarrelsome with his deceptions. What territories exist in our cities that have yet to be penetrated effectively with the truth?

While serving in Youth With A Mission, I have had the privilege of working with thousands of Christians from all ages in different evangelism strategies throughout Chicago. After our team moved to the city sixteen years ago, I began to read about the great evangelists in Chicago's history, like D. L. Moody and Billy Sunday. I wondered if aggressive evangelism could still be effective today. Our purpose at YWAM Chicago has always been to love the city by partnering with churches and ministries engaged in long-term community transformation. Like most in long-term ministry, I wanted to shy away from anything that looked impersonal or non-relational. Is it possible for the church to continue to publicly engage its culture, as it has historically, without feeding the modern perception from church outsiders that Christians are too judgmental and pushy? I have come to believe that a type of evangelism that reignites the "taking it to the streets" vision of the church can play a very important and necessary role alongside our long-term community-transforming strategies. The stories that follow are meant to encourage you toward the same conclusion.

Capturing the Attention of the Urban Culture

Wayne A. Meeks, in his book *The First Urban Christians*, does a great job showing the significance the city plays in the formation and exchange of ideas. He states,

> *The City, then, was the place where the new civilization could be experienced, where novelties would first be encountered. It was the place*

where, if anywhere, change could be met and even sought out. It was where the empire was and where the future began. To become a city dweller meant to be caught up in movement.[3]

These movements are bought and sold in the city's marketplace. It is necessary then that the church enters this marketplace and influences those movements. Over the years we have used creative arts teams to engage the thoughts and worldviews of people in plazas, parks, street corners, and cafés. Street dramas can create a great opportunity to visually display a biblical truth that may speak to the conscience of the city. Similar to the way Jesus used parables in public gatherings, these teams are able to use biblical or modern parables to draw a culture into viewing its world through the eyes of truth. Teams are trained to quickly move into the crowd after the drama to initiate conversation.

When individuals with specific artistic talents come to work with us, we ask the Lord for strategic avenues to witness for Him. One couple, exceptionally talented musically, felt led of the Lord to enter a talent contest at an "open-mic night" in a nearby café. The No Exit Café, a somewhat "alternative" place located near us at the time, was a neighborhood favorite. The couple wrote a song that spoke of God's heart for Chicago. As he played guitar and she sang the words the Lord had given them for the city, the audience was spellbound. Following the performance, several of the patrons immediately asked them about the song, creating an opportunity to speak to them personally of God's heart. They actually won the contest.

Every year there is an "Artist on the Wall" contest along the lakefront in our neighborhood. Dozens of artists pay a small fee to create chalk and washable paint pictures on the concrete breaker wall at the beach. One year, we entered a couple of artists who painted very thought-provoking pictures. They revealed the personal involvement of God in creation, and His broken heart over the fallenness of man's original intent. For hours, people walked by the art and talked to the artists about their work. This also created a great opportunity to talk to people about the Lord.

The city is a place of constant visual stimulus. Throughout the day, countless forms of advertisement and entertainment fight for the city-dweller's attention. It could be said that the modern pulpit is the city, and the modern preacher is the latest and catchiest billboard or street merchant. The city is the medium for the exchange of ideas and value systems. I believe this is the place where the life and message of Christ must be heard. We have used street parables, drum bands, street musicians, and hip hop dance teams to capture the city's attention and provoke them with truth.

Every year we run a performing arts camp in the summer. City kids, ages five to eighteen, come to be trained in creative dance and music. The last couple days of the camp, they perform their songs and choreographed dances along the lakefront, in plazas, and even at Six Flags Great America, an hour north of the city. Following these performances they go out into the crowds to pray for people. Young people with a sincere love for Jesus can influence numerous lives in the city.

Street Worship

One of the ways that we have captured the city's attention has been through teams that worship on street corners and in plazas. The Lord has led us countless times to take worship teams to the NBC plaza next to the Michigan Avenue Bridge in downtown Chicago. I am always amazed at how people walking along the sidewalk respond to a passionate display of public worship. Sometimes the teams are as large as fifty or sixty people singing to the Lord with guitars. Invariably, people stop. Some join in, but most just stare in amazement. I have discovered that one of the greatest ways to minister to the spirit and soul of the city is by inviting the presence of God in unashamed worship. The teams are encouraged not to perform for people but truly worship the Lord. This has allowed the Holy Spirit to draw people into His presence.

God is a creative God. When we make ourselves available to Him, to do whatever He asks, He often leads us to do some unusual things. Several times He has led us to the Uptown neighborhood for an unusual assignment. Though Uptown at one time was a very affluent neighborhood on the North Side, it is home to one of the largest concentrations of the mentally ill and homeless in the city. Several times we have taken worship teams to the corner of Wilson and Broadway avenues in the heart of the neighborhood.

On a few occasions, after worshiping for some time, generally drawing a crowd of homeless and depressed individuals, we have felt led of the Lord to all lay prostrate on the concrete sidewalk and cry out for His life and breath to enter our lives. In a physical display of utter desperation and dependency on God, we spend several minutes individually telling God that we cannot survive or experience life without Him. People stop and gaze at the team in wonder. Many then wait for us to stop so they can talk to us. I believe that through this unique display of humility and worship, the Lord was able to minister to some of the wounds of brokenness and abandonment that existed in that neighborhood.

Identifying with the Religious Pursuit of the City-Dweller

Like Paul in Acts 17, we can recognize and use the existing pursuit of spirituality, evident in many who live in our cities, to identify with and create opportunities to express truth to people. In his book *Taking Our Cities for God*, John Dawson writes, "The city dweller is often an idolater. The city intensifies everything, and this includes devotion to false gods."[4] The city has a way of forcing us to make some philosophical sense out of the brokenness and struggles of humanity. It pushes us to find some form of meaning and security. The average person in the city, because of ethnic culture or urban survival, is quite religious. One tool that we have used in many ethnic communities to initiate conversations is religious surveys. Most immigrants feel a strong desire to be better understood by those around them. A person can immediately take the position of a learner by asking the immigrant to tell about his or her religion. Furthermore, most will feel culturally obligated to hear what we believe after we have honored them with a genuine interest in their culture and beliefs.

We have done thousands of these surveys with teams all over the city. On the average, when sending teams of fifteen out in our North Side neighborhood, Rogers Park, one of the most ethnically diverse neighborhoods in the city, the first fifteen people encountered have thirteen different nationalities represented among them. Of those thirteen, eleven are from the least evangelized countries of the world. These people may never have entered a church building, and in many cases, because of cultural isolation, may have never come in contact with the gospel. In some cases contacts were followed up and relationships built that lead to conversions months or even years later.

One young Muslim man was stopped by one of our team members, Chris. They exchanged religious beliefs and the man showed some curiosity toward the message and life of Jesus. Chris continued to meet with him regularly in the South Asian community of Chicago on Devon Street. Eventually, they began to meet in each other's homes. After months of conversation, Chris showed the *Jesus* film in Urdu. This man was overwhelmed by the life of Jesus but struggled with accepting Him as the Son of God. That night he had a dream in which Jesus visited him. In his dream, Jesus told him to go back and listen to his new friends because what they were telling him was true. The next day the young man came to Chris's home and told him he wanted to become a follower of Jesus. This man is still following the Lord today.

The surveys have questions that are intended to discover what people believe about God. There are questions like: "Do you believe there is a God?"; "How do you think this God feels about you?"; "What do you think this God requires of you?" The teams look for an answer that they can identify with, and then relate their own journey to it. The possibility is the same today as in Paul's time. After Paul had spoken into the spiritual pursuit of the citizens of Athens, many wanted to hear more (Acts 17:32). This created further venues for dialogue.

Connecting Through Urban Need

Perhaps the most effective evangelistic tool over the years has been the use of prayer evangelism to create witnessing opportunities. The megacity can make people feel lost, insecure, vulnerable, and powerless. I have discovered that many people are like seething pots, waiting to boil over on the first person who enters their world. Ten years ago the Lord led us to begin taking teams year round to Daley Plaza, surrounding the main courthouse downtown, and offer to pray for people's needs. We heard of the success of YWAM Metro New York in setting up prayer stations around their city, and decided to try a similar strategy in Chicago. Since that time we have prayed with more than eleven thousand people on this plaza.

Daley Plaza functions as a large gathering place for the downtown business community during lunch hours. The strategy is simple but surprisingly effective. Teams go to the plaza and walk up to people, asking them if they need prayer for anything in their lives. Most people do not know how to handle the offer. After they discover that we are not asking for money, or part of some unusual cult group, many will take a deep breath and begin to tell us how much they need prayer. These times of prayer have led to divine appointments and incredible opportunities to minister to people. Typically a team of fifteen to twenty people will pray with more than a hundred people in a couple of hours. Some are lawyers and judges overwhelmed with a court case. Many are businessmen and businesswomen dealing with broken worlds and family crisis. But most are ordinary people trying to survive the difficulties and traumas of life. I have seen the Lord arrange numerous divinely timed encounters, with people who would normally never consider entering the church for help.

Finding Prepared Ground

Recently, after sending a team around the plaza to pray for people, I looked up and saw a well-dressed woman exiting the courthouse building about fifteen yards away. I felt compelled to ask her if she needed prayer. As I walked toward her she stopped and stared at me. The closer I got the more surprised she looked. She was frozen when I reached her. I told her that a group of us was praying for people in the plaza, and asked her if she needed prayer for anything. She looked at me in amazement and said, "What did you say?" I repeated my previous statement and added that we felt the Lord wanted us to give people hope that day, which is not something I usually say.

Tears formed in her eyes. She said, "I don't know if you believe in this or not, but I think I had a vision of you last night." She began to tell me how she had recently been divorced, lost her job, and was now in court losing custody of her children. The night before, she had decided she no longer wanted to live. Just as she was about to take an overdose of pills, she felt the overwhelming disapproval of God at what she was about to do. Angrily, she told God she was not sure He even existed. But, if He was there, He needed to show Himself somehow or she would kill herself. The next moment, she said she saw a mental picture of someone who looked like me walking up to her in Daley Plaza. In her vision, she heard me say that God had sent me to give her hope. Surprised at the vision, she told God that if this was Him, then make it happen the next day while she was going to court. You can imagine the openness this woman had in hearing God's heart for her. After I talked with her for some time, she wept and said to me, "You just don't understand how much this has changed my life."

One day a married couple on our team encountered another couple going toward the courthouse. When asked if they needed prayer, the woman sarcastically said, "Yeah, you can pray for us; we're going to file for divorce." Our teammates took the man and woman aside separately, offering to pray for them. They spent nearly forty-five minutes praying and sharing the Lord with them. They both decided to ask the Lord into their lives. They then came back together and prayed that God would heal their marriage. At the end of the time, the woman was in tears. They thanked our team members for giving them hope that God could heal their marriage. They then turned around and went home, never entering the courthouse.

Here's one more example of the many instances when it seems we were in the right place at the right time. An ambitious sixteen-year-old boy stopped a well-dressed businessman while he was talking on his cell phone. He told the man that he was in the plaza praying for people and asked if there was any prayer that the man needed. The man told his party, on the other end of the phone, to hold on and asked the boy to repeat himself. The boy told him again what he was there for. The man got back on the phone and said, "You are not going to believe this, but there's this boy here who says he wants to pray for us . . . yeah, that's what I thought . . . well, hold on."

Suddenly, the man handed the phone to the boy. He had been talking to his wife about their teenage son who was getting entangled with gangs and drugs. Now the boy on our team was counseling the woman, on the phone, how to teach their son about God and how the Lord can change their son's life like He had changed his own. The time ended with the boy, the man, and the woman on the cell phone all praying together. The woman kept thanking the boy and telling him how encouraged she was that she had met him that day.

The fact is that people are truly overwhelmed and God is ready to meet with them. As Paul exhorts us in Romans 10:14, "How, then, can they call on the one they have not believed in? And how can they believe in the one of whom they have not heard? And how can they hear without someone preaching to them?" The people of God can be the missing part to this equation. God is ready to create divine appointments for us when we step out in evangelism. Surely we can enter what has been considered the territory of the enemy, and see the church grow and communities transformed.

There are many ways to use the needs of those around us to build bridges for the gospel. We have used teams to give out food in parks, in what we call "Hot Dog Evangelism." Groups have distributed water bottles along the lakefront on hot days as a way to talk to people. One year we blanketed an ethnic neighborhood with flyers offering free services from college students such as computer tutoring, music lessons, house cleaning, etc. A relationship was built through this outreach with a Muslim man that led to him becoming a believer and being baptized nearly two years after we first entered his house.

PRINCIPLES THAT CAN HELP

The church is an aggressive agent for change. Jack Dennison, in his book *City Reaching*, says, "America has never seen the full capabilities of the church unleashed in a major city."[5] What would it look like for the Church to become public in its faith? Unfortunately, Dennison goes on to say later in his book, "Evidence suggests that 95 percent of all Christians in North America will not lead a single person to Christ in their entire lifetime."[6] After working with hundreds of youth teams, I have come to believe that this current generation of believers has an evangelistic gifting. This can be seen, in part, by their strong desire for relevant truth and a commitment to relationships and the valuing of people.

The following principles are lessons that we have learned in seeking to mobilize that generation to once again take the gospel to the streets.

1. Evangelism is a partnership with the Holy Spirit (John 16:7–11; Matt. 10:19–20; Acts 1:8). Allow the Holy Spirit to guide you in an effective strategy for your city and neighborhood. After all, He is the greatest Evangelist. Ask Him for unique methods that will create the environment for dialogue, communicate a sincere interest in people, and give an opportunity to become relationally involved.

2. Effective evangelism must be relevant (Prov. 25:11; Heb. 4:12). Seek the Lord for the unique forms of evangelism that will enable you to build bridges into the people group or neighborhood you are targeting. A relevant strategy can be discovered through prayer, research, and interaction with the community (1

Chron. 12:32). God will often lead in unique ways to bring truth to a culture (Ezek. 4:1–8; 12:1–6). Be obedient and see what He will do.

3. Use strategies that identify with and understand people (Acts 17:22–31). It is the kindness of God that leads us to repentance (Rom. 2:4), and His understanding that causes us to approach Him with our needs (Heb. 4:15–16). Use strategies that build bridges. Jesus either created a situation that made the other person ask a question, or directly asked one Himself (John 4:4–26). In David Kinnaman's book *unChristian*, research shows that most nonbelievers "admit their emotional and intellectual barriers go up when they are around Christians, and they reject Jesus because they feel rejected by Christians."[7]

4. Know your goal (2 Cor. 5:16–21). The goal is reconciliation between God and man. We do not do evangelism to assuage our own consciences. Whatever approach we use must be sincere and personal, enabling people to see God more clearly (John 3:17; Gal. 5:22–23; 6:1–3). This understanding will not only affect our message but also our methodology.

5. Leave the ground fertile for another (1 Cor. 3:10). We must seek to leave people with a greater openness to God as a result of our encounter with them. Most need several encounters with truth before they will respond to the Lord. Our time with people will either advance that process or hinder it, to the degree that we display the heart of God accurately. An effective message, whether proclamational or one on one, can awaken a culture or an individual to truth. Like the ministry of John the Baptist, it can prepare the way for the Lord (Matt. 3:1–3).

6. Be committed to discipleship (Matt. 28:18–20). We must remind ourselves that the Great Commission is to make disciples, not just converts (v. 19). Build into your evangelism strategy a plan for follow-up. Find ways to partner with local churches whenever possible. When targeting a community without a culturally relevant church, be committed to a church-planting strategy. Barnabas and Saul remained in Antioch for a year to teach and disciple those who were coming to the Lord (Acts 11:19–26).

CONCLUSION: NEIGHBORHOOD EVANGELISM

As the peoples and cultures of the nations continue to move into the cities, we are faced with an ever-increasing need for neighborhood evangelism. Because this constant flow of humanity represents great diversity, our evangelism must aggressively enter new territory outside the walls of the church. Roger Greenway, in *Apostles to the City*, exhorts us, "When due to uncertainty or frustration, people engaged in mission work begin to minimize the importance of winning converts from unbelief to saving faith in Christ, something has seriously gone wrong."[8] By the same token, David Kinnaman, in *unChristian*, reminds us, "If you create more barriers with outsiders because of your tactics, you have not been a good steward of the gospel. How we choose to share Christ is as important as our actually doing it."[9] It must be the church's goal to participate in both active and Christlike evangelism. Unless we mobilize relevant and effective evangelism strategies, the Church will lose ground in increasingly post-Christian and unreached urban environments.

Aggressive evangelism, when done well, can expand the ministry of the local church toward city transformation. First, it helps to identify and initiate relationships with those who are isolated from the Church. Second, it allows the Holy Spirit to create divine opportunities to speak the truth of God's Word, in a very personal way, to those in need. Finally, it engages the conscience of a culture or community through relevant and identifiable displays of truth. May we see a new generation that has the passion to take the gospel of our Lord to the streets of our cities.

REFLECTION QUESTIONS

1. What communities in your city may be isolated from the normal influence of the Church? What parts of your city represent key marketplaces, cultural gathering points, or places of recreation that could be used for evangelism strategies?

2. Are there evangelistic models that could build bridges into some of your city's places of need? What evangelism strategies could be used to effectively lay the groundwork for the church in that area?

3. Are there families, youth, or college students in your church who could be trained and mobilized into some of these areas with unique forms of evangelism?

Recommended Reading List

Barna, George. *Evangelism That Works*. Ventura, Calif.: Regal, 1995.

Boyd, Gregory. *Letters from a Skeptic*. Colorado Springs: Chariot Victor, 1994.

Cunningham, Sarah. *Dear Church*. Grand Rapids, Mich.: Zondervan, 2006.

Goodfellow, John. *Streetwise*. Seattle: YWAM, 1991.

McClung, Floyd. *Living on the Devil's Doorstep*. Seattle: YWAM, 1988, 2001.

Silvoso, Ed. *That None Should Perish*. Ventura, Calif.: Regal, 1994.

Tooley, Ross. *We Cannot but Tell*. Seattle: YWAM, 1971, 1993.

Notes

PART 1: CRITICAL ISSUES

Introduction to Critical Issues
by John Fuder

1. Quantitative studies pose a problem and a testable hypothesis, gather numerical data, analyze the data statistically, and draw conclusions. See Robert E. Slavin, *Research Methods in Education*, 2nd ed. (Boston: Allyn and Bacon, 1992), 70–72.

2. Ibid. Qualitative studies immerse researchers in a given social situation, collect "word" data (observations and interviews), form hypotheses inductively in the process, and produce an in-depth analytical description of an intact cultural scene.

3. Leith Anderson, "Practice of Ministry in 21st Century Churches," *Bibliotheca Sacra*, 151. Oct-Dec. 1994, 387.

4. Marvin J. Newell, "Why Is America a Mission Field?" *American Missionary Fellowship*, Fall 2006, Vol. 12, No. 2, 4–6.

5. Robert D. Lupton, *Compassion, Justice and the Christian Life* (Ventura, Calif.: Regal, 2007), 113.

6. Ibid.

7. John Fuder, ed., *A Heart for the City* (Chicago: Moody, 1999).

8. Howard Witt, "Hispanics Lead Pace in Diverse Nation," *Chicago Tribune*, 1 May 2008, 4.

9. Antonio Olivo, "Study: U.S. Population Will Grow Nearly 50% by 2050," *Chicago Tribune*, 12 February 2008, 4.

10. Numerous noteworthy individuals have been cited as the source of this tried and true axiom, the likes of which include (listed alphabetically) Karl Barth, Jonathan Edwards, Reinhold Niebuhr, Charles Spurgeon, and John Stott. We are in good company to practice the same!

11. Ray Quintanilla, "Towns' Melting Pots Boil Anxiety," *Chicago Tribune*, 29 May 2007, 1.

12. Oscar Avila, "City's Future Tied to Mexicans," *Chicago Tribune*, 13 September 2006, 3.

13. See Psalm 146:7–9, among many other verses.

14. See 1 Peter 2:11.

15. Zechariah 7:9–10.

16. Garbi Schmidt, *Islam in Urban America* (Philadelphia: Temple Univ. Press, 2004), 10.

17. Larry A. Poston and Carl F. Ellis Jr., *The Changing Face of Islam in America* (Camp Hill, Pa.: Horizon Books, 2000), 14.

18. Ibid., 268.

19. Ibid., 269.

20. Ibid., 270.

Chapter 1: Gentrification
by Wayne L. Gordon

1. For a more detailed description of the eight key components of Christian community development see John Fuder, ed., *A Heart for the City* (Chicago: Moody, 1999), chapter 5, "A Philosophy of Urban Ministry."
2. Wayne L. Gordon and Randall Frame, *Real Hope in Chicago* (Grand Rapids, Mich.: Zondervan, 1995).
3. Robert D. Lupton, *Renewing the City: Reflections on Community Development and Urban Renewal* (Downers Grove, Ill.: InterVarsity, 2005).

Chapter 2: Working Together to Restore Our Communities
by Noel Castellanos

1. Robert Linthicum, *Transforming Power: Biblical Strategies for Making a Difference in Your Community* (Downers Grove, Ill.: InterVarsity, 2003), 132.

Chapter 3: "Exegeting" Your Community
by John Fuder

1. Ray Bakke, *A Theology as Big as the City* (Downers Grove, Ill.: InterVarsity, 1997), 13.
2. Rachel Zoll, "Illinois Leads Nation in Diversity of Religions," *Chicago Tribune*, 20 September 2002, 8.
3. Ibid.
4. John Fuder, *The Occasional Bulletin*, "Training Students to Exegete the City." Vol. 15, No. 2, Spring 2003, 4–6.
5. *Today in the Word*, February 2002, 4, 36–39.
6. Ibid., 4.
7. Lyle W. Dorsett, *A Passion for Souls* (Chicago: Moody, 1997), 64.
8. John Cook, "Lowlife Highlights," *Chicago Tribune*, 22 December 2002, 6.
9. Dorsett, *Passion for Souls*, 65–66.
10. Ibid., 67, 84.
11. *Today in the Word*, 4, 38–39.
12. Dorsett, *Passion for Souls*, 306, 310, 312.
13. John Fuder, *The World of Green Eyes: Toward a Strategy for Reaching the Homeless*, unpublished paper. Biola University, Spring 1991.
14. Jude Tiersma Watson, et al., of Cambria Community, Innerchange. See details in Charles Van Engen and Jude Tiersma, eds., *God So Loves the City* (Monrovia, Calif.: MARC, 1994).
15. John Fuder, "Becoming an Insider," in *A Heart for the City* (Chicago: Moody, 1999).
16. John Fuder, *The Occasional Bulletin*, "Training Students to Exegete the City." Vol. 15, No. 2, Spring 2003, 4–5.
17. Class notes from SICS 502, Social Organization, Spring 1991.
18. Sherwood G. Lingenfelter and Marvin K. Mayers, "Ministering Cross Culturally," and Judith Lingenfelter, "Getting to Know Your New City," in *Discipling the City*, ed. Roger S. Greenway (Grand Rapids, Mich.: Baker, 1986, rept. 1992).

19. James P. Spradley, *The Ethnographic Interview* and James P. Spradley, *Participant Observation* (New York: Holt, Rinehart and Winston, 1980).

20. John Fuder, *Training Students for Urban Ministry: An Experiential Approach* (Eugene, Ore.: Wipf and Stock), 2001.

21. Elijah Anderson, *A Place on the Corner* (Chicago: Univ. of Chicago, 1978); Elliot Liebow, *Tally's Corner* (Boston: Little, Brown, 1967); William Whyte, *Street Corner Society* (Chicago: Univ. of Chicago, 1955).

22. Mark Van Houten, *God's Inner-City Address* (Grand Rapids: Zondervan, 1988), 20–21. See too *Profane Evangelism* (Grand Rapids: Zondervan, 1989).

23. Ray Bakke, *The Urban Christian* (Downers Grove, Ill.: InterVarsity, 1987), 108–9.

24. Leith Anderson, "Christian Ministry in the 21st Century," lecture delivered at the W. H. Griffith Thomas Lectures at Dallas Theological Seminary, 2–5 February 1993.

25. Roger S. Greenway and Timothy M. Monsma, *Cities: Missions' New Frontier* (Grand Rapids, Mich.: Baker, 2000), 130–38.

26. Harvie M. Conn, *Planting and Growing Urban Churches* (Grand Rapids, Mich.: Baker, 1997), 33.

27. John Holzmann, "Caleb Project Research Expeditions," in *Planting and Growing Urban Churches*, ed. Harvie M. Conn (Grand Rapids, Mich.: Baker, 1997), 53, 57.

28. *Peoples of Yemen: A Prayer Guide* (Littleton, Colo.: Caleb Project, 2005).

29. Harvie M. Conn and Manuel Ortiz, *Urban Ministry* (Downers Grove, Ill.: InterVarsity, 2001), 273.

30. Ibid., 258,

31. Ibid., 274–75.

32. Bob Waymire and Carl Townsend, *Discovering Your City* (Etna, Calif.: LIGHT, 2000).

33. Robert D. Lupton, *Renewing the City* (Downers Grove, Ill.: InterVarsity, 2005).

34. Leith Anderson, "Practice of Ministry in 21st Century Churches," *Bibliotheca Sacra,* 151. October–December 1994, 388.

35. Class projects from GM790: Community Analysis and GS500: Practice of Ministry.

36. Referencing a bipolar, manic-depressive, abused, suicidal, chemically dependent, ex-convict . . . who gave her life to Christ!

37. E. Thomas Brewster and Elizabeth S. Brewster, *Bonding and the Missionary Task: Establishing a Sense of Belonging*, Perspectives on the World Christian Movement, eds. Ralph D. Winter and Steven C. Hawthorne (Pasadena, Calif.: William Carey, 1992), C-107–19.

38. Spradley, *Ethnographic Interview*, 1980, 32–34.

39. Marvin K. Mayers, *Christianity Confronts Culture* (Grand Rapids, Mich.: Zondervan, 1987), 4–7.

40. Oswald Chambers, *My Utmost for His Highest* (Grand Rapids, Mich.: Discovery House, 1992 rpt.), March 3.

Chapter 4: The Border, the Barrio, and the 'Burbs

by Juanita Irizarry

1. Agencia ALPHA, http://www.agenciaalpha.org/, January 29, 2008.

2. Patricia Sobalvarro, written testimony, Spring 2007.

3. Agencia ALPHA website.

4. Kit Danley and Ian Danley, "How Immigration Is Impacting One CCDA Ministry," *Restorer*, Christian Community Development Association, May 2006.

5. Ibid.

6. "Flor Crisostomo ... Nueva Inmigrante en una Vieja Lucha," *El Sol Newspaper*, Year 3, No 82, (February 1, 2008), 11.

7. The church was also the scene of a year-long controversy during 2006 and 2007 around Elvira Arrellano. Sandra Dibble and Anna Cearley, "Deported Activist Vows to Carry On Cause," August 21, 2007, http://www.signonsandiego.com/uniontrib/20070821/news_1m21elvira .html cited December 28, 2007.

8. "Flor Cristosomo ... Nueva Inmigrante en una Vieja Lucha," 11.

9. Richard Fry and Shirin Hakimzadeh, "A Statistical Portrait of Hispanics at Mid-Decade: Pew Hispanic Center Tabulations of 2000 Census and 2005 American Community Survey," October 20, 2006, http://pewhispanic.org/reports/middecade/, cited January 9, 2007, Table 3.

10. Ibid., Table 1.

11. Mark Hugo Lopez, "Electoral Engagement Among Latinos," Latino Research @ ND, Vol. 1, No. 2, December 2003, http://www.nd.edu/~latino/research/pubs/LRNDv1n2.pdf, cited January 9, 2007, 1.

12. J. P. Schmelzer, "Their Future, Our Future," *Chicago Sun-Times*, November 26, 2007.

13. Berenice Alejo and Sylvia Puente, *Forging the Tools for Unity: A Report on Metro Chicago's Mayors Roundtables on Latino Integration*, University of Notre Dame Institute for Latino Studies Center for Metropolitan Chicago Initiatives, and Metropolitan Mayors Caucus, (November 2007), 7.

14. Ibid.

15. Ibid., 2.

16. Beatriz Ponce de Leon, *A Shared Future: The Economic Engagement of Greater Chicago and Its Mexican Community*, Task Force Series (Chicago: The Chicago Council on Global Affairs, 2006), 10.

17. Ibid., 10–11.

18. Alejo and Puente, *Forging the Tools*, 3.

19. "Discrimination in Metropolitan Housing Markets," U.S. Department of Housing and Urban Development, February 2003.

20. (see p.91)

21. Craig Wong, "On Being the Church. The Church's 'Third Rail' of Immigration," PRISM, May/June 2008, No. 3 (Wynnewood, PA: Evangelicals for Social Action).

Chapter 5: A Special Blessing from the Lord?

by Samuel Naaman

1. For detailed information on Muslims in America see Yvonne Yazbeck Haddad, ed., *The Muslims of America* (New York: Oxford Univ. Press, 1991) and Yvonne Yazbeck Haddad and Jane Idleman Smith, *Muslim Communities in North America* (Albany, N.Y.: State Univ. of New York Press, 1994). The number 6 million is often quoted by other electronic communications too. *The Cross or the Crescent: Understanding Islam* is a good video produced by the Southern Baptists.

2. See Ghulam Masih Naaman, *My Grace Is Sufficient for You*, published by The Call of Hope, Germany, for more details of Ghulam's conversion. This can also be found on Answering-Islam.org, in section "Why They Converted."
3. Islamic Shariah law is derived from the teachings of the Quran and Hadith (Saying of the Prophet Muhammad). This law is practiced in Saudi Arabia.
4. Interview with Mr. Haq, a Muslim scholar, in Chicago, 2 Feb. 2008.

Chapter 6: Economic Development in the Hood

by Mary Nelson

1. U.S. Dept. of Justice website (www.usdoj.gov/recidivism) has detailed analysis of the cited statistics and much more, and the DOJ updates the figures regularly.

2. Annie E. Casey Foundation, "Family Economic Success," Workforce Development paper, www.aecf.org/MajorInitiatives/FamilyEconomicSuccess.2007.
3. Christian Community Development Association (CCDA) has Eight Key Components. More information is available at www.ccda.org/aboutus/philosophy.
4. *2003 Key Indicators Report*, published by Bethel New Life, based on the 2000 census figures.
5. Michael Porter, "Competitive Advantage of the Inner City." See also Michael Porter's address at the Willow Creek Leadership Summit 2007, "Doing Well at Doing Good." DVD available at http://www.willowcreek.com/wcaprodsb.asp?invtid=PR30367.
6. CCDA *Restorer* Newsletter, Spring 1992.
7. Luther Snow, *The Power of Asset Mapping: How Your Congregation Can Act on Its Gifts* (Herndon, Va.: The Alban Institute, 2004).
8. A good resource is Joy Skjegstad, *Winning Grants to Strengthen Your Ministry* (Herndon, Va.: The Alban Institute, 2007).
9. *Communities First*, ed. Jay Van Groningen (Grand Rapids, Mich.: CRWRC, 2007), has great resources for congregations moving into action.

Chapter 7: New Wineskins

by Scott Clifton and Jackson Crum

1. Phrase "shadow of the skyline" attributed to founding pastor of Park Community Church, Matt Heard.
2. Chicago Housing Authority FY 2005 Annual Plan. November 1, 2004. Appendix 8, 26–27.
3. Chicago Housing Authority FY 2005 Annual Plan, 35.
4. Mary Schmich, "Key Developer Also Trying to Rebuild Lives," *Chicago Tribune*, 8 July 2004, 2.
5. Mary Schmich, "Everyone Equal in Cabrini-Green Supermarket," *Chicago Tribune*, 4 June 2000. Metro Section, 1.
6. Vincent Donovan, *Christianity Rediscovered* (Maryknoll, N.Y.: Orbis books, 2004), xiii.
7. Leslie Newbigin, *The Gospel in a Pluralist Society* (Grand Rapids. Mich.: Eerdmans, 1989), 213.
8. Robert Coleman, *The Master Plan of Evangelism* (Grand Rapids, Mich.: Revell, 1993), 27.
9. www.kncsb.org/resources/PersonsofPeace.pdf.

10. Ken Blanchard, Patricia Zigarmi, and Drea Zigarmi, *Leadership and the One Minute Manager* (New York: William Morrow and Company, 1985), 44.

11. http://www.ccda.org/philosophy#listening.

12. Henry Blackaby and Claude King, *Experiencing God* (Nashville: Broadman and Holman, 1994), 65.

13. Taken from one-day workshop with Bob Logan, *From Followers to Leaders*. Church Smart Resources, Spring 2008.

14. ccda.org.

15. Robert Lupton, *And You Call Yourself a Christian* (Chicago: CCDA, 2000), 35.

16. Donovan, *Christianity Rediscovered*, 123.

17. Rick Rusaw and Eric Swanson, *The Externally Focused Church* (Loveland, Colo.: Group, 2004), 60–61.

18. Dan Webster, *The Real Deal* (Grand Rapids, Mich.: Custom Printers, 1998), 94.

Chapter 8: Growing a Church Through Prayer

by Al Toledo

1. Andrew Murray, *Teach Me to Pray* (Ada, Mich.: Bethany House, 1982), 27.

2. Bob Griffin Jr., *Firestorms of Revival* (Lake Mary, Fla.: Creation House, 2006), 58.

3. Martin Luther King Jr., *A Testament of Hope: The Essential Writings of Martin Luther King, Jr.*, James M. Washington, ed. (New York: HarperOne, 1990), 220.

4. Dutch Sheets, *The River of God* (Ventura, Calif.: Regal, 1998), 194.

5. Charles Finney, *Experiencing Revival* (New Kensington, Pa.: Whittaker House, 2008 rpt.), 78.

6. Joseph R. Myers, *The Search to Belong: Rethinking Intimacy, Community, and Small Groups* (Grand Rapids, Mich.: Zondervan, 2003), 36.

7. Greg Hawkins, *Reveal: Follow Me* (Barrington, Ill.: Willow Creek Association, 2008), 29.

8. Jim Cymbala, *Fresh Wind, Fresh Fire* (Grand Rapids, Mich.: Zondervan, 1997), 82.

9. Finney, *Experiencing Revival*, 78.

PART 2: CHURCH-PLANTING MODELS

Chapter 9: Jesus on the Mic

by Phil Jackson

1. Michel W. Harris, *The Rise of Gospel Blues: The Music of Thomas Andrew Dorsey in the Urban Church* (New York: Oxford Univ. Press, 1992).

2. James P. Spradley, *Participant Observation* (Orlando: Holt, Rinehart and Winston, 1980).

3. James Cone, *Black Theology and Black Power* (Maryknoll, N.Y.: Orbis Books, 1997), and Gustavo Gutiérrez, *A Theology of Liberation: History, Politics, and Salvation* (Maryknoll, N.Y.: Orbis Books, rev. ed. 1988).

Chapter 10: The Volcanic Model
by Isaías Mercado

1. Harold Recinos, *Hear the Cry: A Latino Pastor Challenges the Church* (Louisville, Ky.: Westminster John Knox, 1989).
2. Martin Luther King Jr., *Strength to Love* (New York: Harper & Row, 1963).
3. Gustavo Gutierrez, *We Drink from Our Own Wells: The Spiritual Journey of a People* (New York: Orbis Books, 1984).
4. Harold J. Recinos, "The Barrio as the Locus of a New Church", In *Hispanic/Latino Theology*, Ada Maria Isasi-Díaz and Fernando F. Segovia, eds. (Minneapolis, Minn.: Augsburg Fortress Publs., 1996), 183.
5. Walter Bruggemann, "Rethinking Church Models Through Scripture", *Theology Today* 48 (July 1991): 128–138.

Chapter 11: Becoming a Chinese Neighbor
by Luke Dudenhofer

1. C. Peter Wagner, *Our Kind of People: The Ethical Dimensions of Church Growth in America* (Atlanta: John Knox Press, 1979), 137.
2. David K. Fremon, *Chicago Politics Ward by Ward* (Bloomington, Ind.: Indiana Univ. Press, 1988), 83–87.
3. Bill and Lori Granger, *Lords of the Last Machine: The Story of Politics in Chicago* (New York: Random House, 1987), 163.
4. "Our Pledge," *Bridgeport News*, 23 April 2008, 4.
5. The Chicago Commission on Race Relations, *The Negro in Chicago: A Study of Race Relations and a Race Riot* (Chicago: Univ. of Chicago Press, 1922).
6. Fremon, *Chicago Politics*, 85.
7. Karen Shields, "Clark Beating Shatters Fragile Racial Alliance," *Chicago Reporter*, April 1999.
8. http://en.wikipedia.org/wiki/Bridgeport%2C_Chicago.
9. Curtiss Paul DeYoung, Michael O. Emerson, George Yancey, and Karen Chai Kim, *United by Faith: The Multiracial Congregation as an Answer to the Problem of Race* (New York: Oxford Univ. Press, 2003), 2.
10. *The Hebrew-Greek Key Study Bible* (Grand Rapids, Mich.: Baker, 1984).
11. Denis Lane, *One World—Two Minds: Eastern and Western Outlooks in a Changing World* (Littleton, Colo.: OMF International, 2000), 46.
12. David J. Hesselgrave, *Communicating Christ Cross-Culturally*, 2nd ed. (Grand Rapids, Mich.: Zondervan, 1991), 603.
13. Lane, *Two Minds*, 43.
14. Hesselgrave, *Cross-Culturally*, 593.
15. Lane, *Two Minds*, 46.
16. Ibid., 36–37.
17. Ibid., 61.
18. Hesselgrave, *Cross-Culturally*, 596.
19. Lane, *Two Minds*, 63.
20. Ibid., 24–25.

21. Hesselgrave, *Cross-Culturally*, 266.

22. Matthew Bigelow, Luke Dudenhofer, Fung Pui Phyllis Mak, and Wing Yu Mary Tang, *Community Analysis of the Chinese in Bridgeport for New Life Community Church*. Unpublished manuscript. Moody Graduate School, Chicago, 2007.

23. Ibid., 8.

24. Harvie M. Conn, *Planting and Growing Urban Churches: From Dream to Reality* (Grand Rapids, Mich.: Baker, 1997), 95.

25. Lane, *Two Minds*, 55.

Chapter 12: Church in Emerging Culture

by Daniel Hill

1. In the book *unChristian* by David Kinnaman and Gabe Lyons (Grand Rapids, Mich.: Baker, 2007), the authors cite research from 2007 showing that 40 percent (24 million) of those ages 16–29 consider themselves "outsiders" to the Christian church. If you take a broader look and stretch the age range from 18–41, the percentage is 37 percent and swells to 34 million overall (p. 18).

2. Some of the books that have influenced my understanding of wholistic ministry, in no particular order, are: *Divided by Faith* (Michael Emerson and Christian Smith), *United by Faith* (Karen Chai Kim, Curtiss Paul DeYoung, Michael O. Emerson, and George Yancey), *Justice for All* (John Perkins), *Race Matters* (Cornel West), *Crisis in the Village* (Robert Franklin), *Being White* (Paula Harris and Doug Schaupp), *A Credible Witness* (Brenda Salter-McNeil), *The Hispanic Challenge: Opportunities Confronting the Church* (Manuel Ortiz), *Reconciliation Blues: A Black Evangelical's Inside View of White Christianity* (Ed Gilbreath), *A Theology as Big as the City* (Ray Bakke), *The Urban Christian* (Ray Bakke and Jim Hart), and *Just Generosity: A New Vision for Overcoming Poverty in America* (Ronald Sider).

3. Ray Bakke, *A Theology as Big as the City* (Downers Grove, Ill.: InterVarsity, 1997).

4. Ibid.

5. Quoted from Dr. Ray Bakke's Keynote Address at the 2005 CCDA conference (www.ccda.org).

6. One of the most substantial actions a group moving toward comprehensive community development can take is to gain a commanding understanding of both the history and soul of the neighborhood they are serving in. There are at least two schools of thought in the Christian Community Development world as to how to do this: asset-based community development (begin by looking for the existing strengths of the community and build upon those) and felt-needs ministry (begin by looking at the requests the local stakeholders have as they strive for progress).

We did our best to be sensitive to both of these schools of thought. We enlisted both volunteers and staff to canvass our community and to humbly ask lots of questions. We met with local politicians (in Chicago each of the fifty wards has an alderman), with the local beat police (in Chicago we have something called CAPS, which is a monthly meeting for concerned neighbors), with the executive leadership of local nonprofit agencies, with the principals and teachers of the local elementary and high schools, with the pastors of the local churches, and with as many neighbors and local stakeholders as possible.

7. Martin Luther King, Jr. wrote the "Letter from Birmingham Jail" on April 16, 1963. King wrote the letter from the city jail after a nonviolent protest against segregation. The letter is a response to a statement made by eight white Alabama clergymen.

Chapter 13: House Church

by Clive Craigen

1. A special thanks to Neil Cole, Dave Guiles, Mike Jentes, and Kurt Miller for stretching and shaping my ecclesiology.
2. See Mike Jentes, "Why House Churches?" 2002, http://www.thequestcolumbus.com/origins.html.
3. Dave Guiles, *The ACTS Strategy* (Winona Lake, Ind.: Grace Brethren International Mission, 2002-2003), 51.
4. Del Birkey, *The House Church: A Missiological Model* (Wheaton, Ill.: House Church Central, 1991), 5.
5. Wolfgang Simson, *Houses That Change the World* (Waynesboro, Ga.: Authentic Media, 2005), 58.
6. Rad Zdero, ed., *Nexus: The World House Church Movement Reader* (Pasadena, Calif.: William Carey Library, 2007), 197.
7. Ibid., 200–201.
8. Simson, *Houses That Change*, 68, and Zdero, *Nexus*, 204.
9. Zdero, *Nexus*, 207–9.
10. Simson, *Houses That Change*, 69–70, and Zdero, *Nexus*, 209–11.
11. Zdero, *Nexus*, 212–15.
12. Ibid., 215–16, and Simson, *Houses That Change*, 70–71.
13. Birkey, *The House Church*, 9–11.
14. David Garrison, *Church Planting Movements: How God Is Redeeming a Lost World* (Bangalore, India: WIGTAKE Resources).
15. Ibid., 191–93.
16. George Barna, "Rapid Increase in Alternative Forms of the Church Are Changing the Religious Landscape," *Barna Update*. Barna Group, Ltd. 24 October 2005. http://www.barna.org/FlexPage.aspx?Page=BarnaUpdate&BarnaUpdateID=202.
17. Ibid.
18. Brian Sanders, *Life After Church* (Downers Grove, Ill.: InterVarsity, 2007).
19. Neil Cole, *Organic Church: Growing Faith Where Life Happens* (San Francisco: Jossey-Bass, 2005).
20. Tony and Felicity Dale, *Simply Church* (Austin, Tex.: Karis Publishing, 2002).
21. Robert D. Lupton, *Theirs Is the Kingdom of God* (San Francisco: HarperCollins, 1989), 120.
22. Jerry White, *The Church and the Parachurch* (Portland, Ore.: Multnomah, 1983), 19.
23. Keith Phillips, *Out of Ashes* (Los Angeles: World Impact Press, 1996).
24. Conversations the author had with students and campus ministry leaders.
25. Kay S. Hymowitz, "Dads in the 'Hood," *City Journal*, 6 December 2004. http://www.city-journal.org/html/14_4_dads_hood.html.
26. Marshall Shelley and Eric Reed, interview with Eugene Rivers, "Community from Scratch," *Leadership*. Winter 1999.

Chapter 14: Hospitality in the City

by Dave and Angie Arnold

1. Alex Kotlowitz, *Never a City So Real* (New York: Crown Publishers, 2004).
2. *The Encyclopedia of Chicago* (Chicago: Univ. of Chicago Press, 2004).
3. Check out http://www.city-data.com/zips/60625.html to get a list of all the nationalities represented in Albany Park.
4. Taken from Theodore Roosevelt Web Page, www.rhsroughriders.org.
5. *Encyclopedia of Chicago*, http://www.encyclopedia.chicagohistory.org/pages/36.html.
6. Christine D. Pohl, *Making Room: Recovering Hospitality as a Christian Tradition* (Grand Rapids: Eerdmans, 1999).
7. Henry T. Blackaby and Claude V. King, *Experiencing God: How to Live the Full Adventure of Knowing and Doing the Will of God* (Nashville: Broadman and Holman, 1994).
8. Michael Frost and Alan Hirsch, *The Shaping of Things to Come* (Peabody, Mass.: Hendrickson, 2003).
9. Between February 2004 and the end of 2007, approximately 11,500 of an approved 12,500 applicants had departed from Russia to relocate to the U.S. About 80 percent of Meskhetian Turks are ethnic Turks, while approximately 20 percent are descendants of indigenous Georgians who became Muslim in the 17th to 18th centuries (research done by Brian White, one of our leaders).
10. CCDA exists to reach urban centers with the gospel through community development. Check out www.ccda.org.
11. Merrill Tenney, *Handy Dictionary of the Bible* (Zondervan: Grand Rapids, 1965).
12. Michael Frost, *Exiles: Living Missionally in a Post-Christian Culture* (Peabody, Mass.: Hendrickson, 2006).
13. According to a web article in Noticias, www.noticas.info.com, as of 2007, half the world's population now lives in cities. I quote: "The commission's report states that some 3.2 billion of the world's 6.5 billion people live in cities today, and the number will climb to 5 billion—an estimated 61 percent of the global population—by 2030."
14. 1998 film, *Les Miserables*, directed by Billie August.

Chapter 15: Healing the Hurting in Humboldt Park

by Wilfredo De Jesus with Pamela Toussaint

1. www.mynewlife.org.
2. Ibid., Mission and Vision page.
3. http://www.cbn.com/cbnnews/337692.aspx, March 2008.
4. Ibid.
5. *Outreach* magazine, November/December 2007, 74.
6. http://www.mynewlife.org/Ministries/aspx?site_id=10087.
7. CBS-2 Chicago news transcript, 19 October 2007.
8. National Hispanic Christian Leadership Conference press release, 4 March 2007.

Chapter 16: "Alternative" Cell Church
by Jon R. Pennington

1. Timothy Keller and J. Allen Thompson, *Church Planter Manual* (New York: Redeemer Church Planting Center, 2002), concept detailed in pages 45–48 and surrounding context.
2. America Fact Finder Sheet, Zip Code Tabulation Area 60657, US Census Bureau, www.factfinder.census.gov.
3. First View 2007 Report and 10 Facts Report, Link2Lead.com, Precept Group Research, based on their own studies, census data, and Claritas.
4. Michael J. Weiss, *The Clustered World* (Boston: Little, Brown, and Company, 2000), 212–13.
5. Richard Lloyd, *Neo-Bohemia* (New York: Routledge, 2006), 53.
6. I have read or heard too many such warnings to list them all here. One that comes to mind is out of an article in Ray Bakke's work *The Urban Christian* (Downers Grove, Ill.: InterVarsity, 1987).
7. Karen Hurston, *Growing the World's Largest Church* (Springfield, Mo.: Chrism, 1994), 12.
8. "Cellebrating," *CellChurch Magazine*, compiled by M. Scott Boren, 2000.
9. David Garrison, *Church Planting Movements* (Richmond, Va.: Office of Overseas Operations, International Missions Board of the Southern Baptist Convention), 59.
10. Ibid., 35.
11. Keller and Thompson, *Church Planter Manual*, 260.

Chapter 17: Church in the City Center
by Tom Kubiak

1. Ray Bakke, *Street Signs* (Birmingham: New Hope, 2006), 135.
2. Ibid.
3. Howard Hendricks, Promise-Keepers Conference, Indianapolis, 1993.
4. David Roeder, "The New Downtown," *Chicago Sun-Times*, 25 August 2005, 13–14.
5. Ibid., 16–17.
6. David Roeder, "The New Downtown by Day," *Chicago Sun-Times*, 26 August 2006.
7. Dennis Rodkin, *Chicago* Magazine, "South Loop Rising," June 2007.
8. Percept Group: Ministry Area Profile, Claritas, Calif., 12 March 2007.
9. Mark Skertic, Lucio Guerrero, and Robert C. Herguth, *Chicago Sun-Times*, 27 August 2002.
10. Percept Group: Ministry Area Profile, Claritas, Calif., 12 March 2007.
11. Ibid.
12. For more detail, visit www.southloopcc.org.
13. Curtiss Paul DeYoung, Michael O. Emerson, George Yancey, and Karen Chai Kim, *United by Faith* (New York: Oxford, 2003), 81–82.
14. Charles Lyons, Armitage Church Summer Urban Workshop, 3–5 June 2005.
15. For more detail, visit www.ccda.org.
16. Percept Group: Ministry Area Profile, Claritas, Calif., 12 March 2007.
17. For more detail, visit www.jonescollegeprep.org.
18. Charles Lyons, Armitage Church Summer Urban Workshop, 3–5 June 2005.

PART THREE – MINISTERING TO SUBURBAN NEEDS

Introduction to Ministering to Suburban Needs

by Glen Kehrein

1. The Naturalization Act of 1790 established a uniform rule of naturalization and created a two-year residency requirement for aliens who are "free white persons" of "good moral character" (March 26, 1790). In essence this was the first "affirmative action" program of the federal government intended to guarantee the new country would maintain its Euro-American majority.
2. The U.S. Constitution was adopted in 1787. Section 9 of Article I states that the importation of "such Persons as any of the States now existing shall think proper to admit," meaning that slavery would be permitted and protected until 1808. Section 2 of Article IV said that a person "held to Service or Labour in one State, under the Laws thereof, escaping into another," meaning fugitive slaves, were to be returned to their owners.
3. In 1965, President Lyndon Johnson signed the Immigration Act of 1965 bill that dramatically changed how immigrants are admitted to America, allowing more individuals from third-world countries to enter the U.S. and also including a separate quota for refugees.
4. On August 13, 2008, ABC News reported: "White people will no longer make up a majority of Americans by 2042, according to new government projections. That's eight years sooner than previous estimates, made in 2004." Based upon newly release U.S. Census projections.
5. *Understanding Church Growth* (Grand Rapids: Eerdmans, 1970, 3rd ed. 1990) co-written by Wagner and McGavran became the strategic manual for church growth in the later twentieth century—the age of the creation of the megachurch.
6. See http://www.thepeaceplan.com.
7. See www.efca.org.

Chapter 18: The Times They Are a-Changing

by Glen Kehrein

1. Nicholas Lemann, *The Promised Land: The Great Black Migration and How It Changed America* (New York: Knopf, 1991), 6.
2. David Cohn, *Where I Was Born and Raised* (New York: Houghton Mifflin, 1948), 32–33.
3. Charles E. Silberman, *Crisis in Black and White* (New York: Random House, 1964), 5.
4. Alexis de Tocqueville, *Democracy in America*, 1885 (New York: A.S. Barnes, 1885), 389.
5. James Madison on Rule of Naturalization, 1st Congress, 3 Feb. 1790.
6. Naturalization Act of 26 March 1790 (1 Stat 103–104).
7. Donald L. Miller, *City of the Century: The Epic of Chicago and the Making of America* (New York: Simon & Schuster, 1996), 17.
8. Joel Ignatiev, *How the Irish Became White* (New York: Routledge, 1995), 35.
9. Ibid., 41.
10. Ibid.
11. Quoted from the (New York) *Irish-American*, 6 January 1850, in Florence E. Gibson, *The Attitudes of the New York Irish Toward State and National Affairs, 1848–1892* (New York: Columbia Univ., 1951), 15.

12. For a full accounting of the advancement of the Irish read the excellent work of Joel Ignatiev, *How the Irish Became White*.
13. *Chicago Defender*, 27 November 1943.
14. Metropolitan Housing Council, Biennial Report 1958–59.
15. Amanda I. Seligman, *Block by Block: Neighborhoods and Public Policy on Chicago's West Side* (Univ. of Chicago Press, 2005), 187.
16. Stephen Meyer, *As Long as They Don't Move Next Door: Segregation and Racial Conflict in American Neighborhoods* (New York: Rowan & Littlefield, 2000), 30.
17. http://www.chicagoreporter.com/index.php/c/Sidebars/d/ Surviving_White_Flight_with_Middle_Class_Diversity.
18. "Tearing Down Cabrini-Green," *60 Minutes*, CBS (Chicago, Ill.), 23 July 2003.
19. http://www.ussf2007.org/en/node/18618 .
20. http://www.housingforall.org/PHA_plan.htm.
21. Alan Berube, Bruce Katz, and Robert E. Lang, *Redefining Urban and Suburban America: Evidence from Census 2000* (New York: Brookings Institutional Press, 2005), 200.

Chapter 19: Seizing the Moment
by Winfred Neely

1. One of the first things I did as a church planter in South Holland was have one-on-one meetings with pastors and other leaders in the village. It was in one of these meetings with a Reformed pastor that I learned firsthand of the crisis of the historic churches in South Holland.
2. What is equally telling about this situation is that a good number of African-Americans are driving from the village to the city on Sunday morning for worship services at their churches. They have relationships at these churches and commitment to them is understandable. The problem here is that these well-meaning Christians are demonstrating that they do not have a "theology of place." Christians should settle down in churches where they live. Strong churches consisting of regenerate Christians who live in the vicinity of the church building are in a better position to deal with and address the problems of a community in transition. For more discussion of the "Theology of Place," see Ray Bakke, *A Theology as Big as the City* (Downers Grove, Ill.: InterVarsity, 1997).
3. At the time of this writing, two of the Reformed churches in South Holland have relocated to more congenial cultural pastures. One of the white historic churches in the village disbanded and sold its property to an African-American congregation, and another historic church has sold its property to the municipality and relocated to a so-called milder cultural climate. In all fairness, it must be stated that some Reformed churches in the village are making a sincere effort to connect with the emerging community, and an independent congregation, the Spirit of God fellowship, under the leadership of Dr. John Sullivan, is having a huge impact in South Holland, and Harvey, Illinois.
4. Walter E. Ziegenhals, *Urban Churches in Transition* (New York: Pilgrim Press, 1978), 9.
5. Ibid., 15.

6. The struggle with class fears is not limited to a particular race or ethnic group. The birth of class fear has already been born among middle-class African-American residents of South Holland. Some of the more recent arrivals of African-Americans in the village are not homeowners, but renters who rent homes through Section 8. There is also a displacement of the poor from the projects of the city of Chicago to the southern suburbs. Middle-class black people are disturbed and concerned about the changes in the community since these other black people have moved in and around the village—the lowering of test scores in the high schools, the increase in violence, the dramatic increase of the presence of children and teenagers, children standing on street corners in the summer half-dressed or wearing a robe and house shoes outside, cars lined up in front of some homes and different people going in and out of these homes through all hours of the night, and the class differences among African-Americans. I have heard Christian African-Americans say they are thinking about moving. I am convinced that instead of moving away, and letting the neighborhood and the public schools deteriorate, churches need to consider how they may win people to Christ and make a difference for the Kingdom in the community and in the public schools. Historically, the trend is this: middle-class white communities become middle-class black communities, and middle-class black communities become poor communities. Churches in the village that are predominantly African-American and historic churches that are adapting must step in and prevent the deterioration of the community. One way to do this is by making a commitment to stay in the community. One does not have to relocate in this scenario; one just has to stay put! But we must do more than stay; we must engage in the village at every level of life in the community.

7. In the text the synagogue rulers say to Paul and Barnabas, "If you have a word of exhortation for the people, say it." The expression "word of exhortation" was a technical term for a sermon.

8. Millard Erickson, *Christian Theology* (Grand Rapids, Mich.: Baker, 1985), 1068.

9. Ibid., 49.

10. Ezra E. Jones and Robert L. Wilson, *What's Ahead for Old First Church* (New York: Harper & Row, 1974), 11.

11. Ibid., 49.

12. Charles Chaney, *Church Planting at the End of the Twentieth Century* (Wheaton, Ill.: Tyndale, 1982), 129.

13. Jere Allen and George W. Bullard, *Hope for the Church in the Changing Community*. Quoted in Chaney, *Church Planting*.

14. John Stott, *Authentic Christianity* (Downers Grove, Ill.: InterVarsity, 1995), 71.

15. J. Herbert Kane, *A Global View of Christian Missions* (Grand Rapids, Mich.: Baker, 1971), 259.

16. Ibid.

17. Sodality is the technical term for missional structures, and modality is the technical term for congregational structures. A local church needs both. Missional structures facilitate engagement in mission, whereas congregational structures are designed to facilitate church life.

18. Ralph Winter, *The Two Structures of God's Redemptive Mission* (South Pasadena, Calif.: William Carey Library, 1974), 132.

19. Stuart Murray, *Church Planting: Laying Foundations* (Stottsdale, Pa.: Herald Press, 2001), 153.

20. Ibid., 129.

21. C. Peter Wagner, *Church Planting for a Greater Harvest* (Ventura, Calif.: Regal, 1984), 59.

22. Steve Sjogren and Rob Lewin, *Community of Kindness* (Ventura, Calif.: Regal, 2003), 132.

Chapter 21: Urban Issues in Suburban Towns?

by Tony Danhelka

1. http://www.city-data.com/city/Elgin-Illinois.html.
2. http://www.aurora-il.org/economicdevelopment/demographics.php.
3. Elgin National Watch Company, http://elginwatches.org.
4. City of Aurora, http://www.aurora-il.org/aboutourcity.php.
5. 2006 Income and Poverty Data Kane County, www.heartlandalliance.org/maip/documents/CensusFactSheet2007Kane.pdf.
6. http://aspe.hhs.gov/poverty/08poverty.shtml .

2008 HHS Poverty Guidelines

PERSONS IN FAMILY OR HOUSEHOLD	48 CONTIGUOUS STATES AND D.C.	ALASKA	HAWAII
1	$10,400	$13,000	$11,960
2	14,000	17,500	16,100
3	17,600	22,000	20,240
4	21,200	26,500	24,380
5	24,800	31,000	28,520
6	28,400	35,500	32,660
7	32,000	40,000	36,800
8	35,600	44,500	40,940
For each additional person, add	3,600	4,500	4,140

7. Bible Verses about Poverty, www.compassion.com/child-advocacy/find-your-voice/what-the-bible-says/poverty/what-the-bible-says-about-poverty.htm.
8. The Advent Christian Church was one of six Christian denominations that grew out of the ministry of William Miller (1782-1849). A U.S. Army Captain who fought in the War of 1812, Miller was converted from deism in 1818. www.areachurches.com/adventinfo.html.
9. Eighty years ago, a group of men and women shared the vision of Christ for hurting, needy people. Recognizing the Lord's mandate to feed the hungry, cloth the naked, shelter the sojourner, and visit the imprisoned, they committed themselves to the practical expression of God's love—and on June 10, 1928, the Wayside Cross Rescue Mission was born. www.waysidecross.org.
10. Harvest Evangelism. We are an inter-denominational ministry committed to the fulfillment of the Great Commission (Matt. 28:19–20). The Harvest team, led by founder and president Ed Silvoso, is dedicated to serving the entire body of Christ around the globe while instilling vision for city, regional, and nationwide transformation. The biblical principles of prayer evangelism (Luke 10:1–9; 1 Timothy 2:1–8), marketplace transformation (Acts 2:17–21), and unity in the body (John 13:35) form the core strategy for our efforts. www.harvestevan.org.

Chapter 22: Becoming a Multi-Ethnic Suburban Church

by Marty Schoenleber

1. Other books included *The Suburban Captivity of the Churches: An Analysis of Protestant Responsibility in the Expanding Metropolis* by Gibson Winter (New York: Macmillan, 1962); *Black Like Me* by John Howard Griffin (New York: Signet, 1960).
2. Martin Luther King, "I Have a Dream," speech delivered at the March on Washington August 28, 1963. (http://www.mlkonline.net/dream.html)
3. A. Scott Moreau, ed., *Evangelical Dictionary of World Missions* (Grand Rapids, Mich.: Baker Academic Books, 2000), 455.
4. I owe the phrasing of this idea to my friend and colleague Dr. Michael Green, seminary professor and current pastor of the English language congregation at the Chinese Christian Union Church in Chicago.
5. "In 1960, there were an estimated 50 million evangelical Christians in the West, and 25 million in the rest of the world; today, there are an estimated 75 million in the West, and 325 million in the rest of the world (representing about 20 percent of the two billion Christians worldwide), according to Robert Kilgore, chairman of the board of the missionary organization *Christar*." Approximately 62 percent of all Christians alive today live in the Global South. (Source: http://prayerfoundation.org/evangelical_christianity_shifting_outside_west.htm)
6. While writing this chapter I learned of a wonderful PCA church that one of our former members has found since leaving us for seminary, New Century Fellowship of St. Louis (http://www.newcity.org). This is exciting at a number of levels. Not only has a former member sought a multi-ethnic fellowship after leaving New Song, but has found one that is much further along in its maturity than we are.

Chapter 23: The Great Community

by Daniel J. Gute

1. C. Peter Wagner, *Your Church Can Be Healthy* (Nashville: Abington Press, 1979).
2. Raleigh Washington and Glen Kehrein, *Breaking Down Walls: A Model for Reconciliation in an Age of Racial Strife* (Chicago, Moody: 1993).
3. Ibid., 113, 125, 141, 155, 169, 185, 197, 209.
4. Ken Ham, Carl Wieland, and Don Batten, *One Blood: The Biblical Answer to Racism* (Green Forest, Ark.: Master Books, 1999).
5. Rod Cooper, "People Just Like Me: Does the Bible Give Us Freedom to Build Deliberately Homogeneous Churches?" in *Building Unity in the Church of the New Millennium*, ed. Dwight Perry (Chicago: Moody, 2002), 154.

PART FOUR – PARACHURCH MINISTRIES

Chapter 24: Loving the Sexually Broken

by John Green

1. Jeffrey Dahmer and John Wayne Gacy were serial killers who preyed upon male prostitutes. One potential reason for this is that men involved in prostitution often have little or no family, friends, or loved ones who will care about their disappearance.
2. Wayne R. Dynes, ed., "Prostitution," *Encyclopedia of Homosexuality* (Chicago: St. James Press, 1990), Vol. 2, 1054–58. This article describes some of the early examples of male prostitution, such as in Ancient Greece where male prostitutes were generally slaves or freedmen since free citizens selling their services as prostitutes could risk losing their civil rights; in Ancient Rome, which saw the existence of male brothels; in the medieval Islamic world, where work as a same-sex male prostitute was restricted to young boys and slaves; and in the Ottoman Empire, where very handsome "rakkas," or young male dancers, dressed in feminine attire and were employed as entertainers and sex workers.
3. John Gonsiorek, Walter Bera, and Donald LeTourneau, *Male Sexual Abuse* (Thousand Oaks, Calif.: Sage Publications, 1994).
4. Mitchell S. Ratner, ed., *Crack Pipe as Pimp* (Idaho Falls: Lexington Books, 1993), 86. (This was an eighteen-month study funded by National Institute on Drug Abuse.)
5. Uniform Crime Reports for the United States (1998), FBI, 215.
6. Ibid.
7. Donald M. Allen, "Young Male Prostitutes: A Psychosocial Study," *Archives of Sexual Behavior*, Vol. 9 (1980), No. 5.
8. Chicago Police Department, Annual Report 2004.
9. Ibid.
10. Manuel Fernandez-Alemany, "Comparative Studies on Male Sex Work in the Era of HIV/ AIDS," *The Journal of Sex Research*, Vol. 37 (2000), 2, 187–90.
11. Norra Macready, "Stress Disorder Is Common Among Prostitutes," *British Medical Journal*, Vol. 317 (1998), 7158.
12. Jacqueline Boles and Elifson Kirk, "Sexual Identity and HIV: The Male Prostitute," *The Journal of Sex Research*, Vol. 31 (1994), No. 1, 39–46.
13. Ibid.
14. Cathy Spatz Widom and M. Ashley Ames, "Criminal Consequences of Childhood Sexual Victimization," *Child Abuse & Neglect*, Vol. 18 (1994), No. 4, 303–18.
15. Jim A. Cates and Jeffrey Markley, "Demographic, Clinical, and Personality Variables Associated with Male Prostitution by Choice," *Adolescence*, Vol. 27 (1992), No. 107.
16. "Sexual Behavior Patterns of Customers of Male Street Prostitutes," *Archives of Sexual Behavior*, Vol. 21 (1992), No. 4, 347–57.
17. From the May 1994 statement, *Evangelicals & Catholics Together: The Christian Mission in the Third Millennium*.
18. Norman Grubb, *C. T. Studd* (Fort Washington, Pa.: Christian Literature Crusade, 1972), 166.

Chapter 25: Heart to God and Hand to Man

by Mary Kim, David and Darlene Harvey

1. Presentation by Judy Minor Jackson, Deputy Commissioner, Chicago Department of Planning and Development, to the RJKCCC Review Board, February 9, 2007. Fenger High School.

2. Chicago Housing Authority, Robert Taylor Homes Study, www.thecha.org/housingdev/robert_taylor.html.

3. At one point in Chicago history more than 63,000 people lived in public housing on Chicago's South Side. These homes, the most famous being the Robert Taylor Homes, have been razed to be replaced by town houses with one-third Section 8 housing, one-third full rent, and one-third mortgaged. The new price of the homes makes it impossible for past residents to live in their old neighborhoods. Rent that was nine hundred dollars per month has given way to condos that sell from $550,000 to $975,000. Homes in Bronzeville now go for $350,000 for a flat. Those displaced families will not be able to afford returning to the center of the city.

4. George Scott Railton, *The Authoritative Life of General William Booth Founder of the Salvation Army* (New York: Reliance Trading Co., 1912), 56.

5. Mission Statement of the Salvation Army. www.salvationarmy.org.

6. "Save Souls, Serve Humanity, Grow Saints," www.usc.salvationarmy.org/usc/prayer.nsf.

7. "Heart to God and Hand to Man." www.salvationarmyusa.org/usn.

8. R. G. Moyles, *Come Join Our Army* (Alexandria: Crest Books, 2007), 5.

9. Ibid., 58.

10. Flora Larsson, *My Best Men Are Women* (London: Holder and Stroughton Limited, 1974), 64.

11. Roger Green, *Catherine Booth* (Grand Rapids, Mich.: Baker Books, 1996), 247.

12. General William Booth, *In Darkest England and the Way Out* (London: Supplies & Purchasing Department, 1984); (first printing 1890), 27.

13. Moyles, *Come Join*, 124–25.

14. Ibid., 119–26.

15. Green, *Catherine Booth*, 247–59.

16. Moyles, *Come Join*, 123.

17. Edward McKinley, *Marching to Glory: The History of the Salvation Army in the United States* (Atlanta: Salvation Army Supplies, 1986), 99.

18. "Doing the Most Good Throughout Chicagoland" (brochure), Metropolitan Division. www.salarmychicago.org.

19. Homeless in Chicago: 2007 Numbers and Demographics Point-In-Time Analysis. www.cityofchicago.org.

20. Human Trafficking Fact Sheet. Department of Health and Human Services. www.salvationarmyusa.org/trafficking and www.acf.hhs.gov/trafficking.

21. Interview with Alderman Carrie M. Austin, Ward 34, Chicago, 22 June 2006. Town Hall meeting at Sheldon Heights Church of God in Christ, Chicago, Illinois.

22. Joan Frankle & Krysten Lynn Ryba. Community Needs Assessment: Kroc Center—July 2006. Metro Chicago Information Center, 17 N. State St., Suite 1600, Chicago, Illinois 60602. www.mcic.org.

23. Ibid.

24. Mayor Richard M. Daley of Chicago, Illinois. "Why Chicago Needs a Kroc Center." Speech given at the Kroc Media Event, 6 November 2007.
25. Interview with Dick Starman, trustee for the late Joan Kroc, 11 November 2005.
26. Community Meeting with the Ward 34 at the Alderman's office on 111th street with 18 community members, 8 March 2006.

Chapter 26: Unleashing the Family
by David Anderson

1. *Chicago Tribune*, 30 December 2007, 5.
2. Fred Wulczyn, Brenda Jones Harden, Ying-Ying T. Yuan, Richard P. Barth, and John Landsverk, *Beyond Common Sense: Child Welfare, Child Well-being, and the Evidence for Policy Reform* (Piscataway, N.J.: Aldine Transaction, 2005).
3. Joseph Stowell, *The Trouble with Jesus* (Chicago: Moody, 2003), 116.
4. Christine D. Pohl, *Making Room: Recovering Hospitality as a Christian Tradition* (Grand Rapids: Eerdmans, 1999), 33.
5. Stowell, *Trouble with Jesus*, 116.
6. Children's Defense Fund Fact Sheet. www.childrensdefense.org. 2007.
7. Ibid.

Chapter 27: In Search of Lost Sheep
by David and Beth Kanelos

1. Jim Rayburn III, *Dance Children Dance* (Wheaton, Ill.: Tyndale, 1984), 139.
2. http://www.younglife.org/AboutYoungLife/FactsAtYourFingertips.htm.
3. Throughout this chapter, the word *kids* will be used. In Young Life, we affectionately refer to teenagers as kids, an informal term for a young person or child, also referring to one especially younger or less experienced. Kids are easily imposed upon, are impressionable, and need guidance and love. They need a protector and guardian.
4. Rayburn, *Dance Children*, 46.
5. Ibid., 45.
6. Denny Rydberg, President of Young Life, *The Young Life Informer*, Dec. 2007.
7. http://www.younglife.org/AboutYoungLife/History.htm.
8. Wally Urban, phone interview, 26 April 2008.
9. Jim Chesney, phone interview, 26 April 2008.
10. Char Meredith, *It's a Sin to Bore a Kid: The Story of Young Life* (Waco, Tex.: Word, 1978), 112–18.
11. John N. Miller, *Back to the Basics of Young Life* (publisher unknown, 1991), 73.
12. Rebecca Pippert, *Out of the Salt Shaker and into the World* (Downers Grove, Ill.: InterVarsity, 1979), 34.
13. "A New Generation Expresses Its Skepticism and Frustration with Christianity," 24 September 2007; http://www.barna.org/Flexpage.aspx?Page=BarnaUpdateNarrow&BarnaUpdateID=280.
14. Meredith, *It's a Sin*, 18.

15. Chap Clark, *Hurt: Inside the World of Today's Teenagers* (Grand Rapids, Mich.: Baker Academic, 2004), 190.
16. Rayburn, *Dance Children*, 50.
17. Miller, *Back to the Basics*, 49.
18. Ibid., 49.
19. Rayburn, *Dance Children*, 74.
20. Young Life has formal partnerships with numerous local churches in the United States. For more information about partnering with Young Life, visit our website: www.younglife.org.

Chapter 28: Using Principles of Excellence to Change Young Lives

by Donnita Travis and Sarah James

1. 2000 Census and Chicago Public Schools.
2. Jay P. Green, "High School Graduation Rates in the United States," Civic Report (November 2001). http//www.manhattan-institute.org/html/cr_baeo.htm.
3. "Literacy Behind Prison Walls," Profiles of the Prison Population from the National Adult Literacy Survey, 1994.
4. Kathleen Cushman, "Democracy and Equity: CES's Tenth Common Principle," Vol. 14 #3 (January 1998). http://www.essentialschools.org/cs/resources/view/ces_res/114.
5. Elaine Allensworth, "Graduation and Dropout Trends in Chicago: A Look at Cohorts of Students from 1991 through 2004" (Consortium on Chicago School Research at University of Chicago, January 2005). http://ccsr.uchicago.edu/content/publications.php?pub_id=61.
6. Henry Levin, Clive Belfield, Peter Muenning, and Cecilia Rouse, "The Costs and Benefits of an Excellent Education for All of America's Children" (Columbia University, January 2007). http://www.cbcse.org/media/download_gallery/Leeds_Report_Final_jan2007.pdf.
7. John Fuder, *Training Students for Urban Ministry* (Eugene, Oreg.: Wipf and Stock, 2001), 21.

Chapter 29: Aggressive Evangelism

by Brad Stanley

1. Aubrey Malphurs, *Planting Growing Churches* (Grand Rapids, Mich.: Baker, 1998), 177.
2. *Webster's New World Dictionary* (New York: Warner Books, 1990), 12.
3. Wayne A. Meeks, *The First Urban Christians* (London: Yale Univ. Press, 1983), 16.
4. John Dawson, *Taking Our Cities for God* (Lake Mary, Fla.: Charisma House, 2001), 29.
5. Jack Dennison, *City Reaching* (Pasadena, Calif.: William Carey Library, 1999), 73.
6. Ibid., 142.
7. David Kinnaman and Gabe Lyons, *unChristian: What a New Generation Really Thinks about Christianity . . . and Why It Matters* (Grand Rapids, Mich.: Baker, 2007), 11.
8. Roger Greenway, *Apostles to the City* (Grand Rapids, Mich.: Baker, 1986), 62.
9. Kinnaman and Lyons, *unChristian*, 71.

About the CCDA Institute

This book is presented by the Christian Community Development Association (CCDA) as a practical tool for assisting ministries to enhance their effectiveness in community building. CCDA is a supportive network of urban practitioners, educators, and churches committed to the work of God's Kingdom, especially as it relates to compassion and justice for the poor.

A driving force behind the growth and influence of the Christian Community Development movement has been the writing of our founder, Dr. John Perkins. Throughout the country and around the world, there are hundreds of ministries that have been born as a result of someone reading one of John's books, among them: *Let Justice Roll Down, Justice for All*, and *Beyond Charity*.

Along with the impact of Dr. Perkins's books have been training events or conferences where Dr. Perkins and other CCD leaders have taught the eight key components of CCD.

After many years of seeing the need for a more formalized way to disseminate the philosophy and heart of Christian Community Development, in late 2004, the Christian Community Development Association launched the CCDA Institute to offer regional training for our members and to introduce others engaged in urban ministry or community development to our unique philosophy based on the eight key components of CCD:

- Relocation: The Theology and Practice of Incarnational Ministry

- Reconciliation in the New Millennium

- Redistribution: Toward a Just Distribution of Resources

- Listening to the Community

- Indigenous Leadership Development

- Church-based Community Development

- Empowerment: Moving from Betterment to Empowerment

- Holistic Ministry: Reaching the Whole Person with the Whole Gospel

The delivery of high-caliber training for emerging leaders and the production of books, curriculum, Web-based resources, and other training materials is of utmost importance if CCDA is going to accomplish our vision and mission.

The mission of CCDA is to inspire and train Christians who seek to bear witness to the Kingdom of God by reclaiming and restoring under-resourced communities. The vision of CCDA is to have wholistically restored communities with Christians fully engaged in the process of transformation.

For information regarding membership, events, and other resources available through CCDA, or to find out how to earn a certificate degree from CCDA in Christian Community Development, please visit our website (www.ccda.org) or contact us at:

Christian Community Development Association
3555 W. Ogden Avenue
Chicago, IL 60623

Website: www.CCDA.org
Phone: 773-762-0994